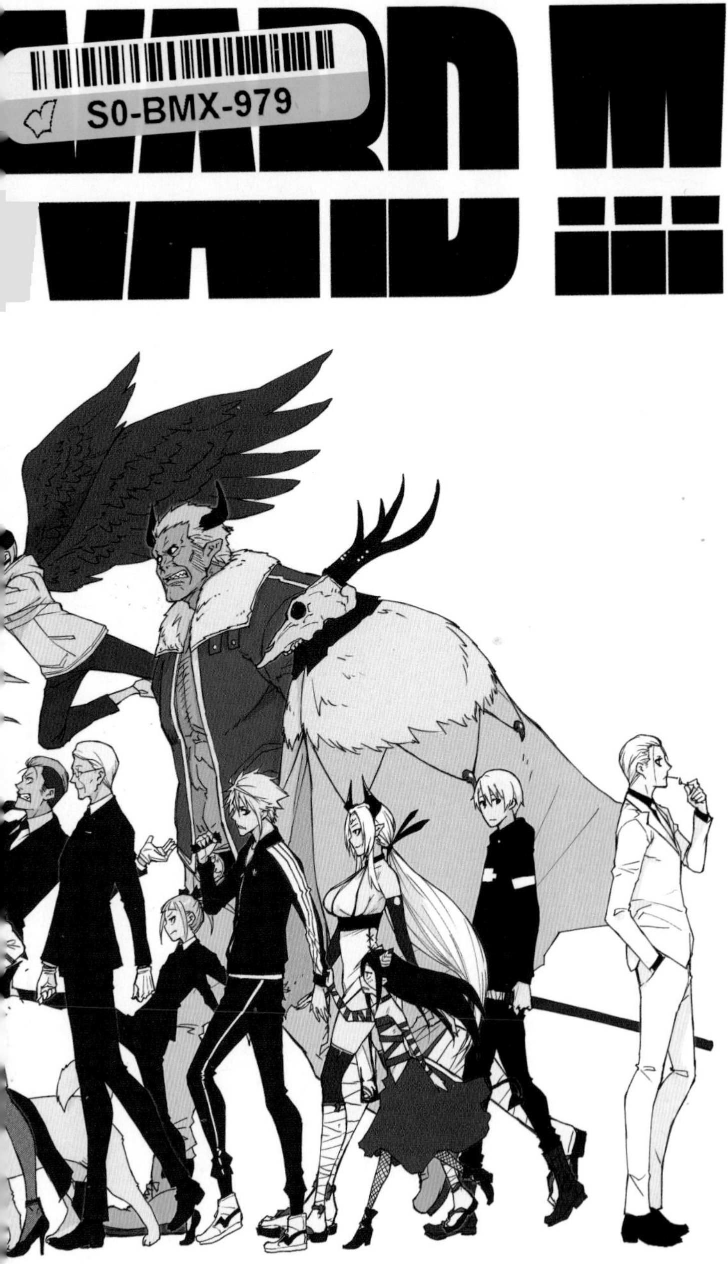

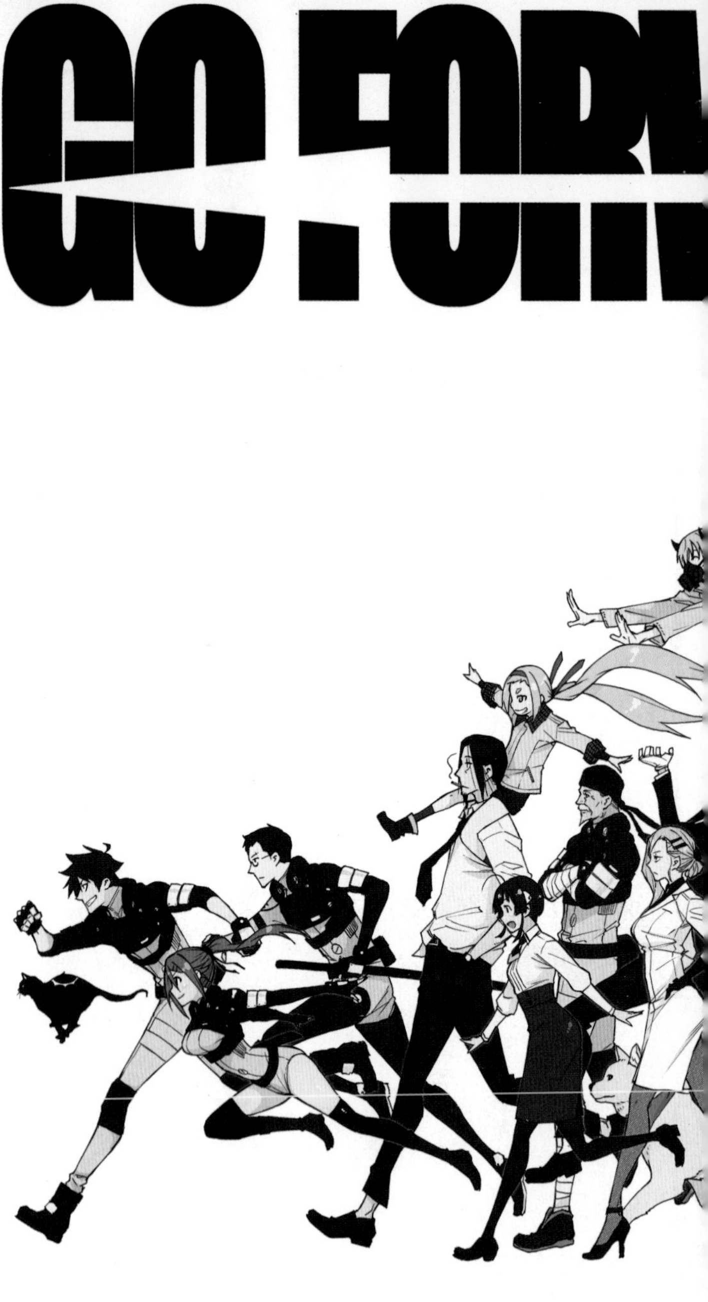
GO FOR

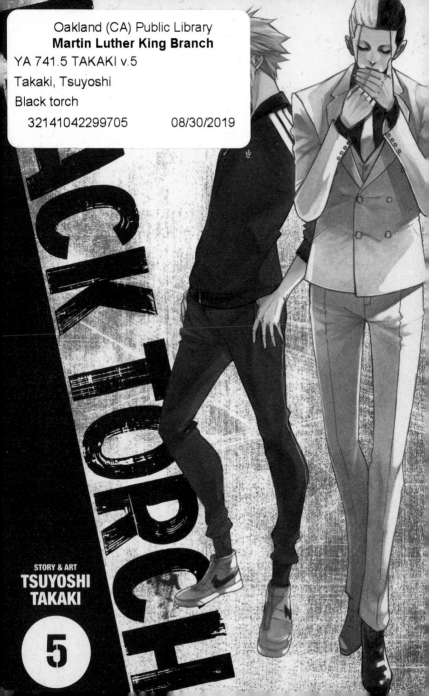

STORY & ART
**TSUYOSHI
TAKAKI**

5

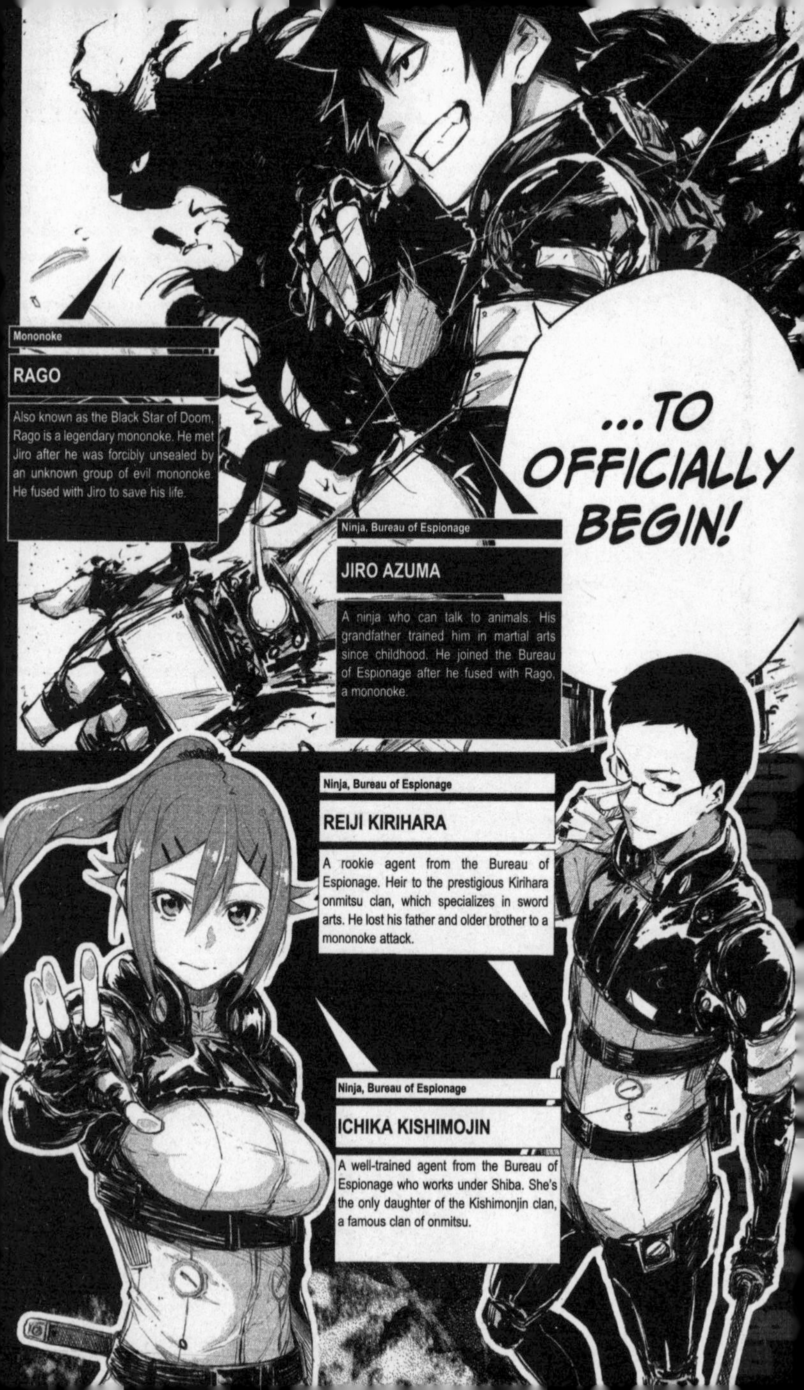
...TO OFFICIALLY BEGIN!
Ninja, Bureau of Espionage
JIRO AZUMA
A ninja who can talk to animals. His grandfather trained him in martial arts since childhood. He joined the Bureau of Espionage after he fused with Rago, a mononoke.
Mononoke
RAGO
Also known as the Black Star of Doom, Rago is a legendary mononoke. He met Jiro after he was forcibly unsealed by an unknown group of evil mononoke. He fused with Jiro to save his life.
Ninja, Bureau of Espionage
REIJI KIRIHARA
A rookie agent from the Bureau of Espionage. Heir to the prestigious Kirihara onmitsu clan, which specializes in sword arts. He lost his father and older brother to a mononoke attack.
Ninja, Bureau of Espionage
ICHIKA KISHIMOJIN
A well-trained agent from the Bureau of Espionage who works under Shiba. She's the only daughter of the Kishimonjin clan, a famous clan of onmitsu.

CHARACTER

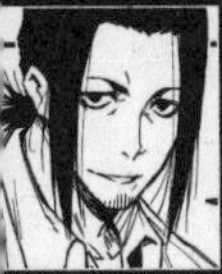

RYOSUKE SHIBA
Ninja, Bureau of Espionage

Chief of Special Operations Division 2 at the Bureau of Espionage, a secret national agency whose mission is the surveillance and disposal of Mononoke. Founder of a new squad, code named Black Torch.

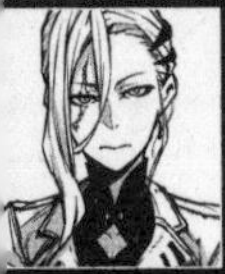

TOKO KUSUMI
Ninja, Bureau of Espionage

Shiba's co-worker and a coldly logical woman, she is Chief of Special Operations Division 1.

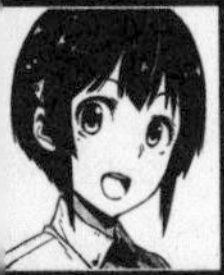

HANA USAMI
Ninja, Bureau of Espionage

One of Shiba's few subordinates, she is a backup member of Black Torch.

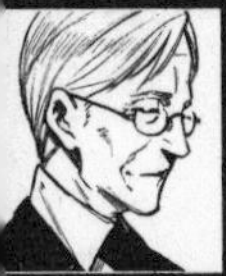

BANJURO TOKIEDA
Ninja, Bureau of Espionage

A capable lieutenant to Kusumi, he can do everything from chauffeur to participate in active battle.

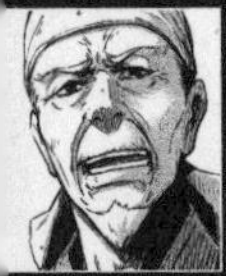

TOKIMASA ASUMA
Former Ninja, Bureau of Espionage

Jiro's grandfather. Descendant of a long line of ninja, he is a former member of the Bureau of Espionage.

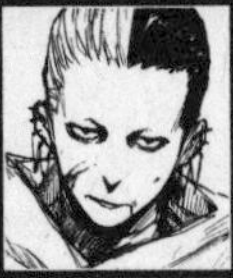

AMAGI

The mastermind behind the current mononoke attacks. Asked Rago to join him back in the Edo period, but Rago refused.

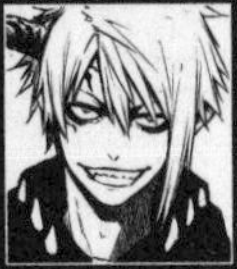

KOUGA

A mononoke. Young and hotheaded, he wants Rago to be his partner.

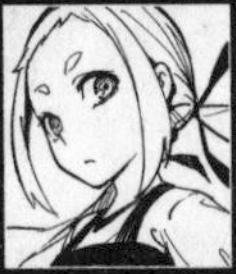

FUYO

A mononoke that looks like a little girl. An ally to humans, she helps Shiba out with various training activities.

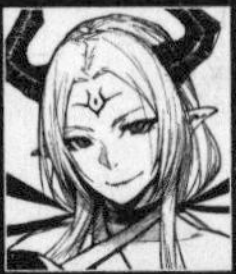

IBUKI

A mononoke. Lives in the Avidya forest with the former onmitsu agent Monjumaru.

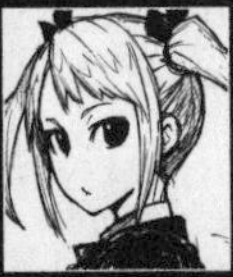

BANRI HIMEZUKA

A member of Black Cloak, an elite unit in Division 1. Is partnered with Inui.

STORY

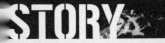

Jiro Azuma, a descendant from a long line of ninja, meets Rago, a mononoke that looks like a small, black cat. After a series of mishaps, Jiro and Rago fuse together and, through an invitation from Ryosuke Shiba, join the secret organization called the Bureau of Espionage to become founding members of the Onmitsu squad called Black Torch.

Together with their new teammates, Jiro and Rago work to defeat a group of mononoke haunting a town. The pair handily defeat their target, but in the process Rago becomes aware of a horrifying truth—in exchange for granting Jiro his powers, he has been unwittingly devouring Jiro's vital energy this entire time!

Before Rago can tell this to Jiro, the two are confronted by Amagi himself! Jiro tries to fight him, but is flattened in a single blow. Amagi, wanting Rago's power for himself, offers to spare Jiro provided Rago comes with him. With little other choice, Rago allows Amagi to undo the possession binding him to Jiro. However, Rago pulls a fast one on Amagi and leaves all of his power behind in Jiro. Enraged that he yet again missed out on getting Rago's power, Amagi lashes out, but Kouga saves Rago. Cooling down, Amagi decides to leave Rago alive and put a different plan into action…

Meanwhile, Jiro is having problems controlling Rago's power. His grandfather, Toshimasa, comes out of retirement to help him, taking him to the Avidya Forest. With the help of the forest's master, Ibuki, Jiro finally starts getting the hang of Rago's power. After a long training session, Ibuki tells Jiro a little about Amagi and his unique ability to strengthen himself by devouring other mononoke!

CONTENTS

5

BLACK TORCH

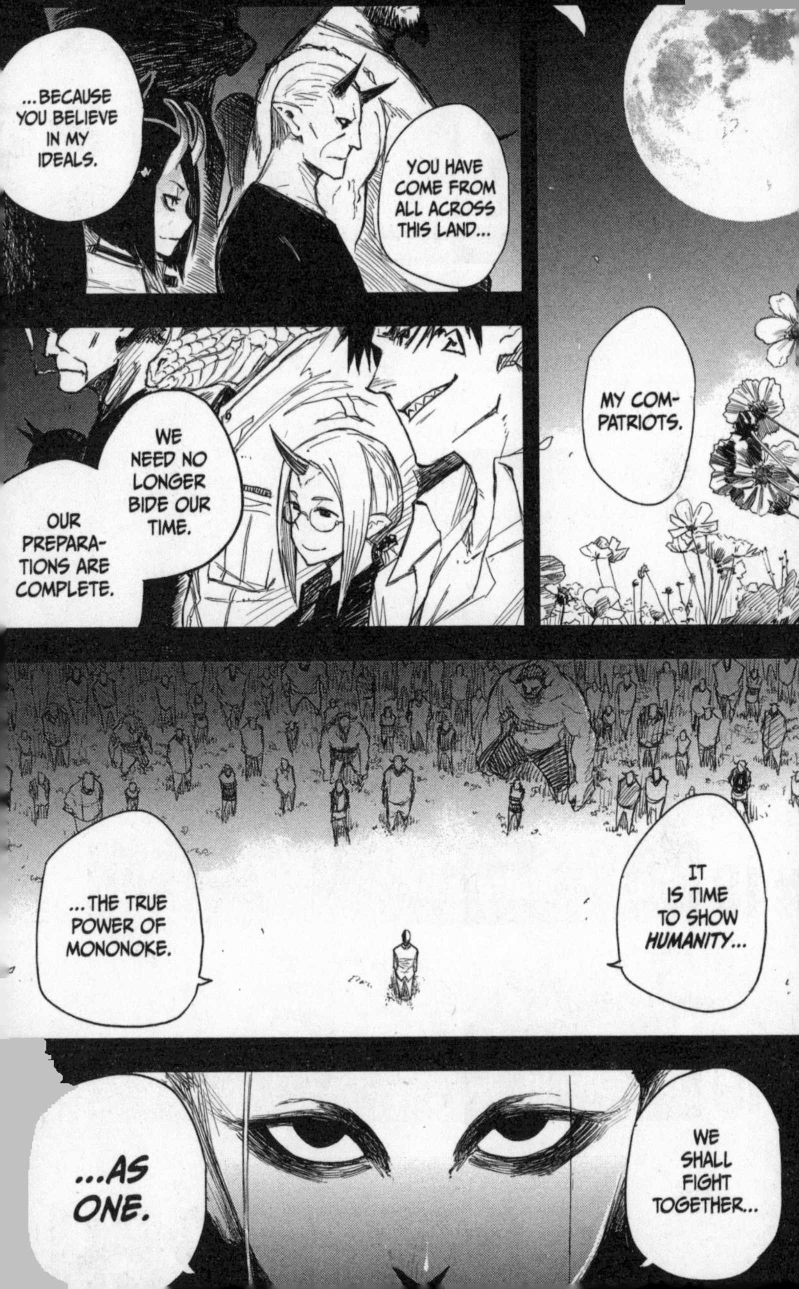
MY COMPATRIOTS.
YOU HAVE COME FROM ALL ACROSS THIS LAND...
...BECAUSE YOU BELIEVE IN MY IDEALS.
WE NEED NO LONGER BIDE OUR TIME.
OUR PREPARATIONS ARE COMPLETE.
IT IS TIME TO SHOW *HUMANITY*...
...THE TRUE POWER OF MONONOKE.
WE SHALL FIGHT TOGETHER...
...AS ONE.

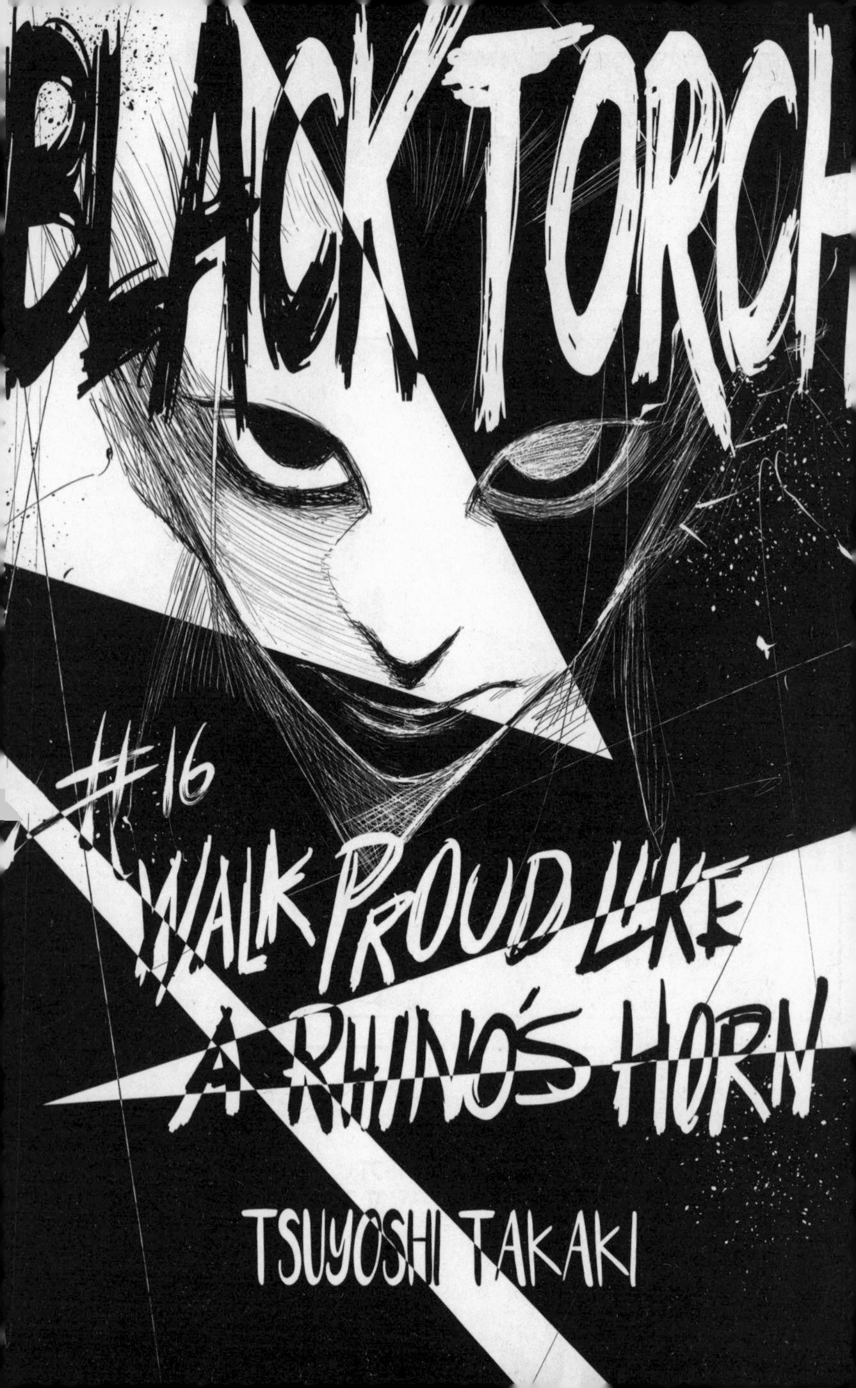
BLACK TORCH
#16
WALK PROUD LIKE A RHINO'S HORN
TSUYOSHI TAKAKI

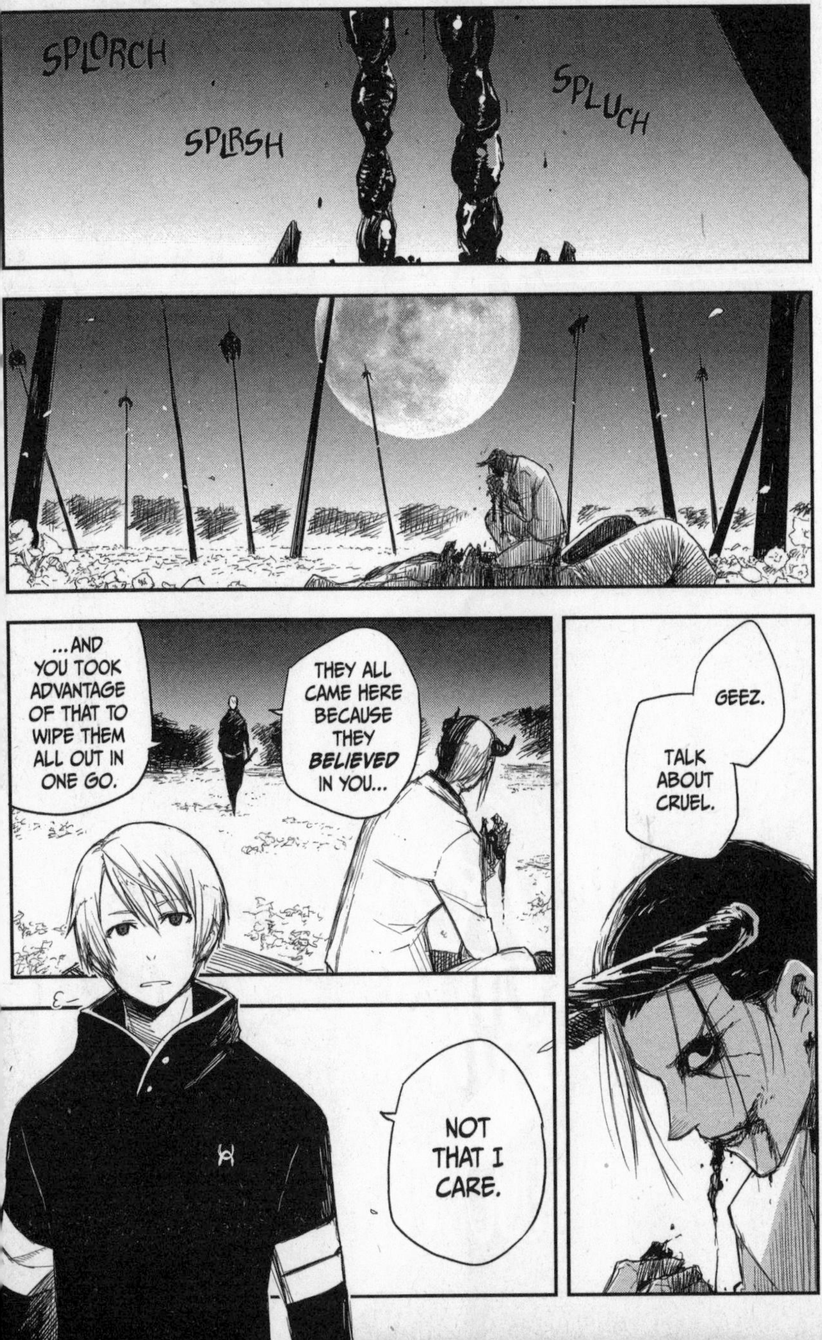
SPLUCH
SPLRSH
SPLORCH
GEEZ.
TALK ABOUT CRUEL.
THEY ALL CAME HERE BECAUSE THEY *BELIEVED* IN YOU...
...AND YOU TOOK ADVANTAGE OF THAT TO WIPE THEM ALL OUT IN ONE GO.
NOT THAT I CARE.

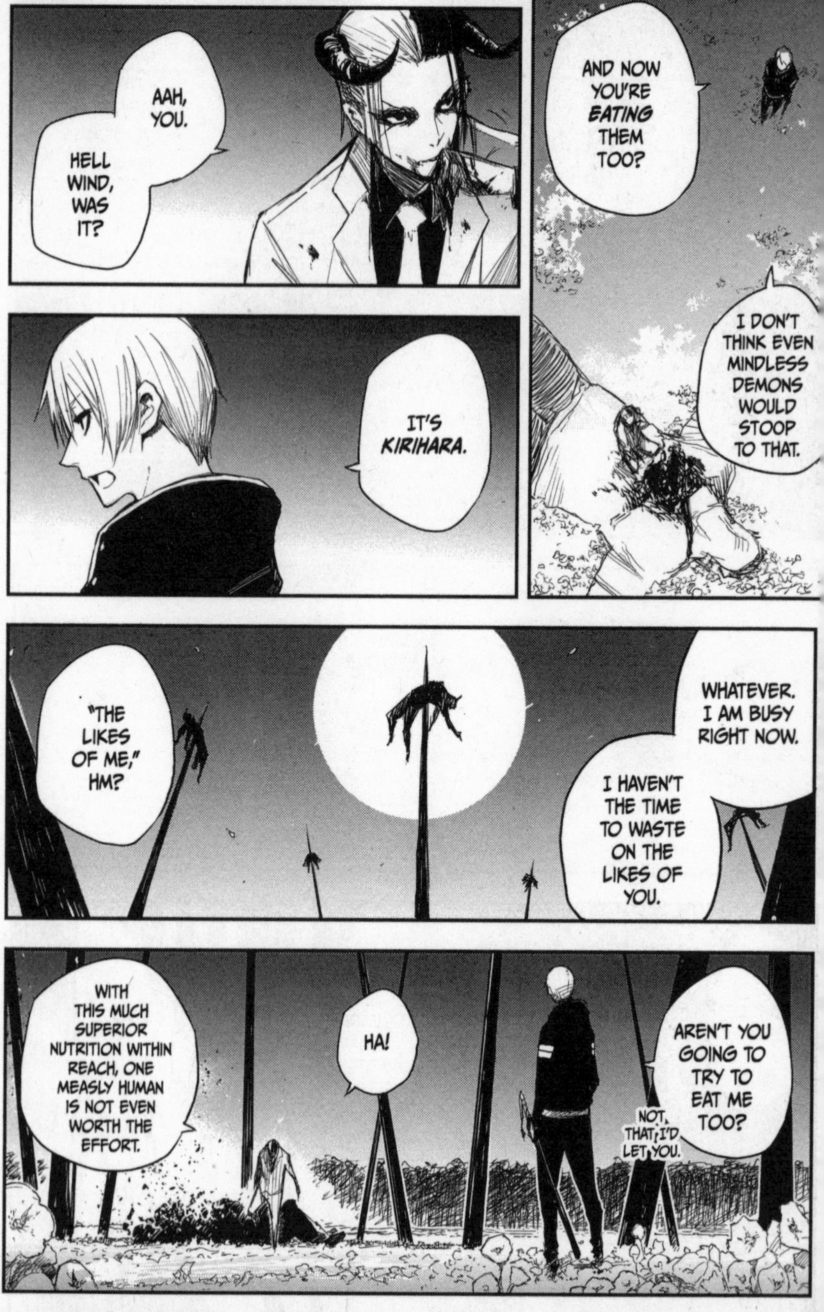
AND NOW YOU'RE *EATING* THEM TOO?
I DON'T THINK EVEN MINDLESS DEMONS WOULD STOOP TO THAT.
AAH, YOU.
HELL WIND, WAS IT?
IT'S *KIRIHARA.*
WHATEVER. I AM BUSY RIGHT NOW.
I HAVEN'T THE TIME TO WASTE ON THE LIKES OF YOU.
"THE LIKES OF ME," HM?
AREN'T YOU GOING TO TRY TO EAT ME TOO?
NOT THAT I'D LET YOU.
HA!
WITH THIS MUCH SUPERIOR NUTRITION WITHIN REACH, ONE MEASLY HUMAN IS NOT EVEN WORTH THE EFFORT.

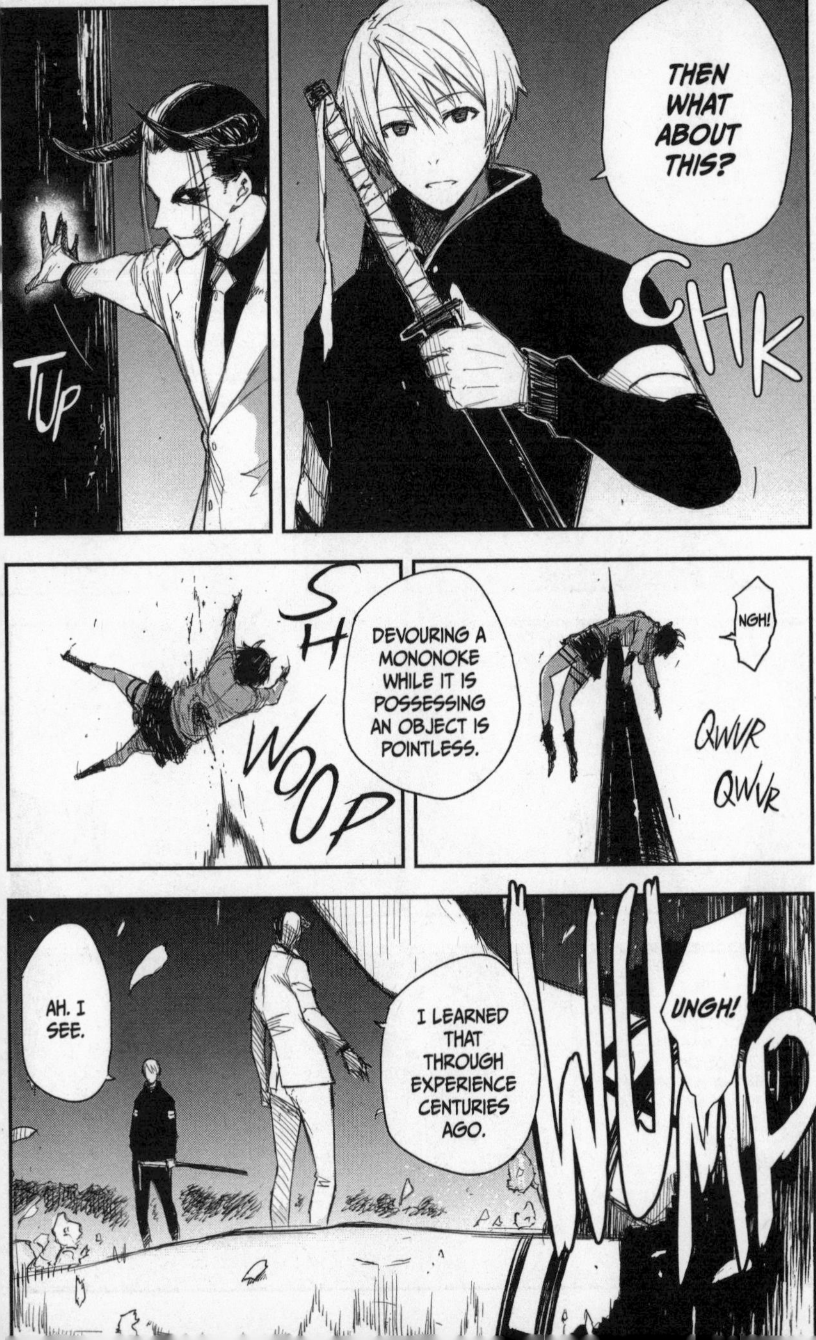
THEN WHAT ABOUT THIS?
CHK
TUP
NGH!
QWVR QWVR
SHWOOP
DEVOURING A MONONOKE WHILE IT IS POSSESSING AN OBJECT IS POINTLESS.
WUMP
UNGH!
I LEARNED THAT THROUGH EXPERIENCE CENTURIES AGO.
AH. I SEE.

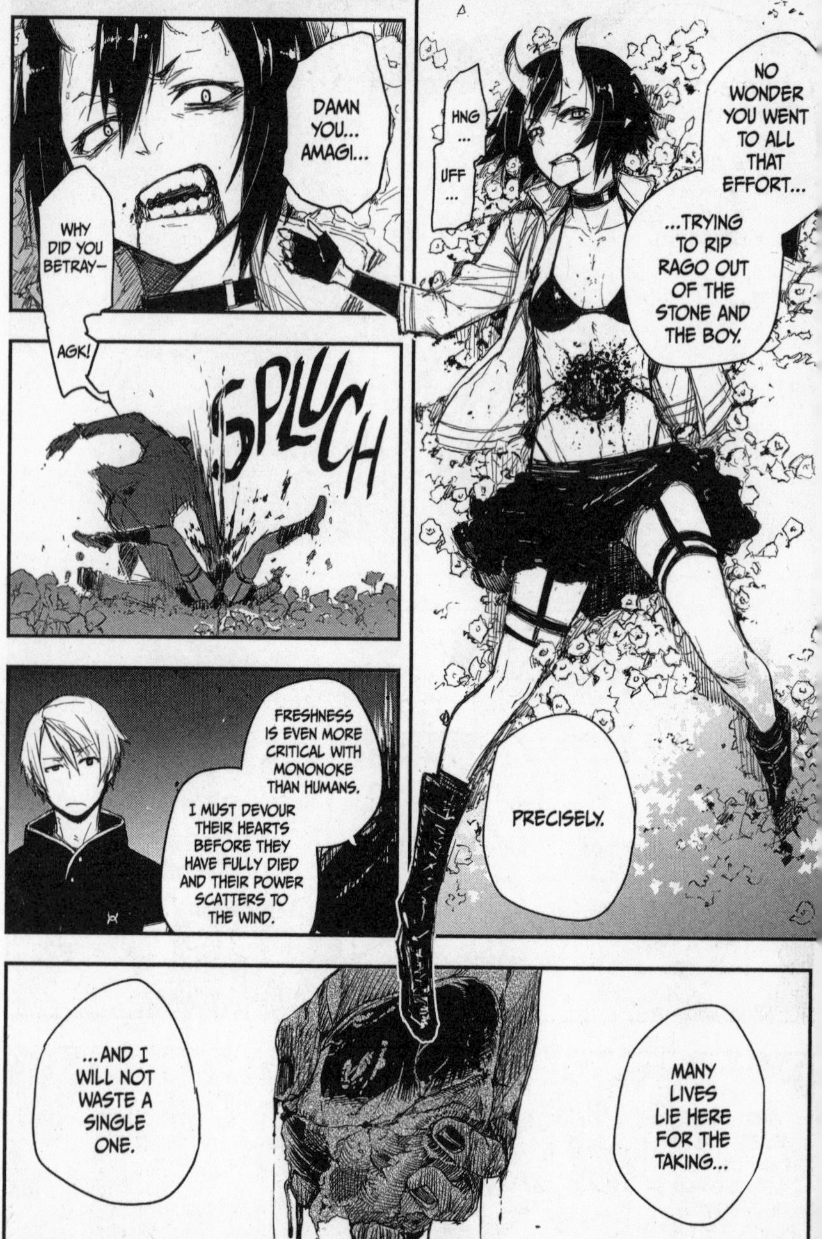
NO WONDER YOU WENT TO ALL THAT EFFORT...
...TRYING TO RIP RAGO OUT OF THE STONE AND THE BOY.
HNG ... UFF ...
PRECISELY.
DAMN YOU... AMAGI...
WHY DID YOU BETRAY—
AGK!
SPLUCH
FRESHNESS IS EVEN MORE CRITICAL WITH MONONOKE THAN HUMANS.
I MUST DEVOUR THEIR HEARTS BEFORE THEY HAVE FULLY DIED AND THEIR POWER SCATTERS TO THE WIND.
MANY LIVES LIE HERE FOR THE TAKING...
...AND I WILL NOT WASTE A SINGLE ONE.

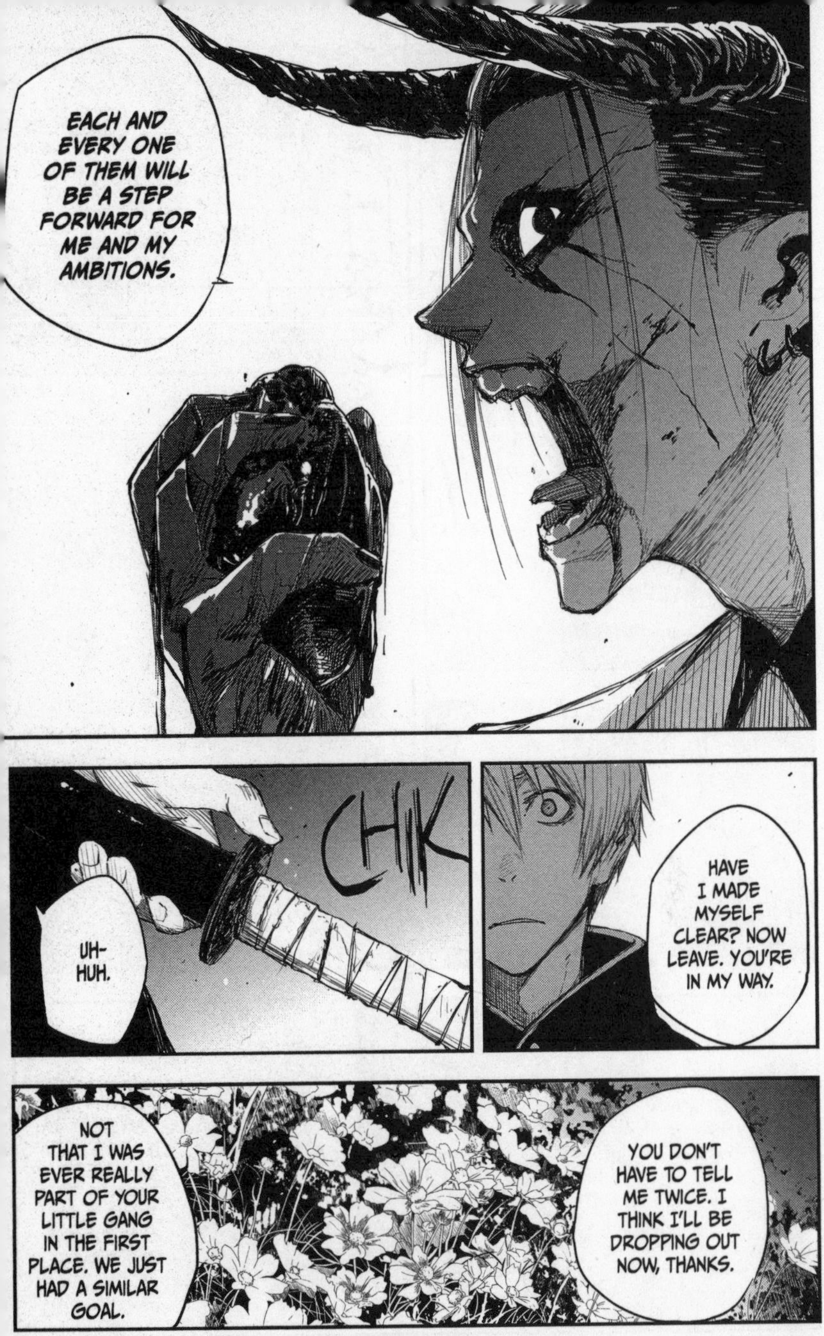
EACH AND EVERY ONE OF THEM WILL BE A STEP FORWARD FOR ME AND MY AMBITIONS.
HAVE I MADE MYSELF CLEAR? NOW LEAVE. YOU'RE IN MY WAY.
CHIK
UH-HUH.
YOU DON'T HAVE TO TELL ME TWICE. I THINK I'LL BE DROPPING OUT NOW, THANKS.
NOT THAT I WAS EVER REALLY PART OF YOUR LITTLE GANG IN THE FIRST PLACE. WE JUST HAD A SIMILAR GOAL.

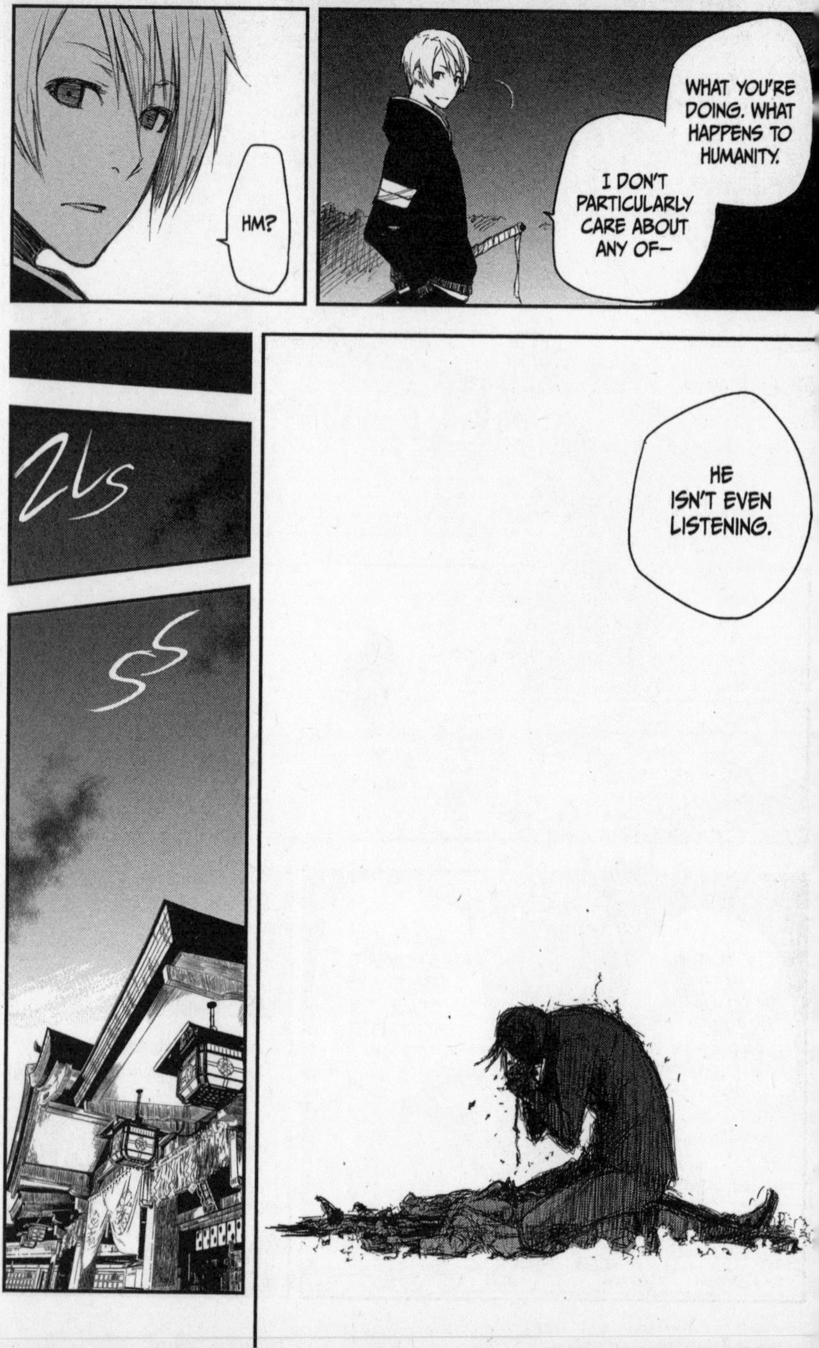
WHAT YOU'RE DOING. WHAT HAPPENS TO HUMANITY.
I DON'T PARTICULARLY CARE ABOUT ANY OF—
HM?
HE ISN'T EVEN LISTENING.
SS

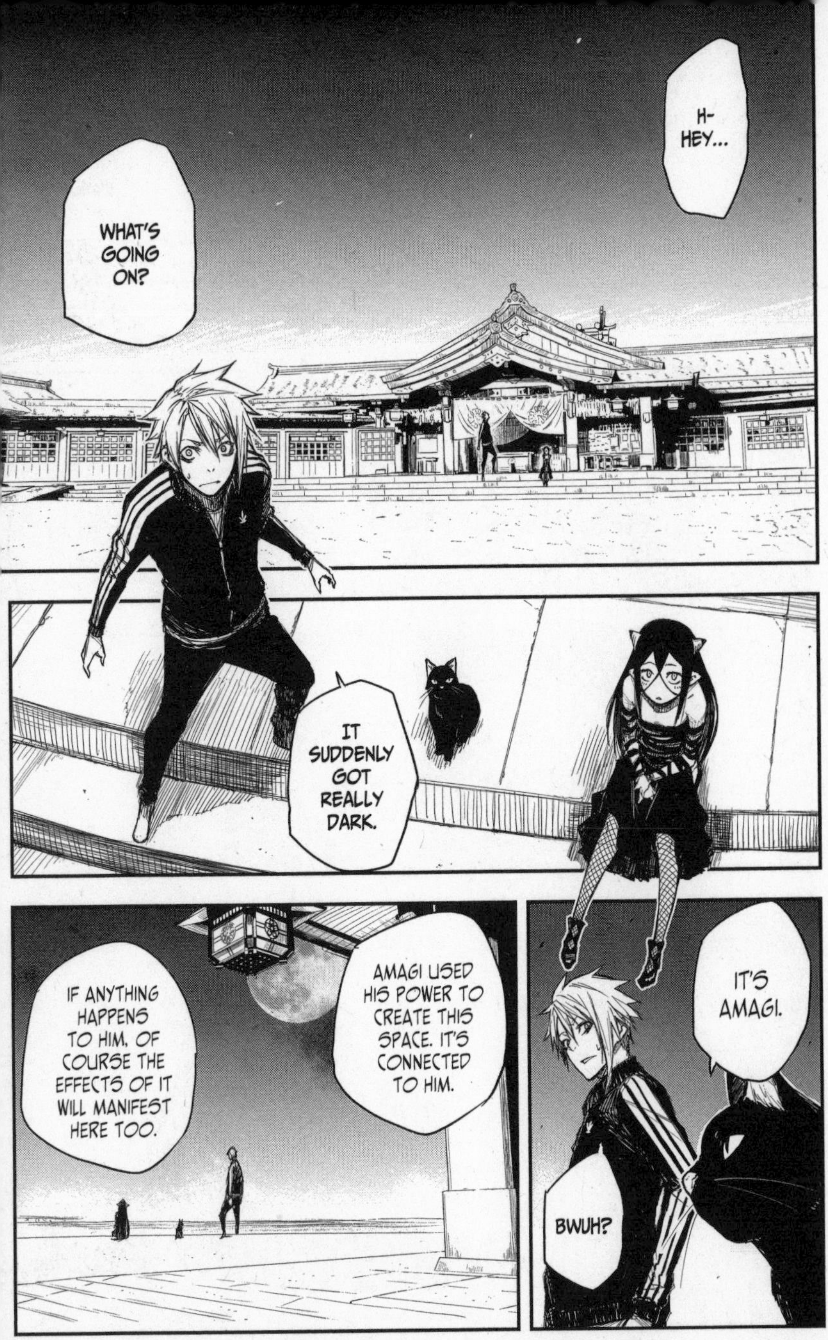
H-HEY...
WHAT'S GOING ON?
IT SUDDENLY GOT REALLY DARK.
IT'S AMAGI.
BWUH?
AMAGI USED HIS POWER TO CREATE THIS SPACE. IT'S CONNECTED TO HIM.
IF ANYTHING HAPPENS TO HIM, OF COURSE THE EFFECTS OF IT WILL MANIFEST HERE TOO.

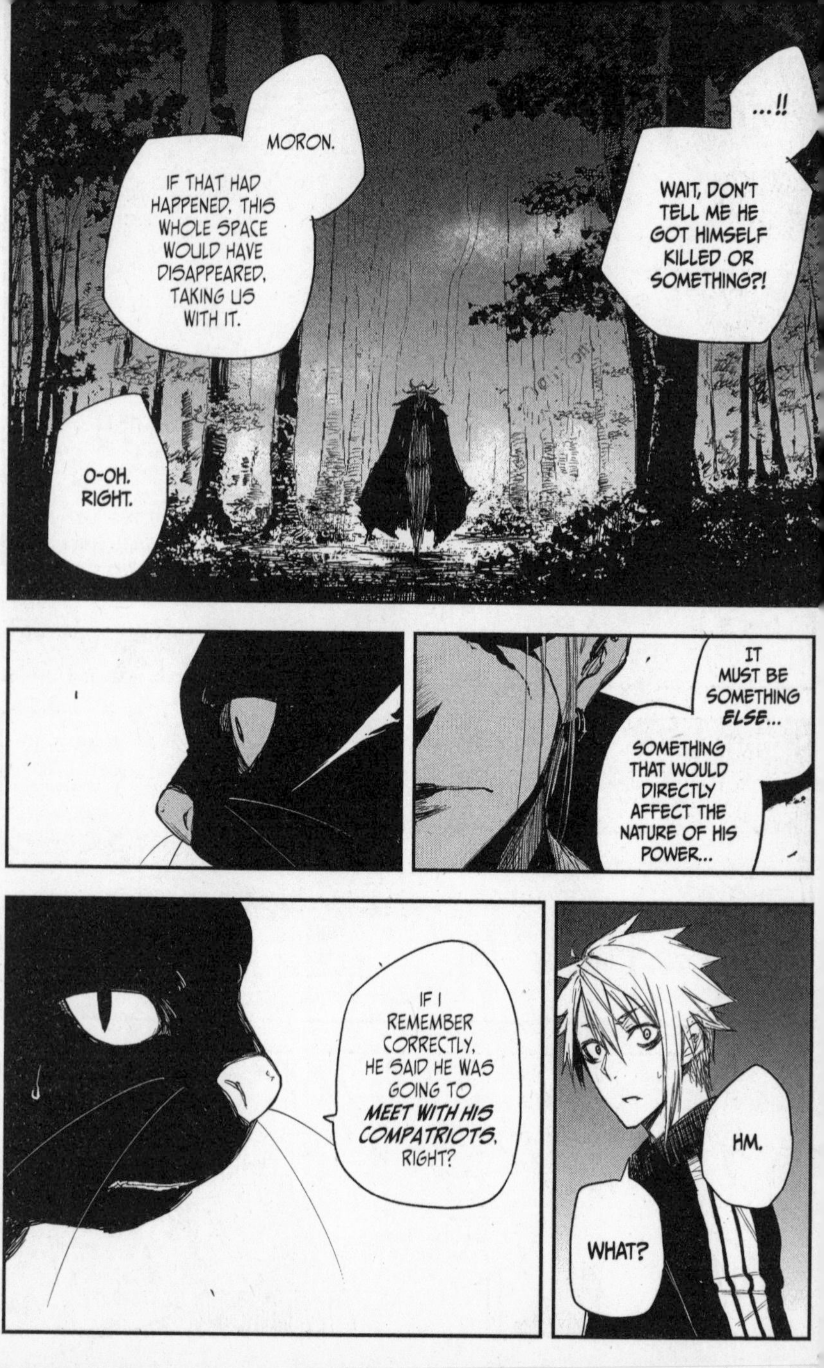
...!!
WAIT, DON'T TELL ME HE GOT HIMSELF KILLED OR SOMETHING?!
MORON.
IF THAT HAD HAPPENED, THIS WHOLE SPACE WOULD HAVE DISAPPEARED, TAKING US WITH IT.
O-OH. RIGHT.
IT MUST BE SOMETHING *ELSE*...
SOMETHING THAT WOULD DIRECTLY AFFECT THE NATURE OF HIS POWER...
HM.
WHAT?
IF I REMEMBER CORRECTLY, HE SAID HE WAS GOING TO *MEET WITH HIS COMPATRIOTS*, RIGHT?

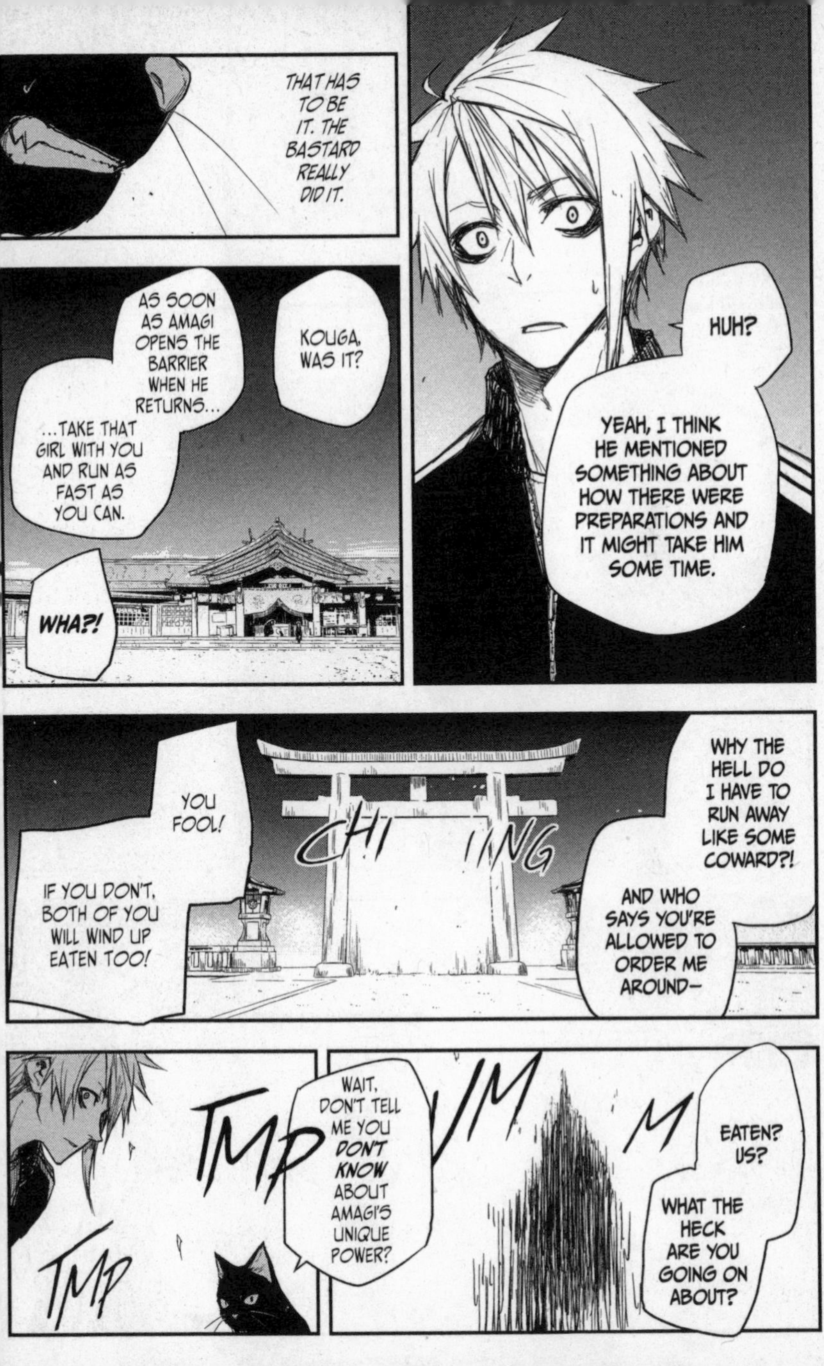
HUH?
YEAH, I THINK HE MENTIONED SOMETHING ABOUT HOW THERE WERE PREPARATIONS AND IT MIGHT TAKE HIM SOME TIME.
THAT HAS TO BE IT. THE BASTARD REALLY DID IT.
KOUGA, WAS IT?
AS SOON AS AMAGI OPENS THE BARRIER WHEN HE RETURNS...
...TAKE THAT GIRL WITH YOU AND RUN AS FAST AS YOU CAN.
WHA?!
WHY THE HELL DO I HAVE TO RUN AWAY LIKE SOME COWARD?!
AND WHO SAYS YOU'RE ALLOWED TO ORDER ME AROUND—
CHI
ING
YOU FOOL!
IF YOU DON'T, BOTH OF YOU WILL WIND UP EATEN TOO!
EATEN? US?
WHAT THE HECK ARE YOU GOING ON ABOUT?
M
VM
WAIT, DON'T TELL ME YOU DON'T KNOW ABOUT AMAGI'S UNIQUE POWER?
TMP
TMP

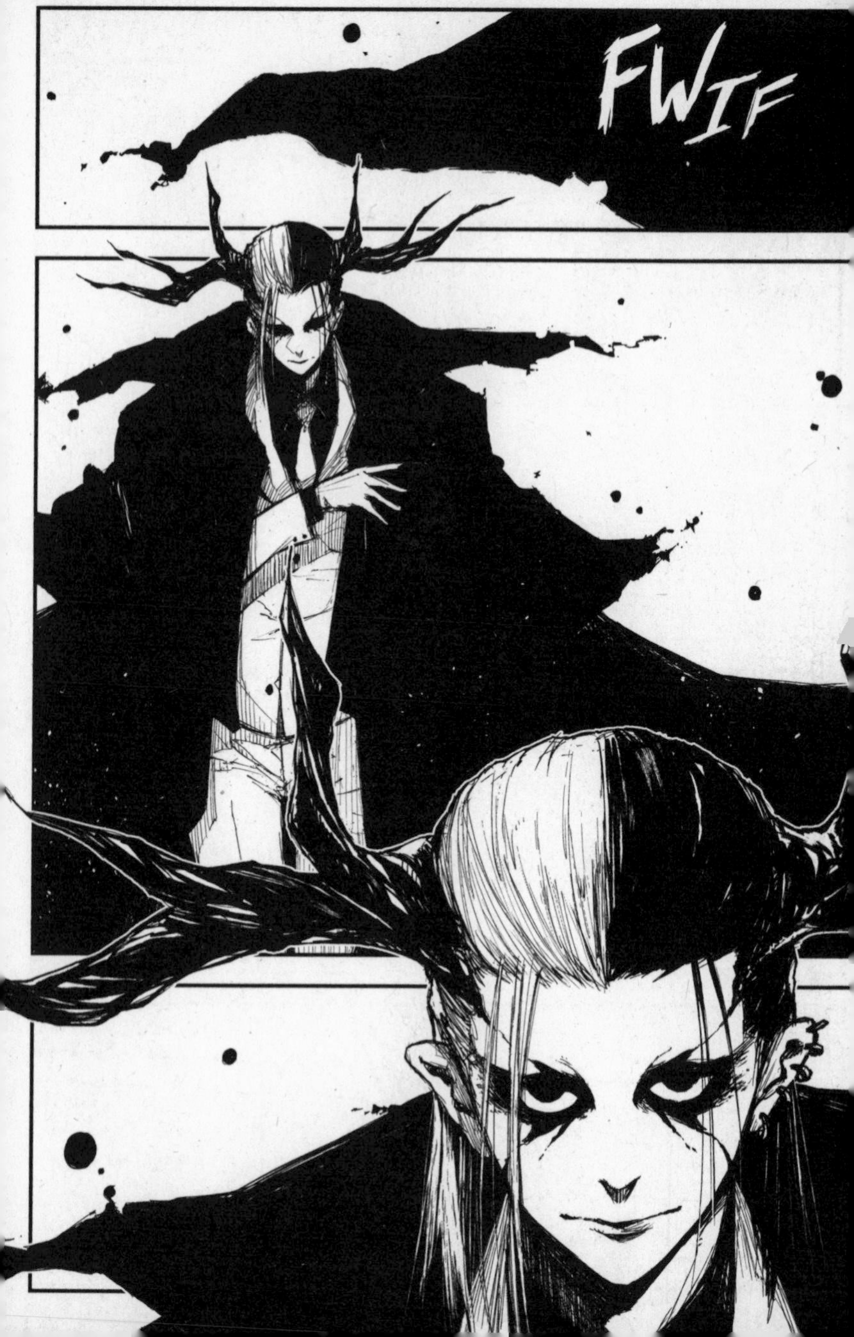
FWIF

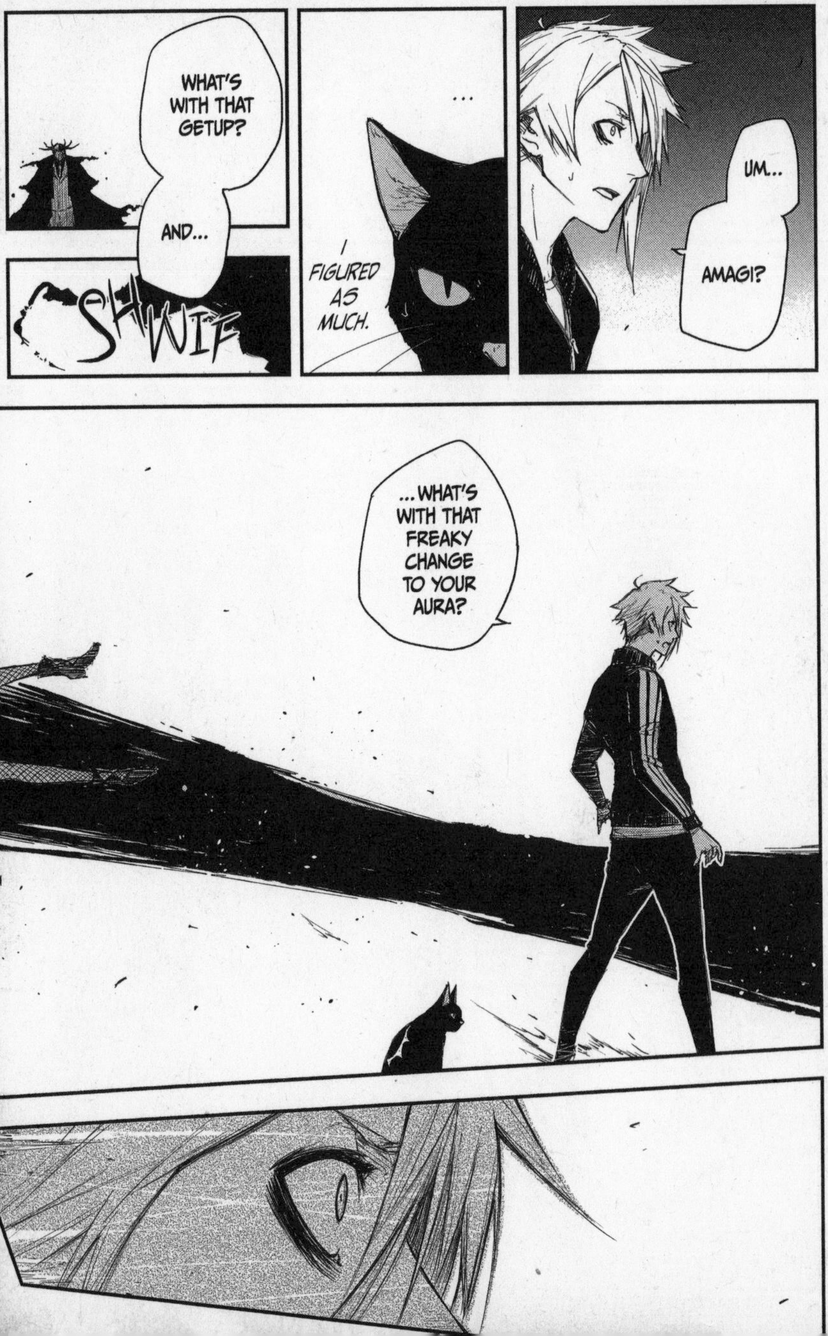
UM...
AMAGI?
...
I FIGURED AS MUCH.
WHAT'S WITH THAT GETUP?
AND...
SHWIF
...WHAT'S WITH THAT FREAKY CHANGE TO YOUR AURA?

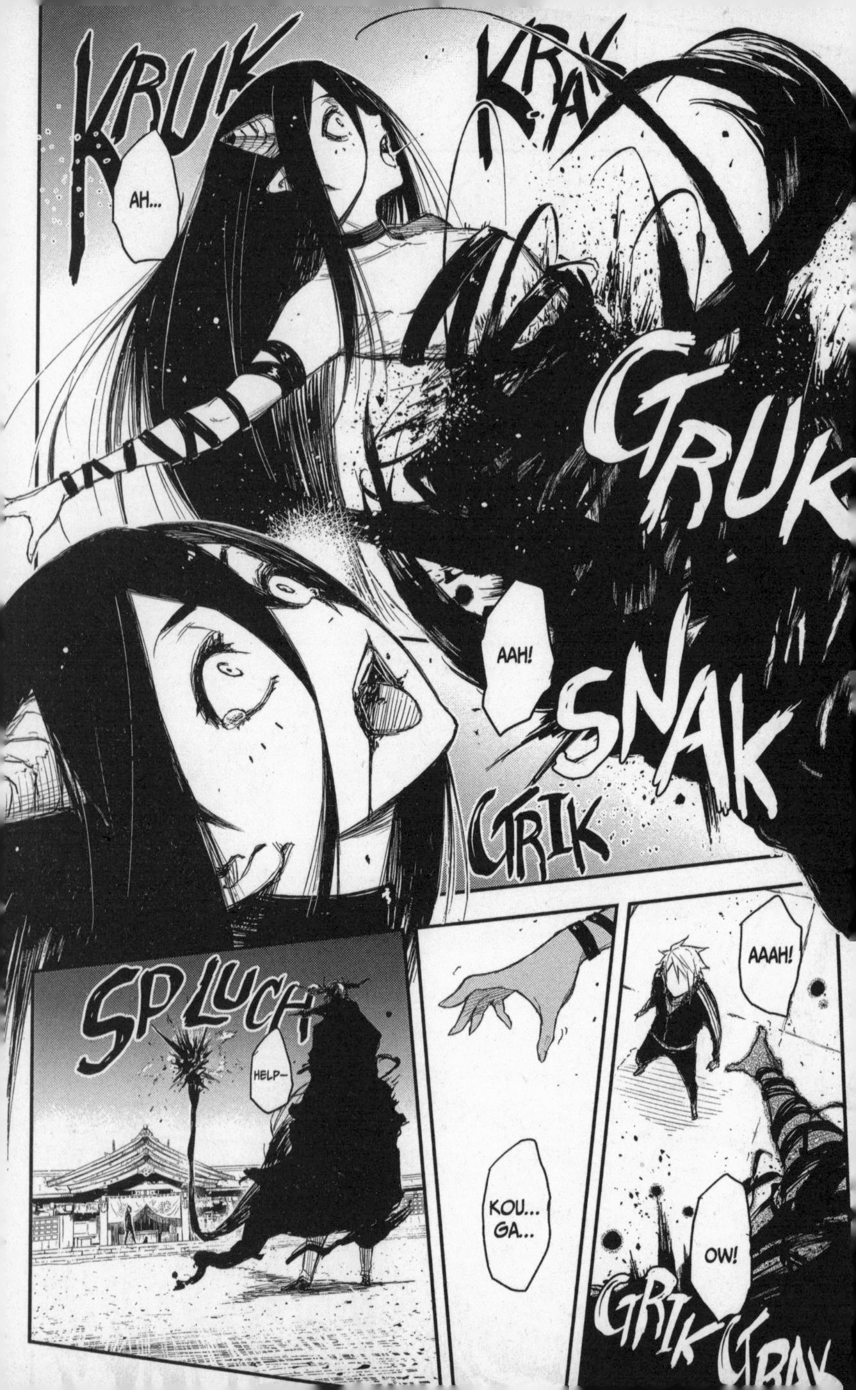
KRAK
KRUK
AH...
GRUK
AAH!
SNAK
GRIK
AAAH!
OW!
GRIK GRAK
KOU... GA...
SPLUCH
HELP-

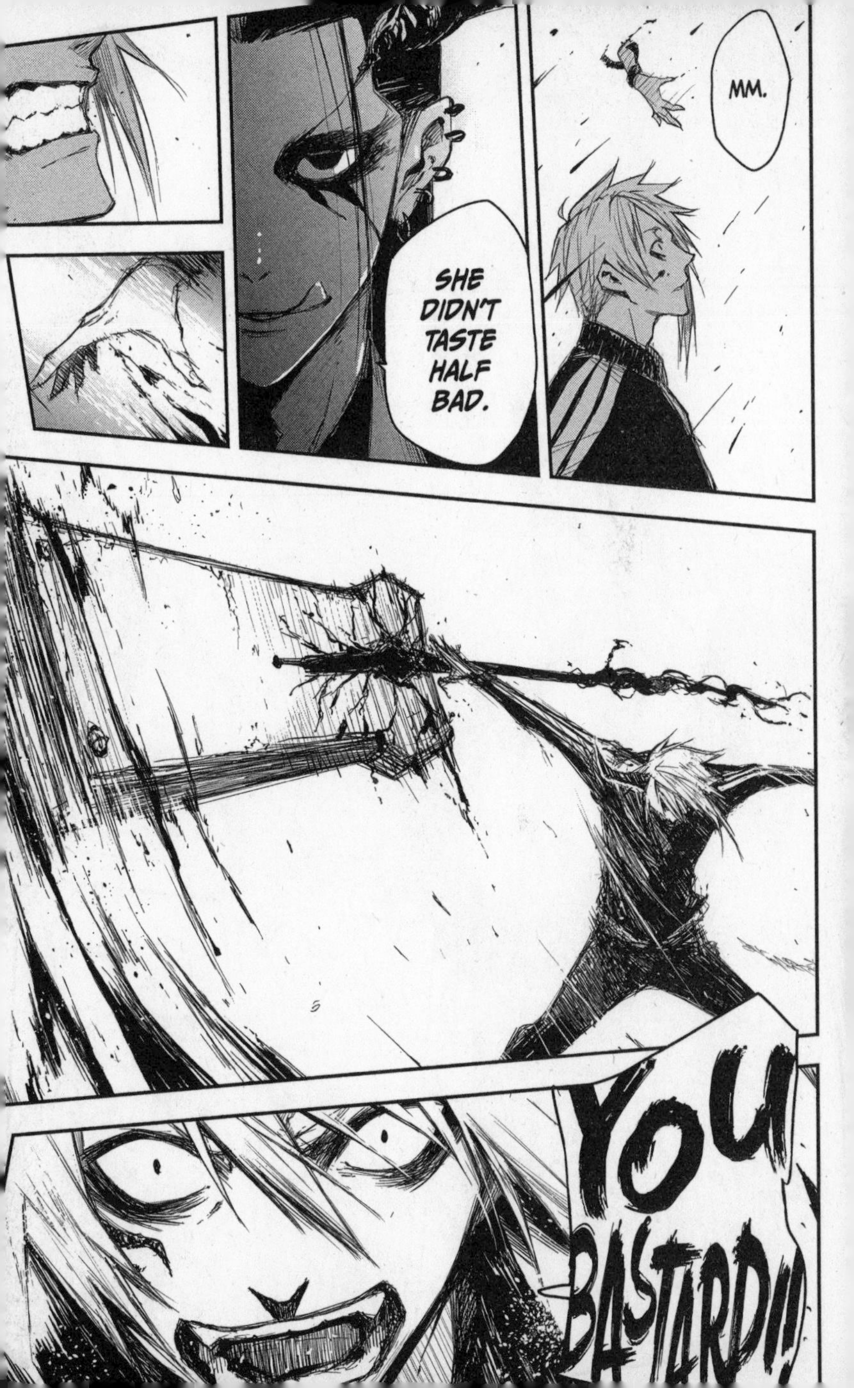
MM.
SHE DIDN'T TASTE HALF BAD.
YOU BASTARD!!

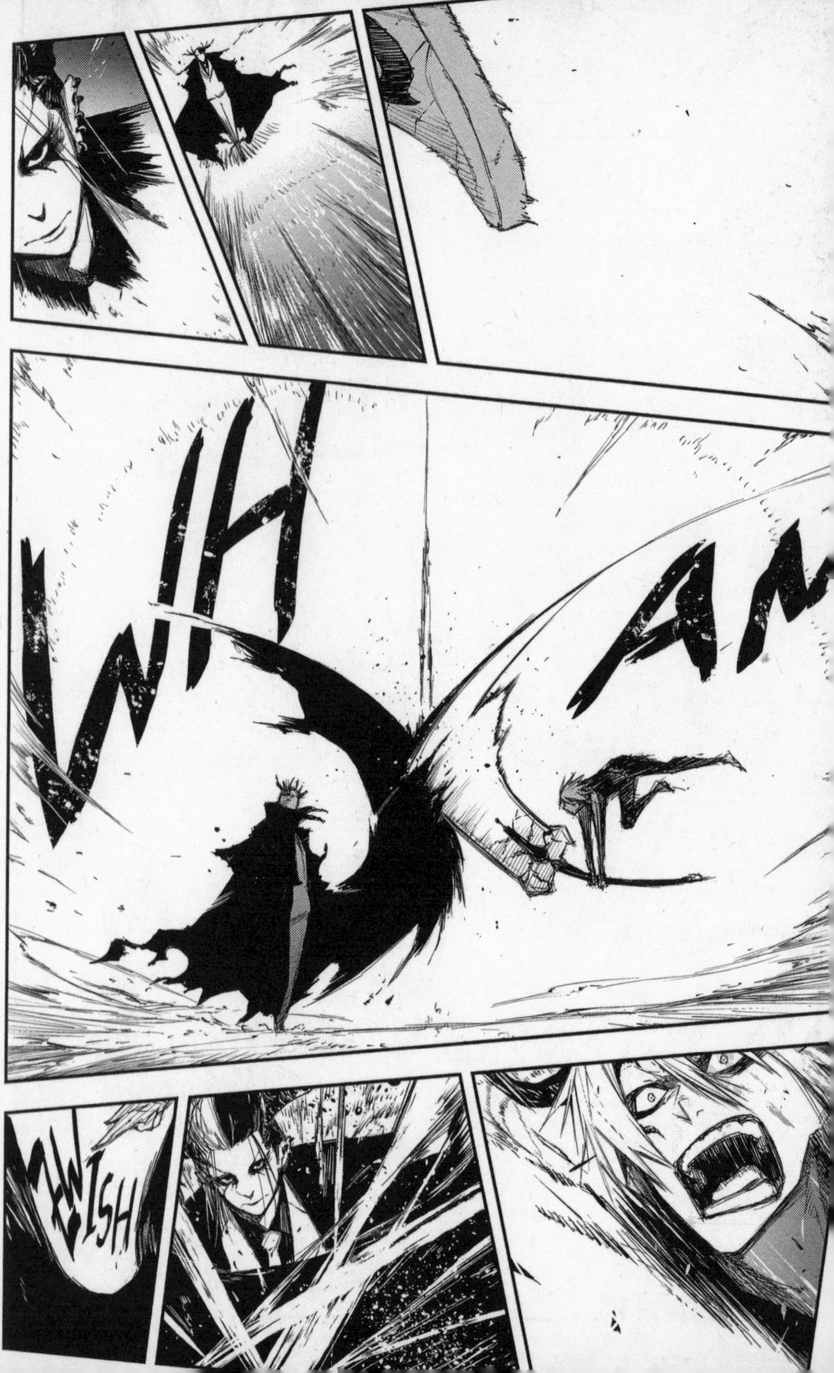
WHAM
SWISH

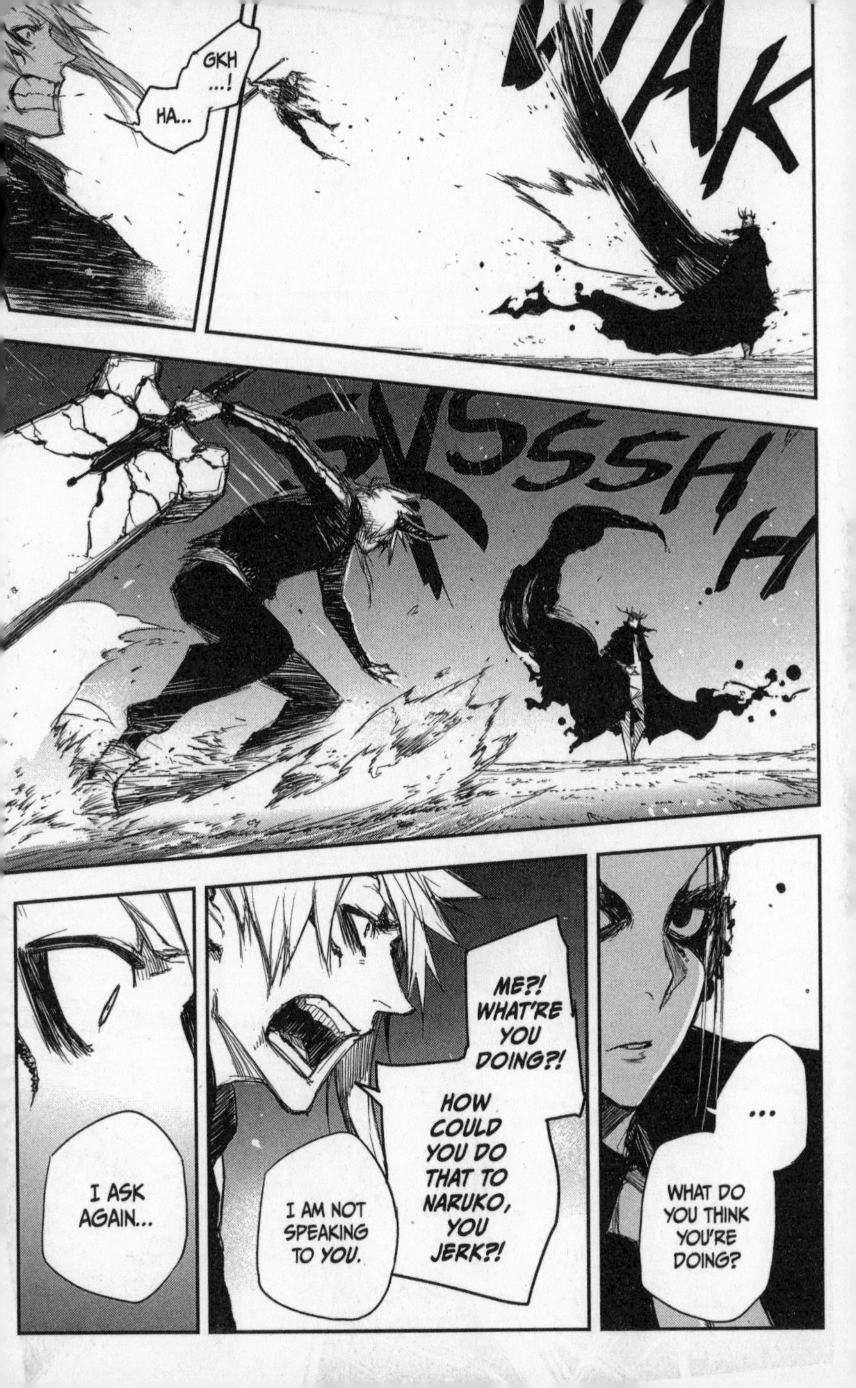
WAK
GKH ...!
HA...
GYSSSHH
...
WHAT DO YOU THINK YOU'RE DOING?
ME?! WHAT'RE YOU DOING?!
HOW COULD YOU DO THAT TO NARUKO, YOU JERK?!
I AM NOT SPEAKING TO YOU.
I ASK AGAIN...

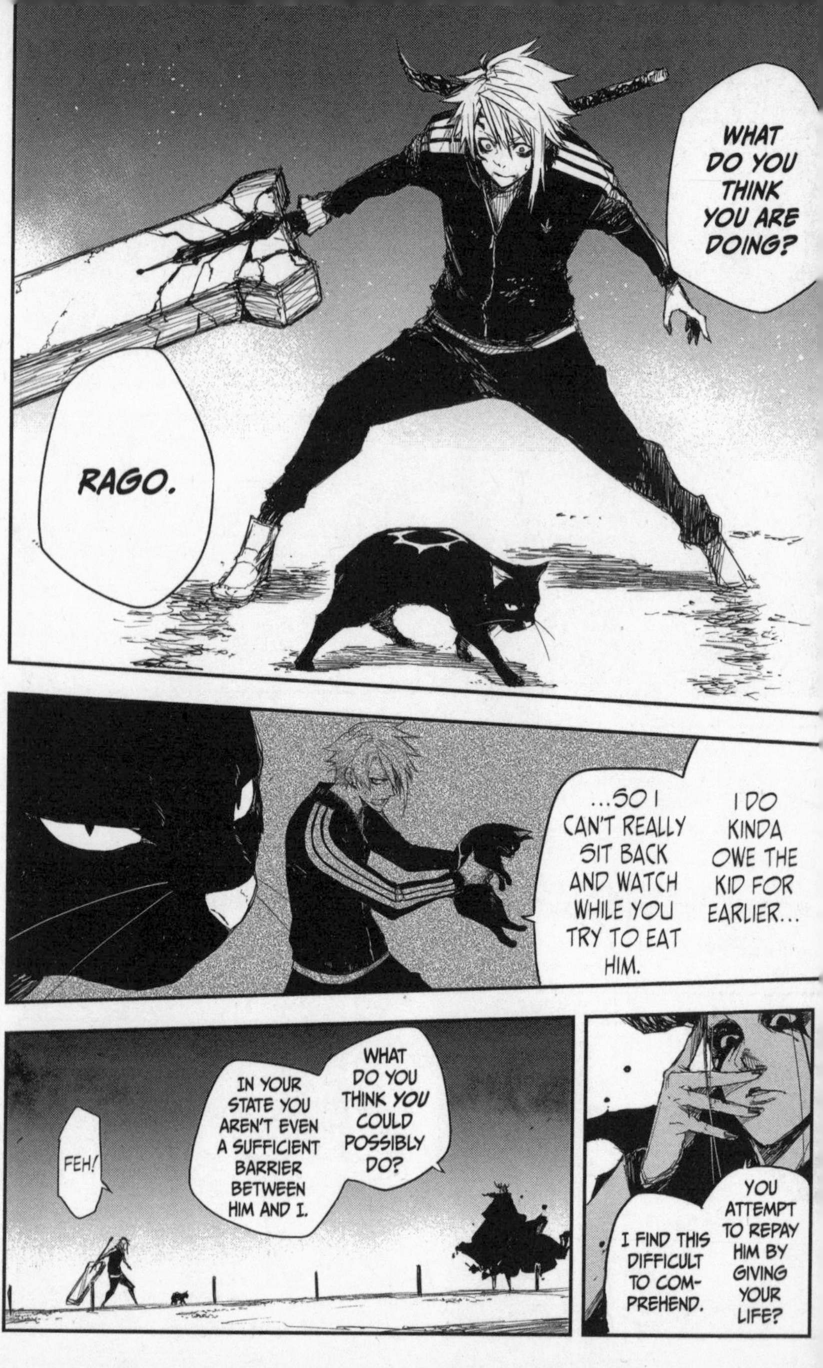
WHAT DO YOU THINK YOU ARE DOING?
RAGO.
I DO KINDA OWE THE KID FOR EARLIER...
...SO I CAN'T REALLY SIT BACK AND WATCH WHILE YOU TRY TO EAT HIM.
YOU ATTEMPT TO REPAY HIM BY GIVING YOUR LIFE?
I FIND THIS DIFFICULT TO COM-PREHEND.
WHAT DO YOU THINK YOU COULD POSSIBLY DO?
IN YOUR STATE YOU AREN'T EVEN A SUFFICIENT BARRIER BETWEEN HIM AND I.
FEH!

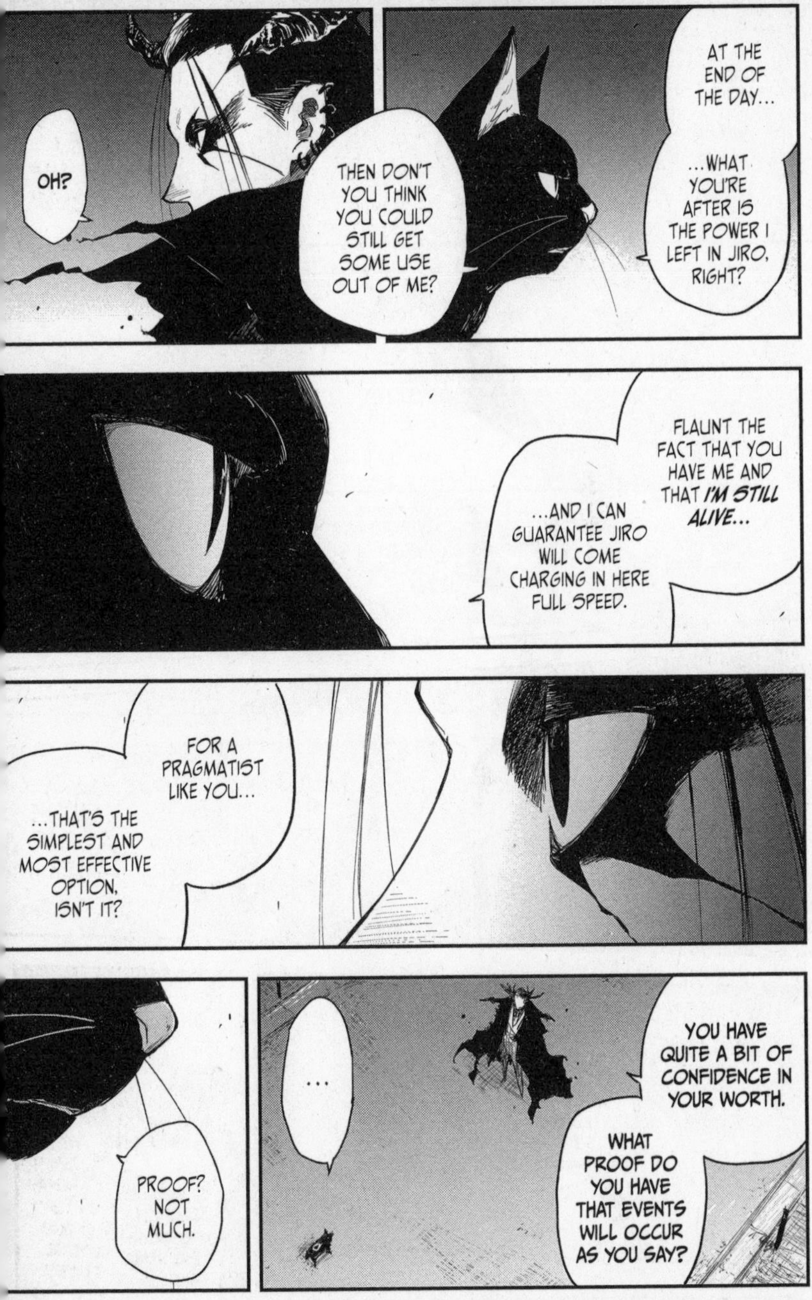

AT THE END OF THE DAY...
...WHAT YOU'RE AFTER IS THE POWER I LEFT IN JIRO, RIGHT?
THEN DON'T YOU THINK YOU COULD STILL GET SOME USE OUT OF ME?
OH?
FLAUNT THE FACT THAT YOU HAVE ME AND THAT *I'M STILL ALIVE...*
...AND I CAN GUARANTEE JIRO WILL COME CHARGING IN HERE FULL SPEED.
FOR A PRAGMATIST LIKE YOU...
...THAT'S THE SIMPLEST AND MOST EFFECTIVE OPTION, ISN'T IT?
YOU HAVE QUITE A BIT OF CONFIDENCE IN YOUR WORTH.
WHAT PROOF DO YOU HAVE THAT EVENTS WILL OCCUR AS YOU SAY?
...
PROOF? NOT MUCH.

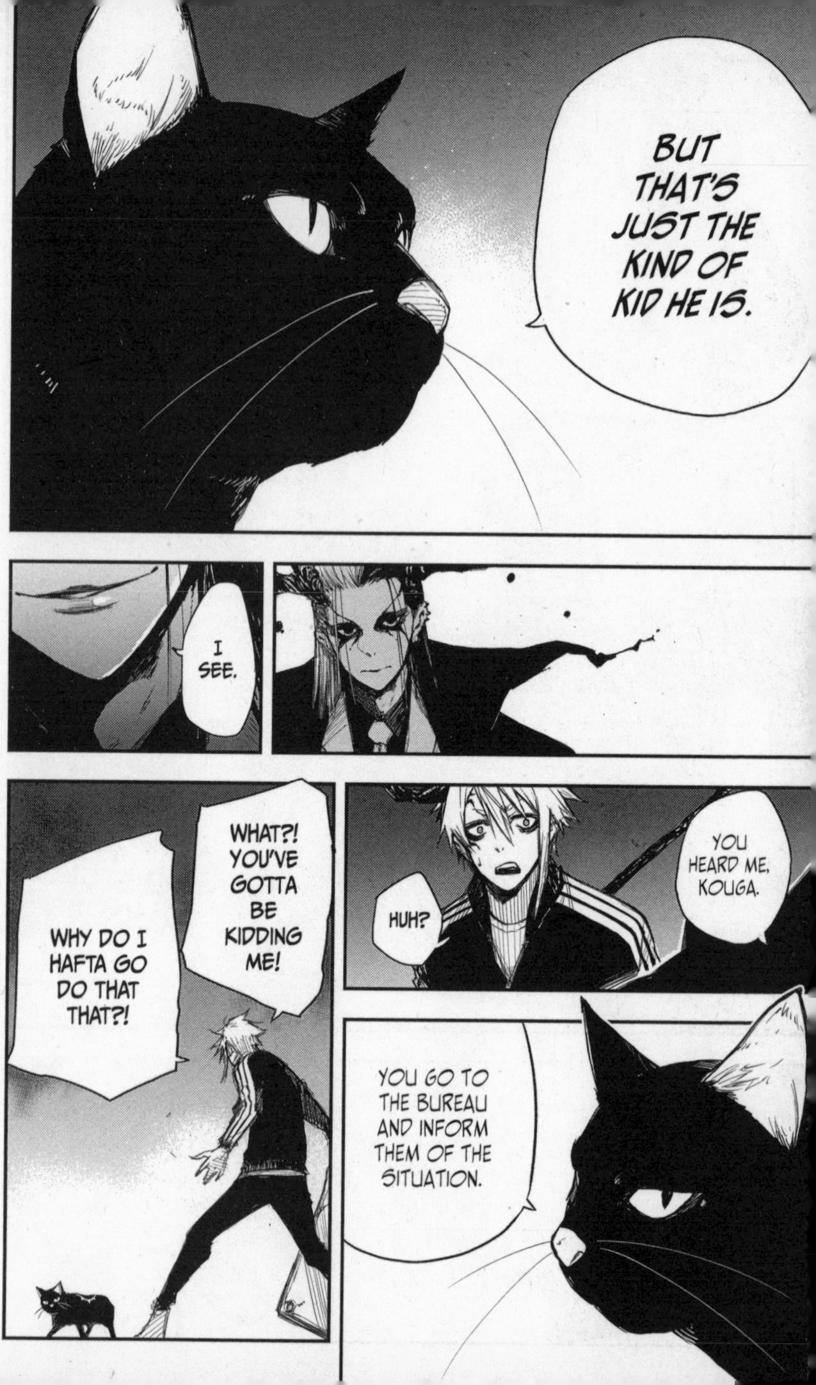
BUT THAT'S JUST THE KIND OF KID HE IS.
I SEE.
YOU HEARD ME, KOUGA.
HUH?
YOU GO TO THE BUREAU AND INFORM THEM OF THE SITUATION.
WHAT?! YOU'VE GOTTA BE KIDDING ME!
WHY DO I HAFTA GO DO THAT THAT?!

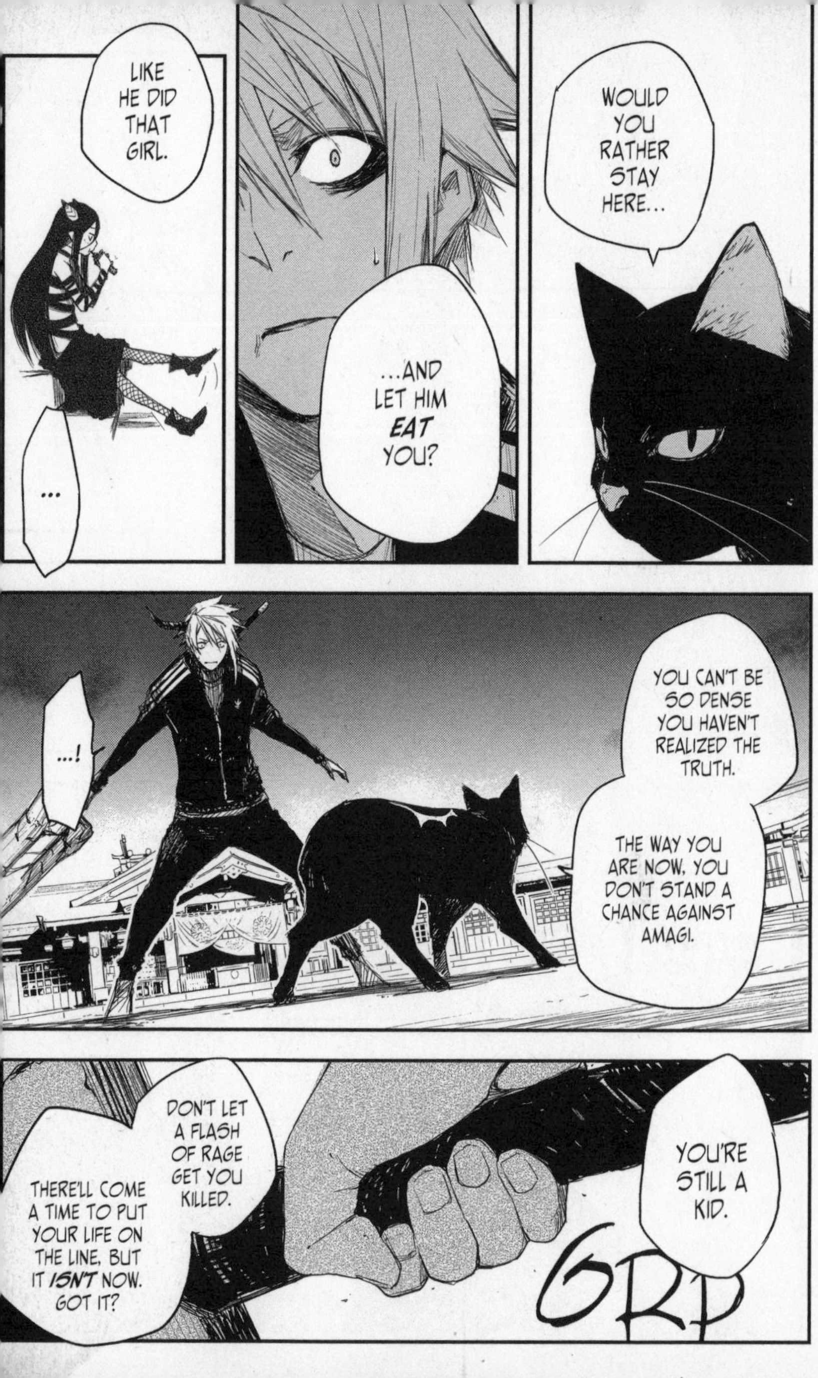
WOULD YOU RATHER STAY HERE...
...AND LET HIM *EAT* YOU?
LIKE HE DID THAT GIRL.
...
YOU CAN'T BE SO DENSE YOU HAVEN'T REALIZED THE TRUTH.
THE WAY YOU ARE NOW, YOU DON'T STAND A CHANCE AGAINST AMAGI.
...!
YOU'RE STILL A KID.
GRP
DON'T LET A FLASH OF RAGE GET YOU KILLED.
THERE'LL COME A TIME TO PUT YOUR LIFE ON THE LINE, BUT IT *ISN'T* NOW. GOT IT?

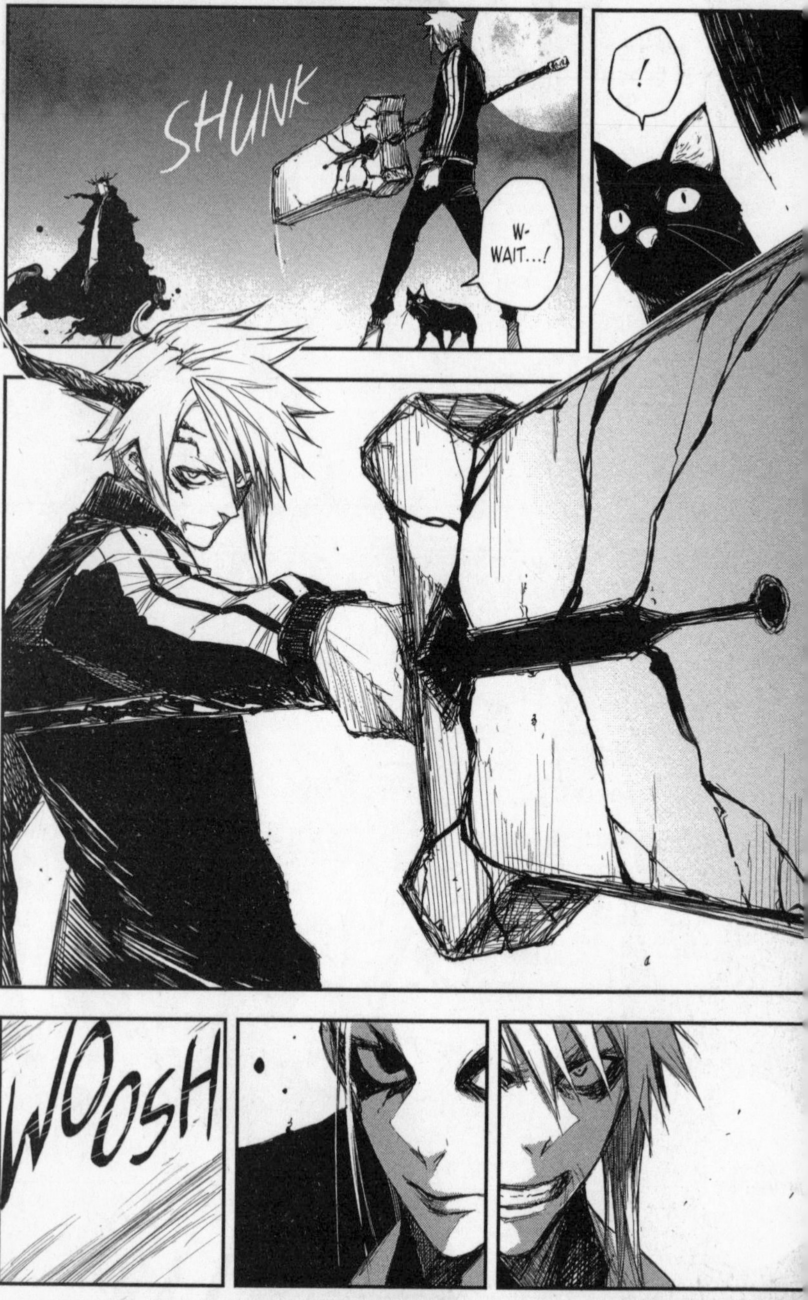
!
SHUNK
W-WAIT...!
WOOSH

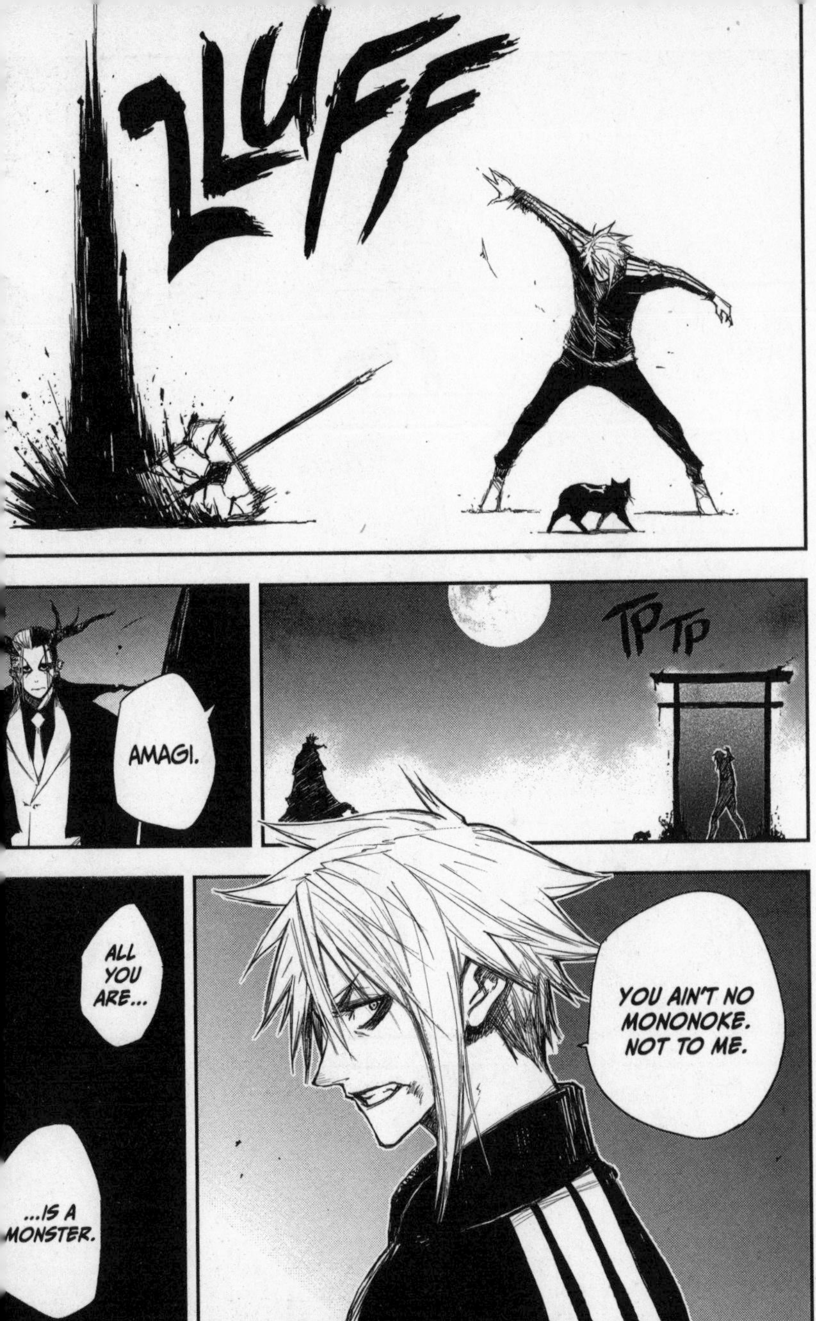
ZUFF
TP TP
AMAGI.
YOU AIN'T NO MONONOKE. NOT TO ME.
ALL YOU ARE...
...IS A MONSTER.

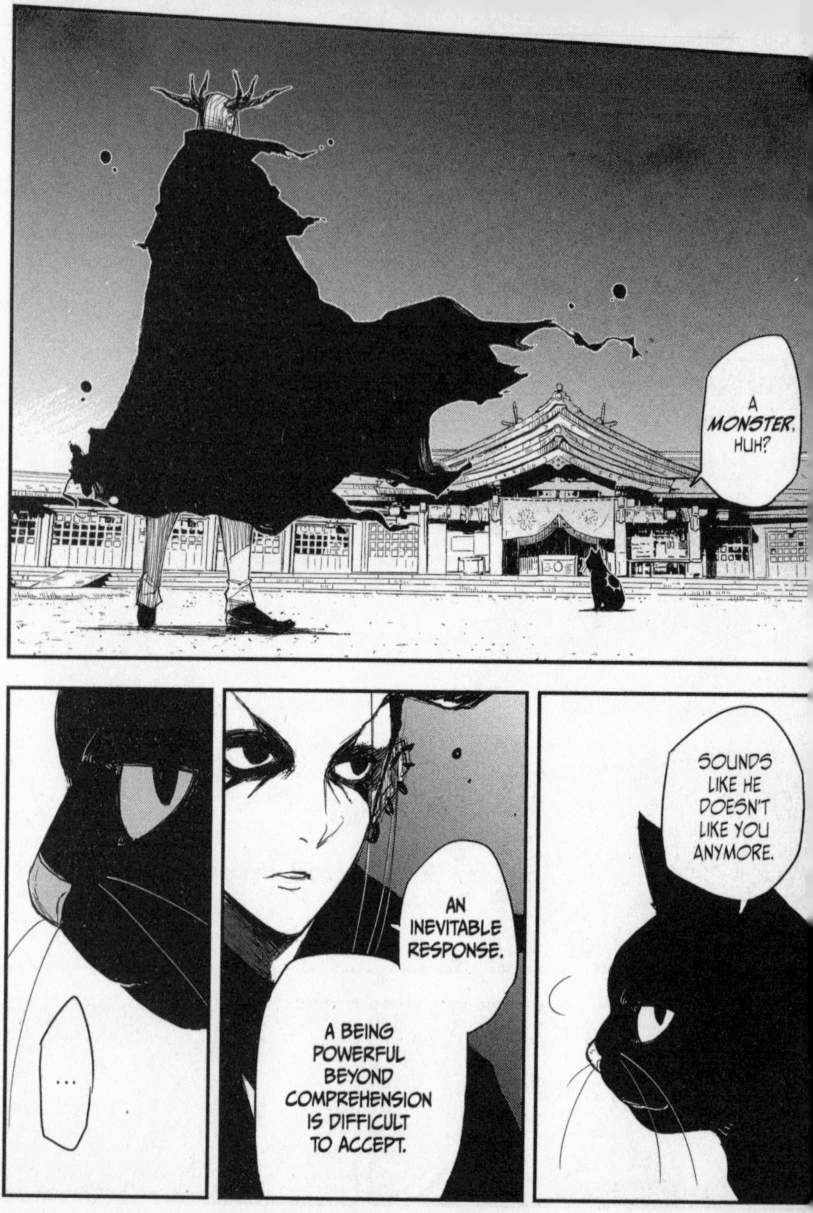
A *MONSTER*, HUH?
SOUNDS LIKE HE DOESN'T LIKE YOU ANYMORE.
AN INEVITABLE RESPONSE.
A BEING POWERFUL BEYOND COMPREHENSION IS DIFFICULT TO ACCEPT.
...

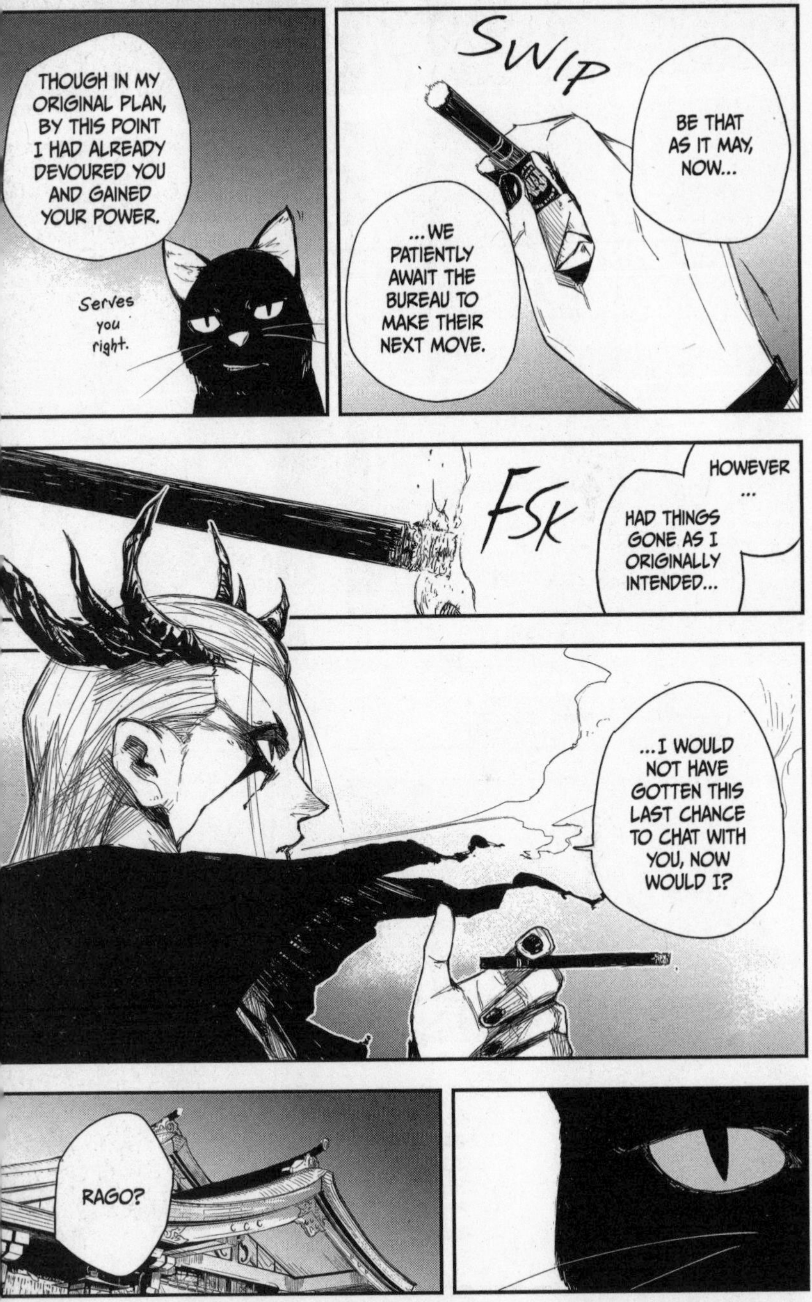
SWIP
BE THAT AS IT MAY, NOW...
...WE PATIENTLY AWAIT THE BUREAU TO MAKE THEIR NEXT MOVE.
THOUGH IN MY ORIGINAL PLAN, BY THIS POINT I HAD ALREADY DEVOURED YOU AND GAINED YOUR POWER.
Serves you right.
FSK
HOWEVER ...
HAD THINGS GONE AS I ORIGINALLY INTENDED...
...I WOULD NOT HAVE GOTTEN THIS LAST CHANCE TO CHAT WITH YOU, NOW WOULD I?
RAGO?

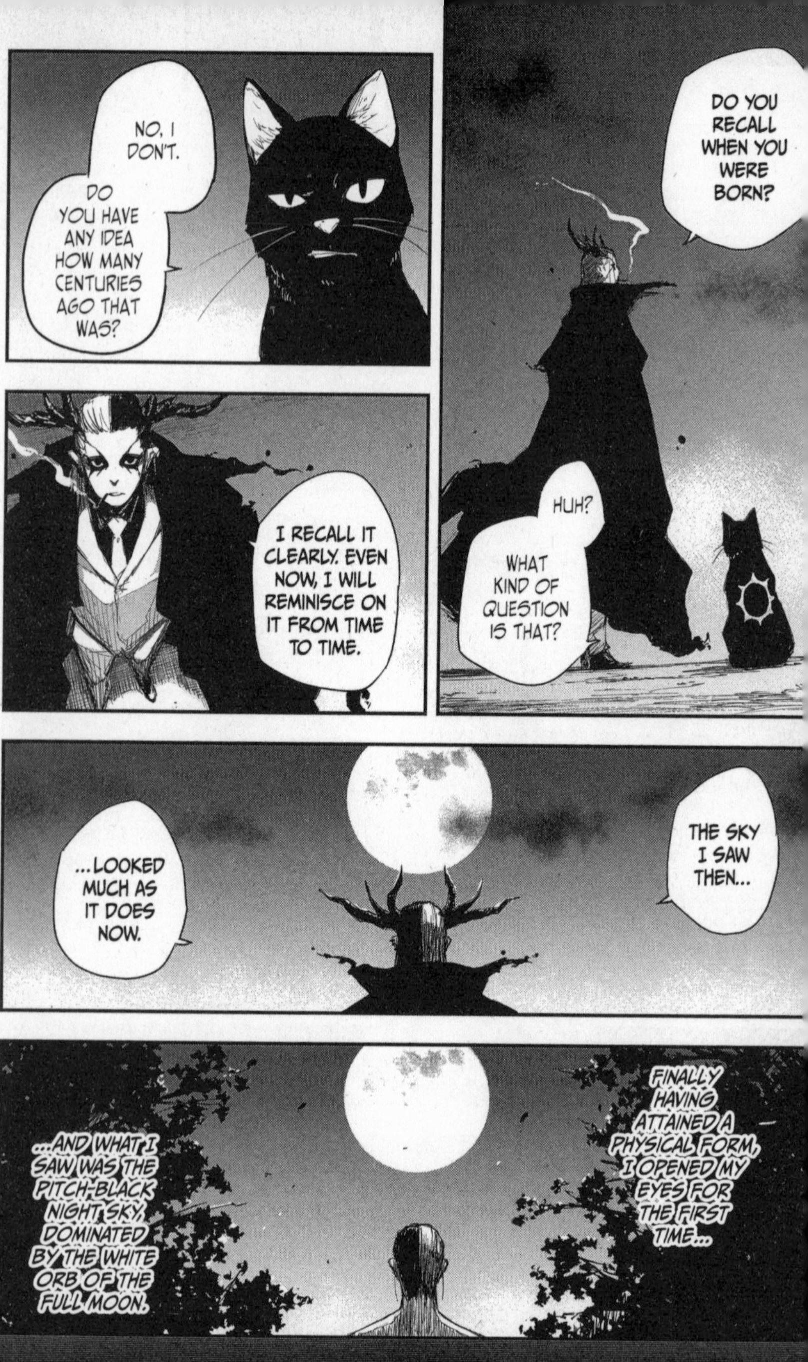
DO YOU RECALL WHEN YOU WERE BORN?
HUH?
WHAT KIND OF QUESTION IS THAT?
NO, I DON'T.
DO YOU HAVE ANY IDEA HOW MANY CENTURIES AGO THAT WAS?
I RECALL IT CLEARLY. EVEN NOW, I WILL REMINISCE ON IT FROM TIME TO TIME.
THE SKY I SAW THEN...
...LOOKED MUCH AS IT DOES NOW.
FINALLY HAVING ATTAINED A PHYSICAL FORM, I OPENED MY EYES FOR THE FIRST TIME...
...AND WHAT I SAW WAS THE PITCH-BLACK NIGHT SKY, DOMINATED BY THE WHITE ORB OF THE FULL MOON.

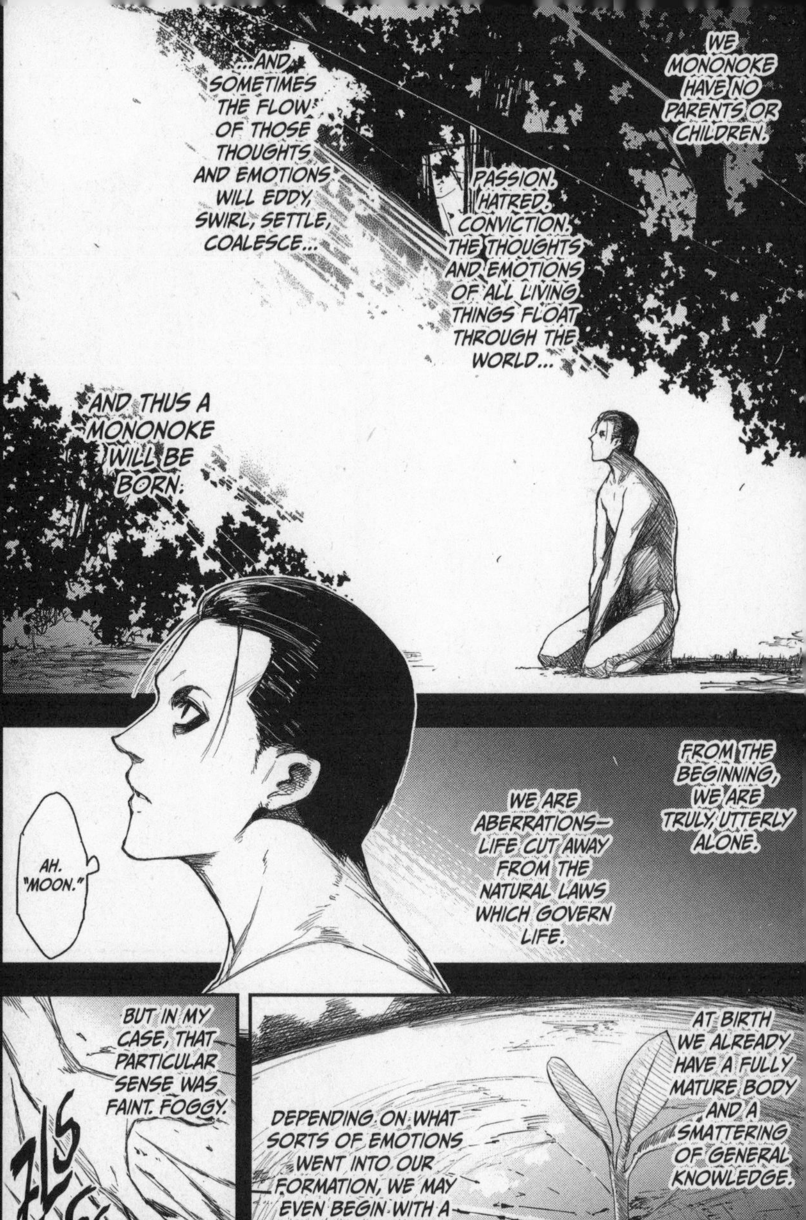
WE MONONOKE HAVE NO PARENTS OR CHILDREN.
PASSION. HATRED. CONVICTION. THE THOUGHTS AND EMOTIONS OF ALL LIVING THINGS FLOAT THROUGH THE WORLD...
...AND SOMETIMES THE FLOW OF THOSE THOUGHTS AND EMOTIONS WILL EDDY, SWIRL, SETTLE, COALESCE...
AND THUS A MONONOKE WILL BE BORN.
FROM THE BEGINNING, WE ARE TRULY, UTTERLY ALONE.
WE ARE ABERRATIONS—LIFE CUT AWAY FROM THE NATURAL LAWS WHICH GOVERN LIFE.
AH. "MOON."
AT BIRTH WE ALREADY HAVE A FULLY MATURE BODY AND A SMATTERING OF GENERAL KNOWLEDGE.
DEPENDING ON WHAT SORTS OF EMOTIONS WENT INTO OUR FORMATION, WE MAY EVEN BEGIN WITH A CLEAR IDEA OF OUR INDIVIDUAL SELF.
BUT IN MY CASE, THAT PARTICULAR SENSE WAS FAINT. FOGGY.
ZLSSS

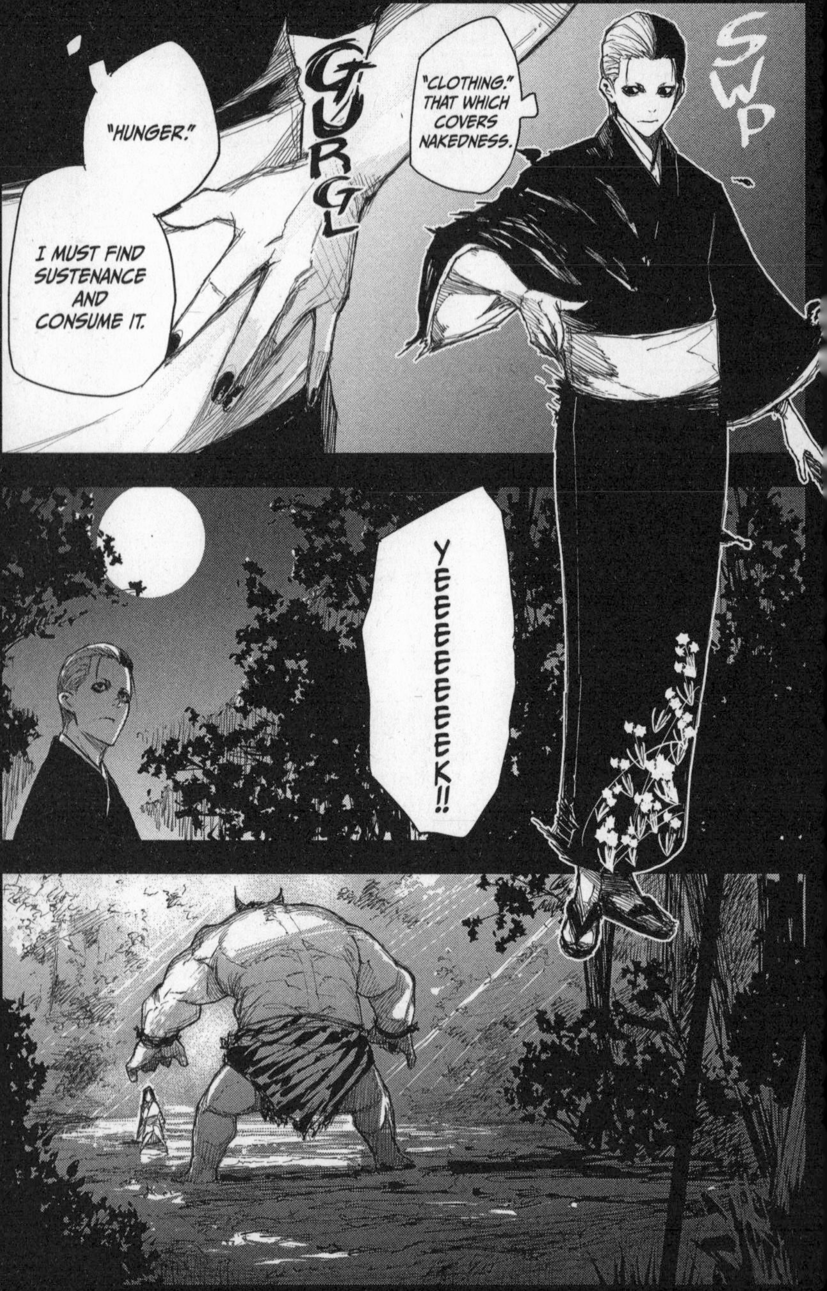
SWP
"CLOTHING." THAT WHICH COVERS NAKEDNESS.
GURGL
"HUNGER."
I MUST FIND SUSTENANCE AND CONSUME IT.
YEEEEEEEK!!

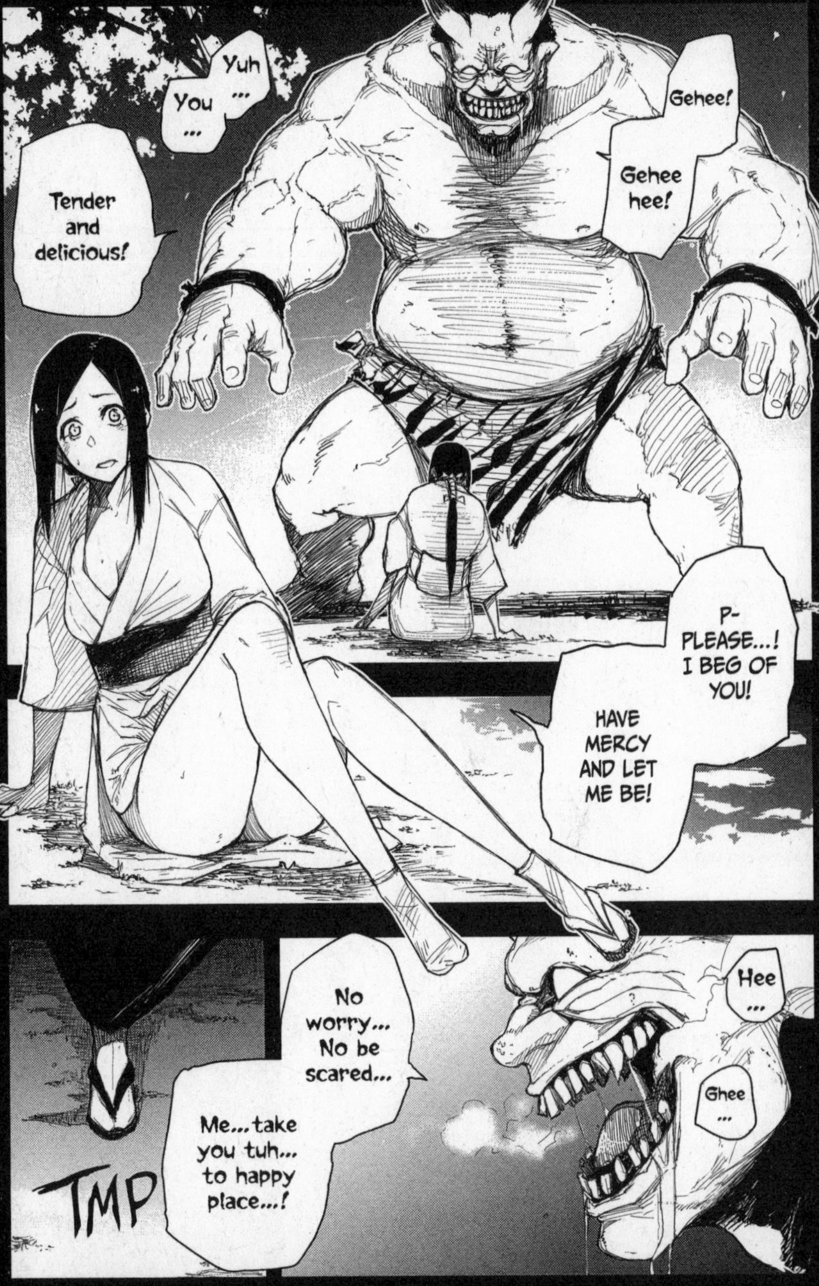
Gehee!
Gehee hee!
Yuh ...
You ...
Tender and delicious!
P- PLEASE...! I BEG OF YOU!
HAVE MERCY AND LET ME BE!
Hee ...
Ghee ...
No worry... No be scared...
Me...take you tuh... to happy place...!
TMP

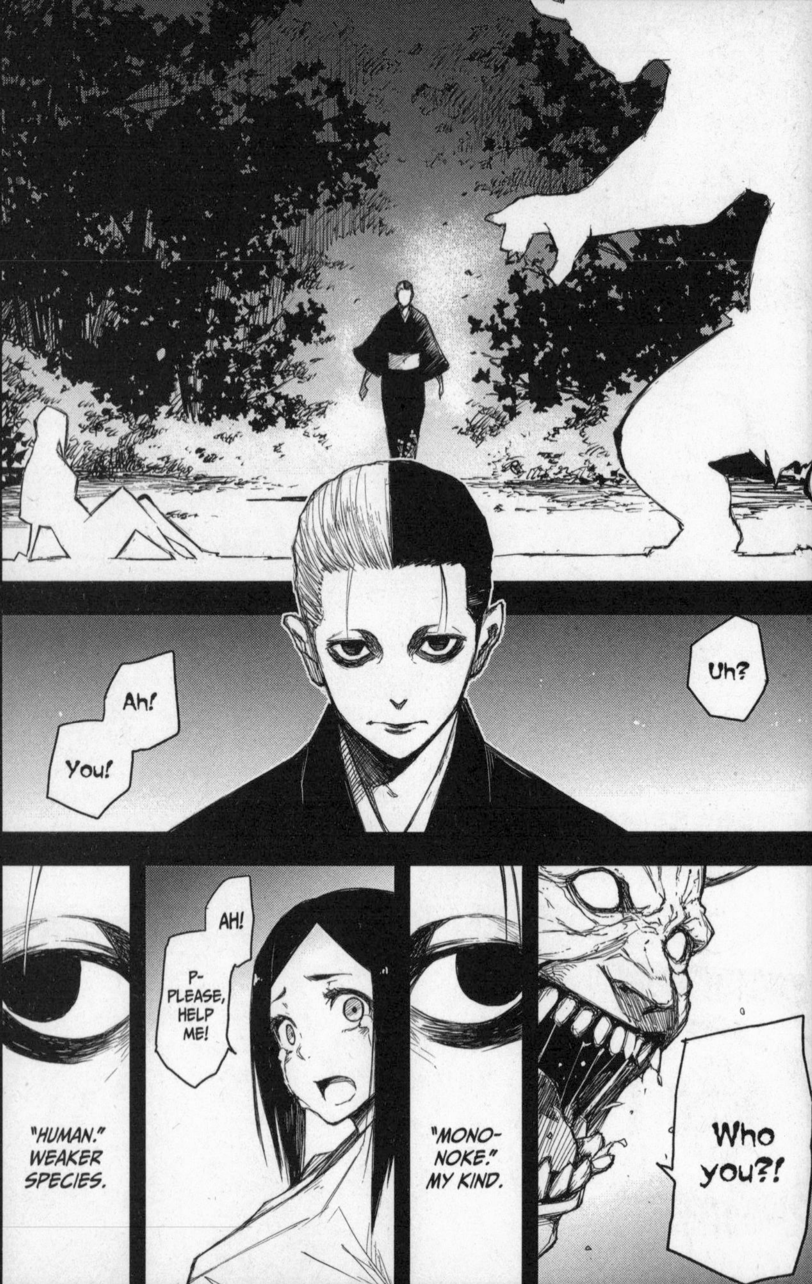
Uh?
Ah!
You!
Who you?!
"MONO-NOKE." MY KIND.
AH!
P-PLEASE, HELP ME!
"HUMAN." WEAKER SPECIES.

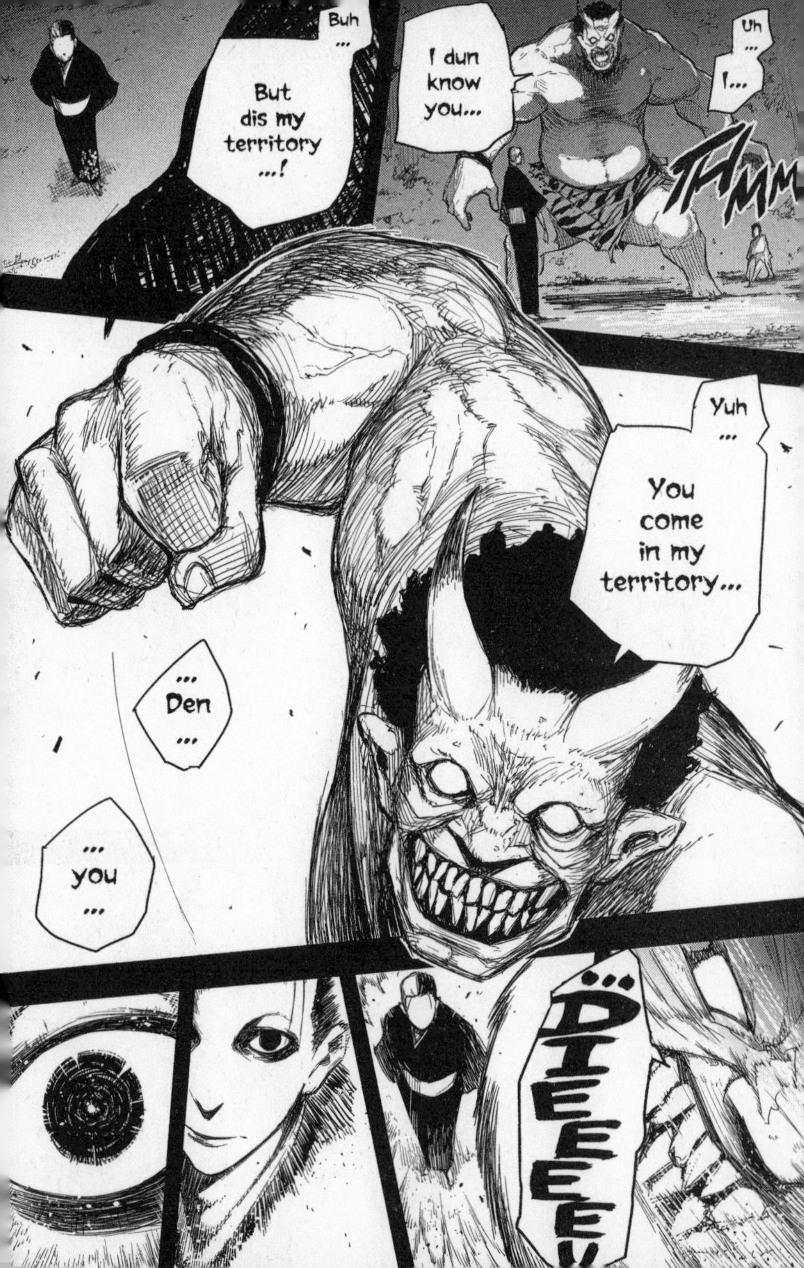
Uh ... I...
I dun know you...
TAMM
Buh ...
But dis my territory ...!
Yuh ...
You come in my territory...
... Den ...
... you ...
...DIEEEEV

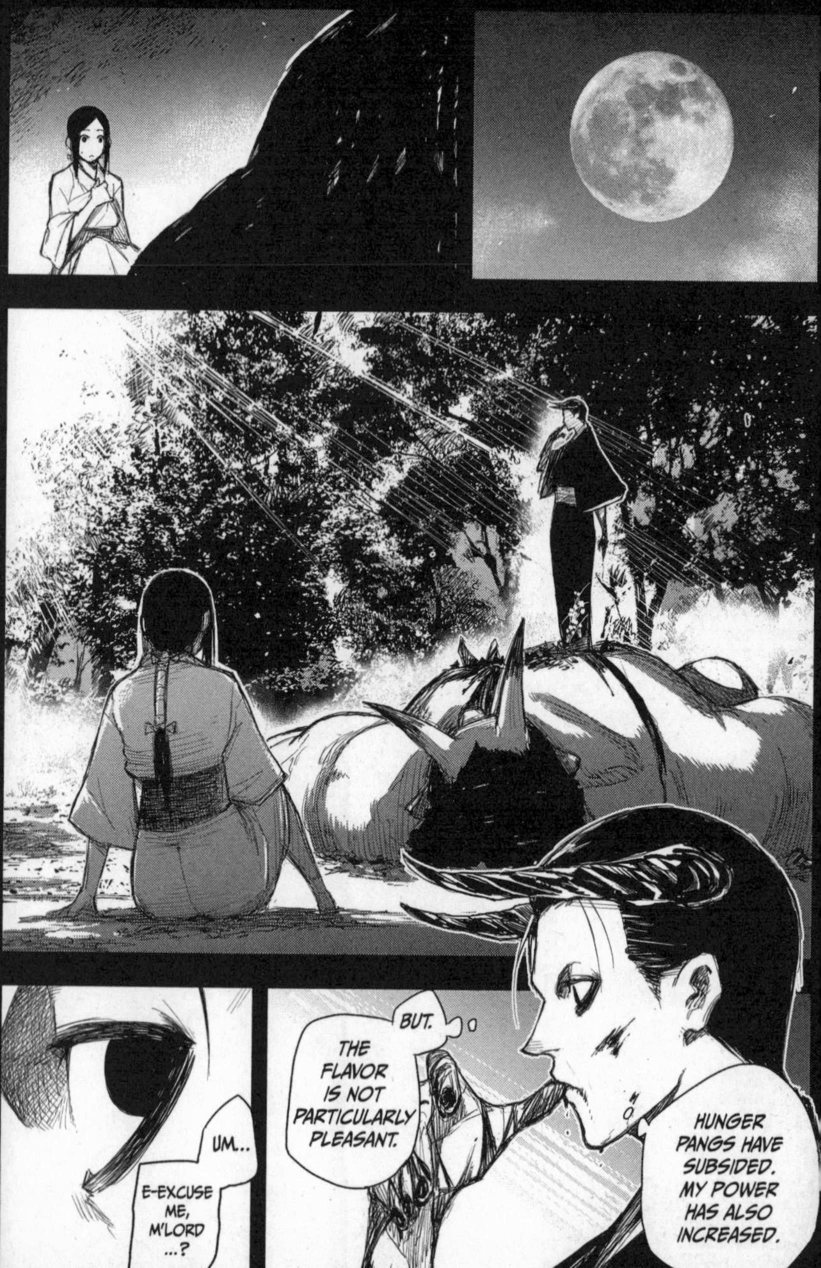
HUNGER PANGS HAVE SUBSIDED. MY POWER HAS ALSO INCREASED.
BUT.
THE FLAVOR IS NOT PARTICULARLY PLEASANT.
UM...
E-EXCUSE ME, M'LORD ...?

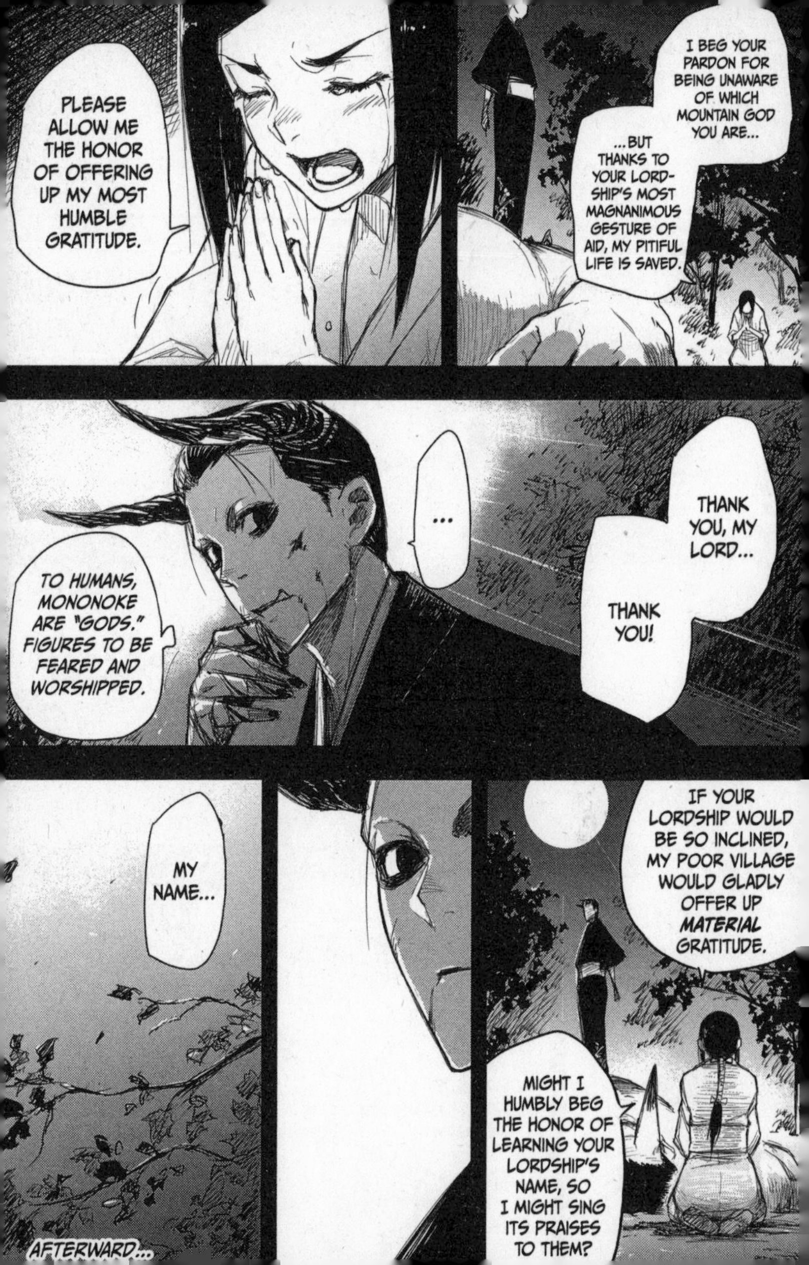
I BEG YOUR PARDON FOR BEING UNAWARE OF WHICH MOUNTAIN GOD YOU ARE...
...BUT THANKS TO YOUR LORDSHIP'S MOST MAGNANIMOUS GESTURE OF AID, MY PITIFUL LIFE IS SAVED.
PLEASE ALLOW ME THE HONOR OF OFFERING UP MY MOST HUMBLE GRATITUDE.
THANK YOU, MY LORD...
THANK YOU!
...
TO HUMANS, MONONOKE ARE "GODS." FIGURES TO BE FEARED AND WORSHIPPED.
IF YOUR LORDSHIP WOULD BE SO INCLINED, MY POOR VILLAGE WOULD GLADLY OFFER UP MATERIAL GRATITUDE.
MIGHT I HUMBLY BEG THE HONOR OF LEARNING YOUR LORDSHIP'S NAME, SO I MIGHT SING ITS PRAISES TO THEM?
MY NAME...
AFTERWARD...

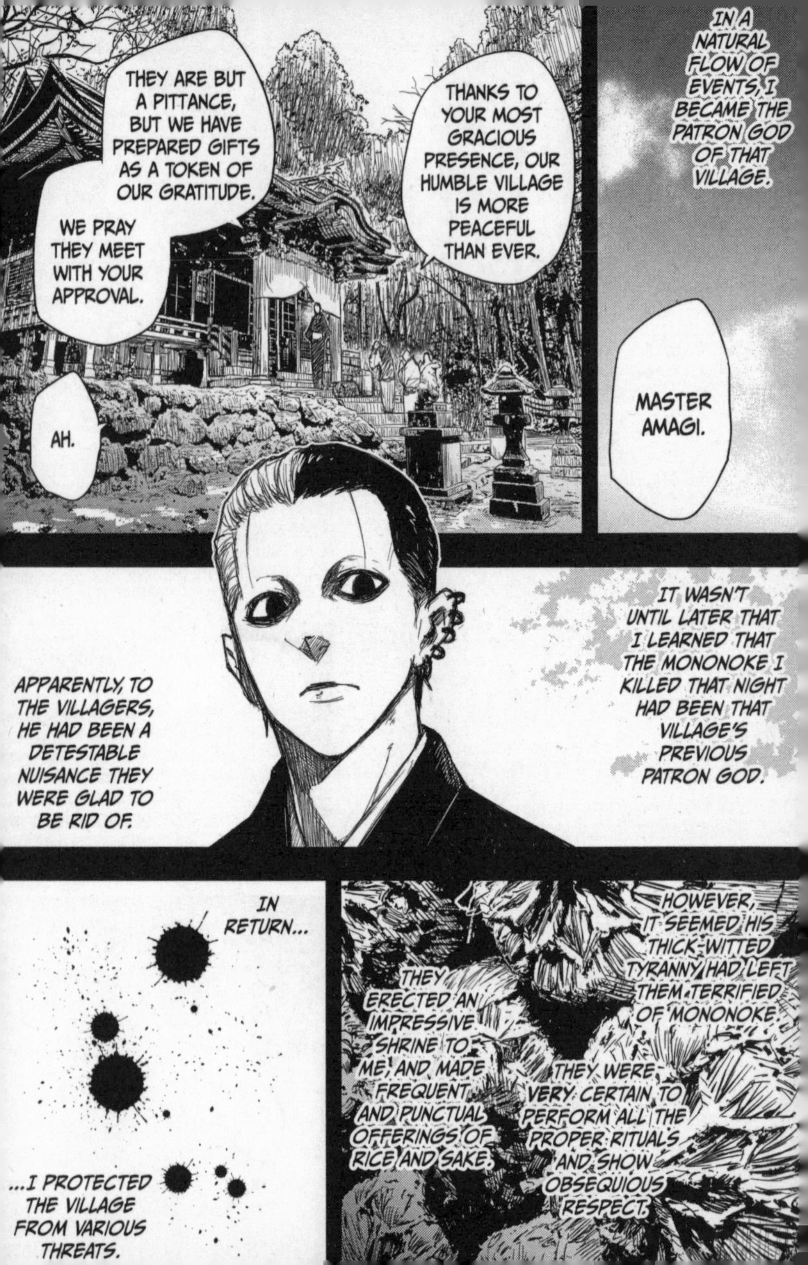
IN A NATURAL FLOW OF EVENTS, I BECAME THE PATRON GOD OF THAT VILLAGE.
MASTER AMAGI.
THANKS TO YOUR MOST GRACIOUS PRESENCE, OUR HUMBLE VILLAGE IS MORE PEACEFUL THAN EVER.
THEY ARE BUT A PITTANCE, BUT WE HAVE PREPARED GIFTS AS A TOKEN OF OUR GRATITUDE.
WE PRAY THEY MEET WITH YOUR APPROVAL.
AH.
IT WASN'T UNTIL LATER THAT I LEARNED THAT THE MONONOKE I KILLED THAT NIGHT HAD BEEN THAT VILLAGE'S PREVIOUS PATRON GOD.
APPARENTLY, TO THE VILLAGERS, HE HAD BEEN A DETESTABLE NUISANCE THEY WERE GLAD TO BE RID OF.
HOWEVER, IT SEEMED HIS THICK-WITTED TYRANNY HAD LEFT THEM TERRIFIED OF MONONOKE.
THEY ERECTED AN IMPRESSIVE SHRINE TO ME, AND MADE FREQUENT AND PUNCTUAL OFFERINGS OF RICE AND SAKE.
THEY WERE VERY CERTAIN TO PERFORM ALL THE PROPER RITUALS AND SHOW OBSEQUIOUS RESPECT.
IN RETURN...
...I PROTECTED THE VILLAGE FROM VARIOUS THREATS.

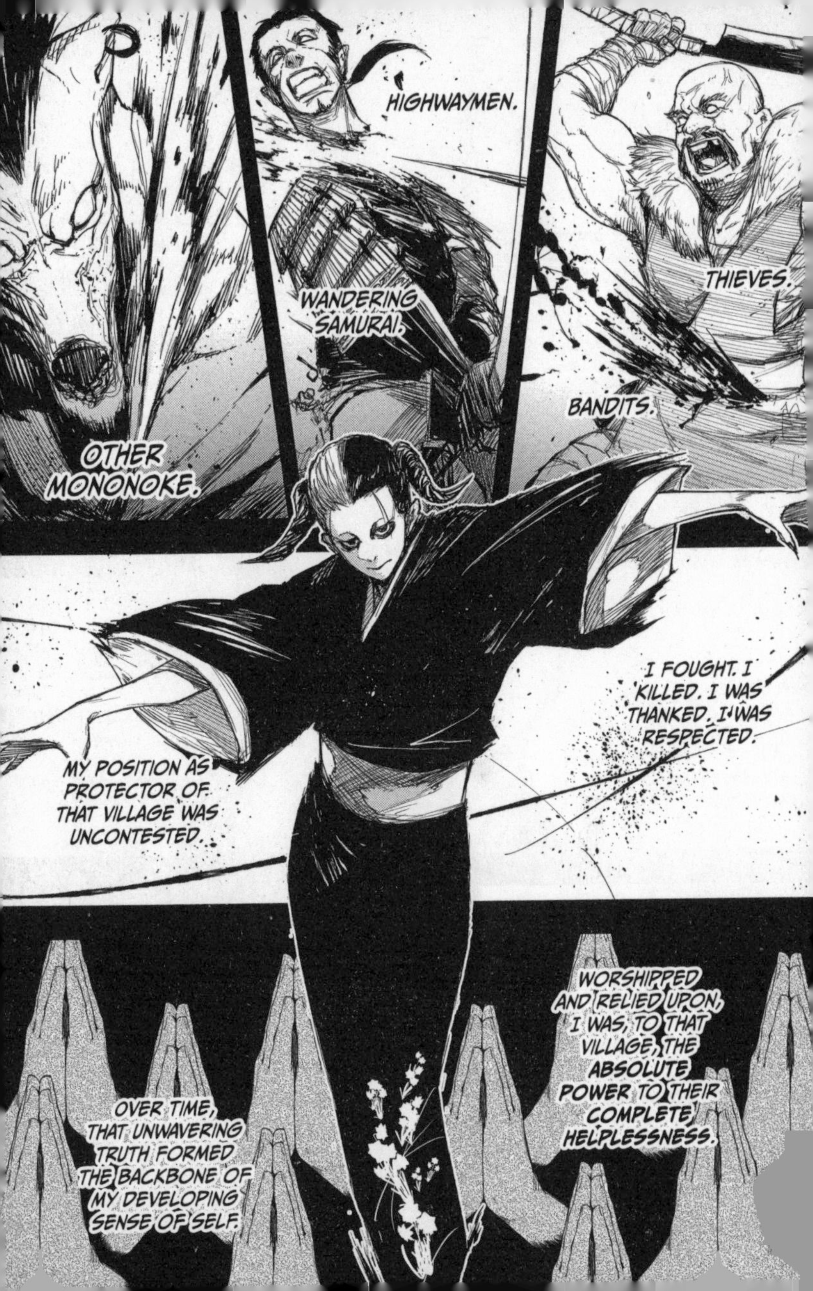
THIEVES.
BANDITS.
HIGHWAYMEN.
WANDERING SAMURAI.
OTHER MONONOKE.
I FOUGHT. I KILLED. I WAS THANKED. I WAS RESPECTED.
MY POSITION AS PROTECTOR OF THAT VILLAGE WAS UNCONTESTED.
WORSHIPPED AND RELIED UPON, I WAS, TO THAT VILLAGE, THE ABSOLUTE POWER TO THEIR COMPLETE HELPLESSNESS.
OVER TIME, THAT UNWAVERING TRUTH FORMED THE BACKBONE OF MY DEVELOPING SENSE OF SELF.

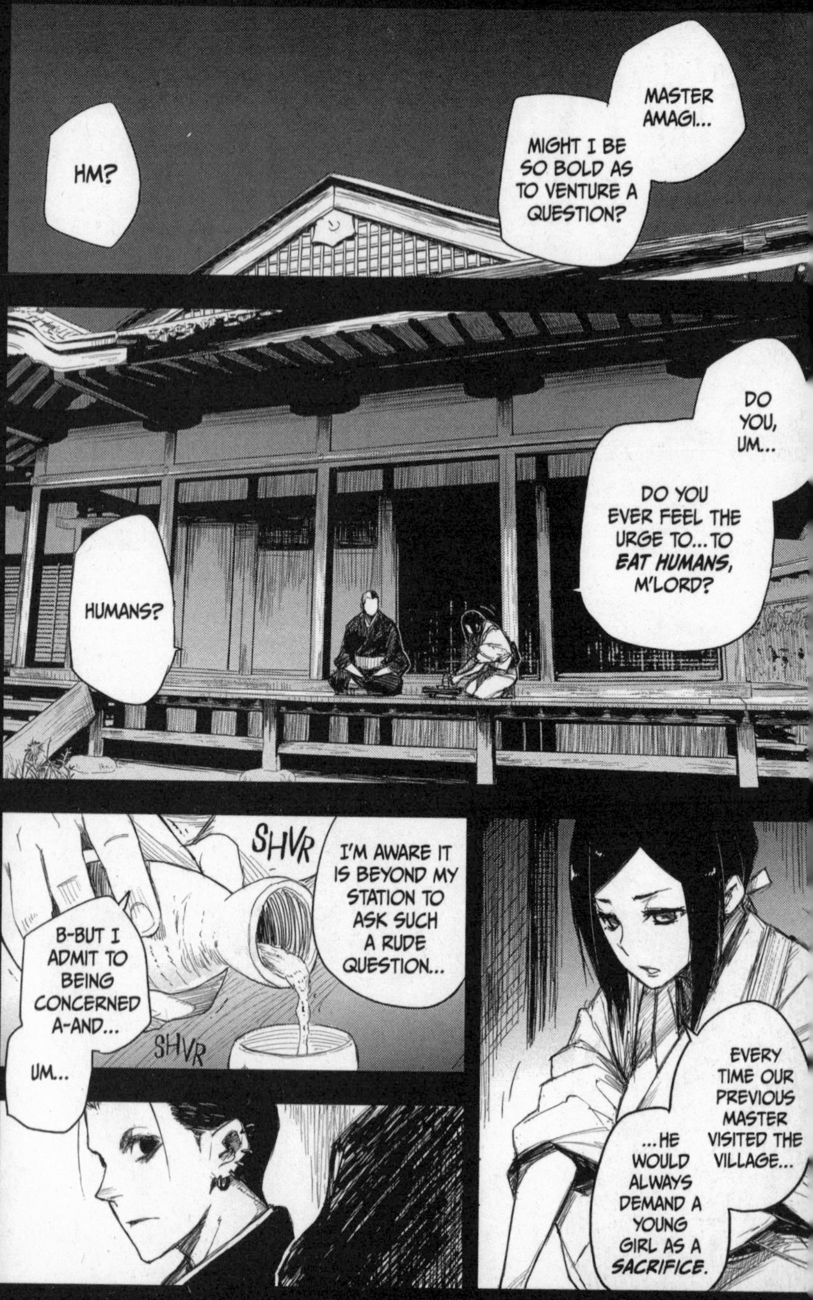
MASTER AMAGI...
MIGHT I BE SO BOLD AS TO VENTURE A QUESTION?
HM?
DO YOU, UM...
DO YOU EVER FEEL THE URGE TO...TO *EAT HUMANS*, M'LORD?
HUMANS?
EVERY TIME OUR PREVIOUS MASTER VISITED THE VILLAGE...
...HE WOULD ALWAYS DEMAND A YOUNG GIRL AS A *SACRIFICE*.
SHVR
I'M AWARE IT IS BEYOND MY STATION TO ASK SUCH A RUDE QUESTION...
B-BUT I ADMIT TO BEING CONCERNED A-AND...
SHVR
UM...

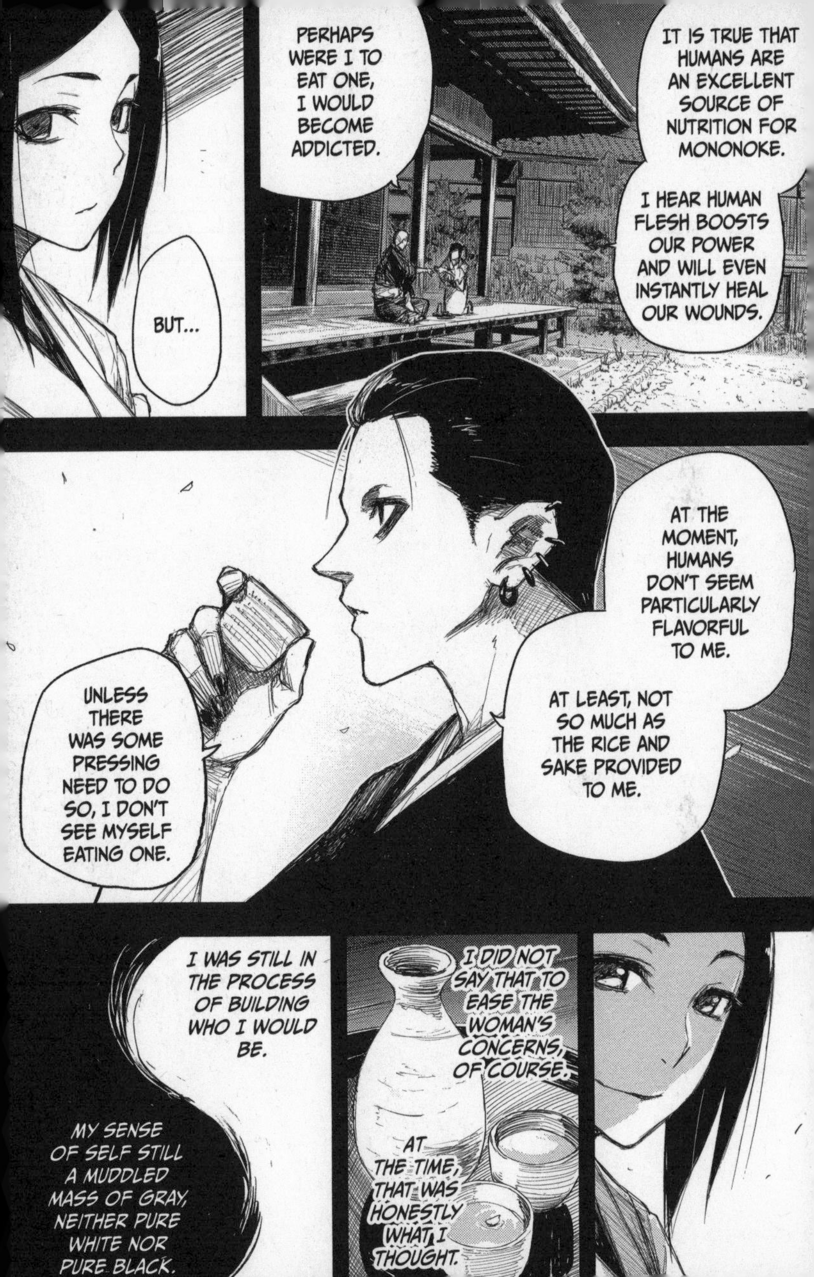
IT IS TRUE THAT HUMANS ARE AN EXCELLENT SOURCE OF NUTRITION FOR MONONOKE.
I HEAR HUMAN FLESH BOOSTS OUR POWER AND WILL EVEN INSTANTLY HEAL OUR WOUNDS.
PERHAPS WERE I TO EAT ONE, I WOULD BECOME ADDICTED.
BUT...
AT THE MOMENT, HUMANS DON'T SEEM PARTICULARLY FLAVORFUL TO ME.
AT LEAST, NOT SO MUCH AS THE RICE AND SAKE PROVIDED TO ME.
UNLESS THERE WAS SOME PRESSING NEED TO DO SO, I DON'T SEE MYSELF EATING ONE.
I DID NOT SAY THAT TO EASE THE WOMAN'S CONCERNS, OF COURSE.
AT THE TIME, THAT WAS HONESTLY WHAT I THOUGHT.
I WAS STILL IN THE PROCESS OF BUILDING WHO I WOULD BE.
MY SENSE OF SELF STILL A MUDDLED MASS OF GRAY, NEITHER PURE WHITE NOR PURE BLACK.

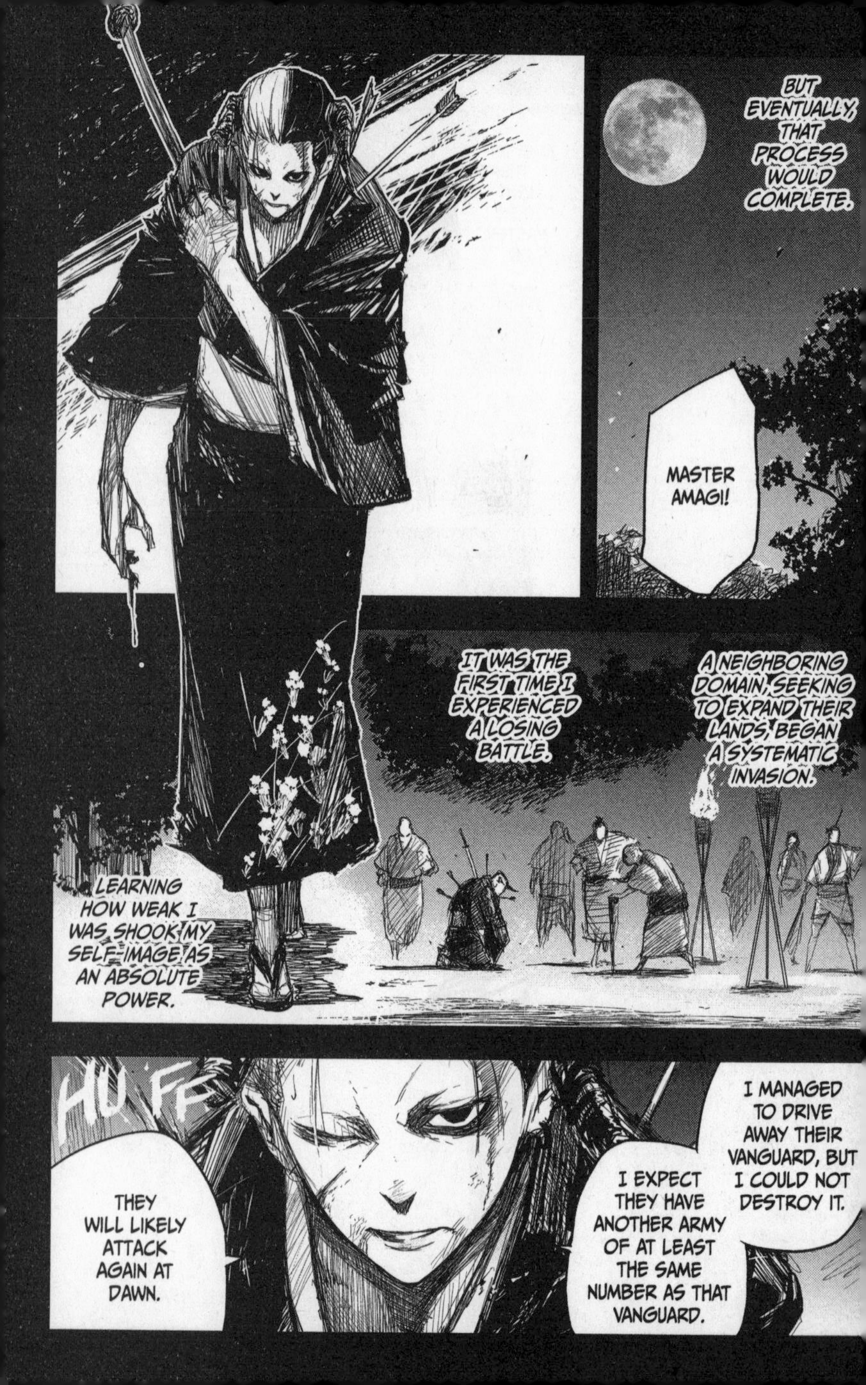
BUT EVENTUALLY, THAT PROCESS WOULD COMPLETE.
MASTER AMAGI!
A NEIGHBORING DOMAIN, SEEKING TO EXPAND THEIR LANDS, BEGAN A SYSTEMATIC INVASION.
IT WAS THE FIRST TIME I EXPERIENCED A LOSING BATTLE.
LEARNING HOW WEAK I WAS SHOOK MY SELF-IMAGE AS AN ABSOLUTE POWER.
I MANAGED TO DRIVE AWAY THEIR VANGUARD, BUT I COULD NOT DESTROY IT.
HUFF
I EXPECT THEY HAVE ANOTHER ARMY OF AT LEAST THE SAME NUMBER AS THAT VANGUARD.
THEY WILL LIKELY ATTACK AGAIN AT DAWN.

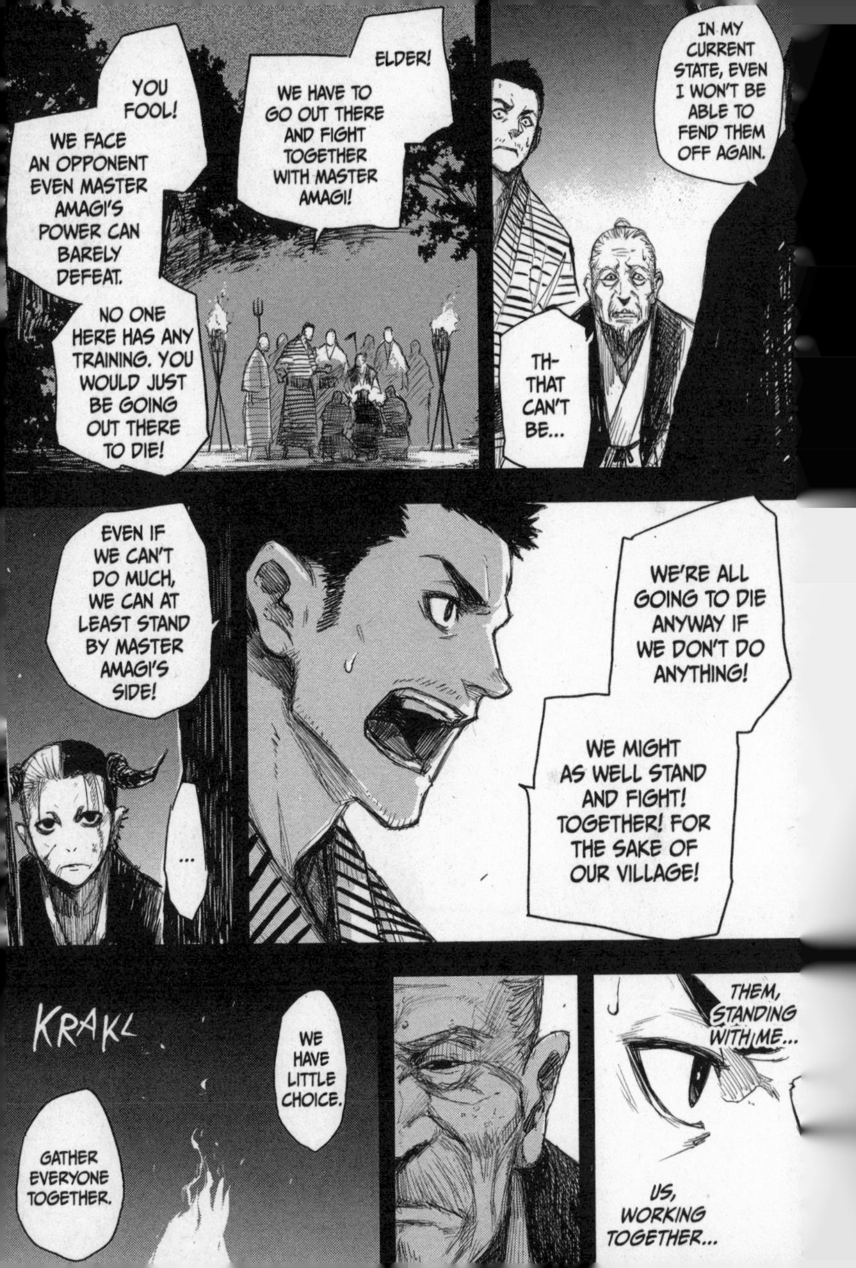
IN MY CURRENT STATE, EVEN I WON'T BE ABLE TO FEND THEM OFF AGAIN.
TH- THAT CAN'T BE...
ELDER!
WE HAVE TO GO OUT THERE AND FIGHT TOGETHER WITH MASTER AMAGI!
YOU FOOL!
WE FACE AN OPPONENT EVEN MASTER AMAGI'S POWER CAN BARELY DEFEAT.
NO ONE HERE HAS ANY TRAINING. YOU WOULD JUST BE GOING OUT THERE TO DIE!
WE'RE ALL GOING TO DIE ANYWAY IF WE DON'T DO ANYTHING!
WE MIGHT AS WELL STAND AND FIGHT! TOGETHER! FOR THE SAKE OF OUR VILLAGE!
EVEN IF WE CAN'T DO MUCH, WE CAN AT LEAST STAND BY MASTER AMAGI'S SIDE!
...
THEM, STANDING WITH ME...
US, WORKING TOGETHER...
WE HAVE LITTLE CHOICE.
KRAKL
GATHER EVERYONE TOGETHER.

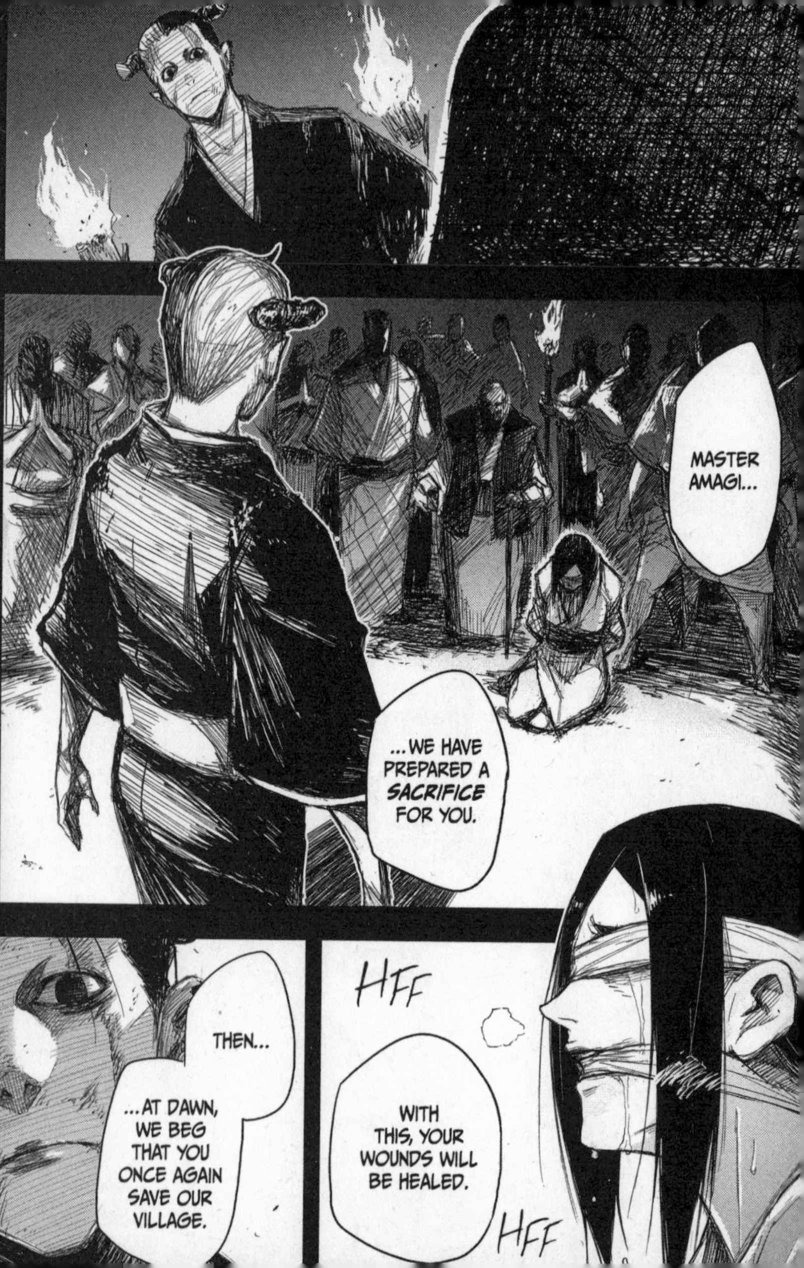
MASTER AMAGI...
...WE HAVE PREPARED A *SACRIFICE* FOR YOU.
HFF
WITH THIS, YOUR WOUNDS WILL BE HEALED.
HFF
THEN...
...AT DAWN, WE BEG THAT YOU ONCE AGAIN SAVE OUR VILLAGE.

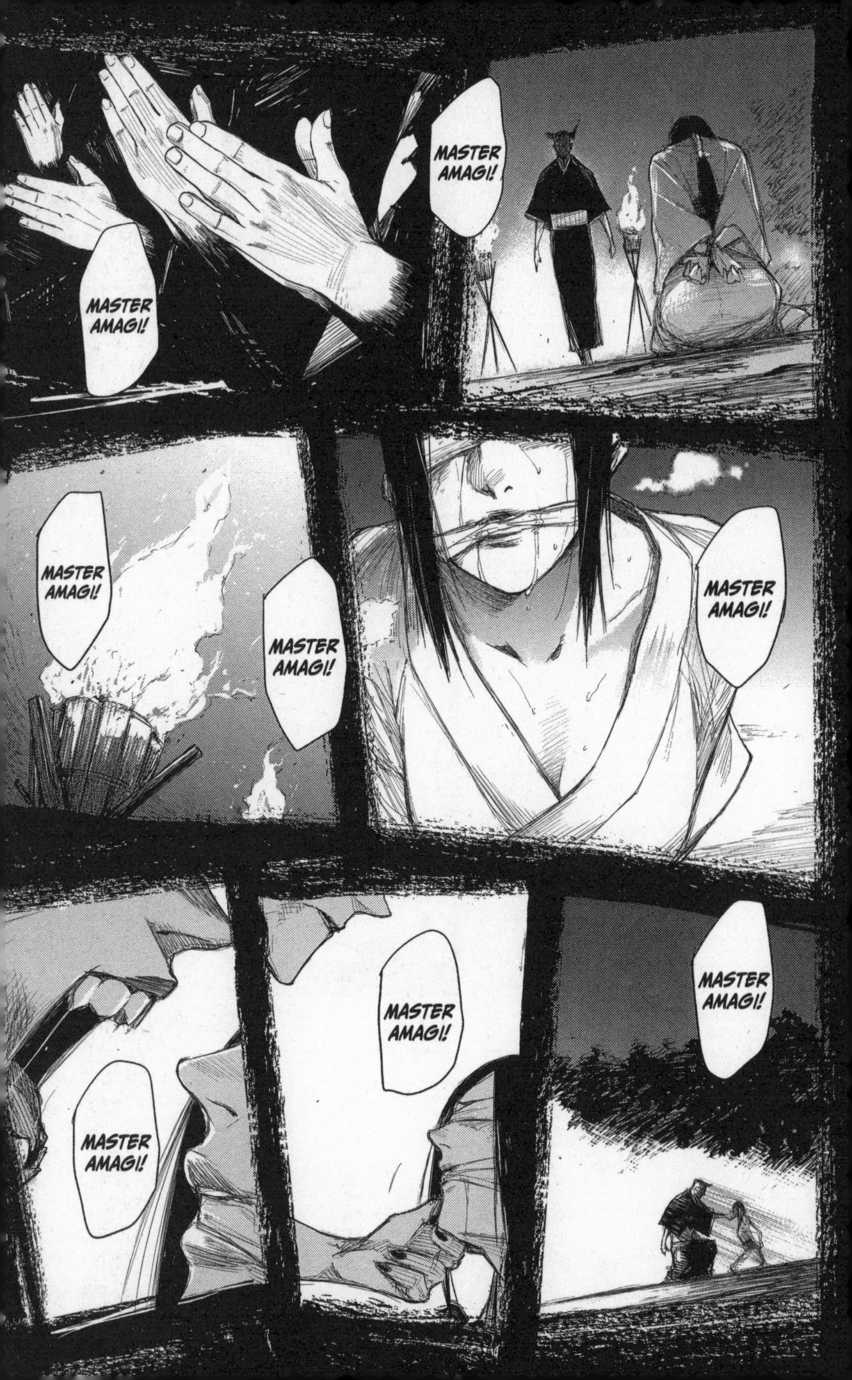
MASTER AMAGI!
MASTER AMAGI!
MASTER AMAGI!
MASTER AMAGI!
MASTER AMAGI!
MASTER AMAGI!
MASTER AMAGI!
MASTER AMAGI!

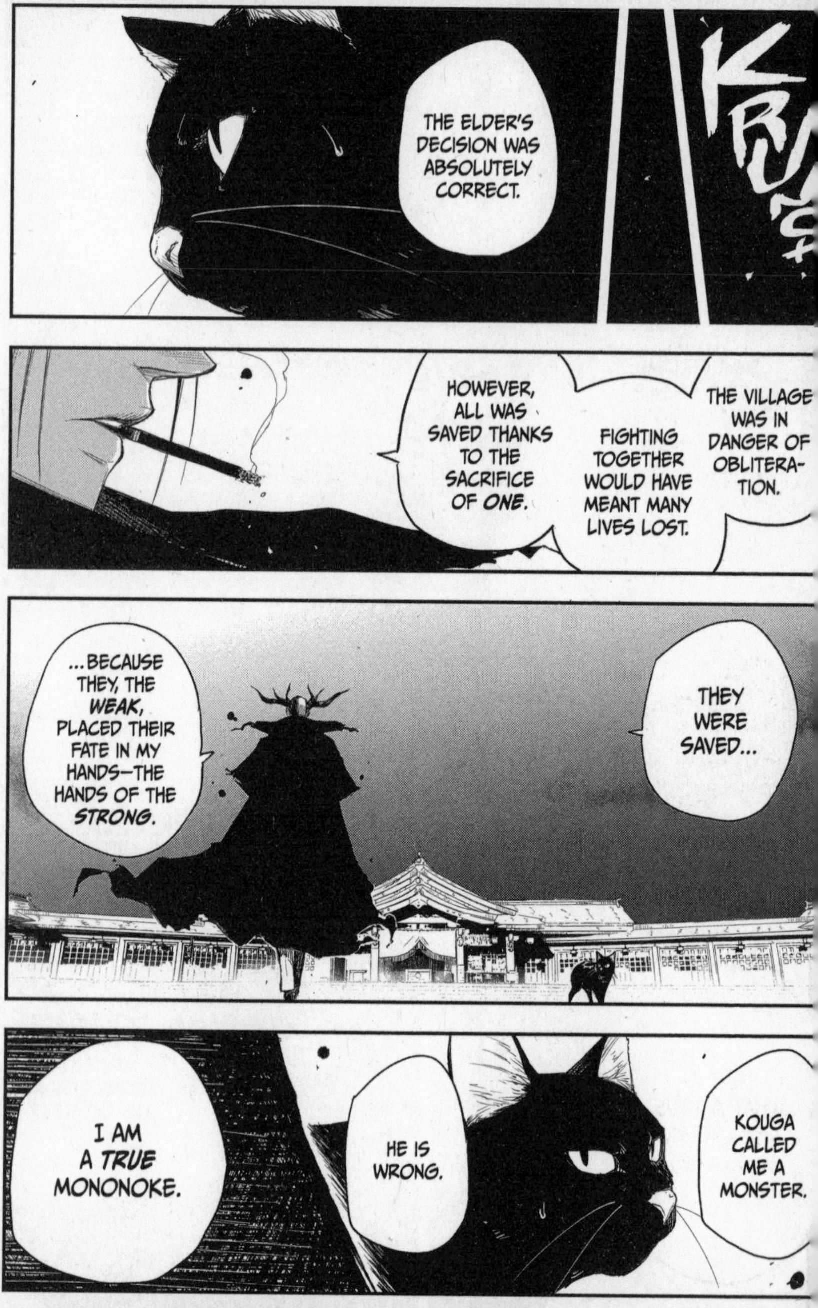
KRU
THE ELDER'S DECISION WAS ABSOLUTELY CORRECT.
THE VILLAGE WAS IN DANGER OF OBLITERATION.
FIGHTING TOGETHER WOULD HAVE MEANT MANY LIVES LOST.
HOWEVER, ALL WAS SAVED THANKS TO THE SACRIFICE OF ONE.
THEY WERE SAVED...
...BECAUSE THEY, THE WEAK, PLACED THEIR FATE IN MY HANDS—THE HANDS OF THE STRONG.
KOUGA CALLED ME A MONSTER.
HE IS WRONG.
I AM A TRUE MONONOKE.

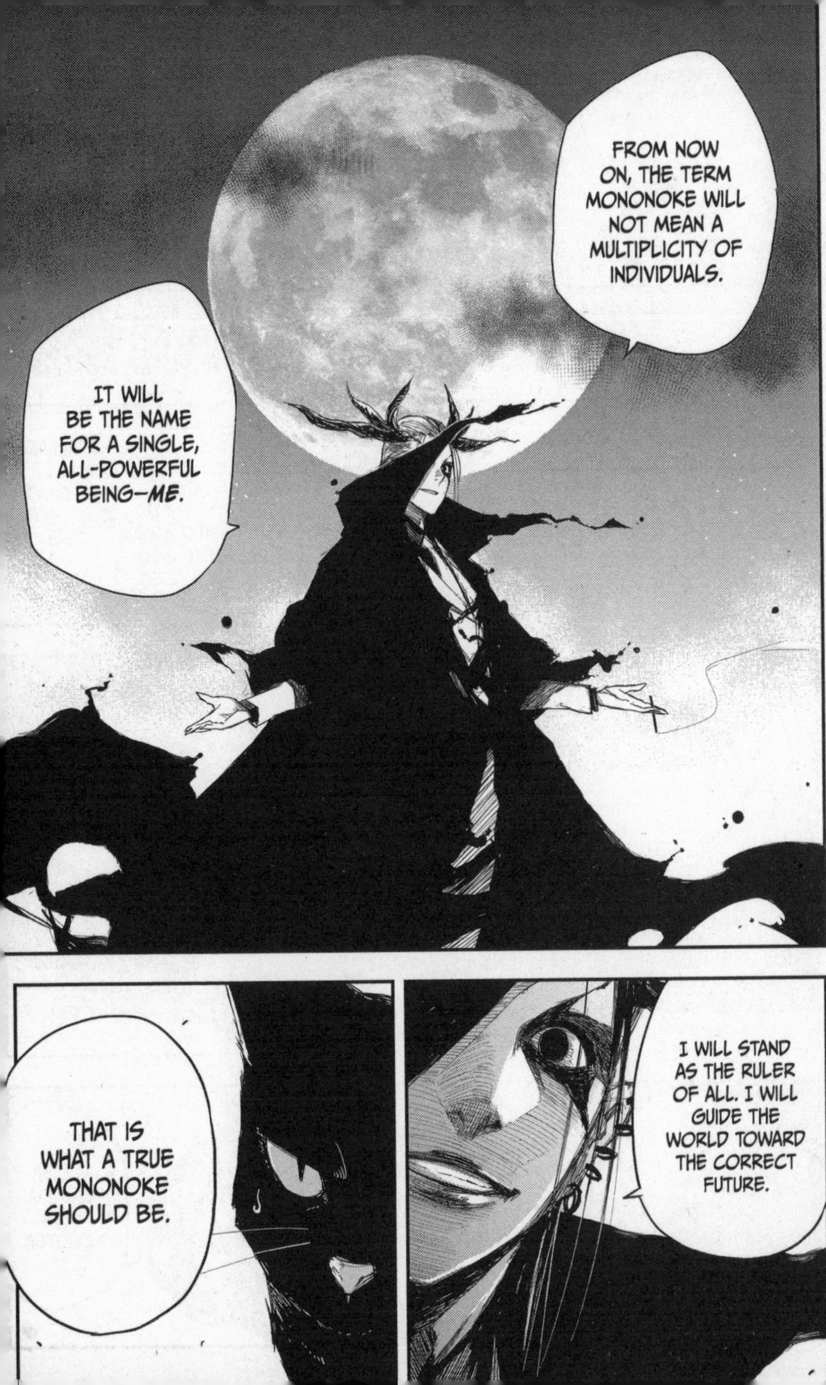
FROM NOW ON, THE TERM MONONOKE WILL NOT MEAN A MULTIPLICITY OF INDIVIDUALS.
IT WILL BE THE NAME FOR A SINGLE, ALL-POWERFUL BEING—*ME*.
I WILL STAND AS THE RULER OF ALL. I WILL GUIDE THE WORLD TOWARD THE CORRECT FUTURE.
THAT IS WHAT A TRUE MONONOKE SHOULD BE.

BLACK TORCH

#17 Unstoppable

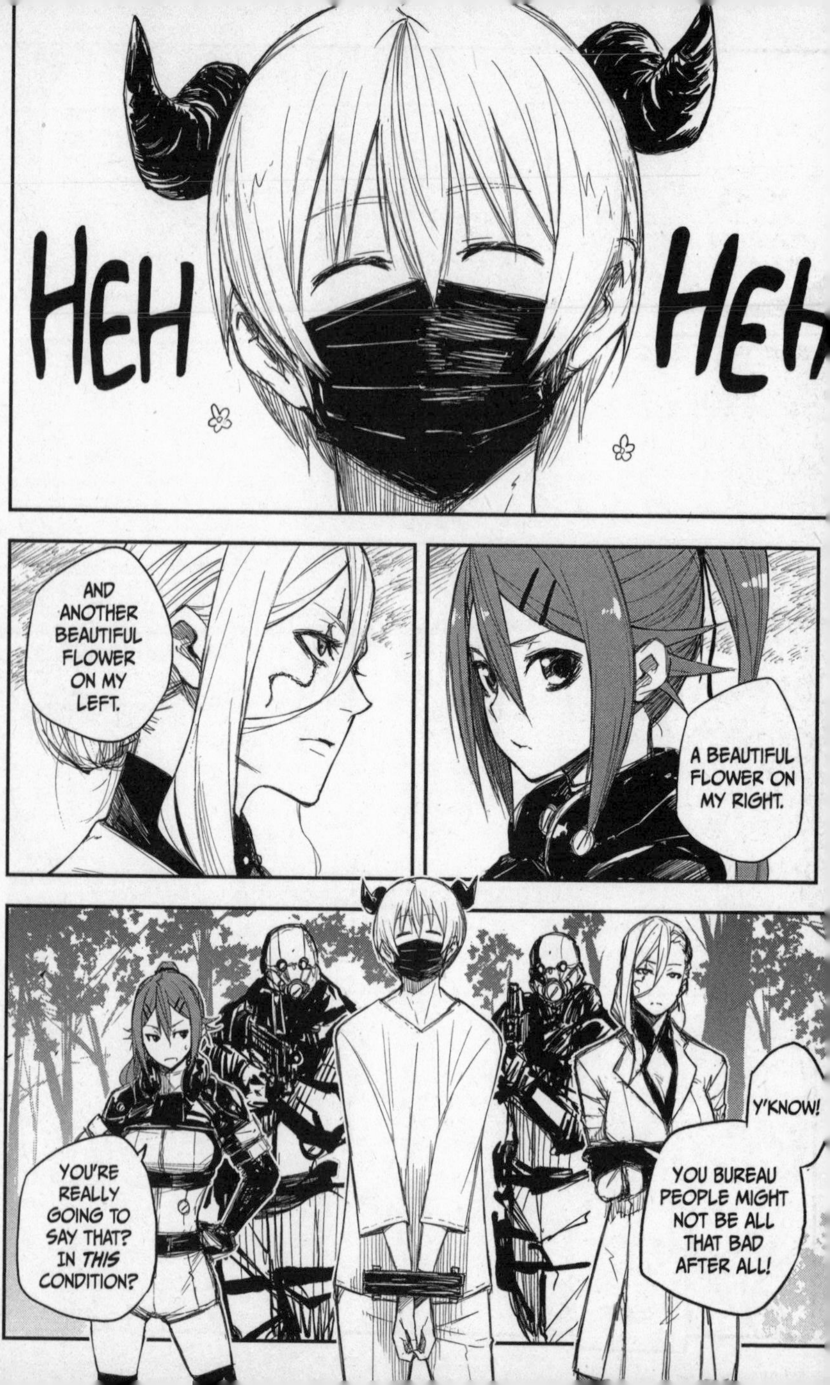
HEH
HEH
A BEAUTIFUL FLOWER ON MY RIGHT.
AND ANOTHER BEAUTIFUL FLOWER ON MY LEFT.
Y'KNOW!
YOU BUREAU PEOPLE MIGHT NOT BE ALL THAT BAD AFTER ALL!
YOU'RE REALLY GOING TO SAY THAT? IN *THIS* CONDITION?

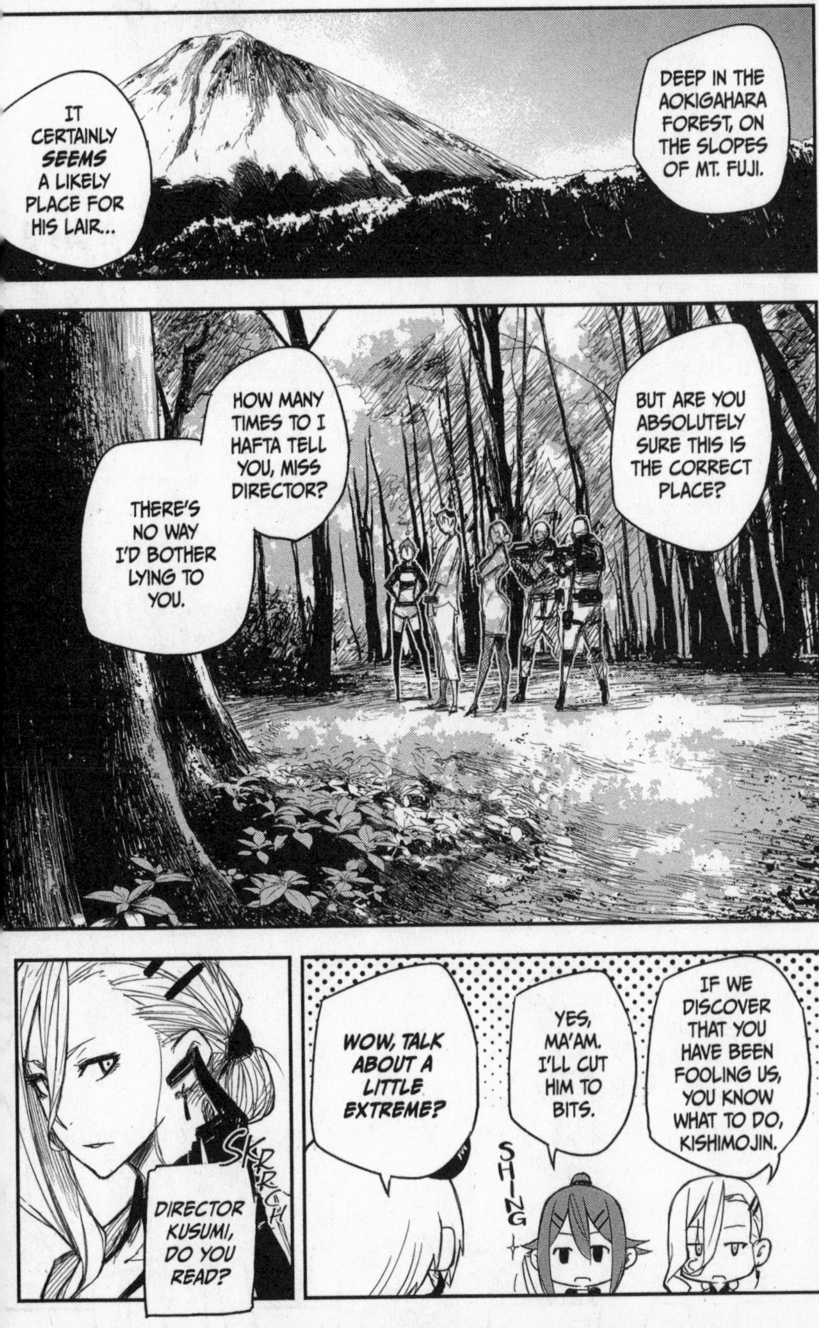
DEEP IN THE AOKIGAHARA FOREST, ON THE SLOPES OF MT. FUJI.
IT CERTAINLY SEEMS A LIKELY PLACE FOR HIS LAIR...
BUT ARE YOU ABSOLUTELY SURE THIS IS THE CORRECT PLACE?
HOW MANY TIMES TO I HAFTA TELL YOU, MISS DIRECTOR?
THERE'S NO WAY I'D BOTHER LYING TO YOU.
IF WE DISCOVER THAT YOU HAVE BEEN FOOLING US, YOU KNOW WHAT TO DO, KISHIMOJIN.
YES, MA'AM. I'LL CUT HIM TO BITS.
SHING
WOW, TALK ABOUT A LITTLE EXTREME?
SKRRCH
DIRECTOR KUSUMI, DO YOU READ?

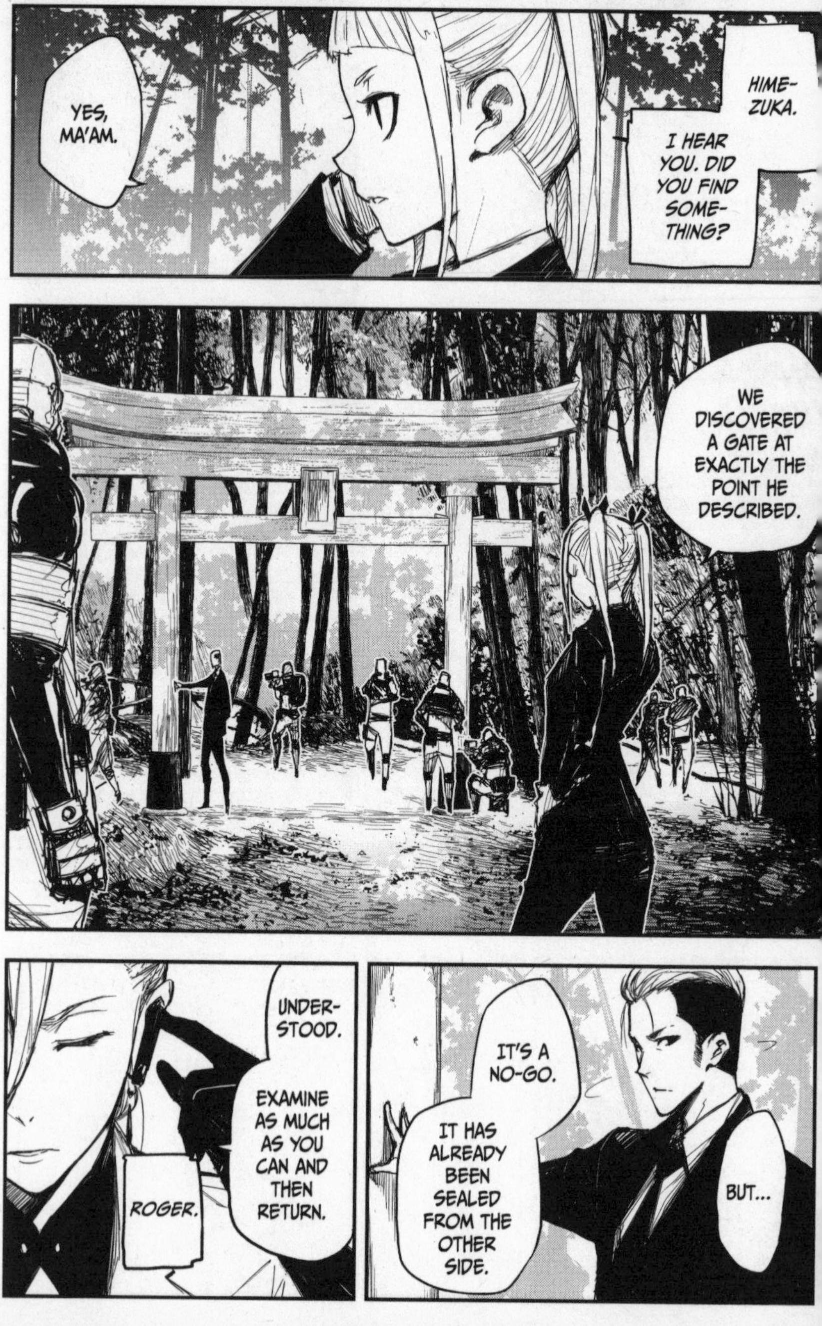
HIME-ZUKA.
I HEAR YOU. DID YOU FIND SOME-THING?
YES, MA'AM.
WE DISCOVERED A GATE AT EXACTLY THE POINT HE DESCRIBED.
IT'S A NO-GO.
IT HAS ALREADY BEEN SEALED FROM THE OTHER SIDE.
BUT...
UNDER-STOOD.
EXAMINE AS MUCH AS YOU CAN AND THEN RETURN.
ROGER.

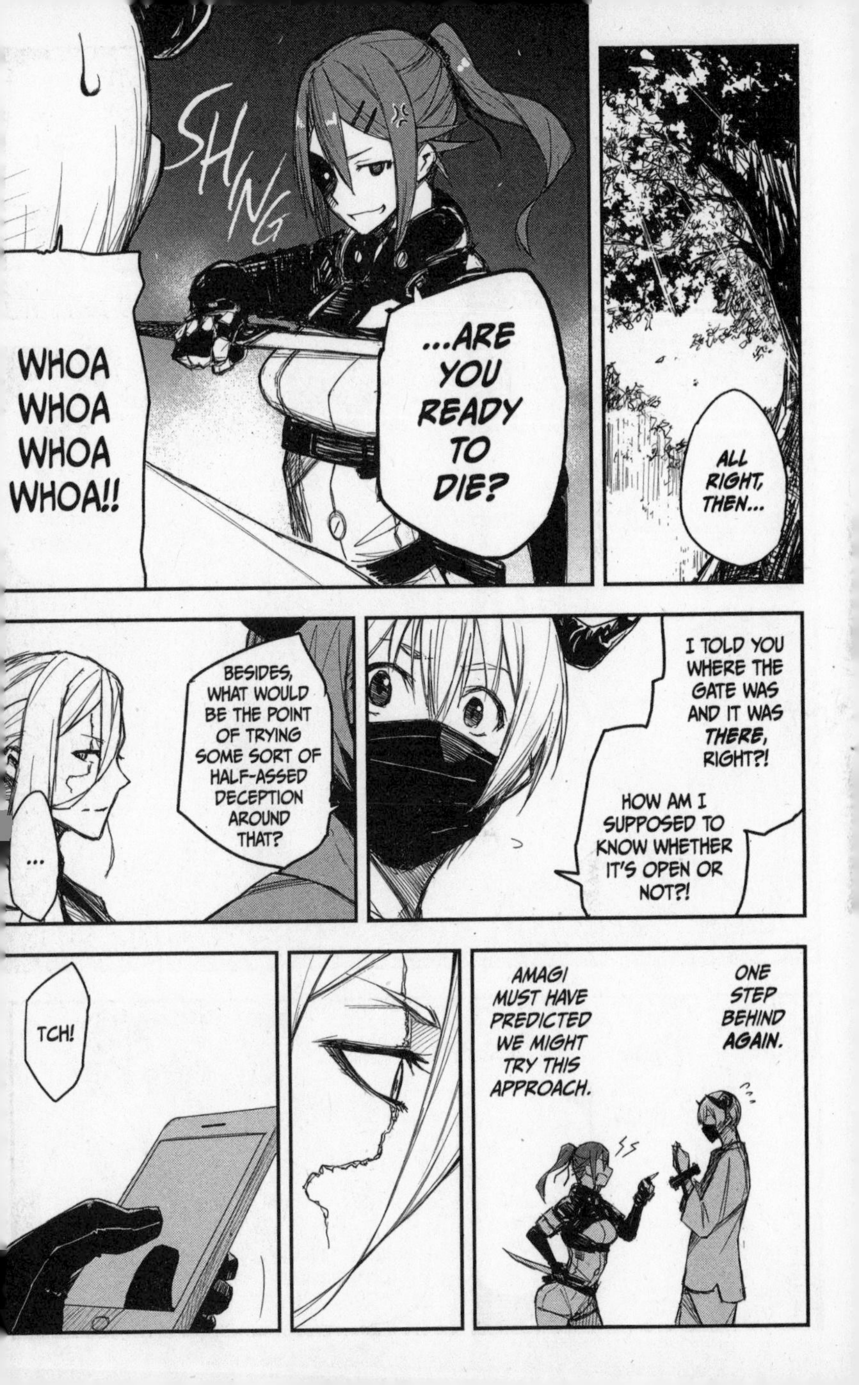
ALL RIGHT, THEN...
SHING
...ARE YOU READY TO DIE?
WHOA WHOA WHOA WHOA!!
I TOLD YOU WHERE THE GATE WAS AND IT WAS THERE, RIGHT?!
HOW AM I SUPPOSED TO KNOW WHETHER IT'S OPEN OR NOT?!
BESIDES, WHAT WOULD BE THE POINT OF TRYING SOME SORT OF HALF-ASSED DECEPTION AROUND THAT?
...
ONE STEP BEHIND AGAIN.
AMAGI MUST HAVE PREDICTED WE MIGHT TRY THIS APPROACH.
TCH!

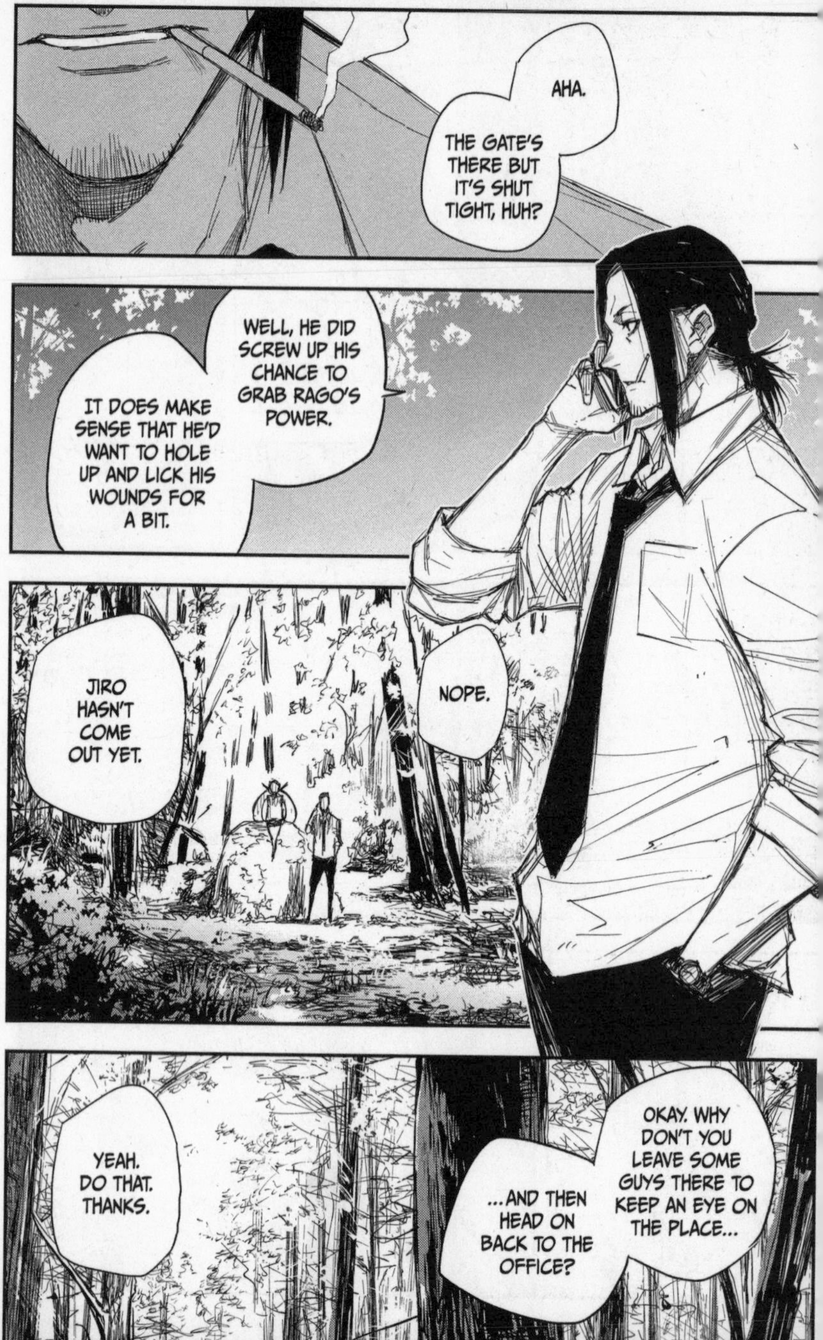
AHA.
THE GATE'S THERE BUT IT'S SHUT TIGHT, HUH?
WELL, HE DID SCREW UP HIS CHANCE TO GRAB RAGO'S POWER.
IT DOES MAKE SENSE THAT HE'D WANT TO HOLE UP AND LICK HIS WOUNDS FOR A BIT.
NOPE.
JIRO HASN'T COME OUT YET.
OKAY. WHY DON'T YOU LEAVE SOME GUYS THERE TO KEEP AN EYE ON THE PLACE...
...AND THEN HEAD ON BACK TO THE OFFICE?
YEAH. DO THAT. THANKS.

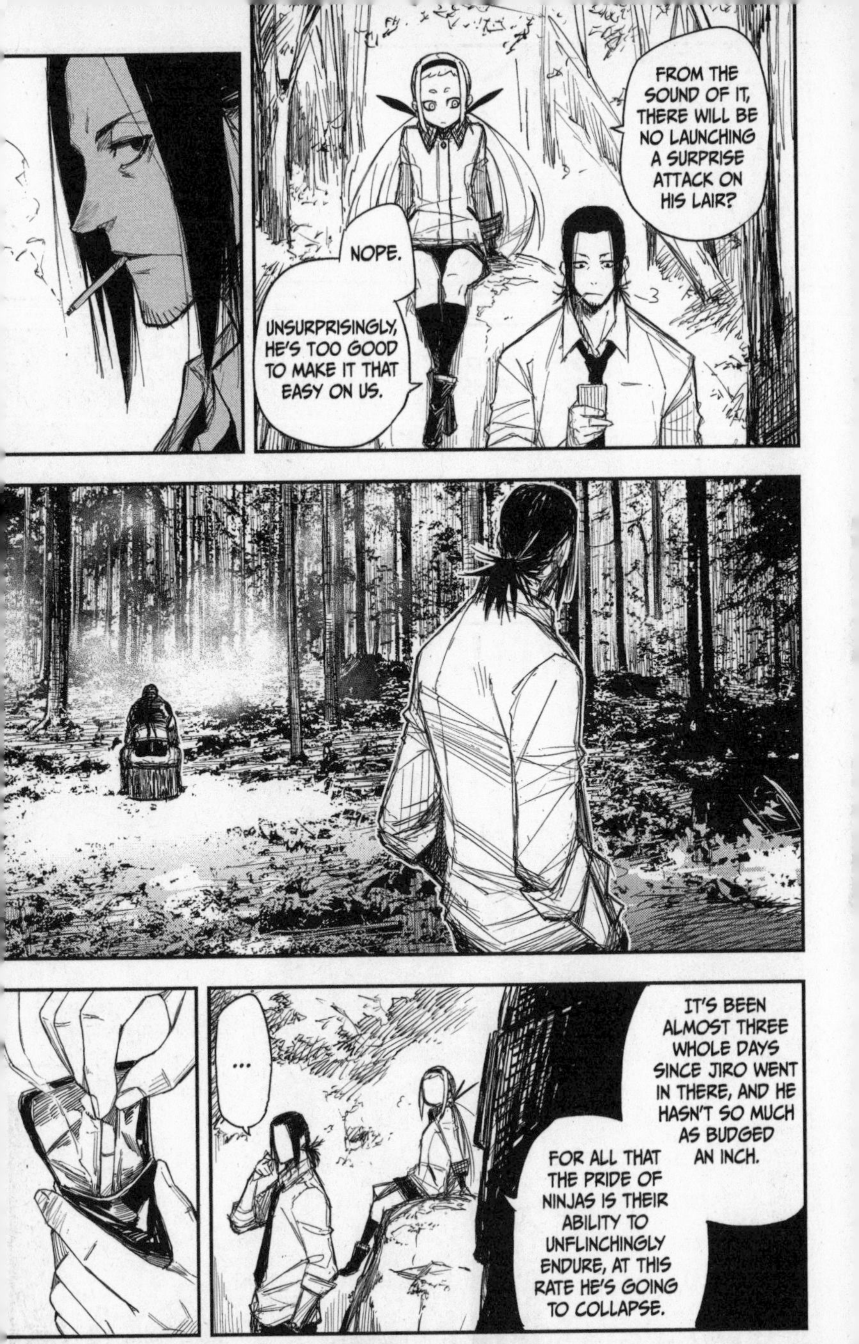
FROM THE SOUND OF IT, THERE WILL BE NO LAUNCHING A SURPRISE ATTACK ON HIS LAIR?
NOPE.
UNSURPRISINGLY, HE'S TOO GOOD TO MAKE IT THAT EASY ON US.
IT'S BEEN ALMOST THREE WHOLE DAYS SINCE JIRO WENT IN THERE, AND HE HASN'T SO MUCH AS BUDGED AN INCH.
FOR ALL THAT THE PRIDE OF NINJAS IS THEIR ABILITY TO UNFLINCHINGLY ENDURE, AT THIS RATE HE'S GOING TO COLLAPSE.
...

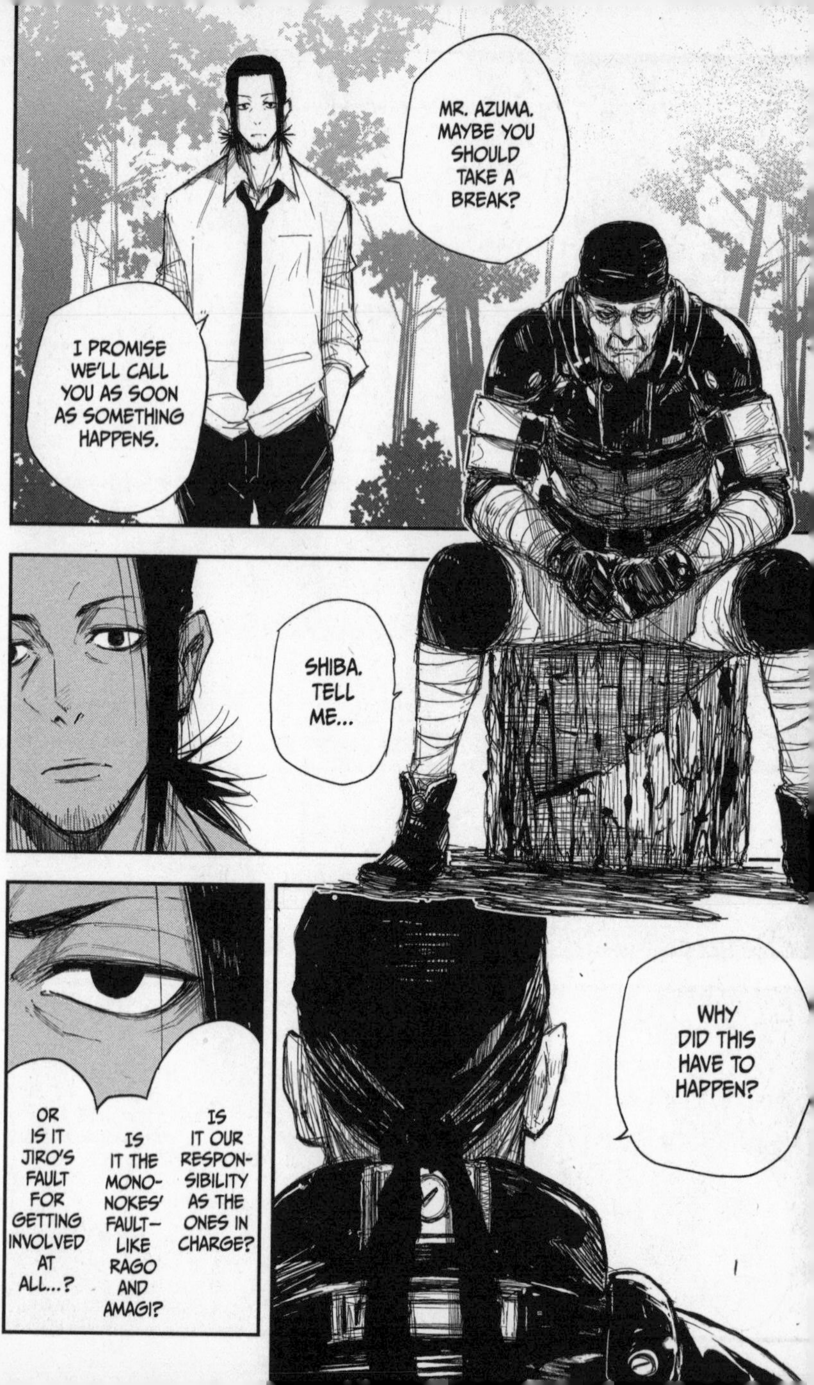
MR. AZUMA. MAYBE YOU SHOULD TAKE A BREAK?
I PROMISE WE'LL CALL YOU AS SOON AS SOMETHING HAPPENS.
SHIBA. TELL ME...
WHY DID THIS HAVE TO HAPPEN?
IS IT OUR RESPON-SIBILITY AS THE ONES IN CHARGE?
IS IT THE MONO-NOKES' FAULT— LIKE RAGO AND AMAGI?
OR IS IT JIRO'S FAULT FOR GETTING INVOLVED AT ALL...?

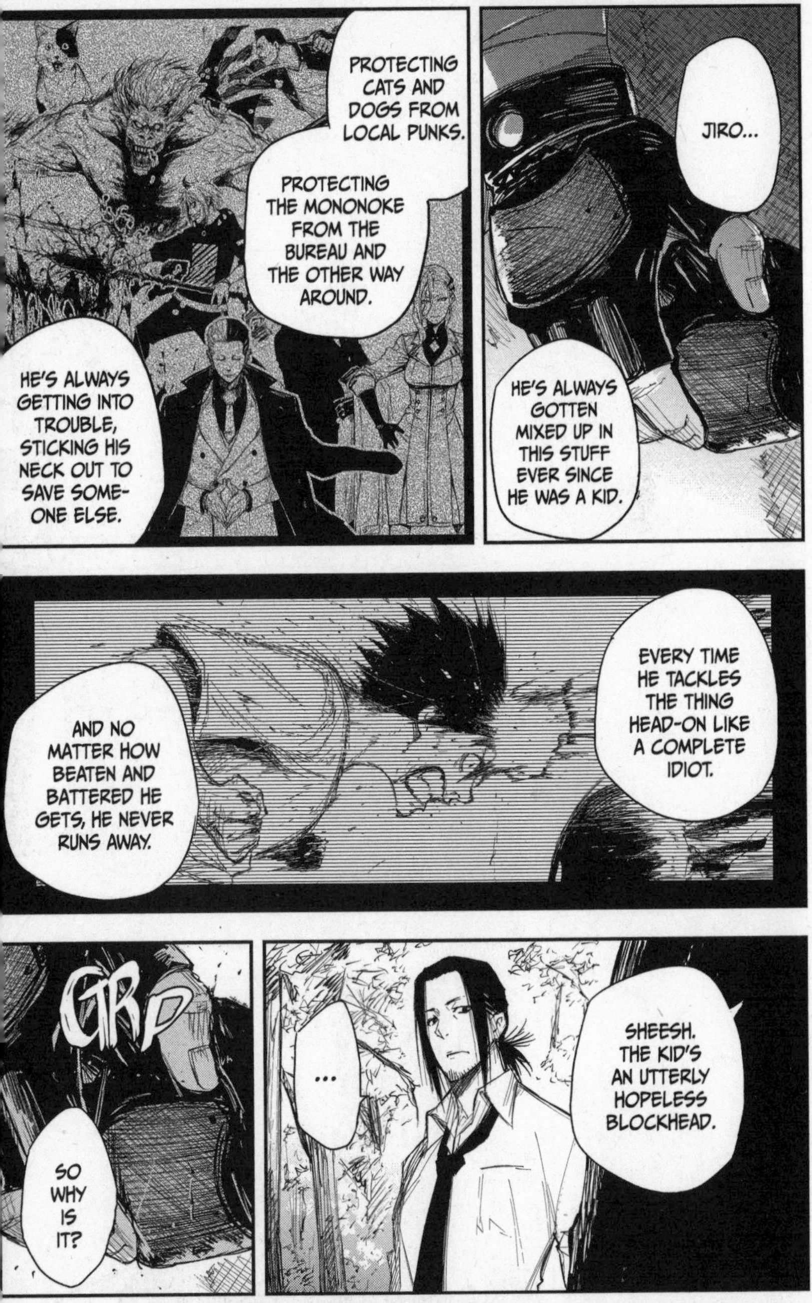

JIRO...
HE'S ALWAYS GOTTEN MIXED UP IN THIS STUFF EVER SINCE HE WAS A KID.
PROTECTING CATS AND DOGS FROM LOCAL PUNKS.
PROTECTING THE MONONOKE FROM THE BUREAU AND THE OTHER WAY AROUND.
HE'S ALWAYS GETTING INTO TROUBLE, STICKING HIS NECK OUT TO SAVE SOME-ONE ELSE.
EVERY TIME HE TACKLES THE THING HEAD-ON LIKE A COMPLETE IDIOT.
AND NO MATTER HOW BEATEN AND BATTERED HE GETS, HE NEVER RUNS AWAY.
SHEESH. THE KID'S AN UTTERLY HOPELESS BLOCKHEAD.
...
GRD
SO WHY IS IT?

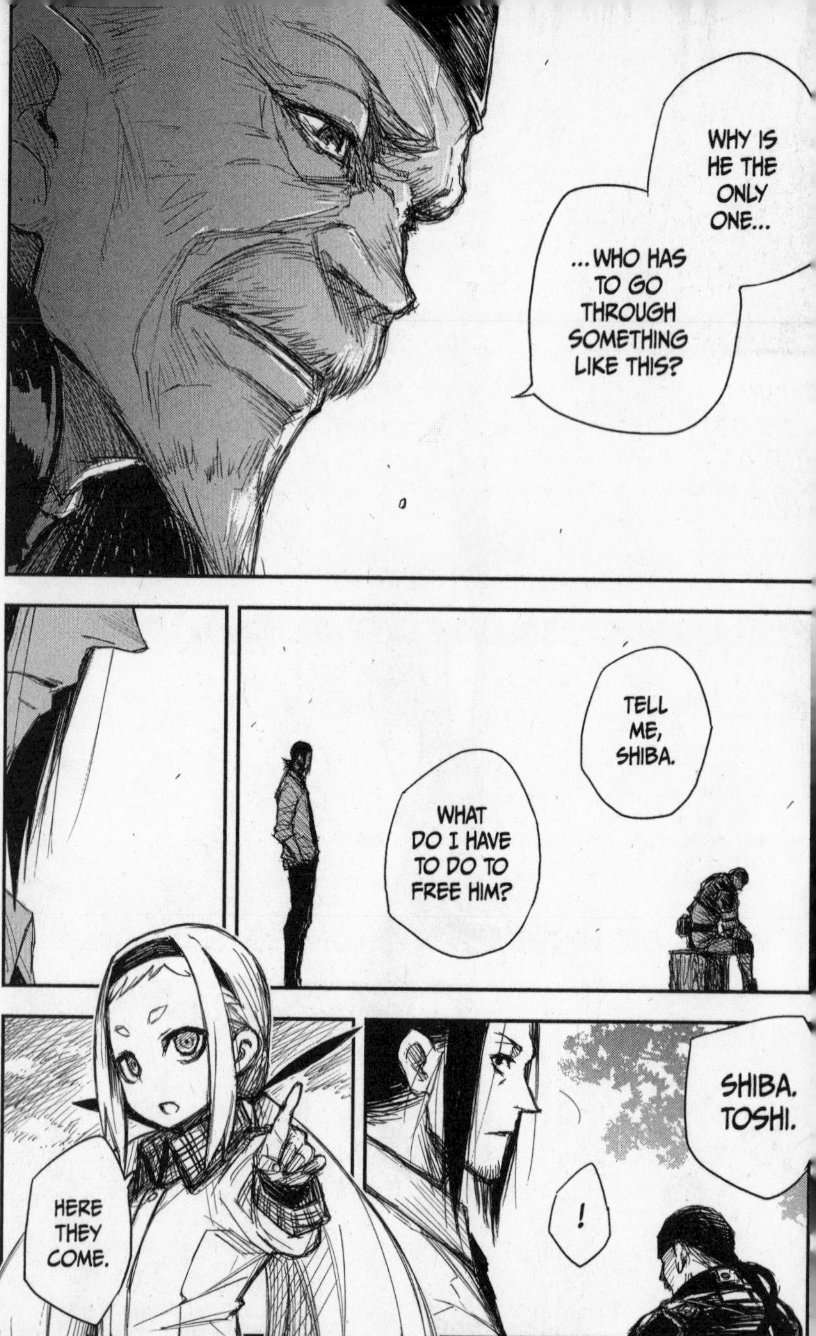
WHY IS HE THE ONLY ONE...
...WHO HAS TO GO THROUGH SOMETHING LIKE THIS?
TELL ME, SHIBA.
WHAT DO I HAVE TO DO TO FREE HIM?
SHIBA. TOSHI.
!
HERE THEY COME.

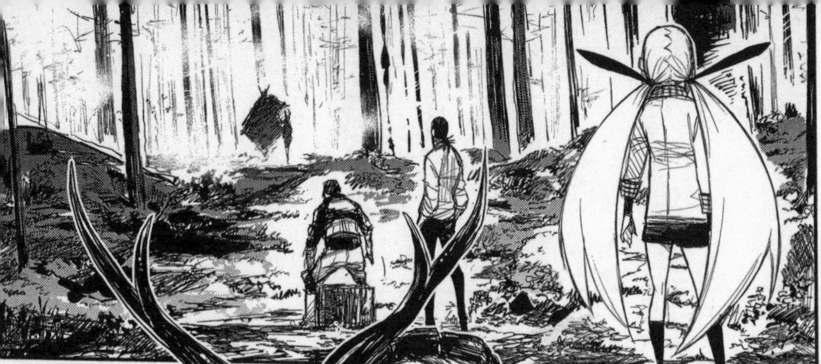
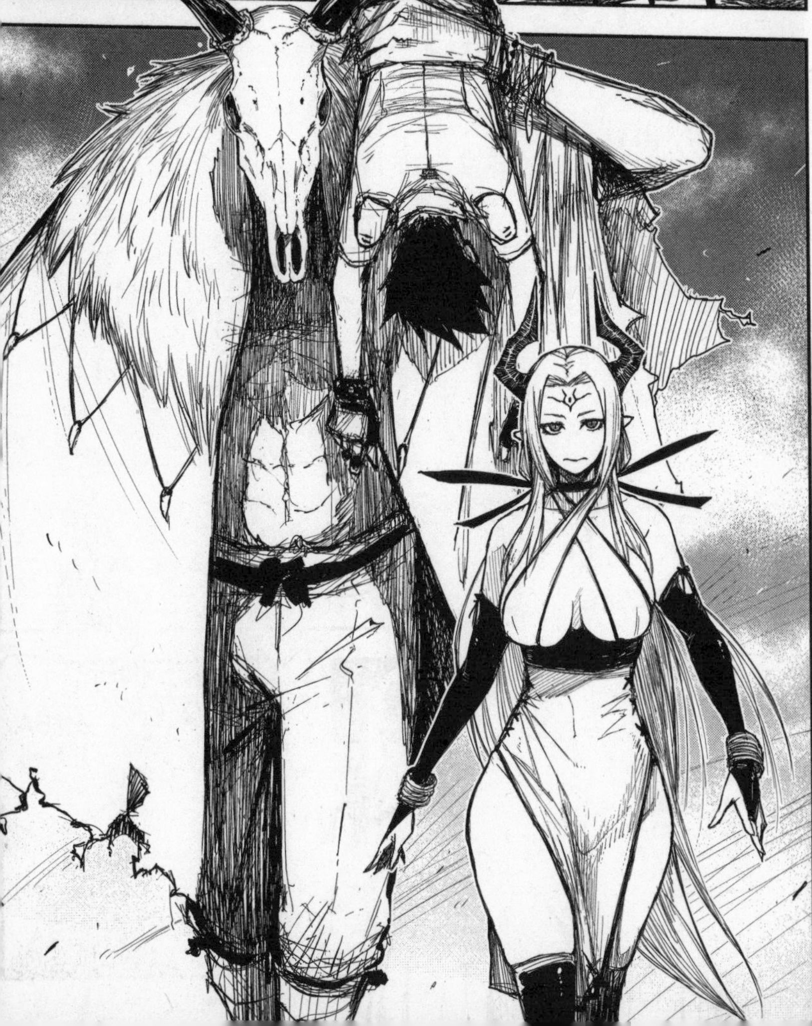

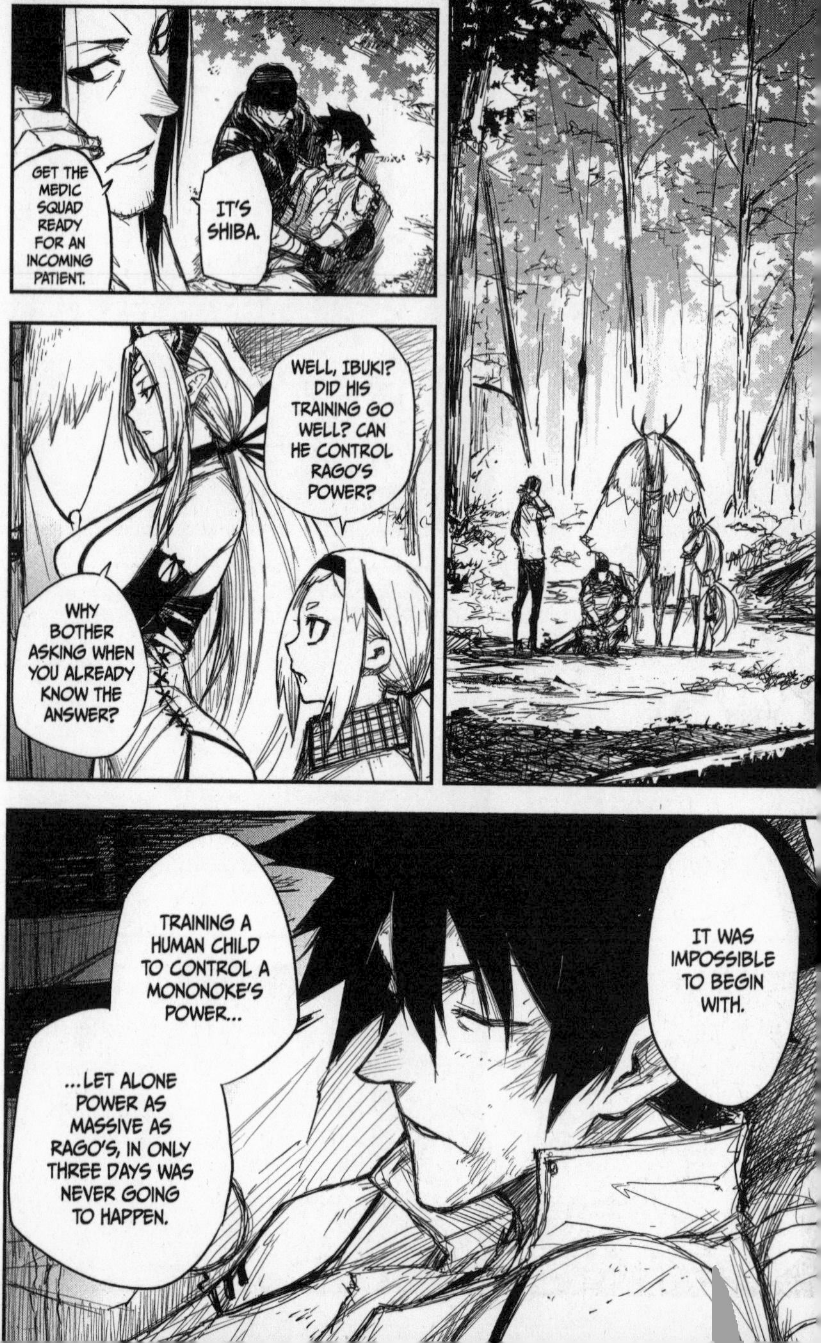
IT'S SHIBA.
GET THE MEDIC SQUAD READY FOR AN INCOMING PATIENT.
WELL, IBUKI? DID HIS TRAINING GO WELL? CAN HE CONTROL RAGO'S POWER?
WHY BOTHER ASKING WHEN YOU ALREADY KNOW THE ANSWER?
IT WAS IMPOSSIBLE TO BEGIN WITH.
TRAINING A HUMAN CHILD TO CONTROL A MONONOKE'S POWER...
...LET ALONE POWER AS MASSIVE AS RAGO'S, IN ONLY THREE DAYS WAS NEVER GOING TO HAPPEN.

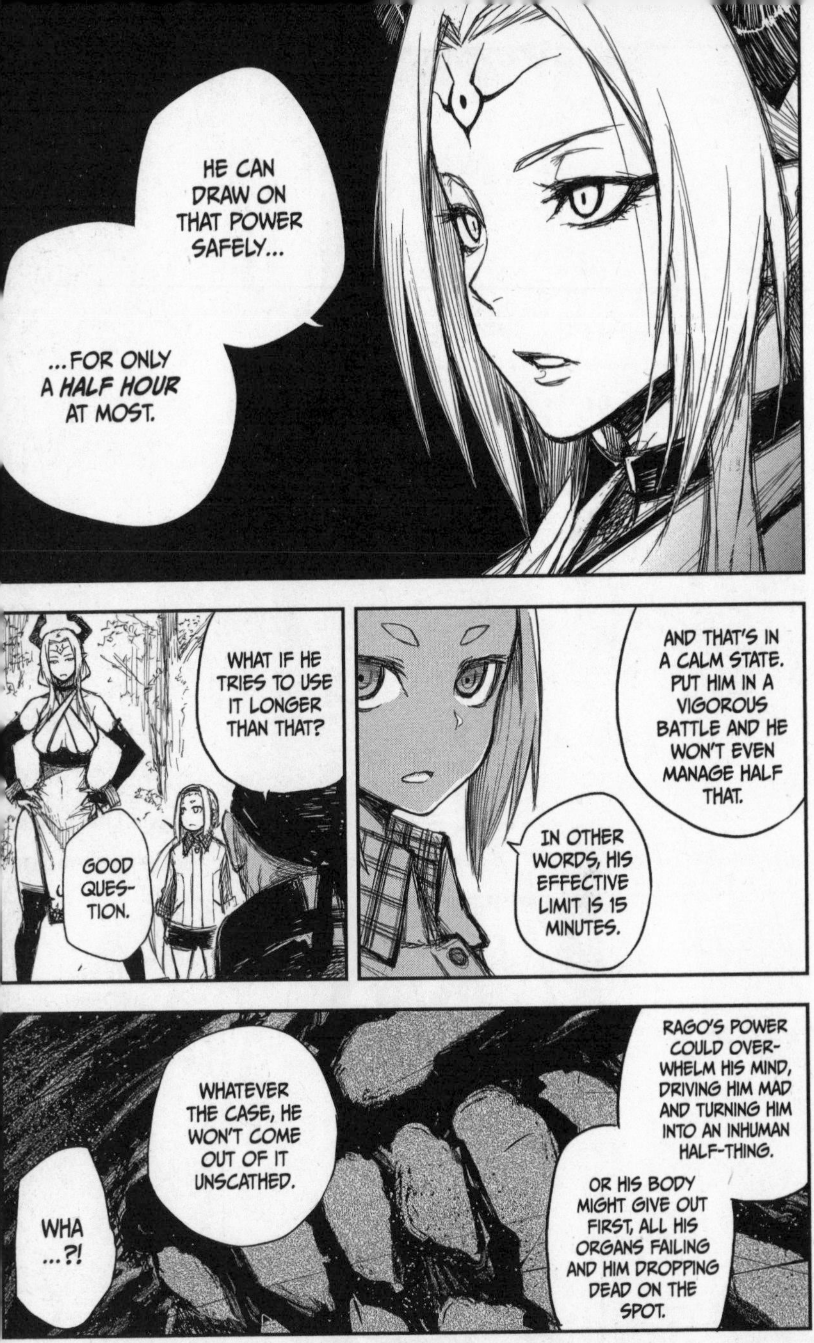
HE CAN DRAW ON THAT POWER SAFELY...
...FOR ONLY A *HALF HOUR* AT MOST.
AND THAT'S IN A CALM STATE. PUT HIM IN A VIGOROUS BATTLE AND HE WON'T EVEN MANAGE HALF THAT.
IN OTHER WORDS, HIS EFFECTIVE LIMIT IS 15 MINUTES.
WHAT IF HE TRIES TO USE IT LONGER THAN THAT?
GOOD QUES-TION.
RAGO'S POWER COULD OVER-WHELM HIS MIND, DRIVING HIM MAD AND TURNING HIM INTO AN INHUMAN HALF-THING.
OR HIS BODY MIGHT GIVE OUT FIRST, ALL HIS ORGANS FAILING AND HIM DROPPING DEAD ON THE SPOT.
WHATEVER THE CASE, HE WON'T COME OUT OF IT UNSCATHED.
WHA ...?!

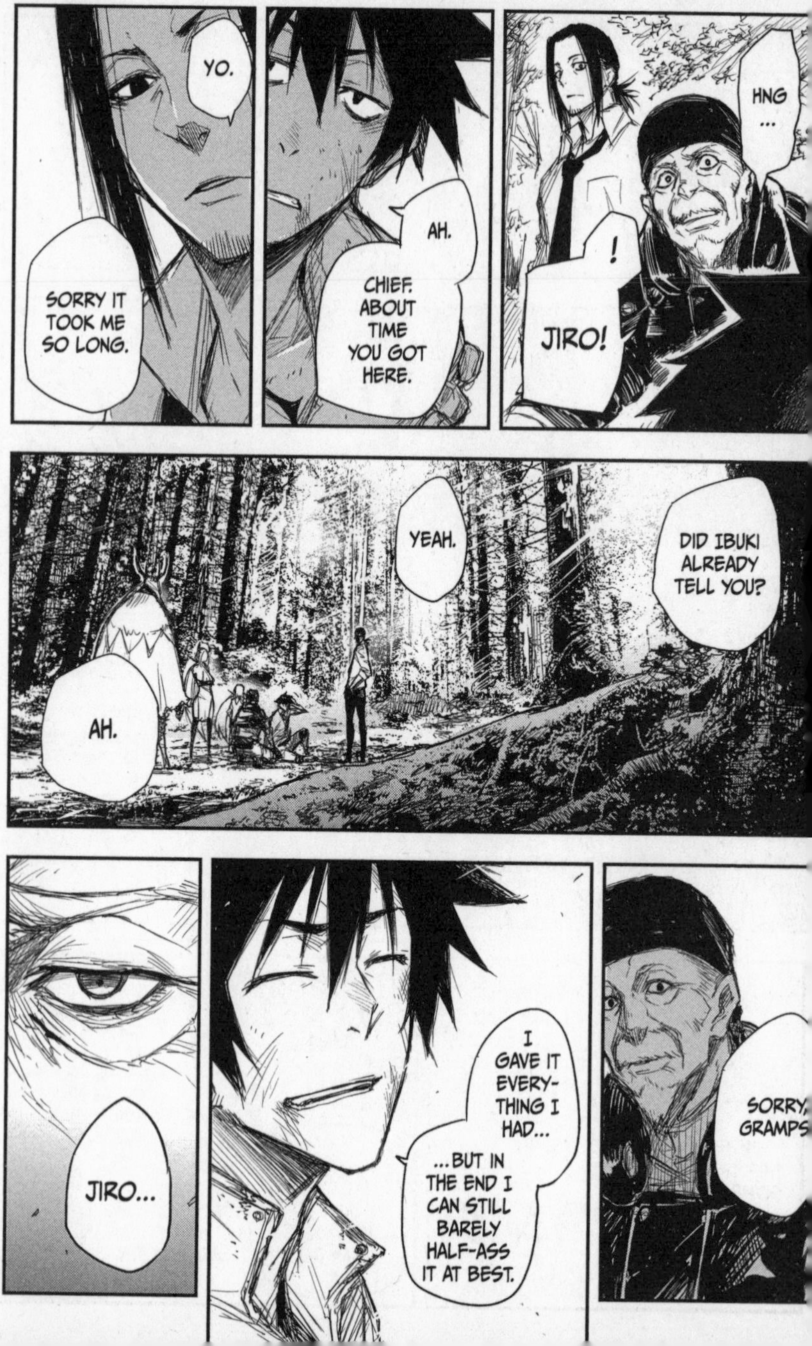
HNG ...
!
JIRO!
AH.
CHIEF. ABOUT TIME YOU GOT HERE.
YO.
SORRY IT TOOK ME SO LONG.
DID IBUKI ALREADY TELL YOU?
YEAH.
AH.
SORRY, GRAMPS
I GAVE IT EVERYTHING I HAD...
...BUT IN THE END I CAN STILL BARELY HALF-ASS IT AT BEST.
JIRO...

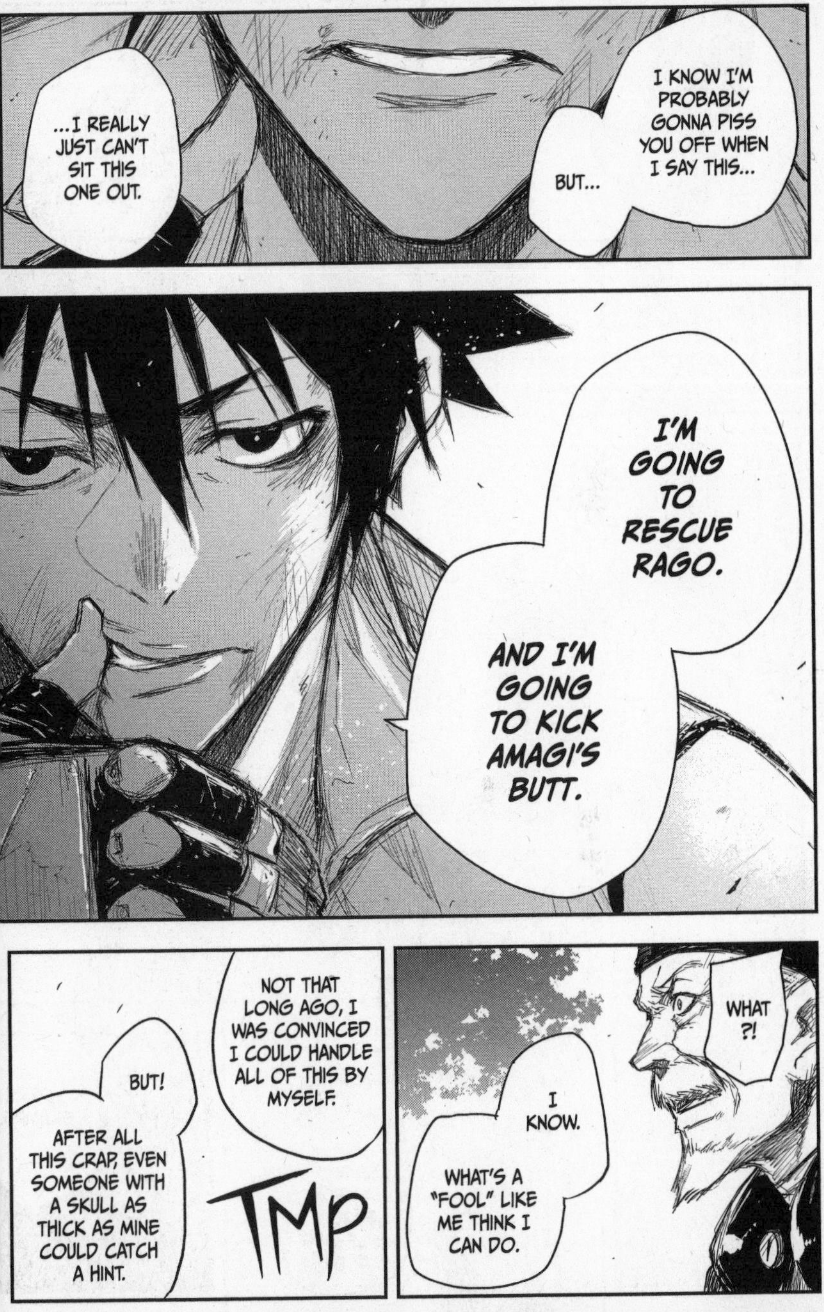
I KNOW I'M PROBABLY GONNA PISS YOU OFF WHEN I SAY THIS...
BUT...
...I REALLY JUST CAN'T SIT THIS ONE OUT.
I'M GOING TO RESCUE RAGO.
AND I'M GOING TO KICK AMAGI'S BUTT.
WHAT ?!
I KNOW.
WHAT'S A "FOOL" LIKE ME THINK I CAN DO.
NOT THAT LONG AGO, I WAS CONVINCED I COULD HANDLE ALL OF THIS BY MYSELF.
BUT!
AFTER ALL THIS CRAP, EVEN SOMEONE WITH A SKULL AS THICK AS MINE COULD CATCH A HINT.
TMP

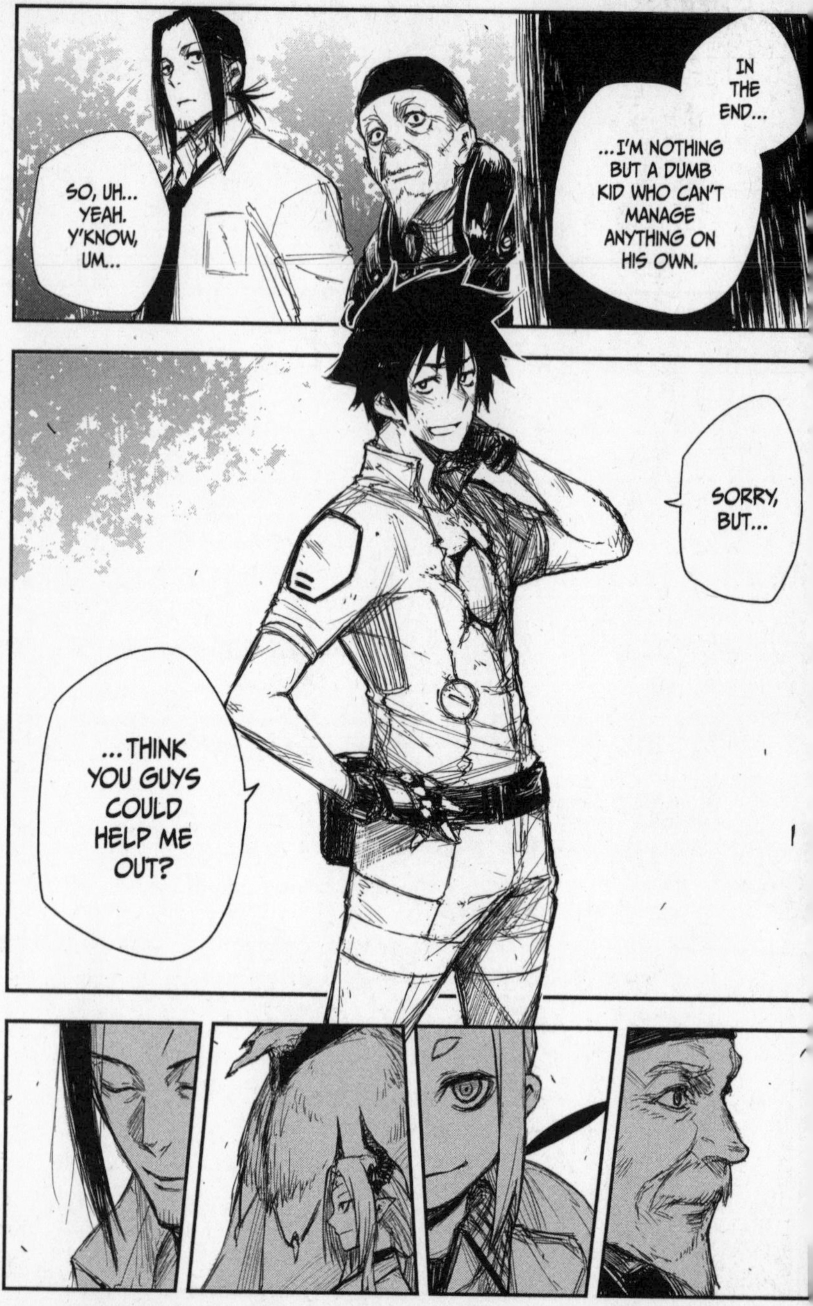
IN THE END...
...I'M NOTHING BUT A DUMB KID WHO CAN'T MANAGE ANYTHING ON HIS OWN.
SO, UH... YEAH. Y'KNOW, UM...
SORRY, BUT...
...THINK YOU GUYS COULD HELP ME OUT?

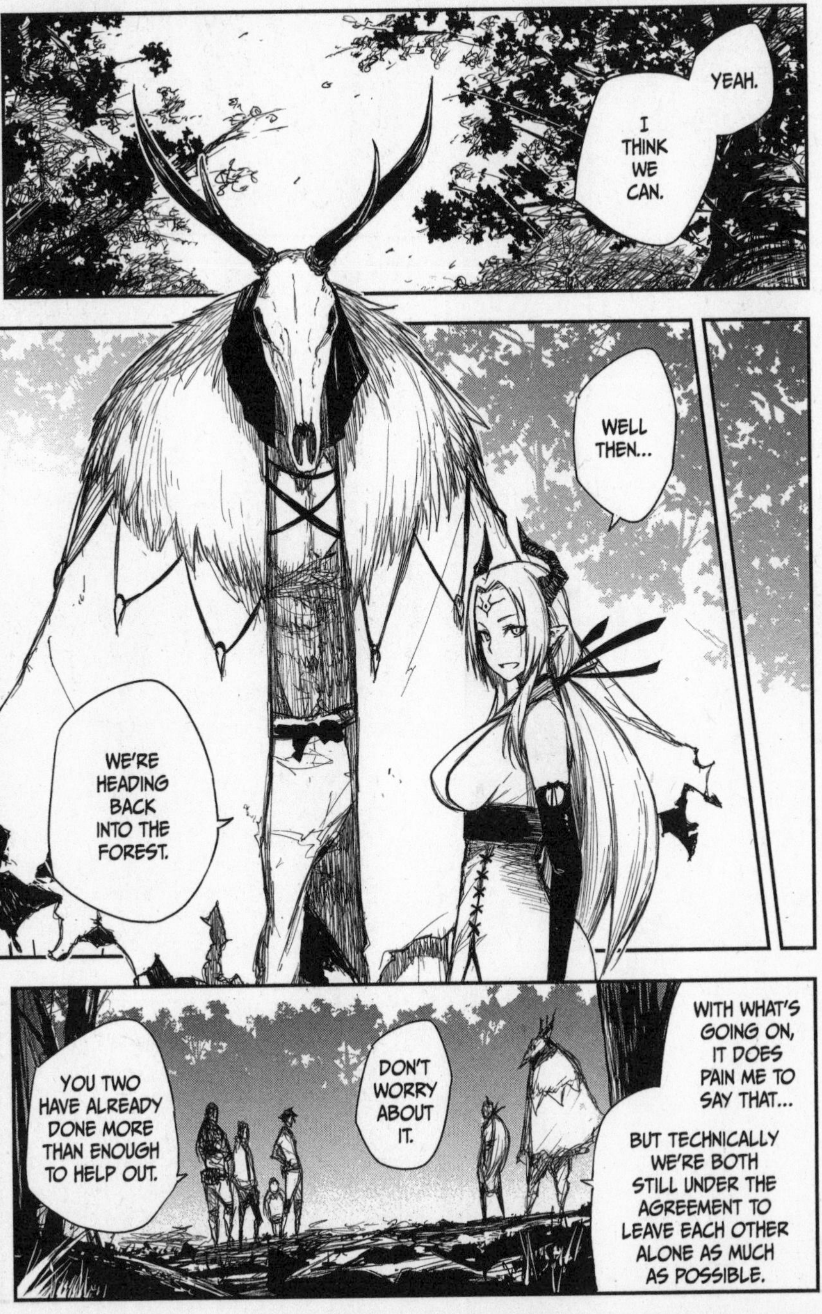
YEAH.
I THINK WE CAN.
WELL THEN...
WE'RE HEADING BACK INTO THE FOREST.
WITH WHAT'S GOING ON, IT DOES PAIN ME TO SAY THAT...
BUT TECHNICALLY WE'RE BOTH STILL UNDER THE AGREEMENT TO LEAVE EACH OTHER ALONE AS MUCH AS POSSIBLE.
DON'T WORRY ABOUT IT.
YOU TWO HAVE ALREADY DONE MORE THAN ENOUGH TO HELP OUT.

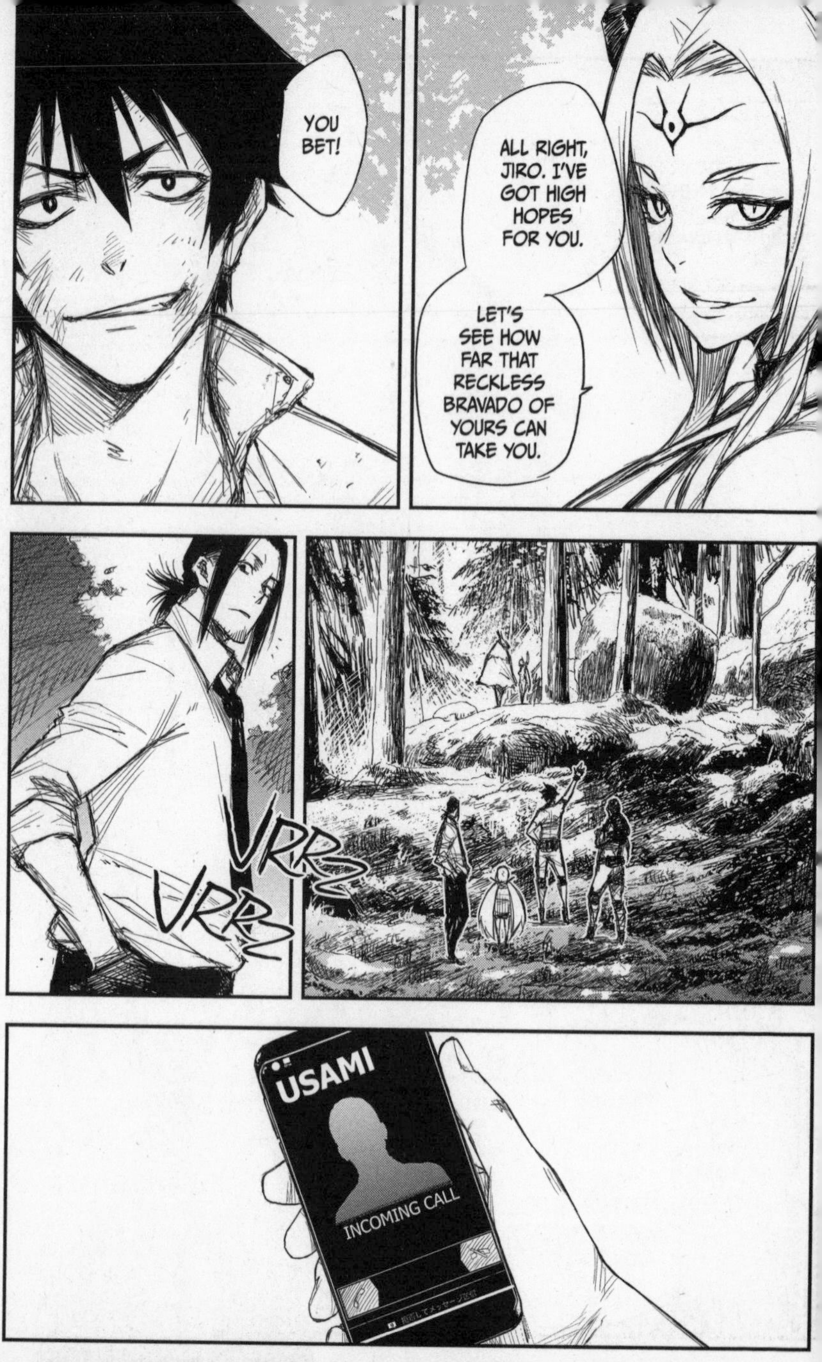
ALL RIGHT, JIRO. I'VE GOT HIGH HOPES FOR YOU.
LET'S SEE HOW FAR THAT RECKLESS BRAVADO OF YOURS CAN TAKE YOU.
YOU BET!
VRRZ VRRZ
USAMI
INCOMING CALL

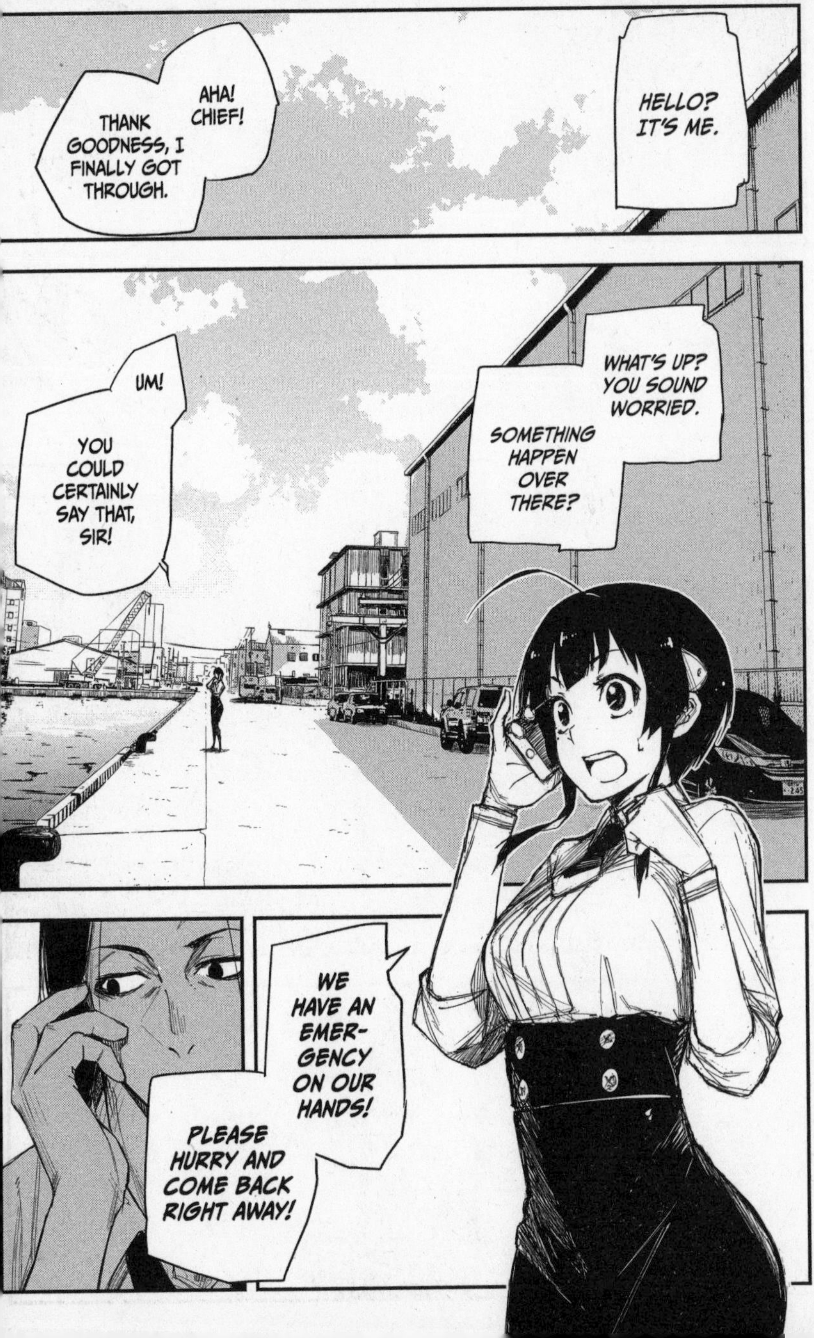
HELLO? IT'S ME.
AHA! CHIEF!
THANK GOODNESS, I FINALLY GOT THROUGH.
WHAT'S UP? YOU SOUND WORRIED.
SOMETHING HAPPEN OVER THERE?
UM!
YOU COULD CERTAINLY SAY THAT, SIR!
WE HAVE AN EMER-GENCY ON OUR HANDS!
PLEASE HURRY AND COME BACK RIGHT AWAY!

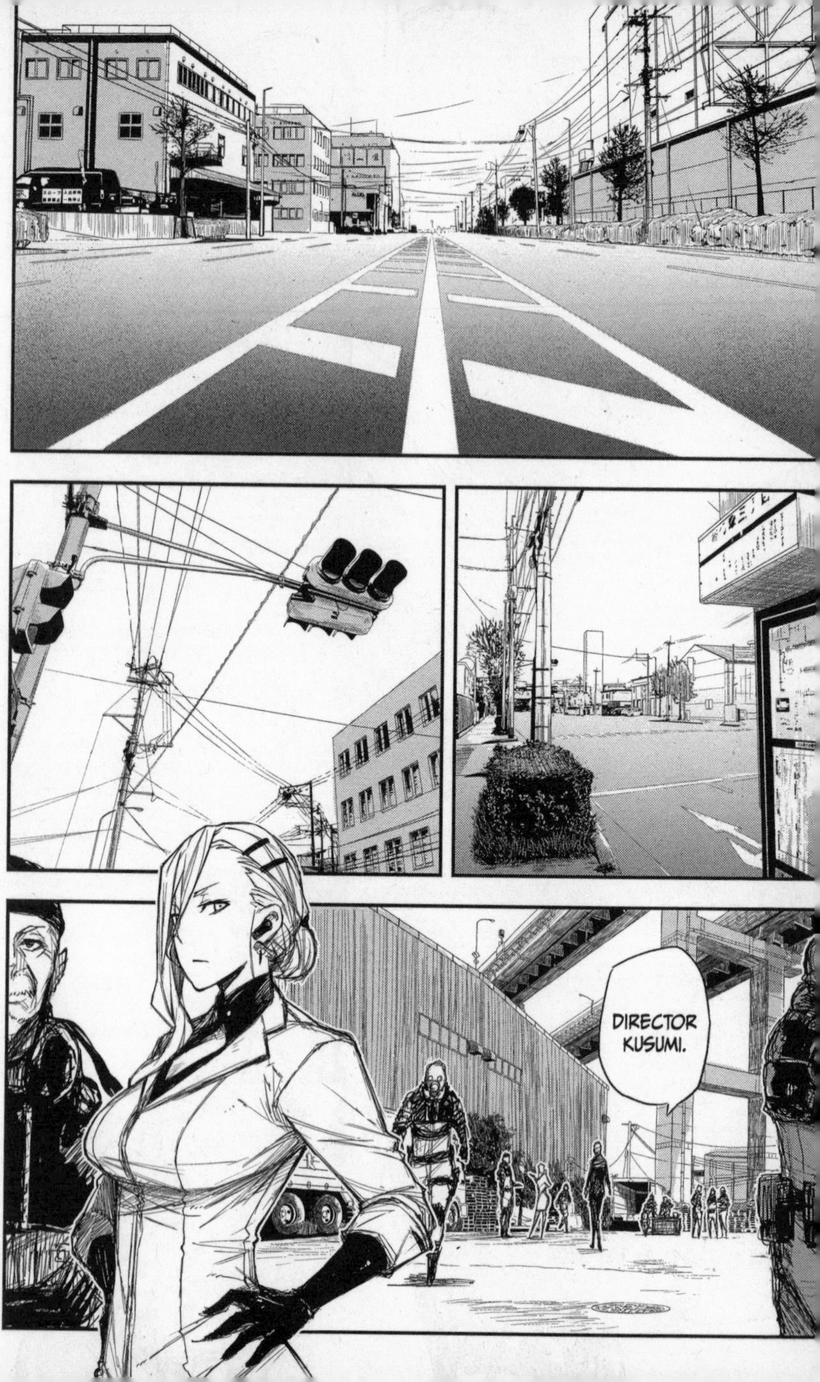
DIRECTOR KUSUMI.

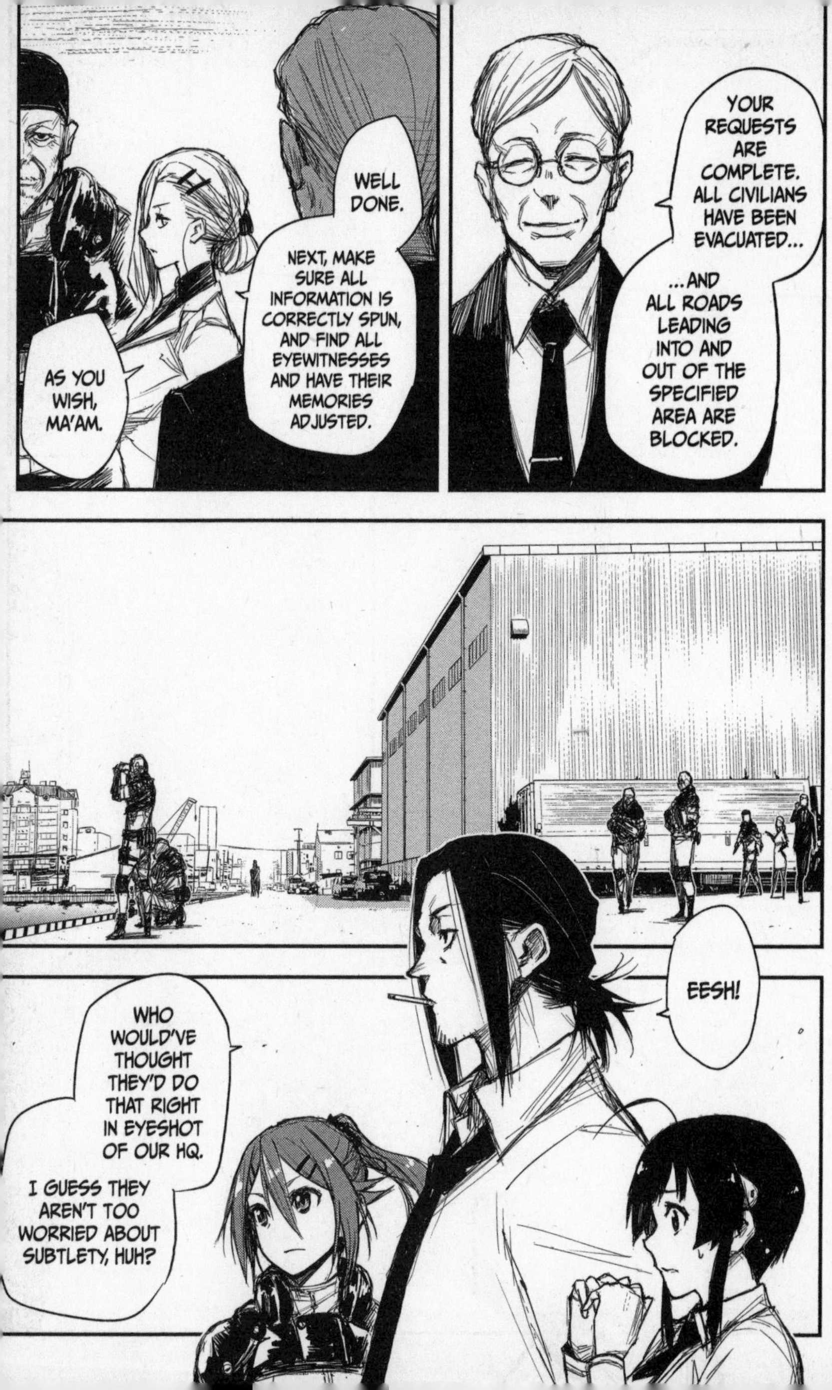
YOUR REQUESTS ARE COMPLETE. ALL CIVILIANS HAVE BEEN EVACUATED...
...AND ALL ROADS LEADING INTO AND OUT OF THE SPECIFIED AREA ARE BLOCKED.
WELL DONE.
NEXT, MAKE SURE ALL INFORMATION IS CORRECTLY SPUN, AND FIND ALL EYEWITNESSES AND HAVE THEIR MEMORIES ADJUSTED.
AS YOU WISH, MA'AM.
EESH!
WHO WOULD'VE THOUGHT THEY'D DO THAT RIGHT IN EYESHOT OF OUR HQ.
I GUESS THEY AREN'T TOO WORRIED ABOUT SUBTLETY, HUH?

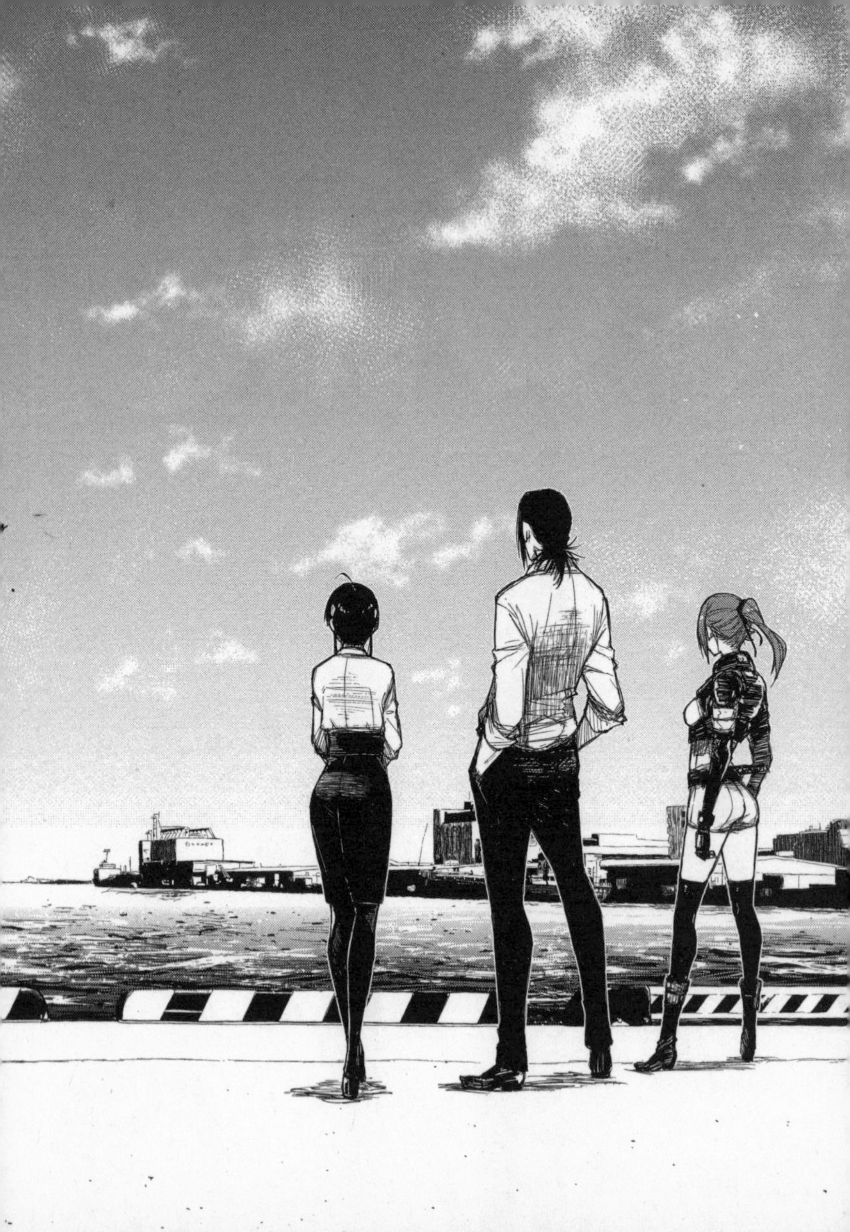

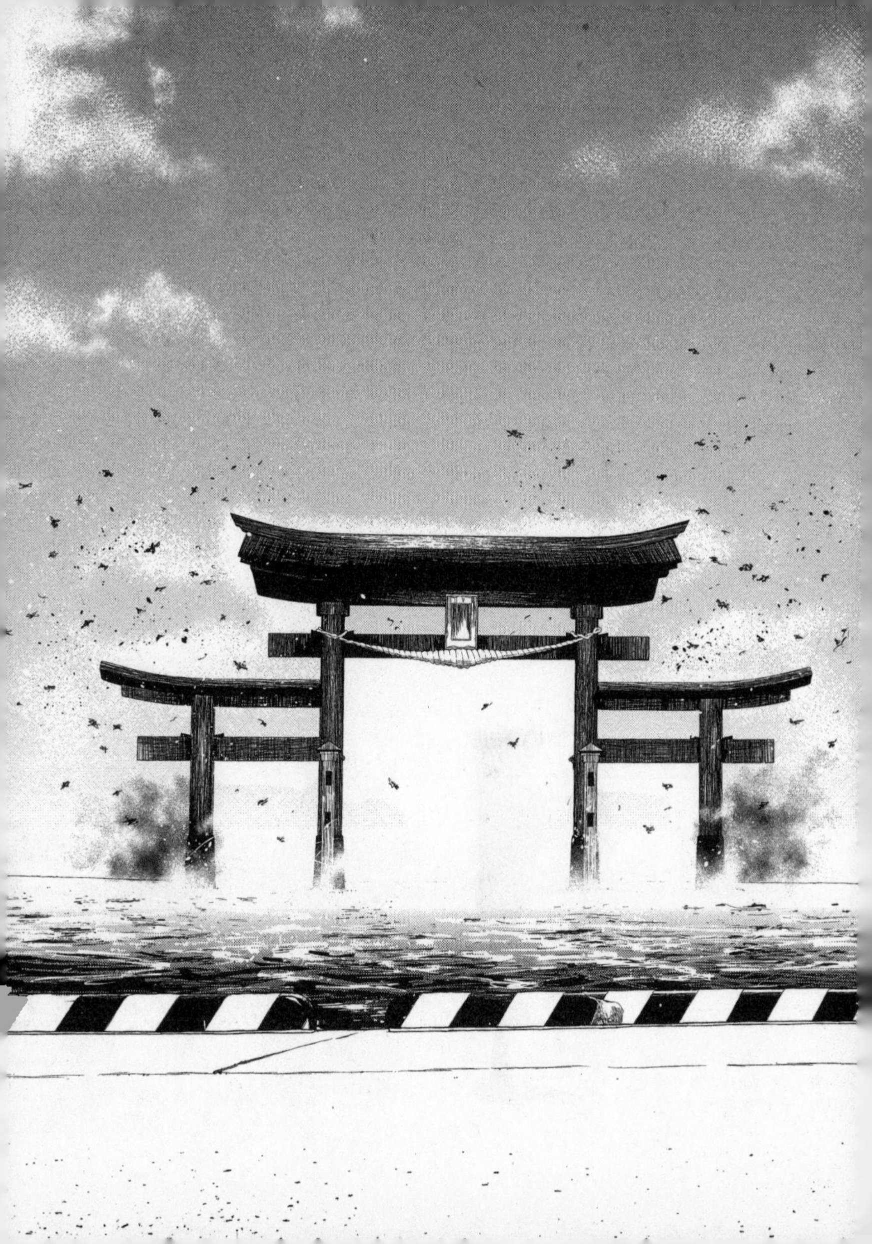

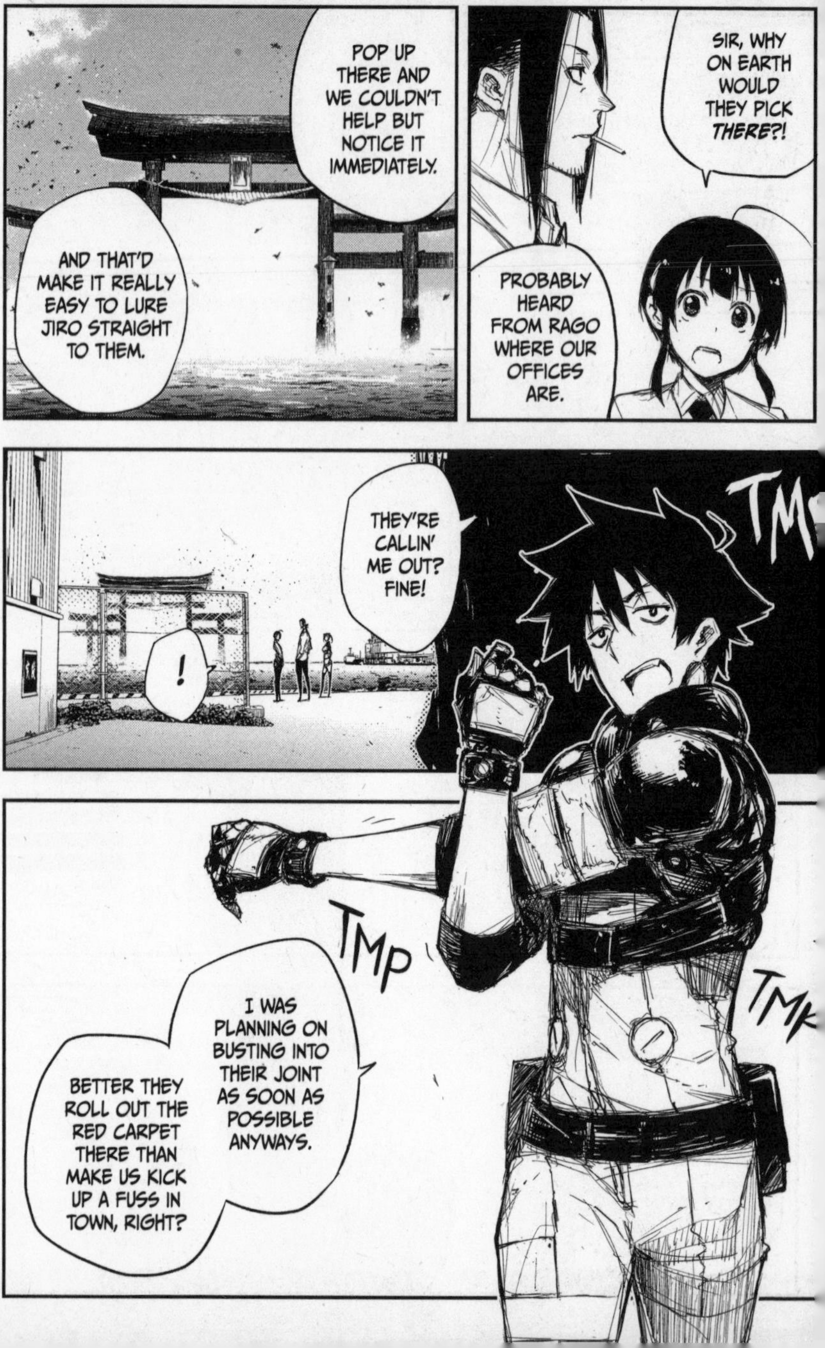
SIR, WHY ON EARTH WOULD THEY PICK *THERE?!*
PROBABLY HEARD FROM RAGO WHERE OUR OFFICES ARE.
POP UP THERE AND WE COULDN'T HELP BUT NOTICE IT IMMEDIATELY.
AND THAT'D MAKE IT REALLY EASY TO LURE JIRO STRAIGHT TO THEM.
THEY'RE CALLIN' ME OUT? FINE!
!
TMP
I WAS PLANNING ON BUSTING INTO THEIR JOINT AS SOON AS POSSIBLE ANYWAYS.
BETTER THEY ROLL OUT THE RED CARPET THERE THAN MAKE US KICK UP A FUSS IN TOWN, RIGHT?

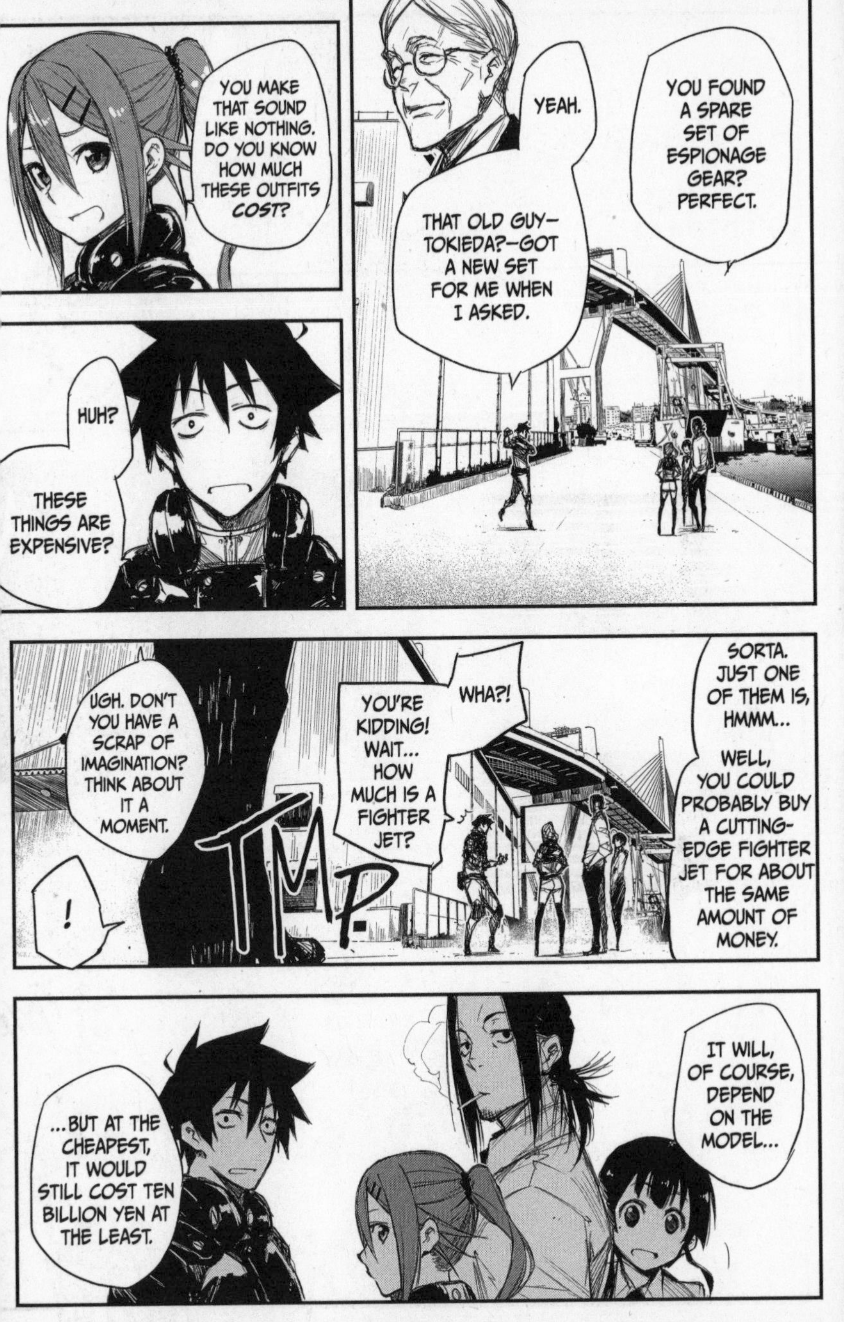
YOU FOUND A SPARE SET OF ESPIONAGE GEAR? PERFECT.
YEAH.
THAT OLD GUY—TOKIEDA?—GOT A NEW SET FOR ME WHEN I ASKED.
YOU MAKE THAT SOUND LIKE NOTHING. DO YOU KNOW HOW MUCH THESE OUTFITS COST?
HUH?
THESE THINGS ARE EXPENSIVE?
SORTA. JUST ONE OF THEM IS, HMMM...
WELL, YOU COULD PROBABLY BUY A CUTTING-EDGE FIGHTER JET FOR ABOUT THE SAME AMOUNT OF MONEY.
WHA?!
YOU'RE KIDDING! WAIT... HOW MUCH IS A FIGHTER JET?
UGH. DON'T YOU HAVE A SCRAP OF IMAGINATION? THINK ABOUT IT A MOMENT.
TMP
!
IT WILL, OF COURSE, DEPEND ON THE MODEL...
...BUT AT THE CHEAPEST, IT WOULD STILL COST TEN BILLION YEN AT THE LEAST.

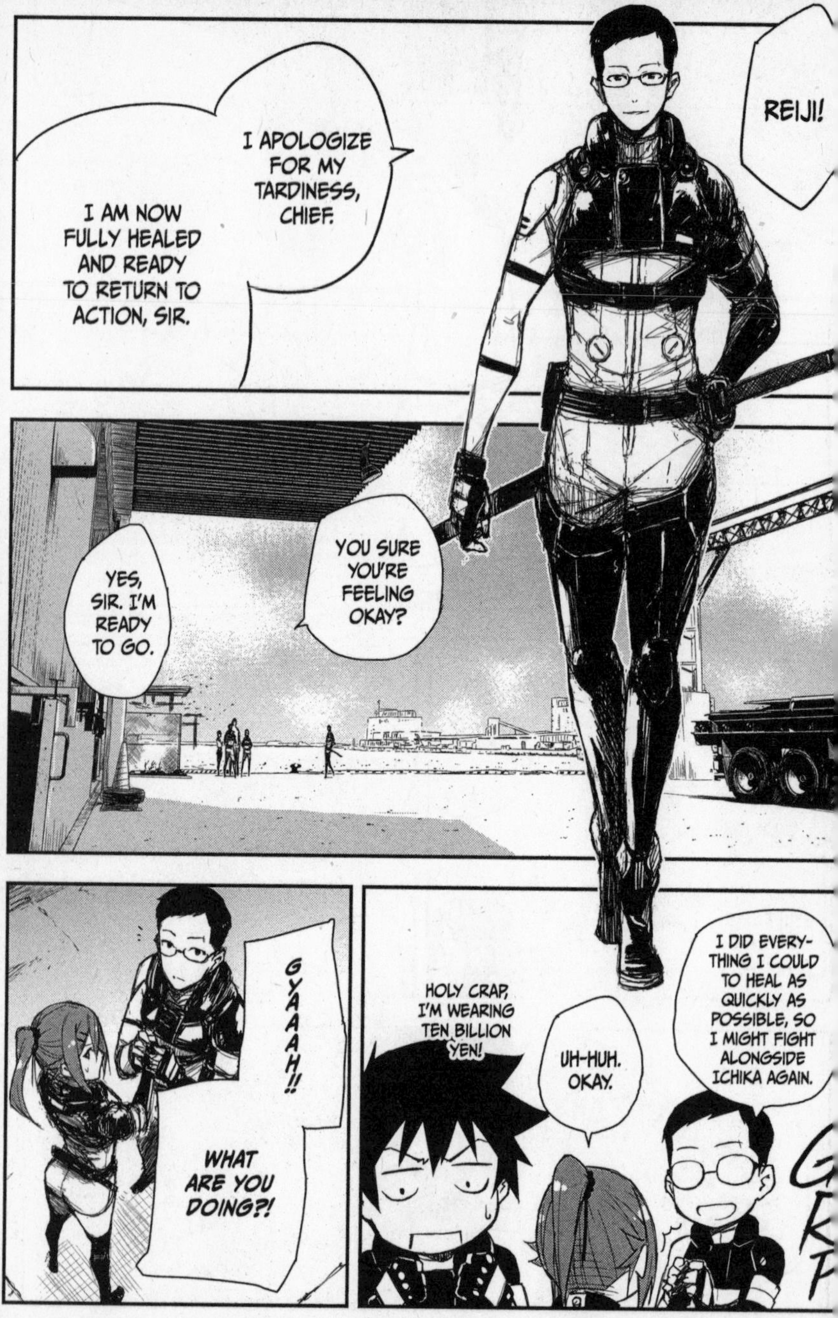
REIJI!
I APOLOGIZE FOR MY TARDINESS, CHIEF.
I AM NOW FULLY HEALED AND READY TO RETURN TO ACTION, SIR.
YOU SURE YOU'RE FEELING OKAY?
YES, SIR. I'M READY TO GO.
I DID EVERYTHING I COULD TO HEAL AS QUICKLY AS POSSIBLE, SO I MIGHT FIGHT ALONGSIDE ICHIKA AGAIN.
UH-HUH. OKAY.
HOLY CRAP, I'M WEARING TEN BILLION YEN!
GYAAAAH!!
WHAT ARE YOU DOING?!

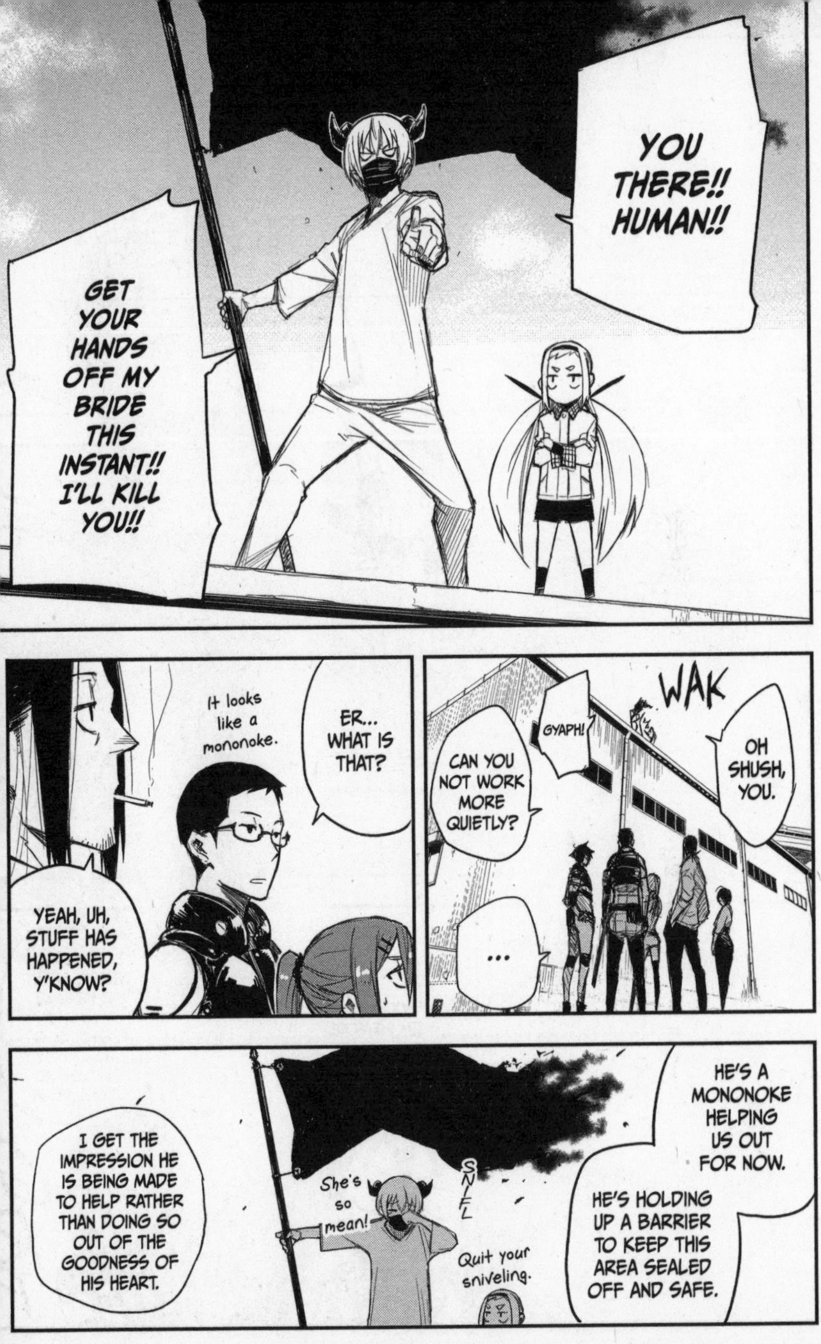
YOU THERE!! HUMAN!!
GET YOUR HANDS OFF MY BRIDE THIS INSTANT!! I'LL KILL YOU!!
WAK
OH SHUSH, YOU.
GYAPH!
CAN YOU NOT WORK MORE QUIETLY?
...
ER... WHAT IS THAT?
It looks like a mononoke.
YEAH, UH, STUFF HAS HAPPENED, Y'KNOW?
HE'S A MONONOKE HELPING US OUT FOR NOW.
HE'S HOLDING UP A BARRIER TO KEEP THIS AREA SEALED OFF AND SAFE.
SNIFL
Quit your sniveling.
She's so mean!
I GET THE IMPRESSION HE IS BEING MADE TO HELP RATHER THAN DOING SO OUT OF THE GOODNESS OF HIS HEART.

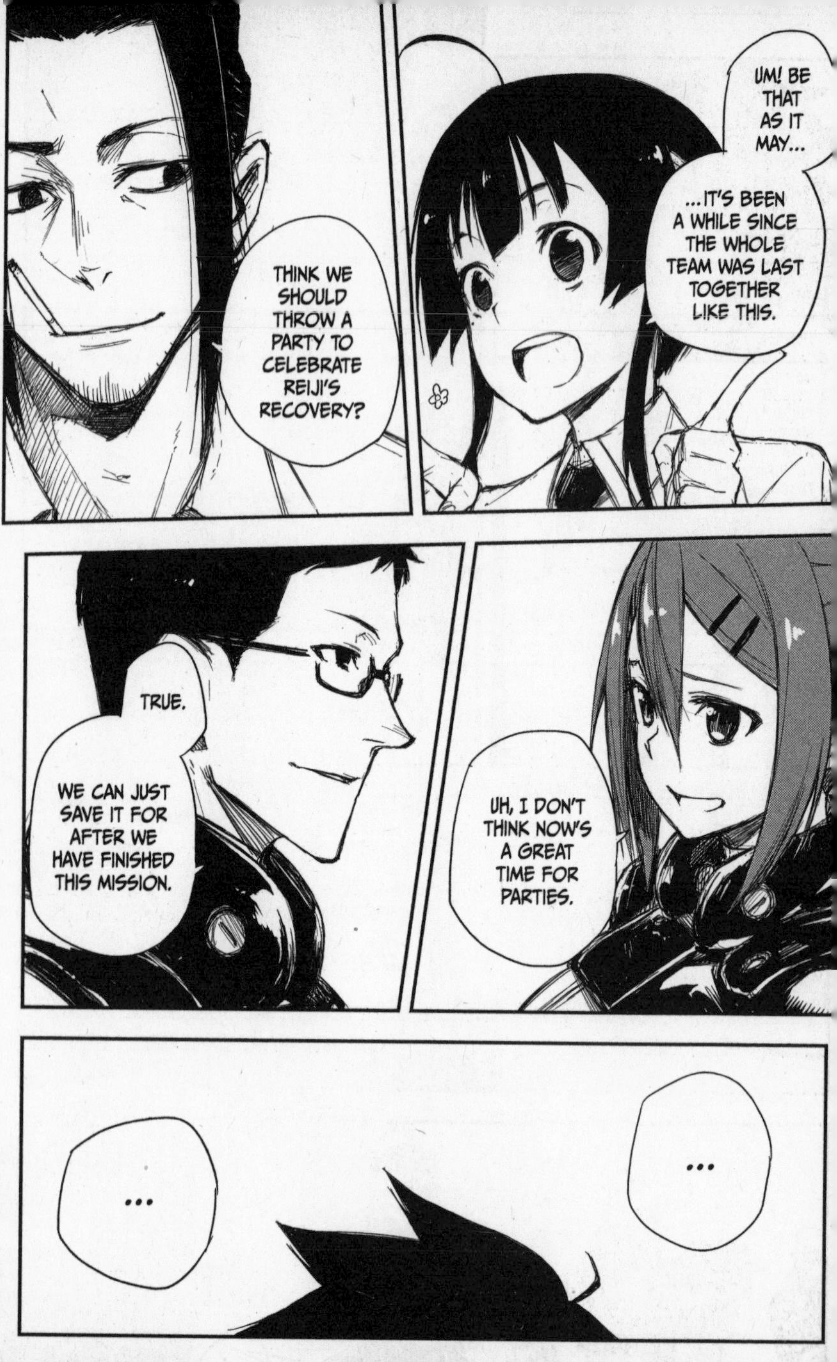
UM! BE THAT AS IT MAY...
...IT'S BEEN A WHILE SINCE THE WHOLE TEAM WAS LAST TOGETHER LIKE THIS.
THINK WE SHOULD THROW A PARTY TO CELEBRATE REIJI'S RECOVERY?
UH, I DON'T THINK NOW'S A GREAT TIME FOR PARTIES.
TRUE.
WE CAN JUST SAVE IT FOR AFTER WE HAVE FINISHED THIS MISSION.
...
...

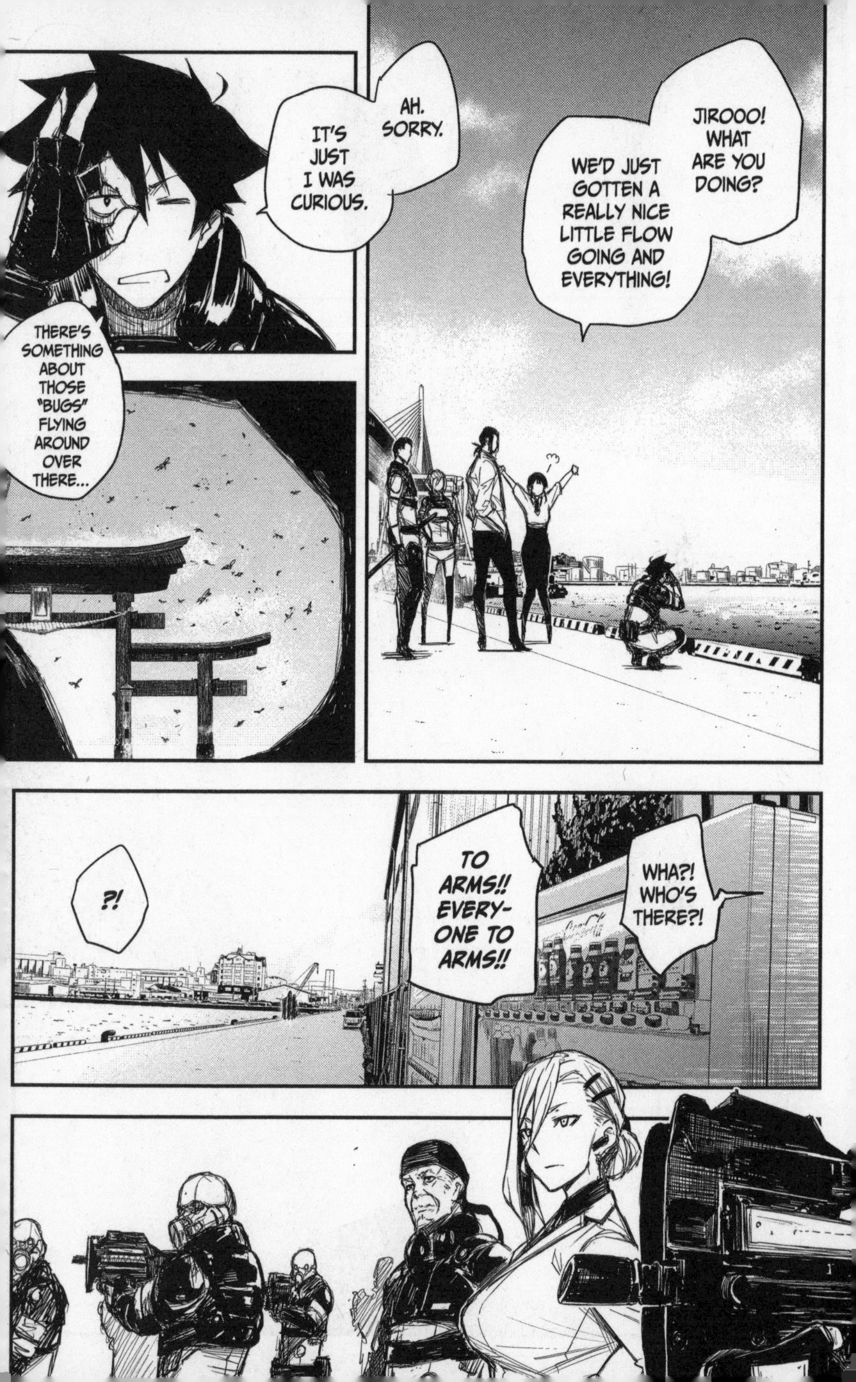
JIROOO! WHAT ARE YOU DOING?
WE'D JUST GOTTEN A REALLY NICE LITTLE FLOW GOING AND EVERYTHING!
AH. SORRY.
IT'S JUST I WAS CURIOUS.
THERE'S SOMETHING ABOUT THOSE "BUGS" FLYING AROUND OVER THERE...
WHA?! WHO'S THERE?!
TO ARMS!! EVERY-ONE TO ARMS!!
?!

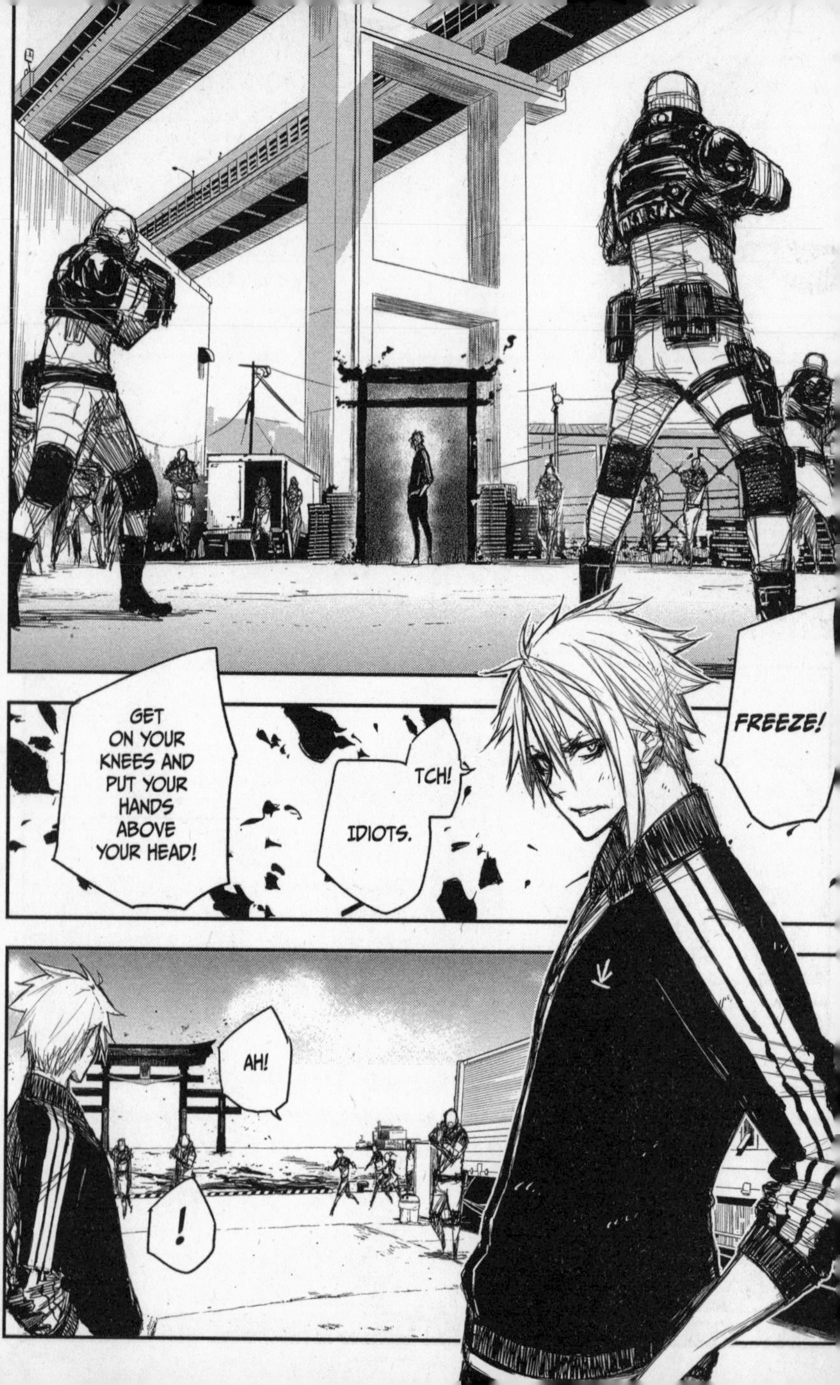
FREEZE!
TCH!
IDIOTS.
GET ON YOUR KNEES AND PUT YOUR HANDS ABOVE YOUR HEAD!
AH!
!

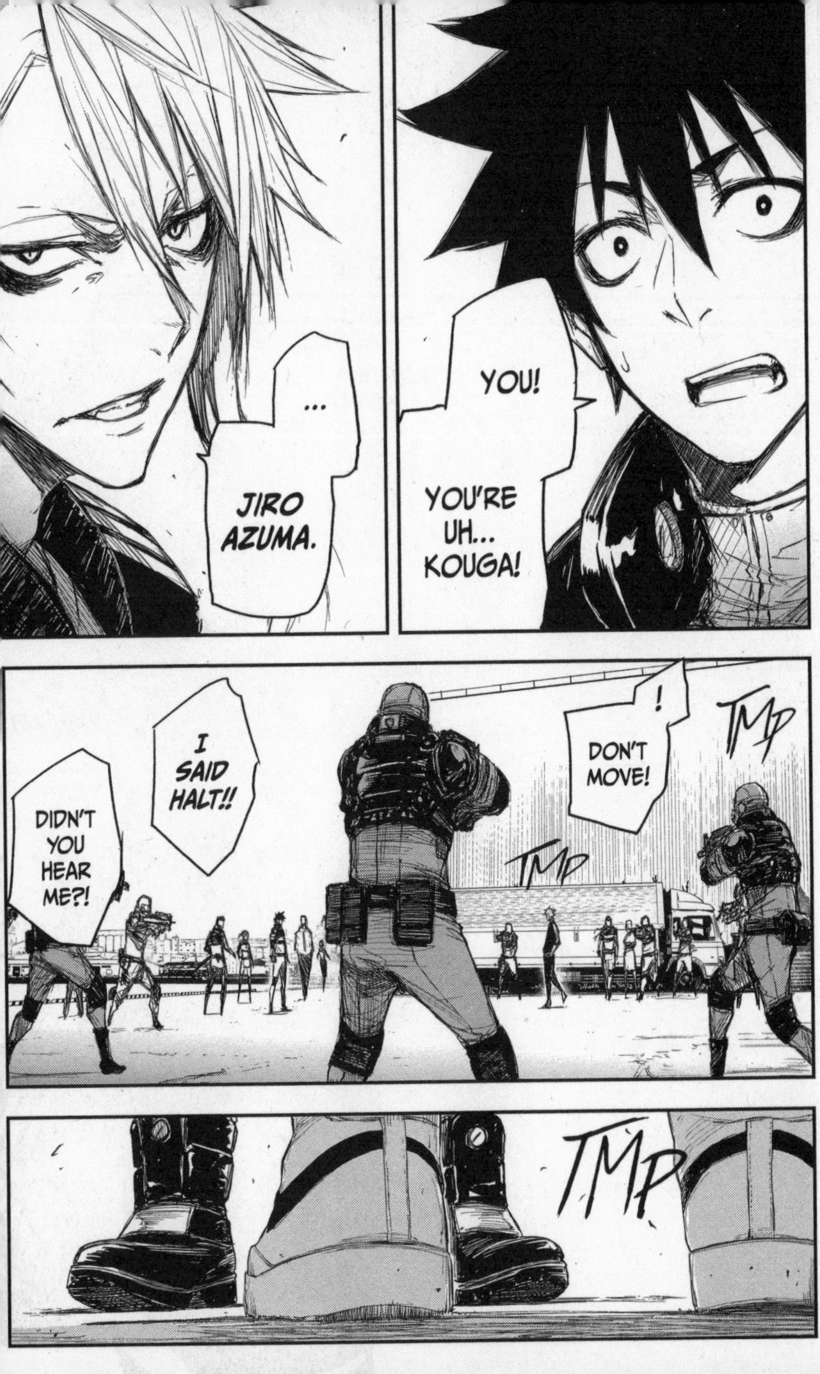
YOU!
YOU'RE UH... KOUGA!
...
JIRO AZUMA.
!
DON'T MOVE!
TMP
TMP
I SAID HALT!!
DIDN'T YOU HEAR ME?!
TMP

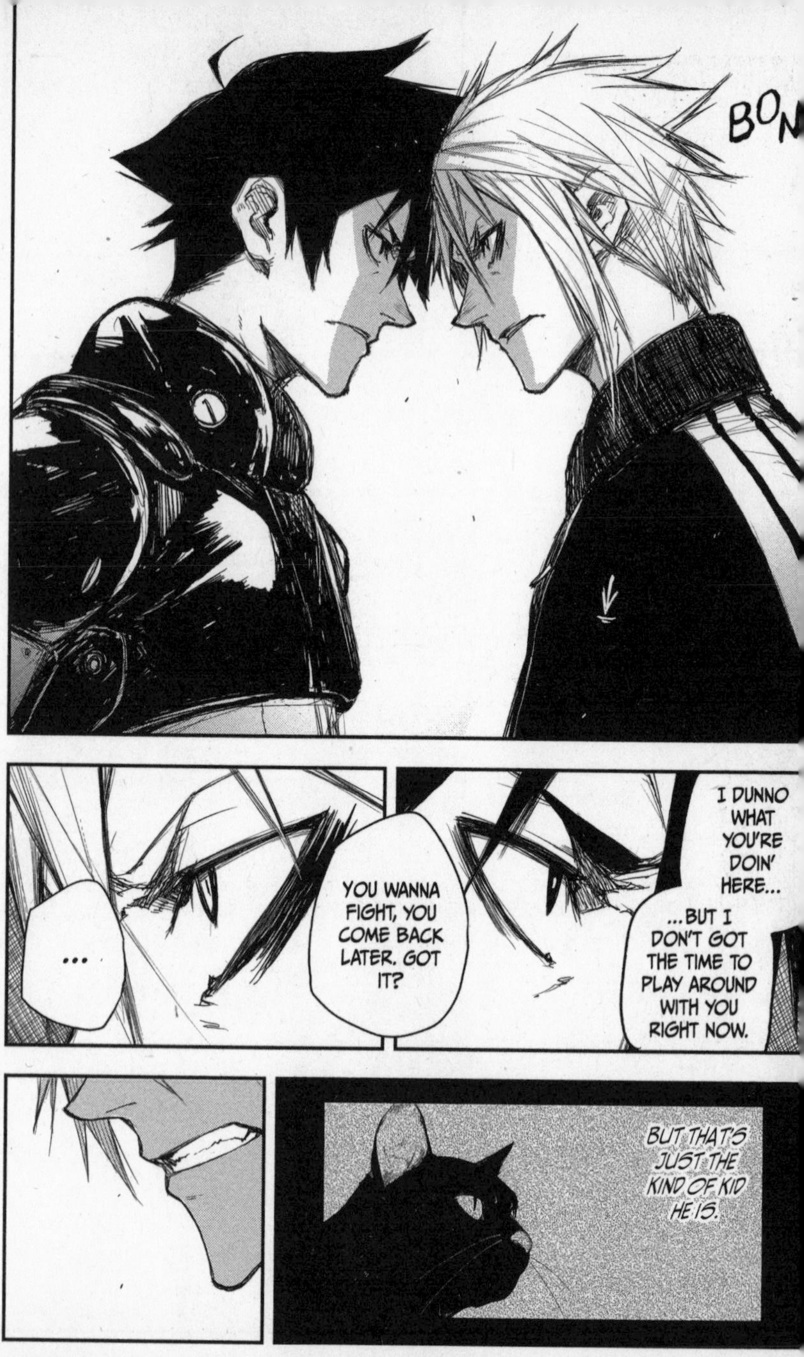
BON
I DUNNO WHAT YOU'RE DOIN' HERE...
...BUT I DON'T GOT THE TIME TO PLAY AROUND WITH YOU RIGHT NOW.
YOU WANNA FIGHT, YOU COME BACK LATER. GOT IT?
...
BUT THAT'S JUST THE KIND OF KID HE IS.

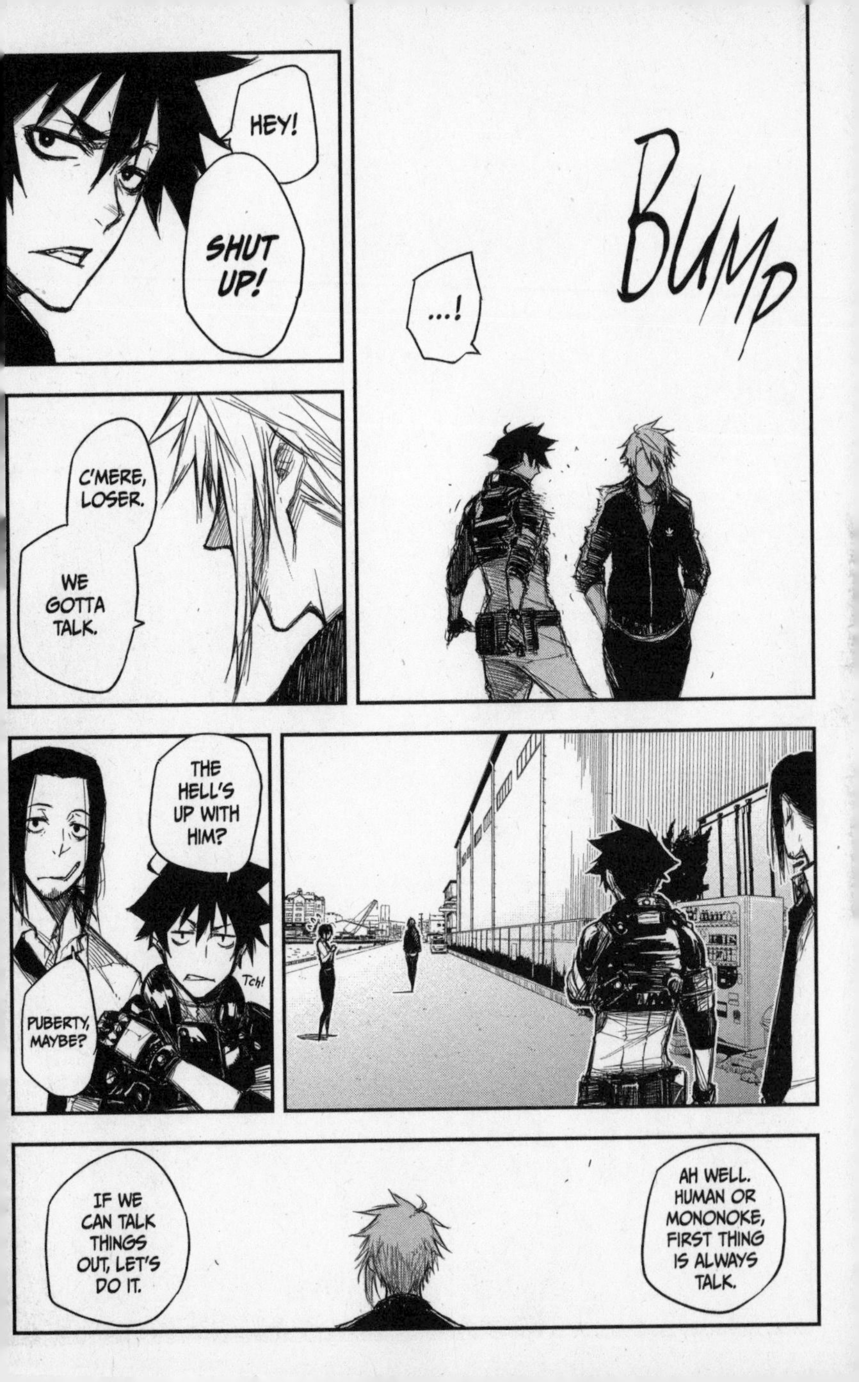
BUMP
...!
HEY!
SHUT UP!
C'MERE, LOSER.
WE GOTTA TALK.
THE HELL'S UP WITH HIM?
Tch!
PUBERTY, MAYBE?
AH WELL. HUMAN OR MONONOKE, FIRST THING IS ALWAYS TALK.
IF WE CAN TALK THINGS OUT, LET'S DO IT.

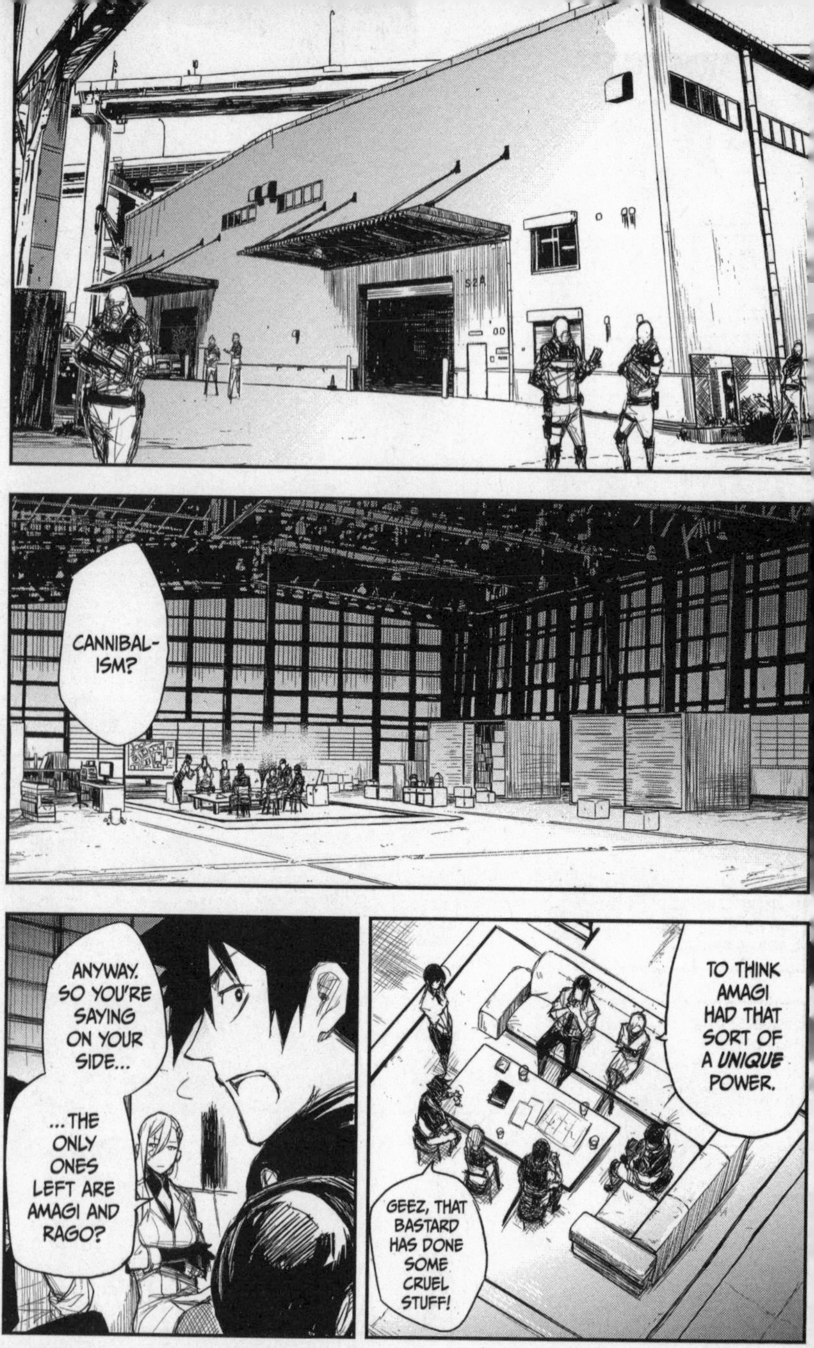
S2A
CANNIBALISM?
TO THINK AMAGI HAD THAT SORT OF A *UNIQUE* POWER.
GEEZ, THAT BASTARD HAS DONE SOME CRUEL STUFF!
ANYWAY. SO YOU'RE SAYING ON YOUR SIDE...
...THE ONLY ONES LEFT ARE AMAGI AND RAGO?

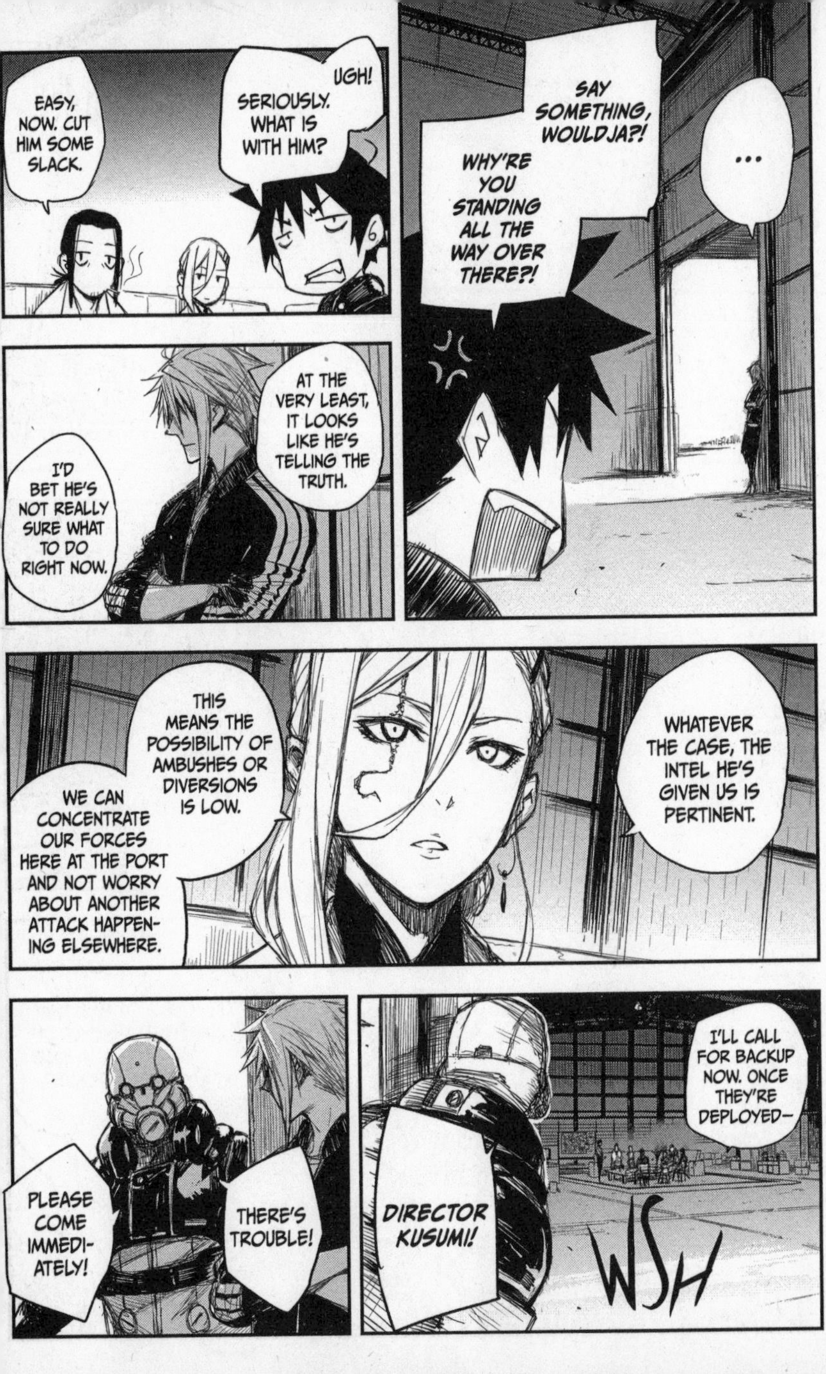
...
SAY SOMETHING, WOULDJA?!
WHY'RE YOU STANDING ALL THE WAY OVER THERE?!
UGH!
SERIOUSLY. WHAT IS WITH HIM?
EASY, NOW. CUT HIM SOME SLACK.
AT THE VERY LEAST, IT LOOKS LIKE HE'S TELLING THE TRUTH.
I'D BET HE'S NOT REALLY SURE WHAT TO DO RIGHT NOW.
WHATEVER THE CASE, THE INTEL HE'S GIVEN US IS PERTINENT.
THIS MEANS THE POSSIBILITY OF AMBUSHES OR DIVERSIONS IS LOW.
WE CAN CONCENTRATE OUR FORCES HERE AT THE PORT AND NOT WORRY ABOUT ANOTHER ATTACK HAPPEN-ING ELSEWHERE.
I'LL CALL FOR BACKUP NOW. ONCE THEY'RE DEPLOYED—
DIRECTOR KUSUMI!
WSH
THERE'S TROUBLE!
PLEASE COME IMMEDI-ATELY!

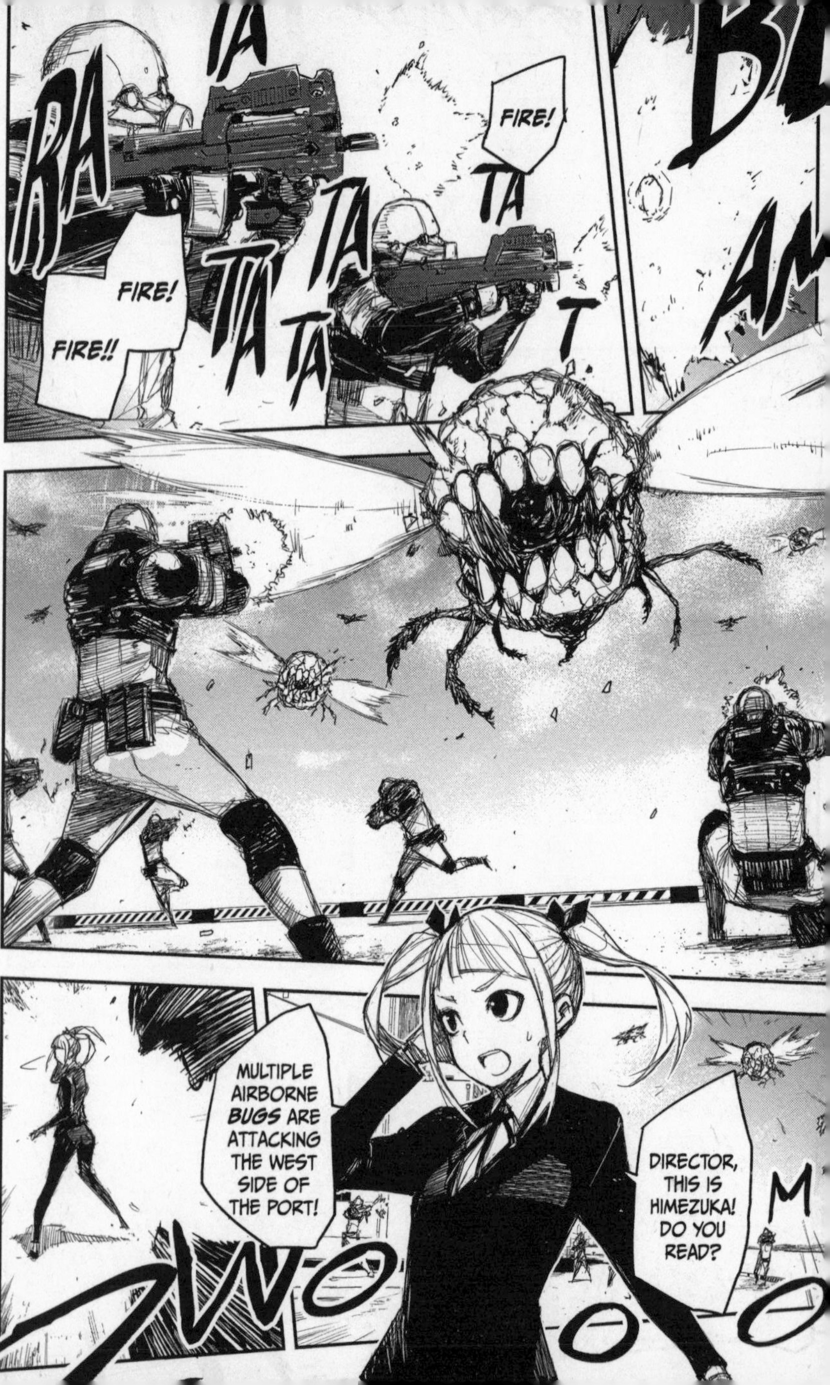

FIRE!
FIRE!
FIRE!!
DIRECTOR, THIS IS HIMEZUKA! DO YOU READ?
MULTIPLE AIRBORNE BUGS ARE ATTACKING THE WEST SIDE OF THE PORT!

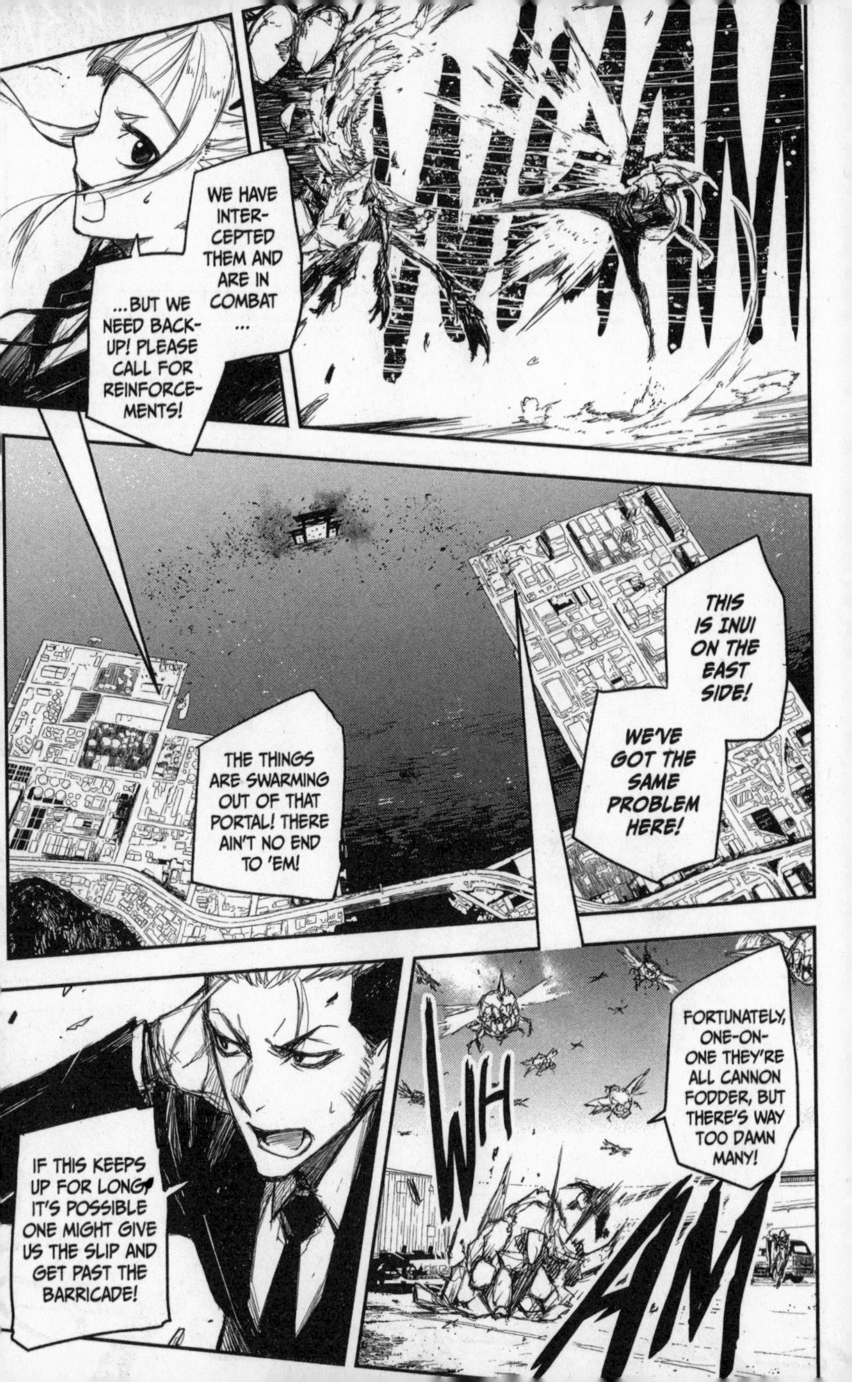
WE HAVE INTER-
CEPTED
THEM AND
ARE IN
COMBAT
...
...BUT WE NEED BACK-UP! PLEASE CALL FOR REINFORCE-MENTS!
THIS IS INUI ON THE EAST SIDE!
WE'VE GOT THE SAME PROBLEM HERE!
THE THINGS ARE SWARMING OUT OF THAT PORTAL! THERE AIN'T NO END TO 'EM!
FORTUNATELY, ONE-ON-ONE THEY'RE ALL CANNON FODDER, BUT THERE'S WAY TOO DAMN MANY!
WHAM
IF THIS KEEPS UP FOR LONG, IT'S POSSIBLE ONE MIGHT GIVE US THE SLIP AND GET PAST THE BARRICADE!

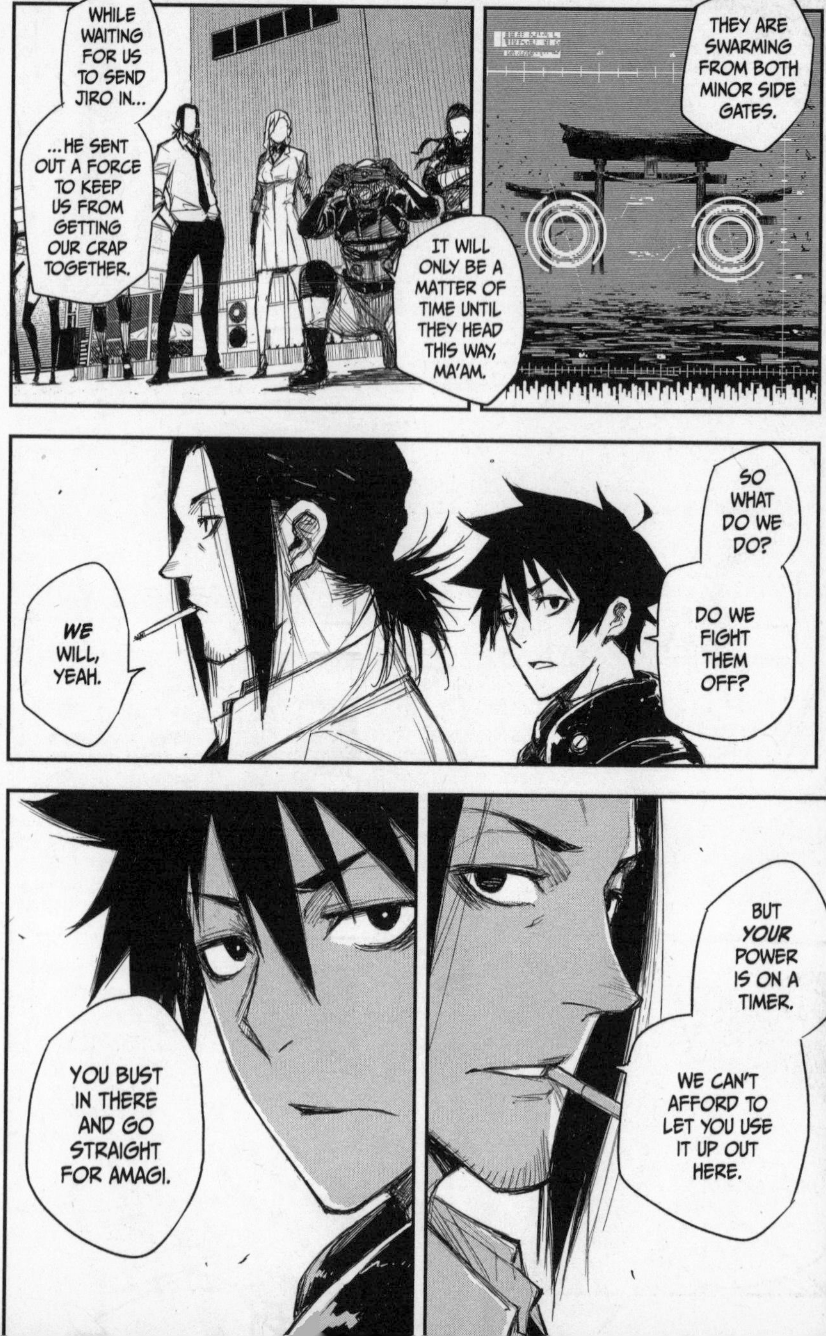
THEY ARE SWARMING FROM BOTH MINOR SIDE GATES.
IT WILL ONLY BE A MATTER OF TIME UNTIL THEY HEAD THIS WAY, MA'AM.
WHILE WAITING FOR US TO SEND JIRO IN...
...HE SENT OUT A FORCE TO KEEP US FROM GETTING OUR CRAP TOGETHER.
SO WHAT DO WE DO?
DO WE FIGHT THEM OFF?
WE WILL, YEAH.
BUT *YOUR* POWER IS ON A TIMER.
WE CAN'T AFFORD TO LET YOU USE IT UP OUT HERE.
YOU BUST IN THERE AND GO STRAIGHT FOR AMAGI.

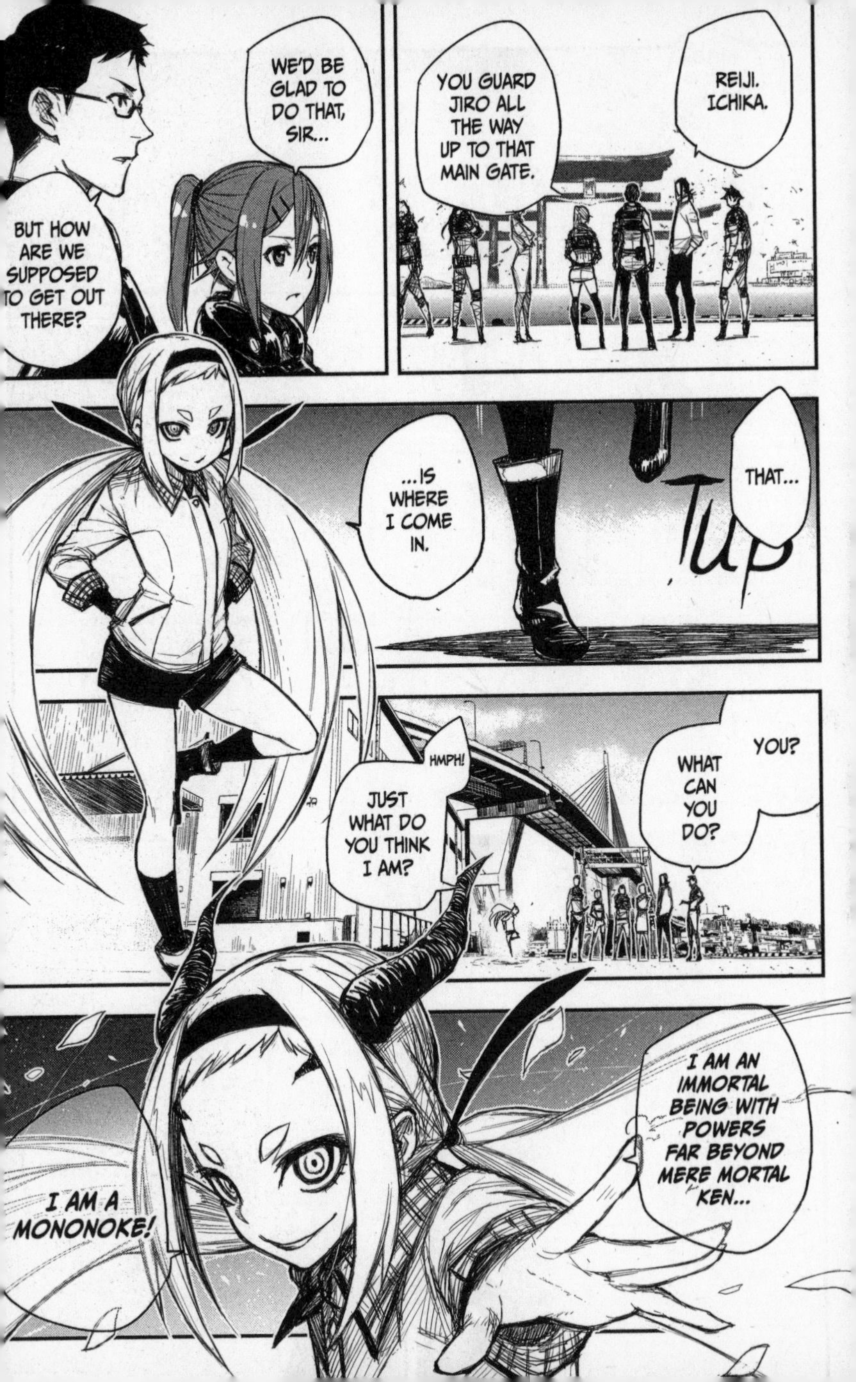
REIJI. ICHIKA.
YOU GUARD JIRO ALL THE WAY UP TO THAT MAIN GATE.
WE'D BE GLAD TO DO THAT, SIR...
BUT HOW ARE WE SUPPOSED TO GET OUT THERE?
THAT...
TUP
...IS WHERE I COME IN.
YOU? WHAT CAN YOU DO?
HMPH!
JUST WHAT DO YOU THINK I AM?
I AM AN IMMORTAL BEING WITH POWERS FAR BEYOND MERE MORTAL KEN...
I AM A MONONOKE!

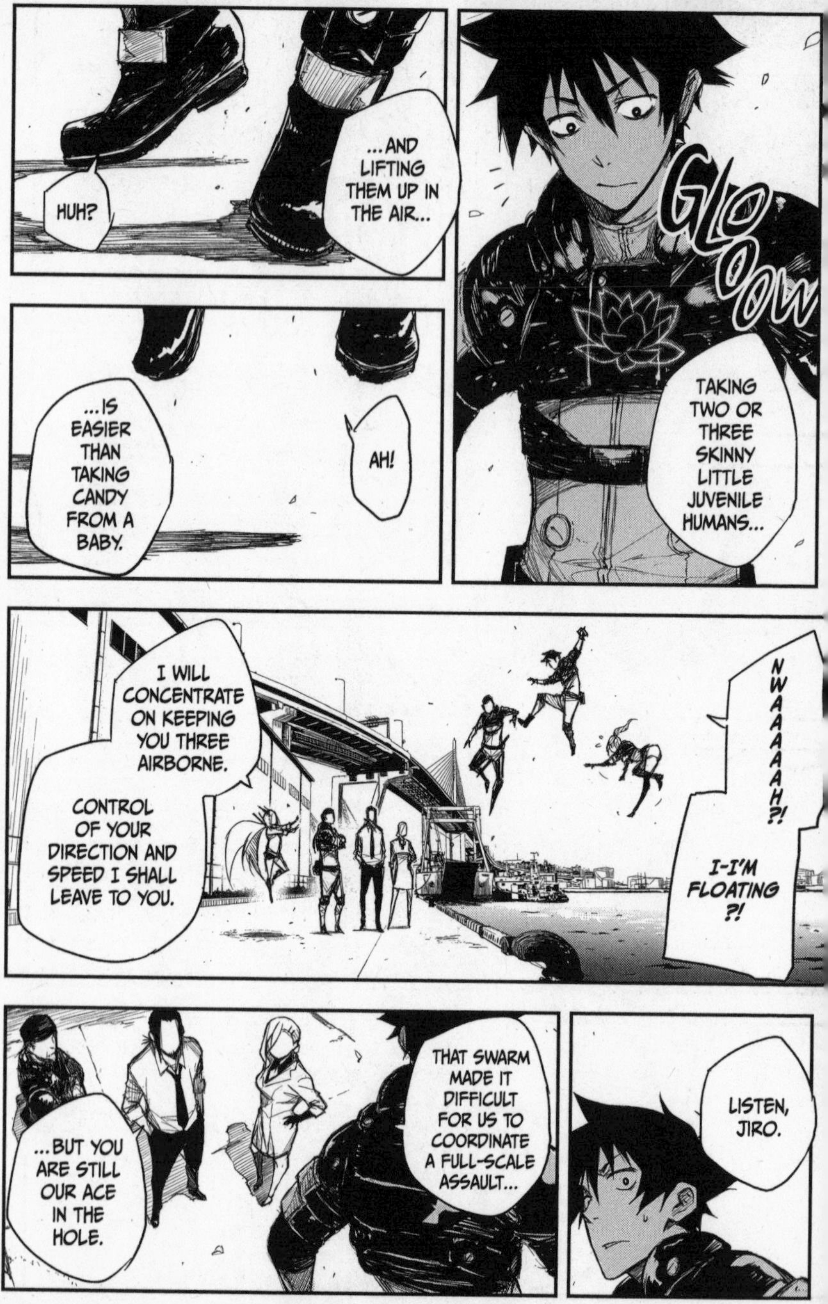
GLOOOW
TAKING TWO OR THREE SKINNY LITTLE JUVENILE HUMANS...
...AND LIFTING THEM UP IN THE AIR...
HUH?
AH!
...IS EASIER THAN TAKING CANDY FROM A BABY.
NWAAAAAAH?!
I-I'M FLOATING ?!
I WILL CONCENTRATE ON KEEPING YOU THREE AIRBORNE.
CONTROL OF YOUR DIRECTION AND SPEED I SHALL LEAVE TO YOU.
LISTEN, JIRO.
THAT SWARM MADE IT DIFFICULT FOR US TO COORDINATE A FULL-SCALE ASSAULT...
...BUT YOU ARE STILL OUR ACE IN THE HOLE.

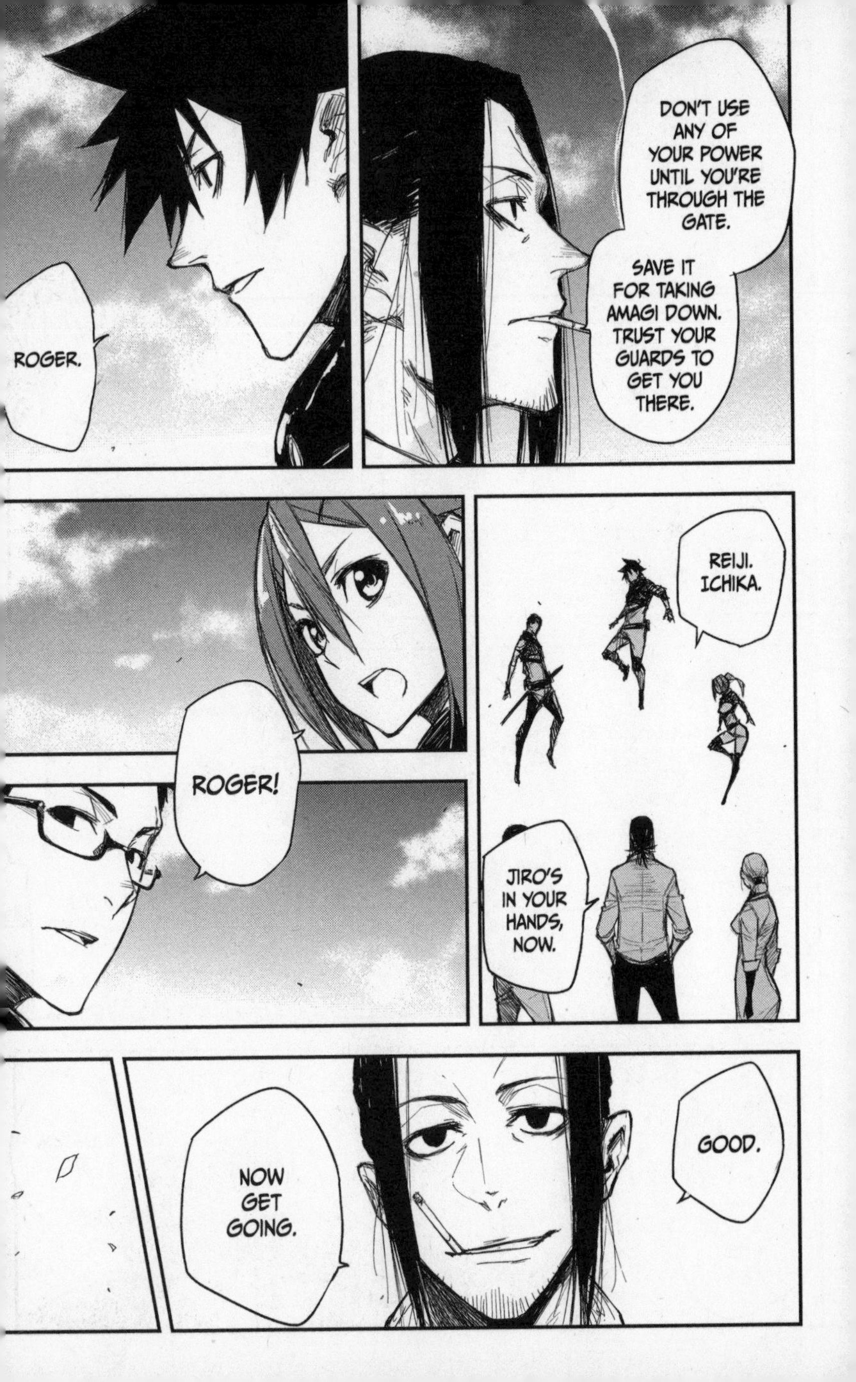
DON'T USE ANY OF YOUR POWER UNTIL YOU'RE THROUGH THE GATE.
SAVE IT FOR TAKING AMAGI DOWN. TRUST YOUR GUARDS TO GET YOU THERE.
ROGER.
REIJI. ICHIKA.
JIRO'S IN YOUR HANDS, NOW.
ROGER!
GOOD.
NOW GET GOING.

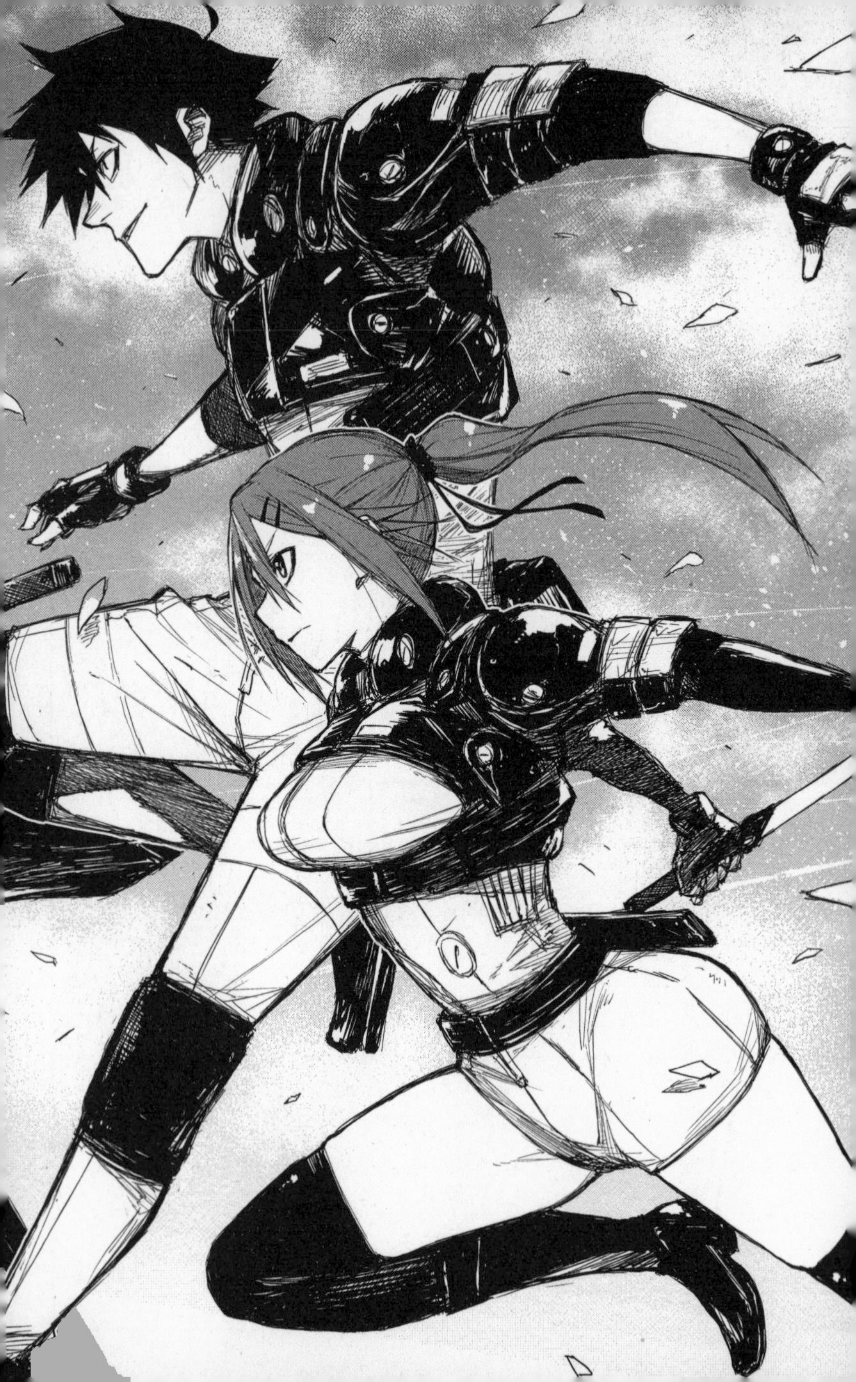

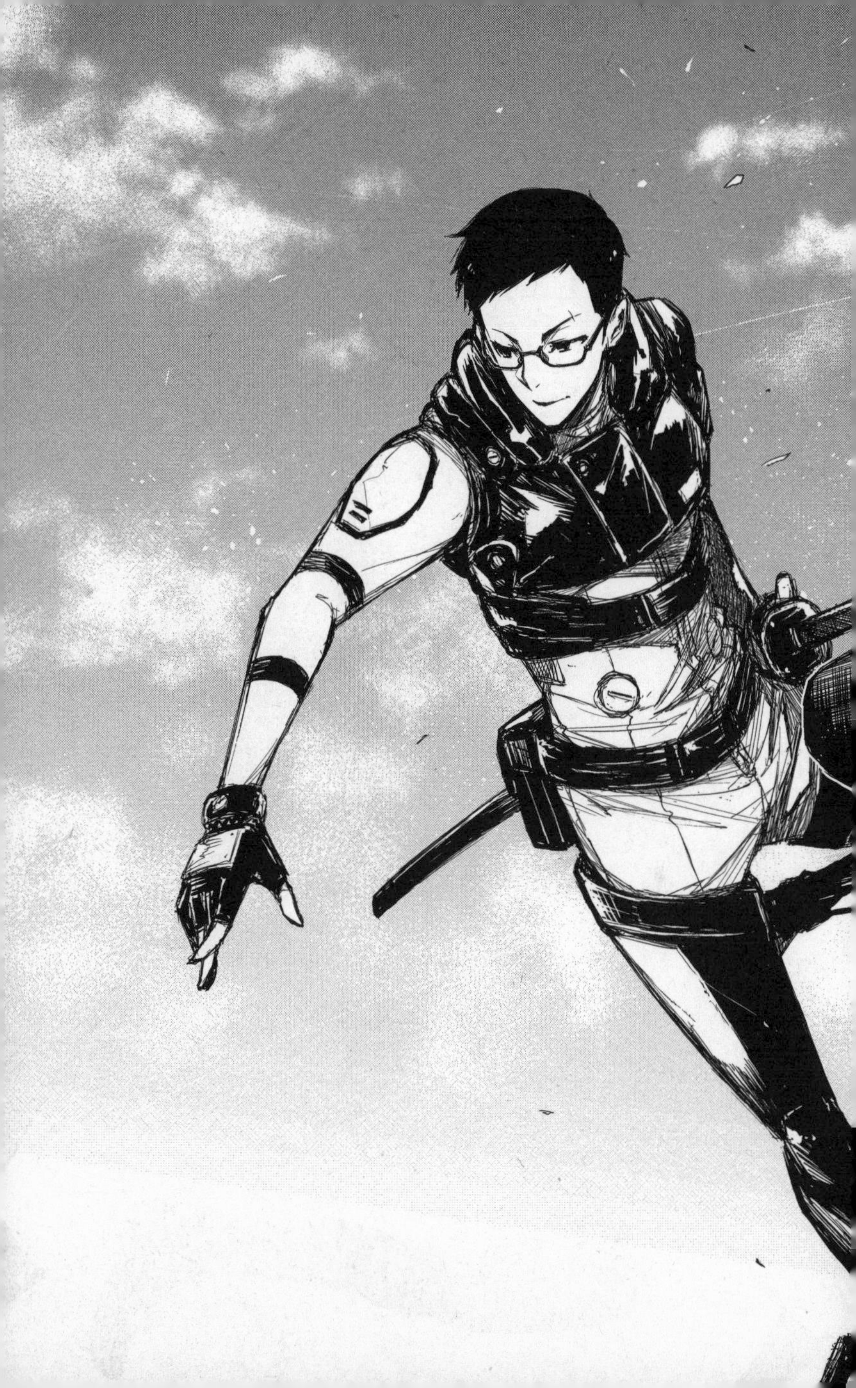

BLACK TORCH

#18 Black or White

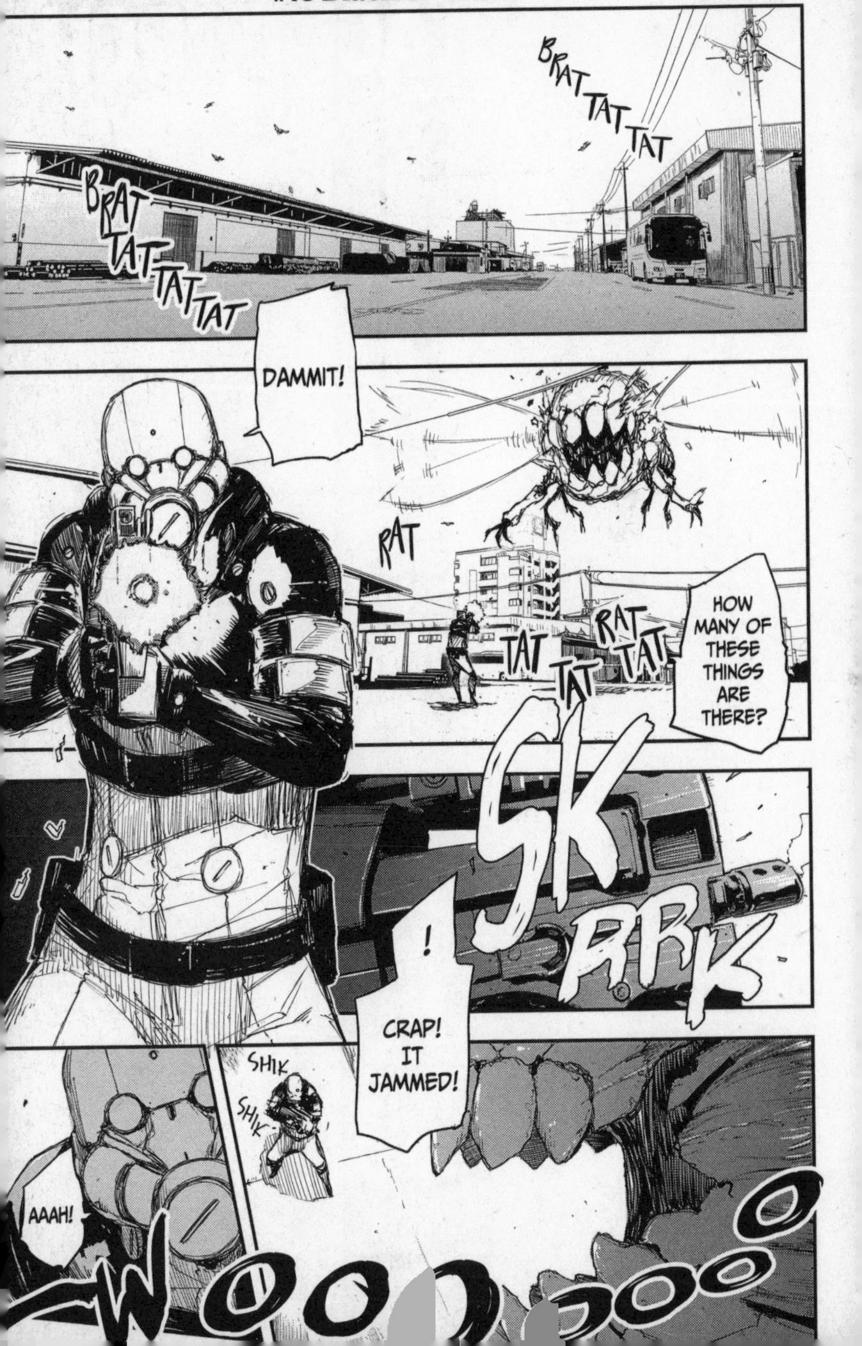

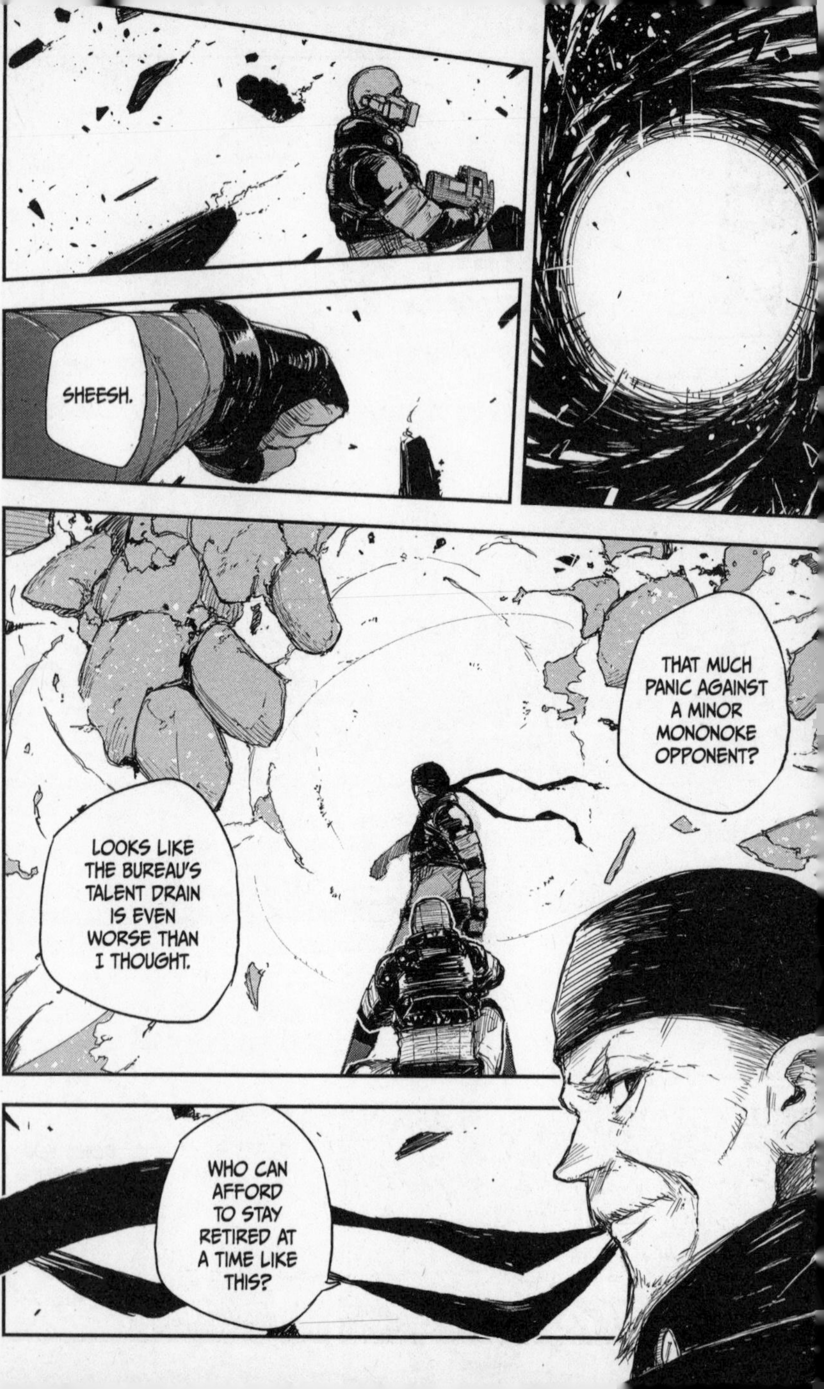
SHEESH.
THAT MUCH PANIC AGAINST A MINOR MONONOKE OPPONENT?
LOOKS LIKE THE BUREAU'S TALENT DRAIN IS EVEN WORSE THAN I THOUGHT.
WHO CAN AFFORD TO STAY RETIRED AT A TIME LIKE THIS?

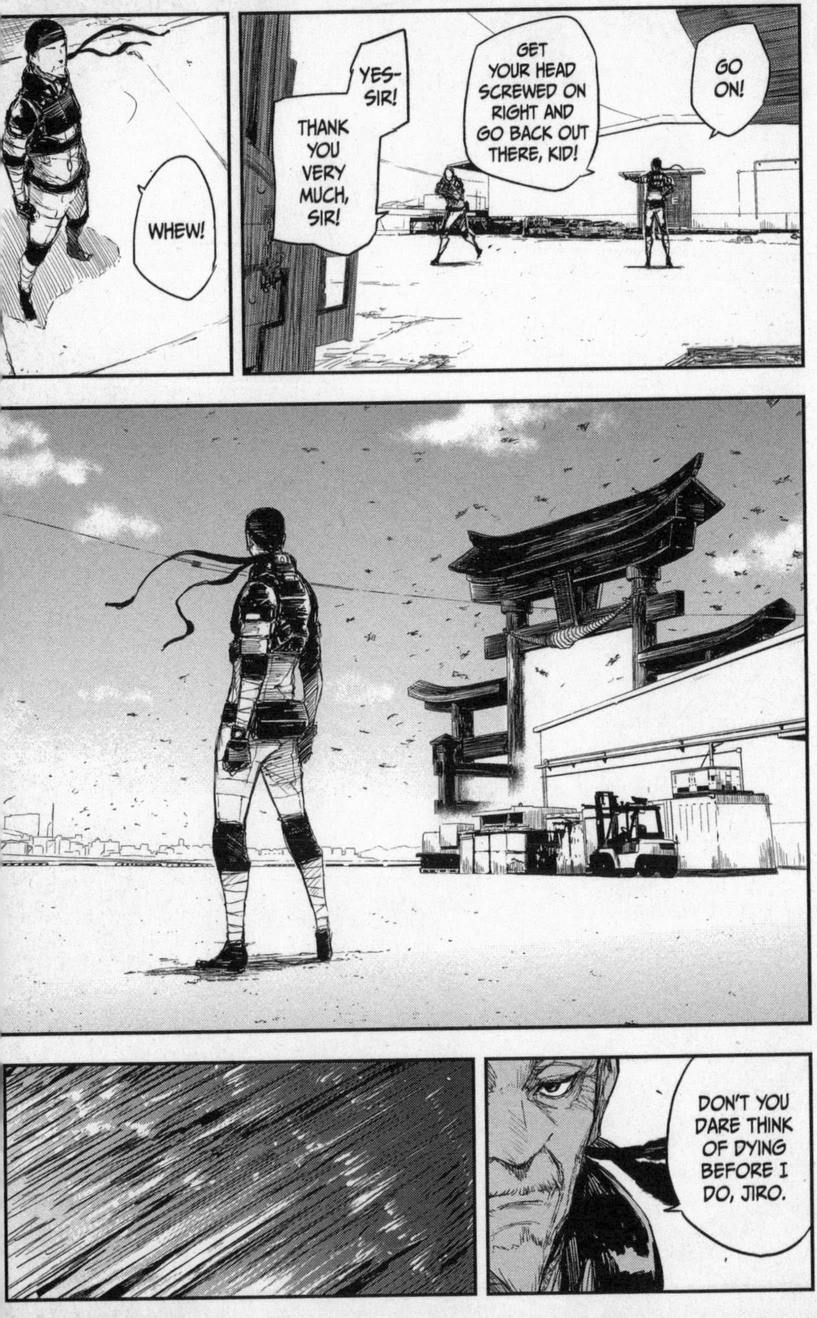
GO ON!
GET YOUR HEAD SCREWED ON RIGHT AND GO BACK OUT THERE, KID!
YES-SIR!
THANK YOU VERY MUCH, SIR!
WHEW!
DON'T YOU DARE THINK OF DYING BEFORE I DO, JIRO.

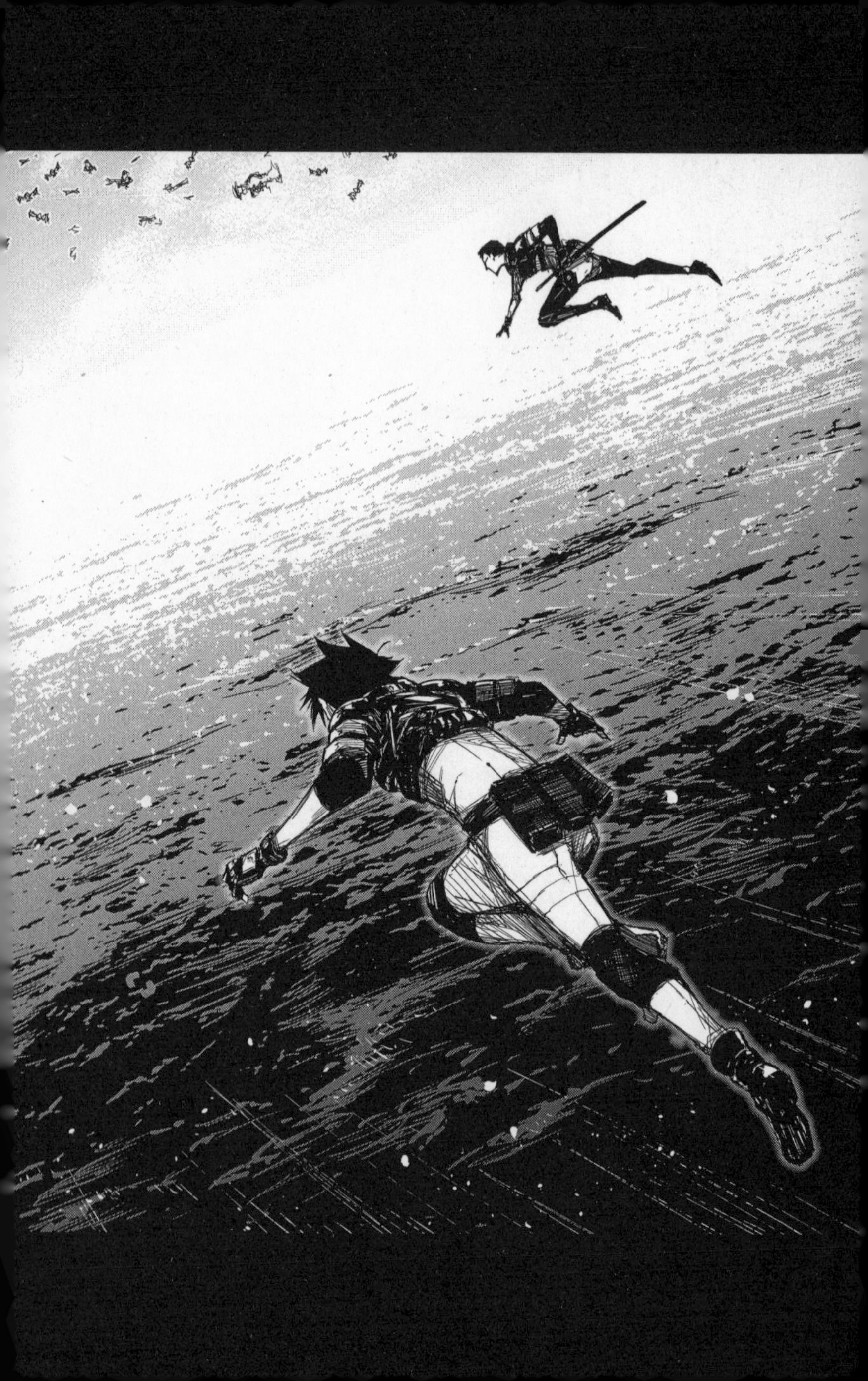

#18 Black or White

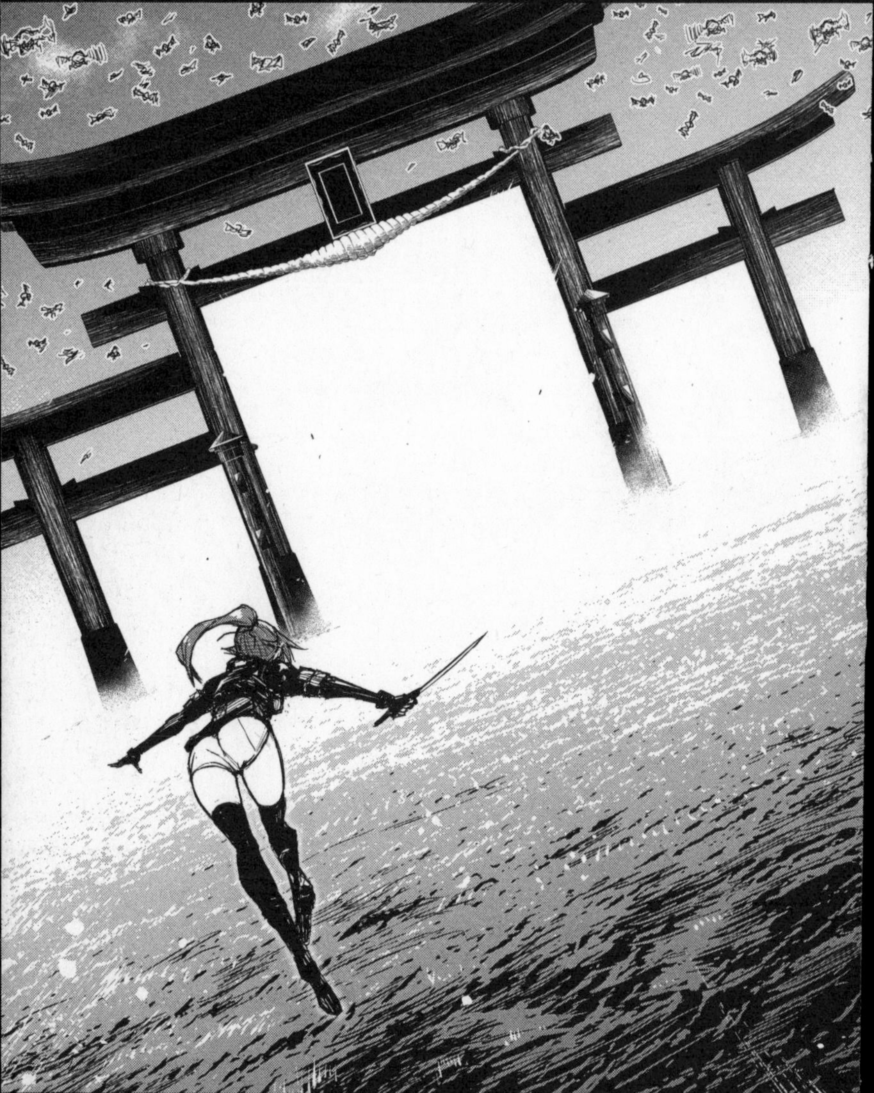

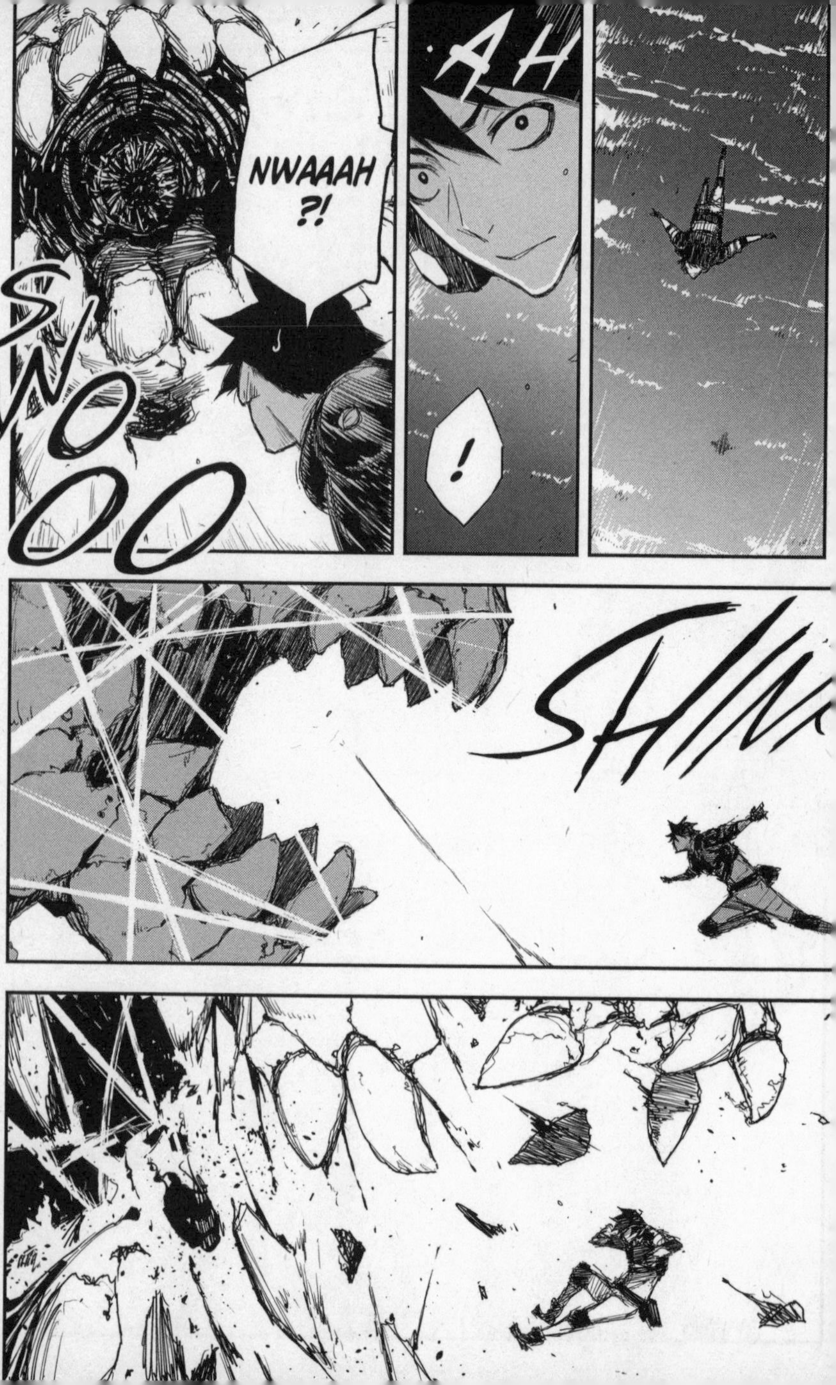
AH
!
NWAAAH ?!
SWOOO
SHIN

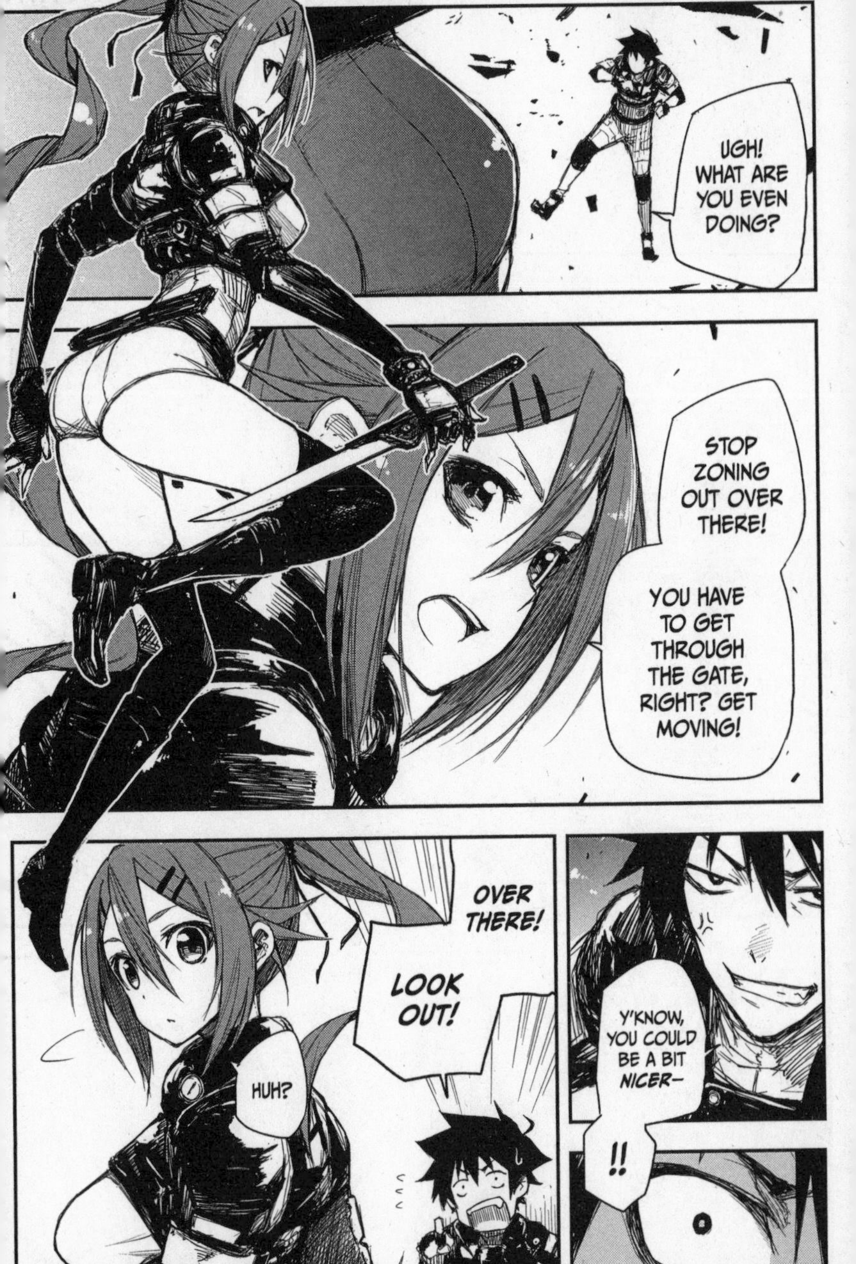
UGH! WHAT ARE YOU EVEN DOING?
STOP ZONING OUT OVER THERE!
YOU HAVE TO GET THROUGH THE GATE, RIGHT? GET MOVING!
Y'KNOW, YOU COULD BE A BIT *NICER*–
!!
OVER THERE!
LOOK OUT!
HUH?

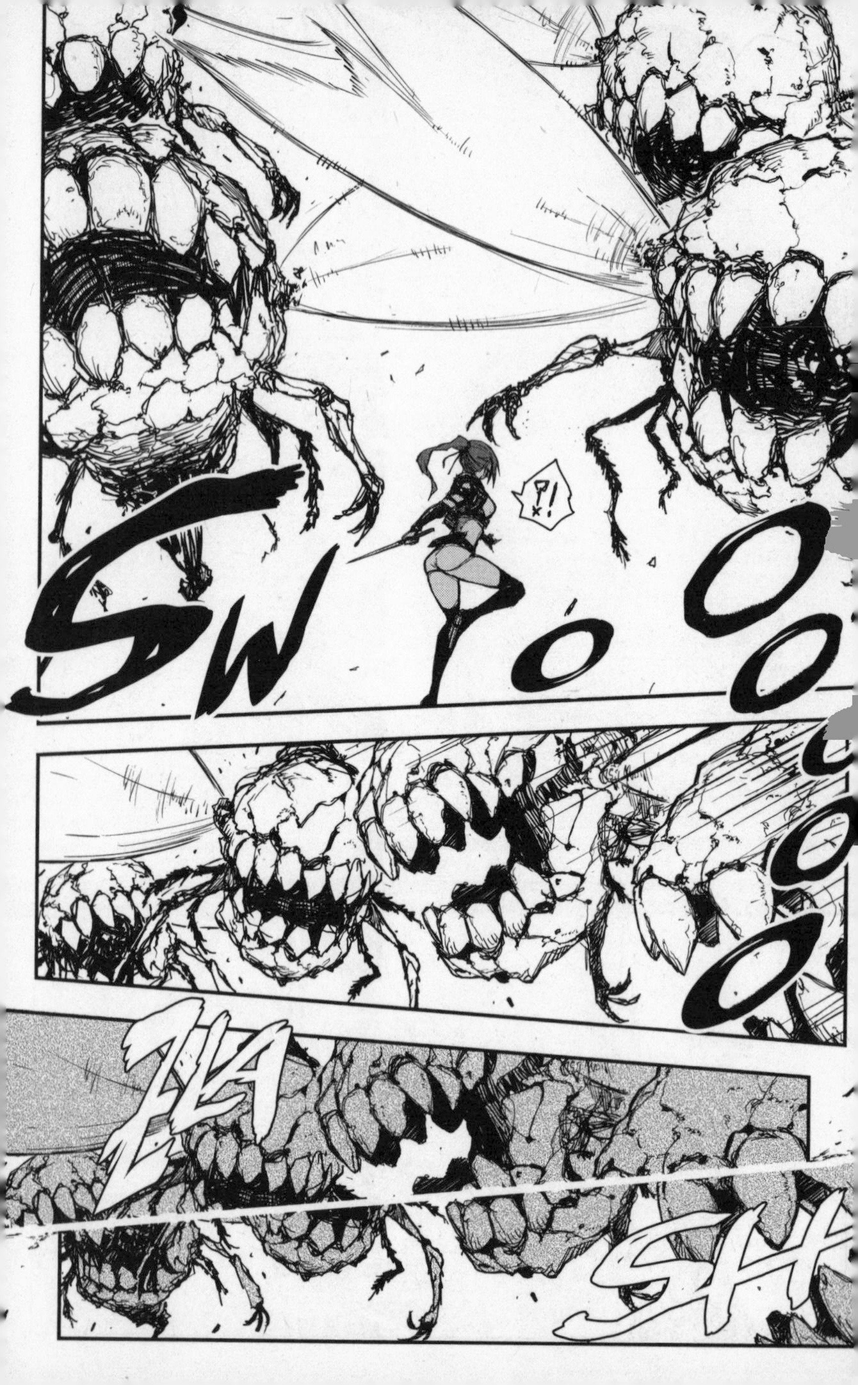
?!
SWOOOOOOO
ZZA
SH

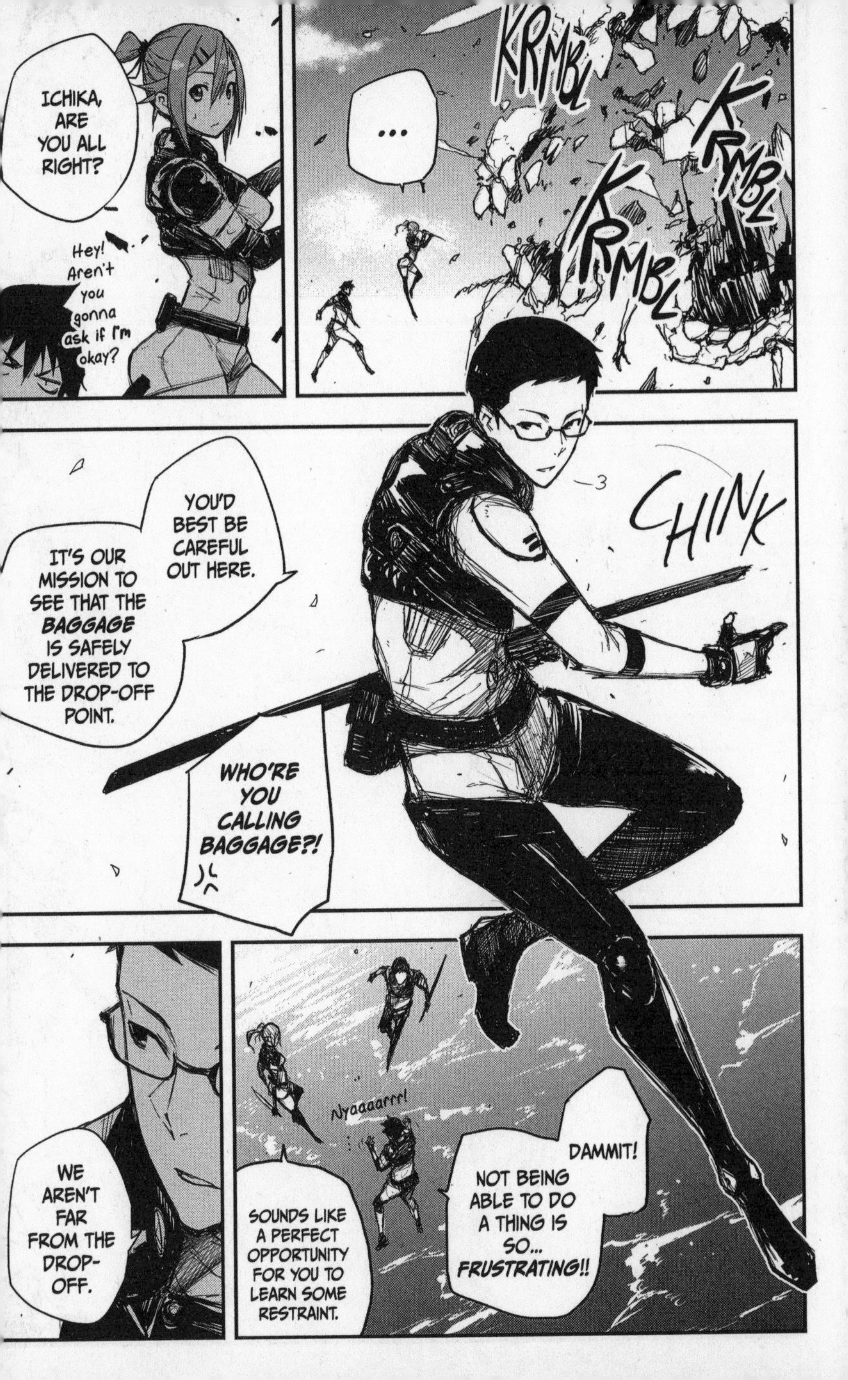
KRMBL
KRMBL
KRMBL
...
ICHIKA, ARE YOU ALL RIGHT?
Hey! Aren't you gonna ask if I'm okay?
CHINK
YOU'D BEST BE CAREFUL OUT HERE.
IT'S OUR MISSION TO SEE THAT THE *BAGGAGE* IS SAFELY DELIVERED TO THE DROP-OFF POINT.
WHO'RE YOU CALLING BAGGAGE?!
DAMMIT!
NOT BEING ABLE TO DO A THING IS SO... *FRUSTRATING!!*
Nyaaaarrr!
SOUNDS LIKE A PERFECT OPPORTUNITY FOR YOU TO LEARN SOME RESTRAINT.
WE AREN'T FAR FROM THE DROP-OFF.

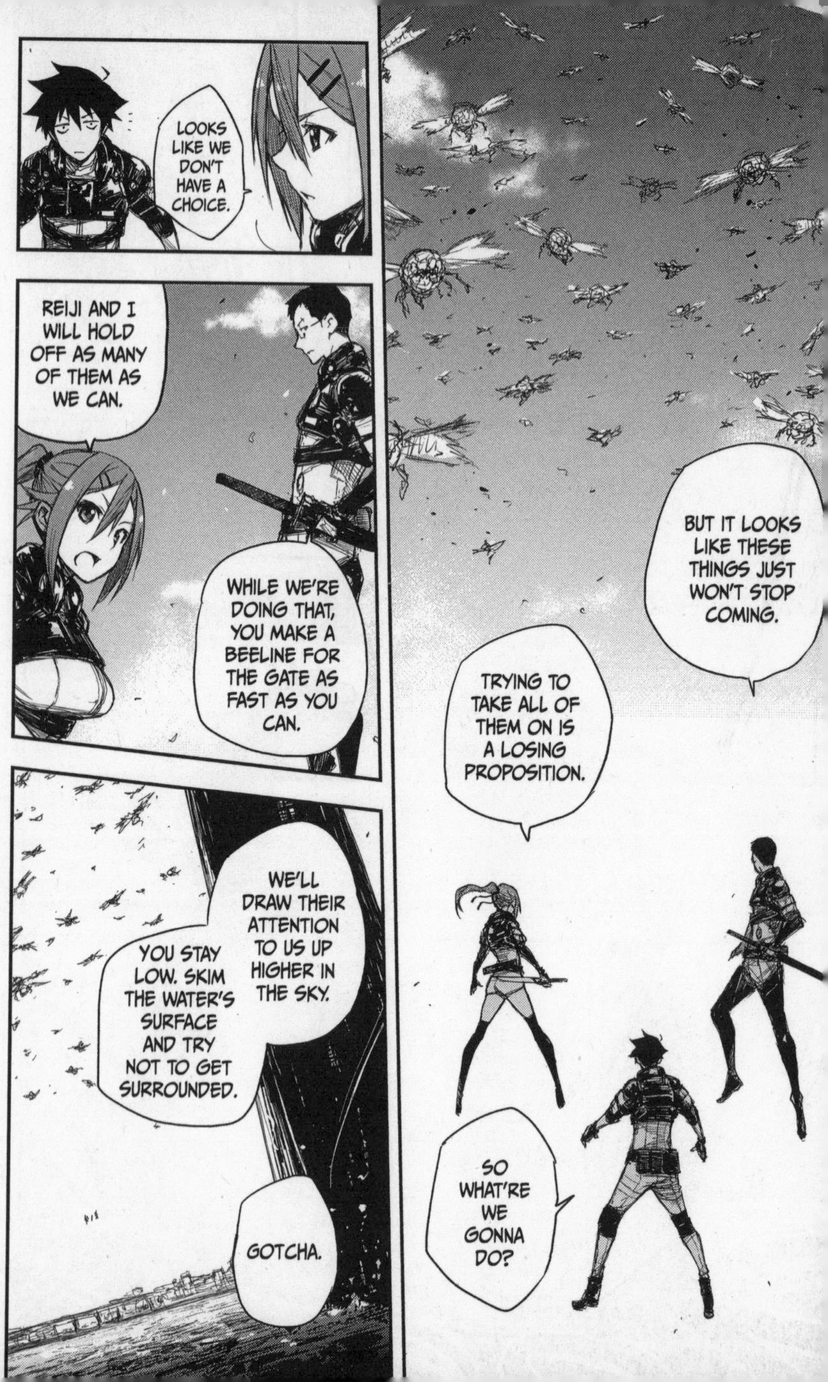
BUT IT LOOKS LIKE THESE THINGS JUST WON'T STOP COMING.
TRYING TO TAKE ALL OF THEM ON IS A LOSING PROPOSITION.
SO WHAT'RE WE GONNA DO?
LOOKS LIKE WE DON'T HAVE A CHOICE.
REIJI AND I WILL HOLD OFF AS MANY OF THEM AS WE CAN.
WHILE WE'RE DOING THAT, YOU MAKE A BEELINE FOR THE GATE AS FAST AS YOU CAN.
WE'LL DRAW THEIR ATTENTION TO US UP HIGHER IN THE SKY.
YOU STAY LOW. SKIM THE WATER'S SURFACE AND TRY NOT TO GET SURROUNDED.
GOTCHA.

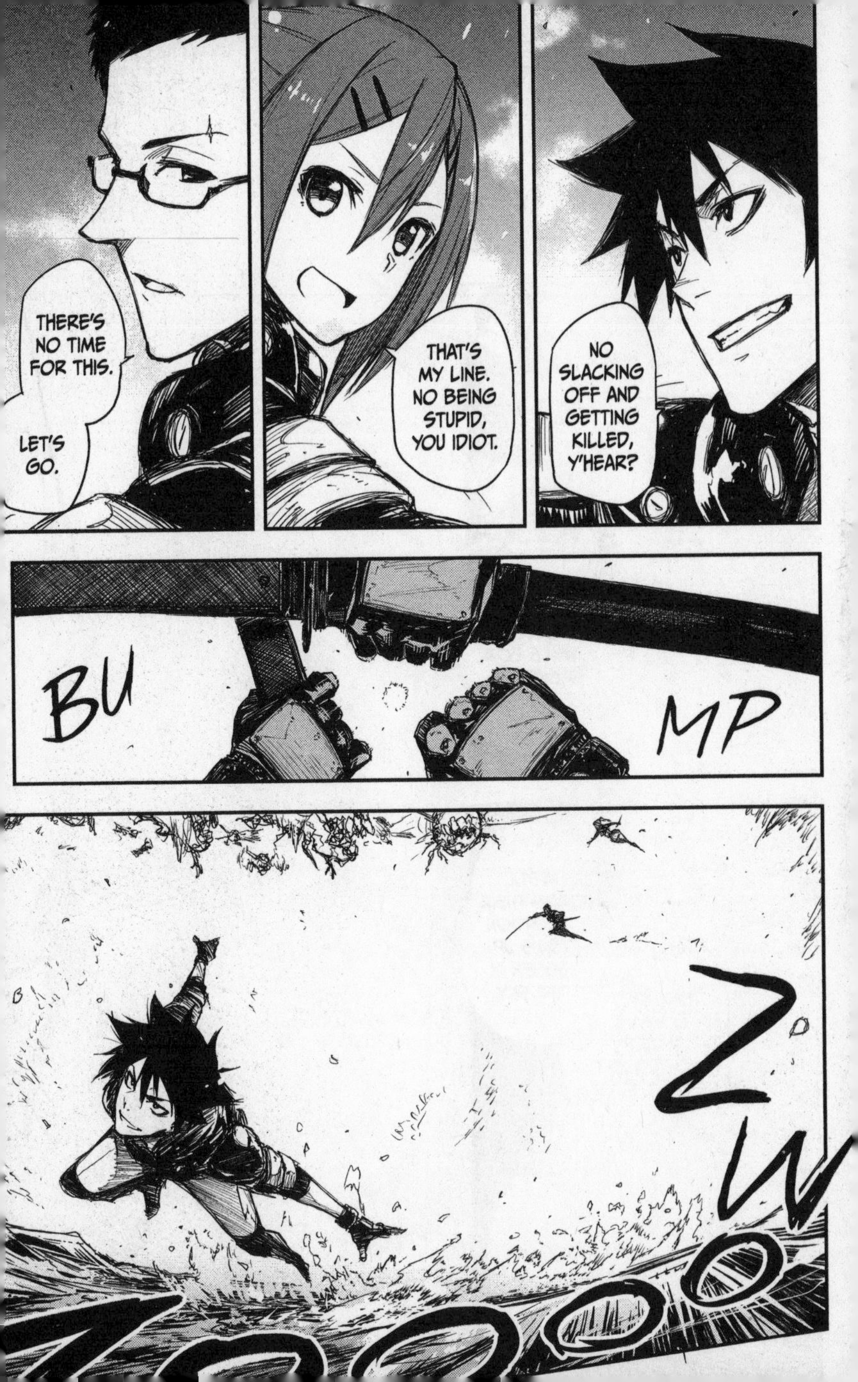
NO SLACKING OFF AND GETTING KILLED, Y'HEAR?
THAT'S MY LINE. NO BEING STUPID, YOU IDIOT.
THERE'S NO TIME FOR THIS.
LET'S GO.
BU MP
ZWOOOO

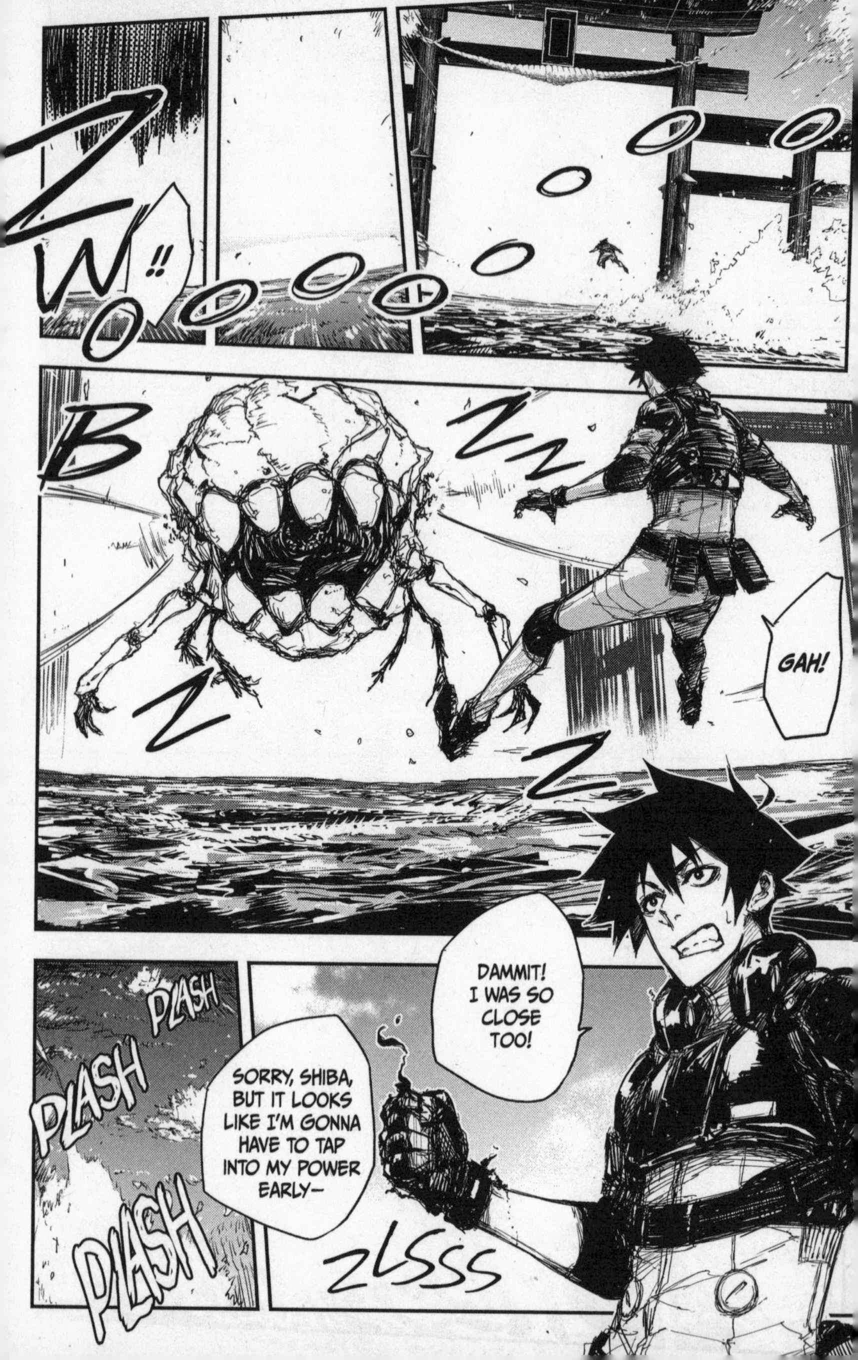
ZWOOOOOOOOOOO!!
GAH!
BZZZZZ
DAMMIT! I WAS SO CLOSE TOO!
SORRY, SHIBA, BUT IT LOOKS LIKE I'M GONNA HAVE TO TAP INTO MY POWER EARLY—
ZLSSS
PLASH
PLASH
PLASH
PLASH

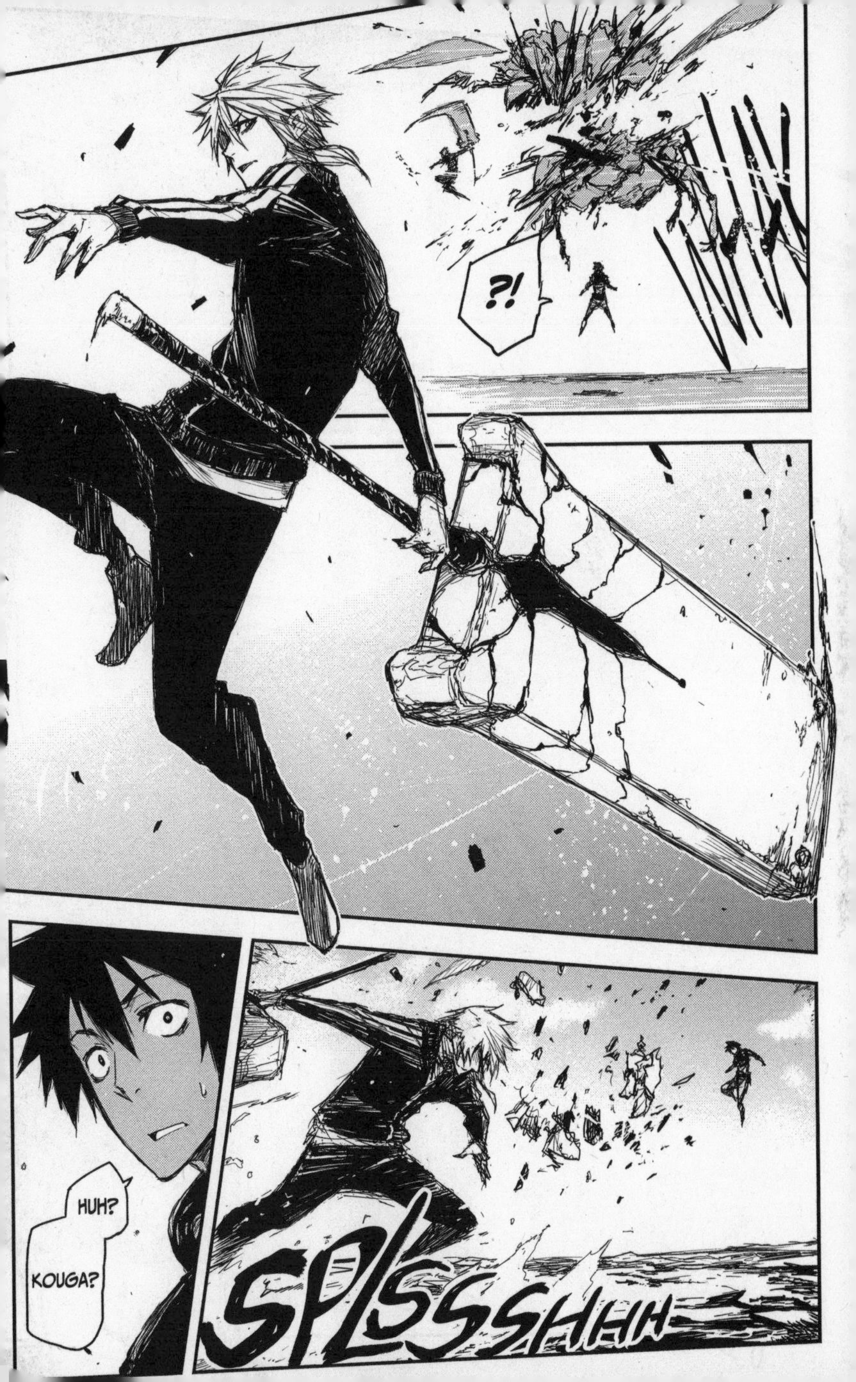
?!
SPLSSSHHH
HUH?
KOUGA?

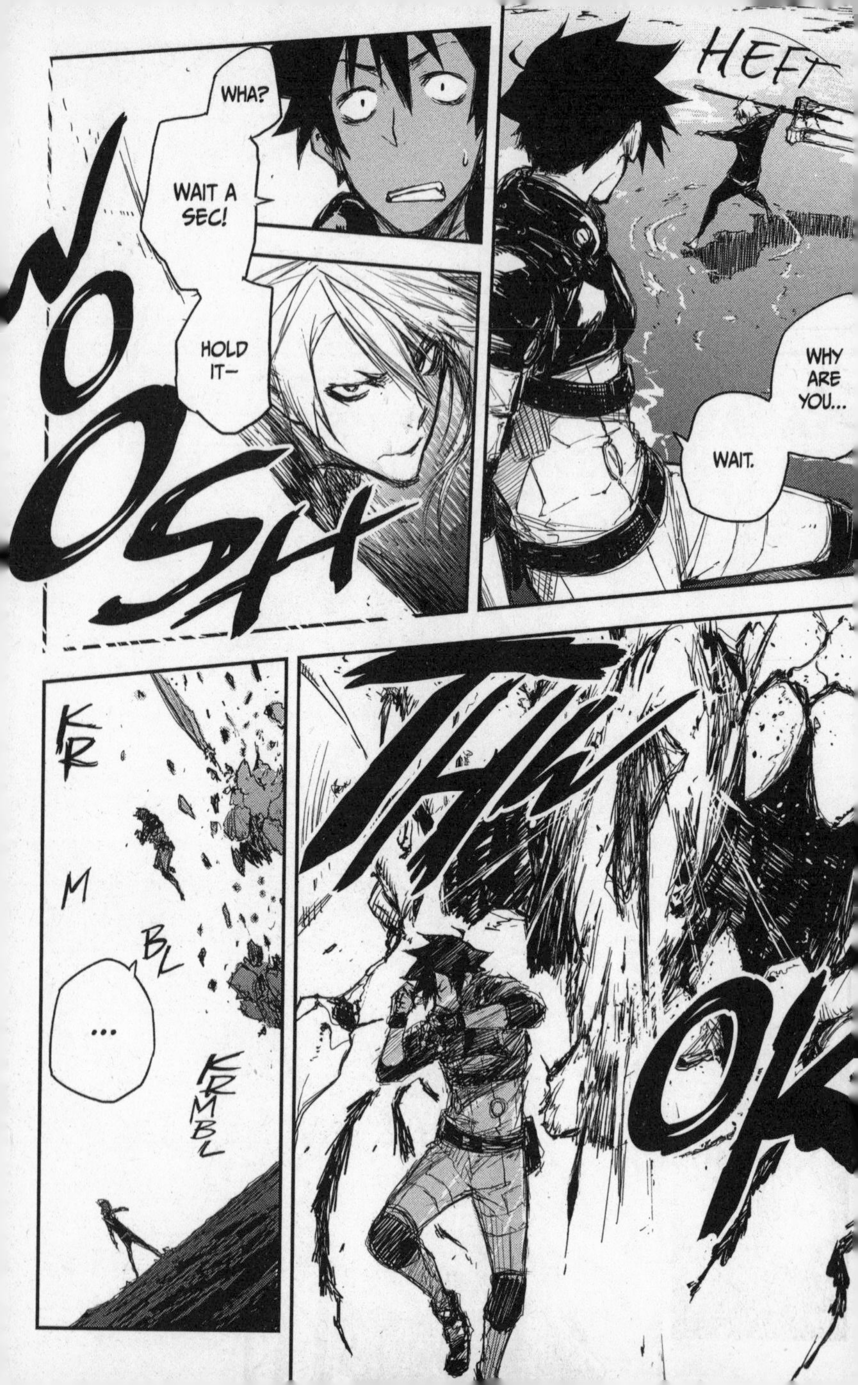
HEFT
WHY ARE YOU...
WAIT.
WHA?
WAIT A SEC!
HOLD IT—
WOOSH
THWOK
KRMBL
...
KRMBL

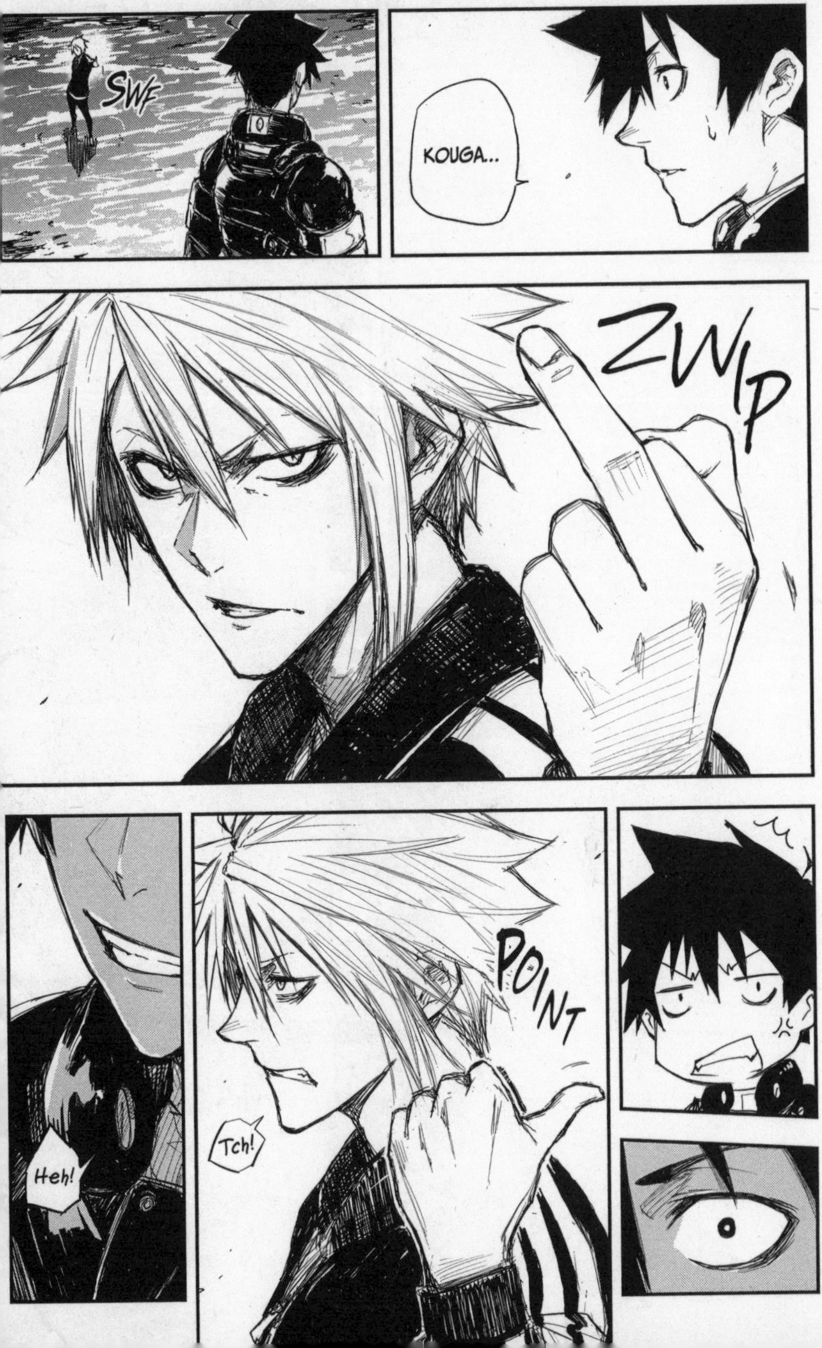
KOUGA...
SWF
ZWIP
POINT
Tch!
Heh!

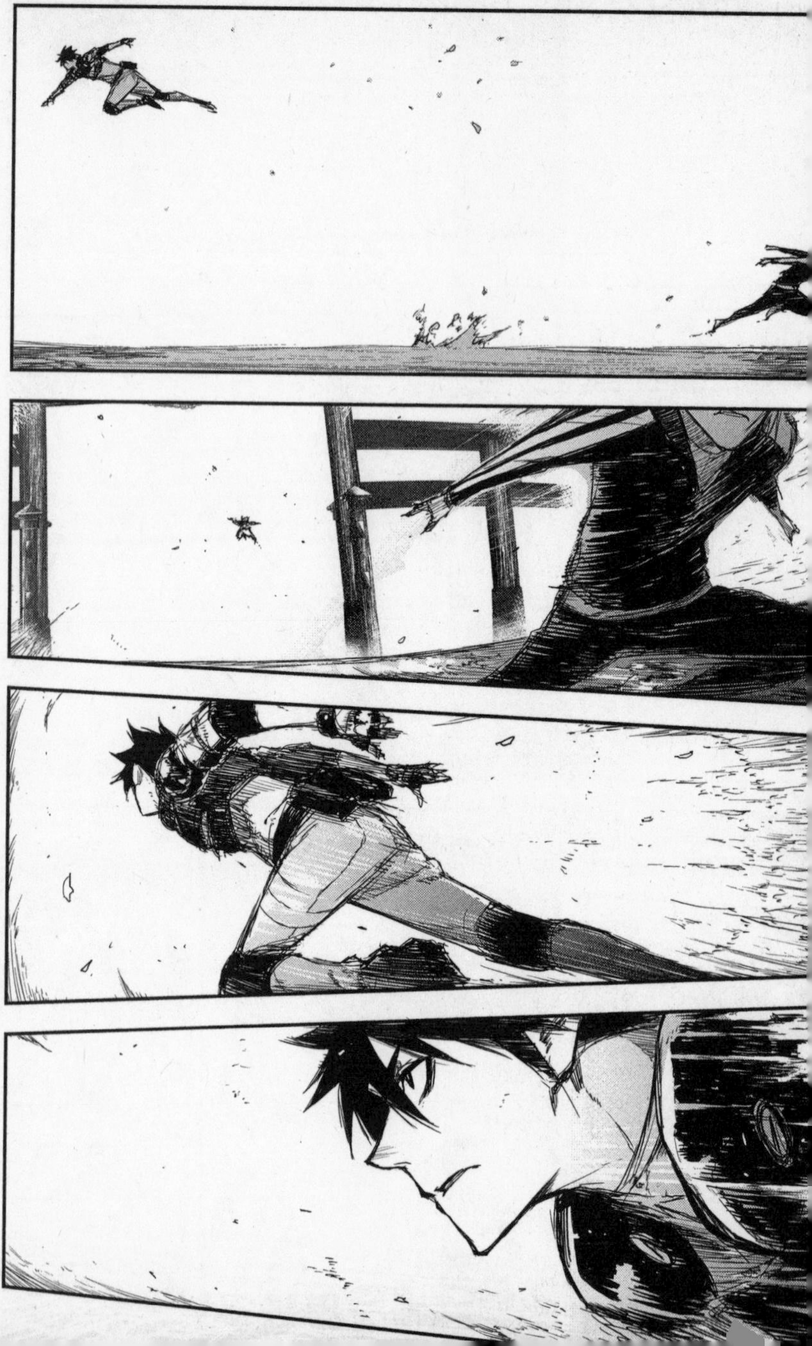

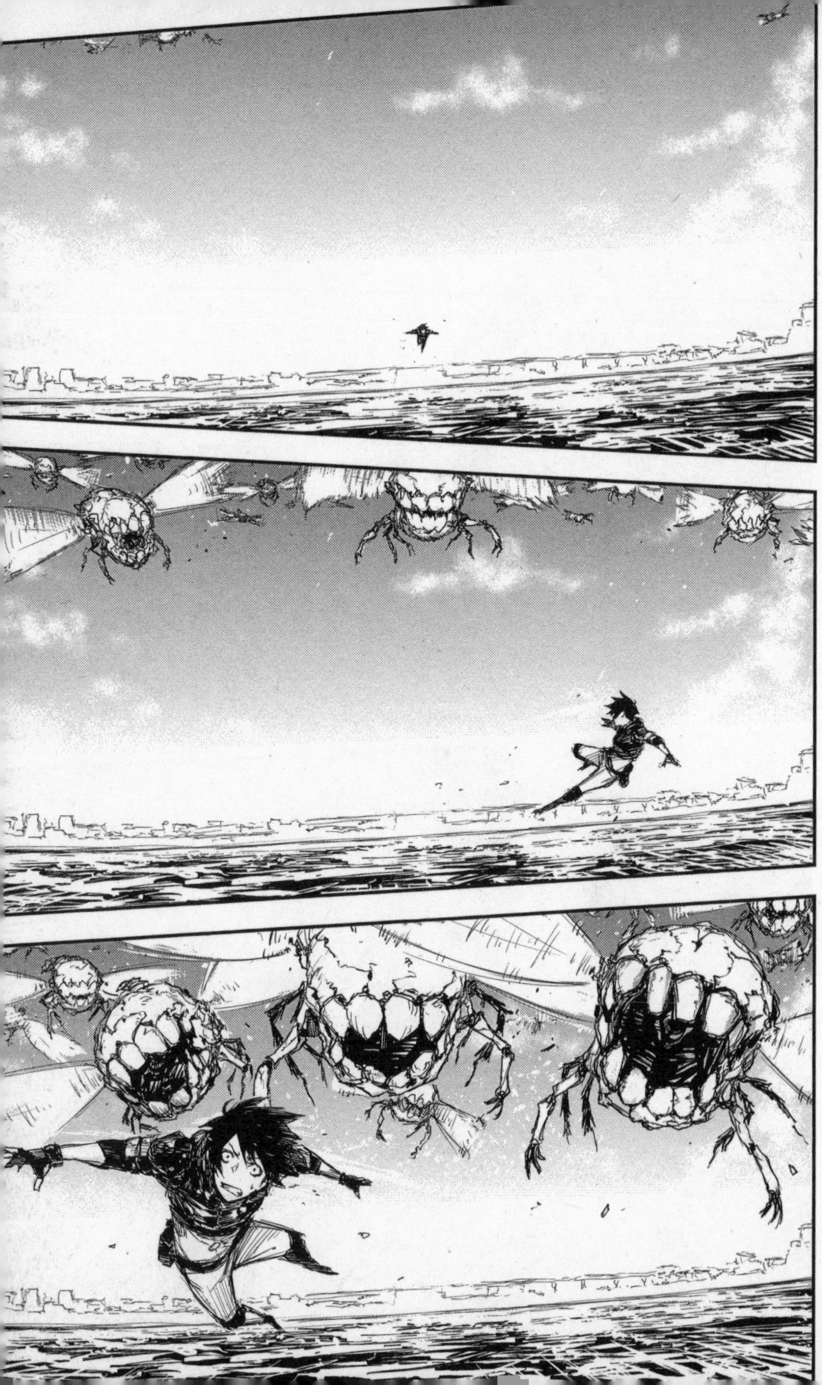

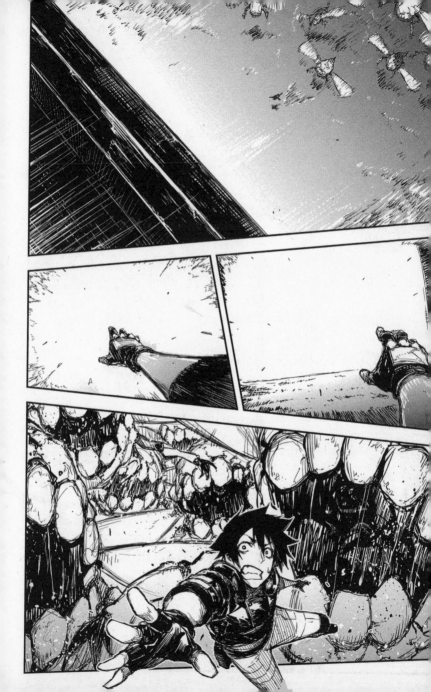

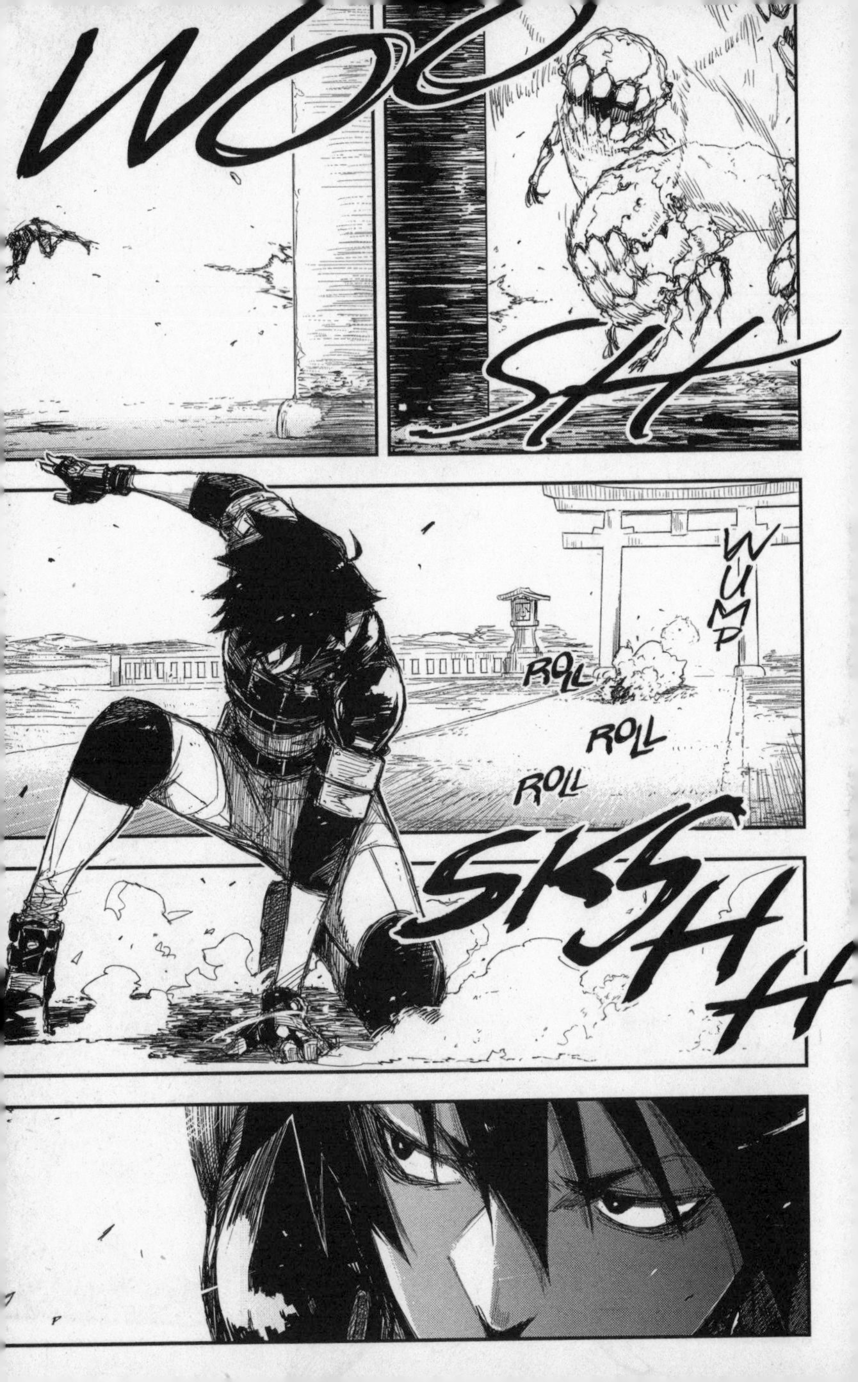
SH
WOO
WUMP
ROLL
ROLL
ROLL
SKSHH

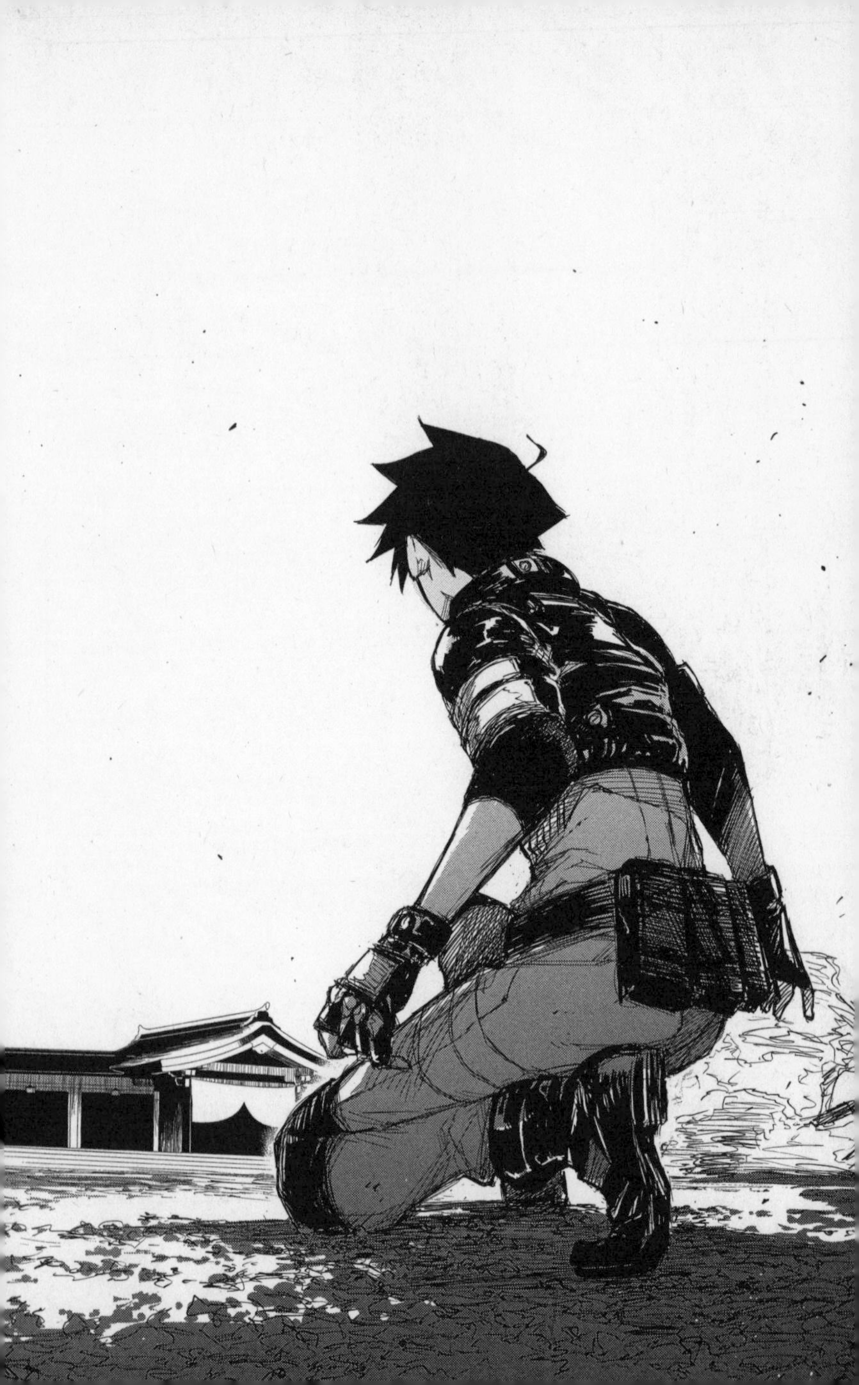

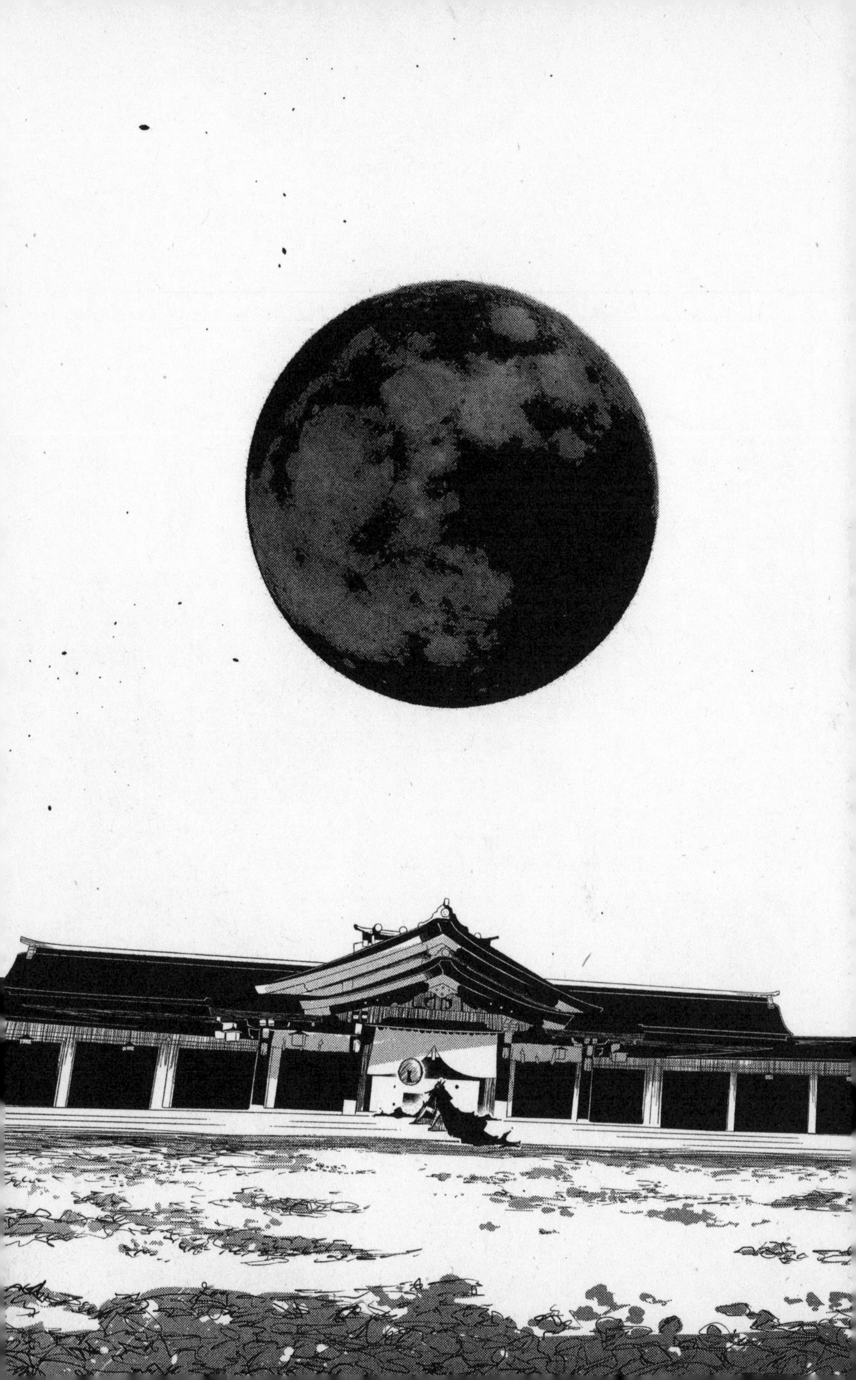

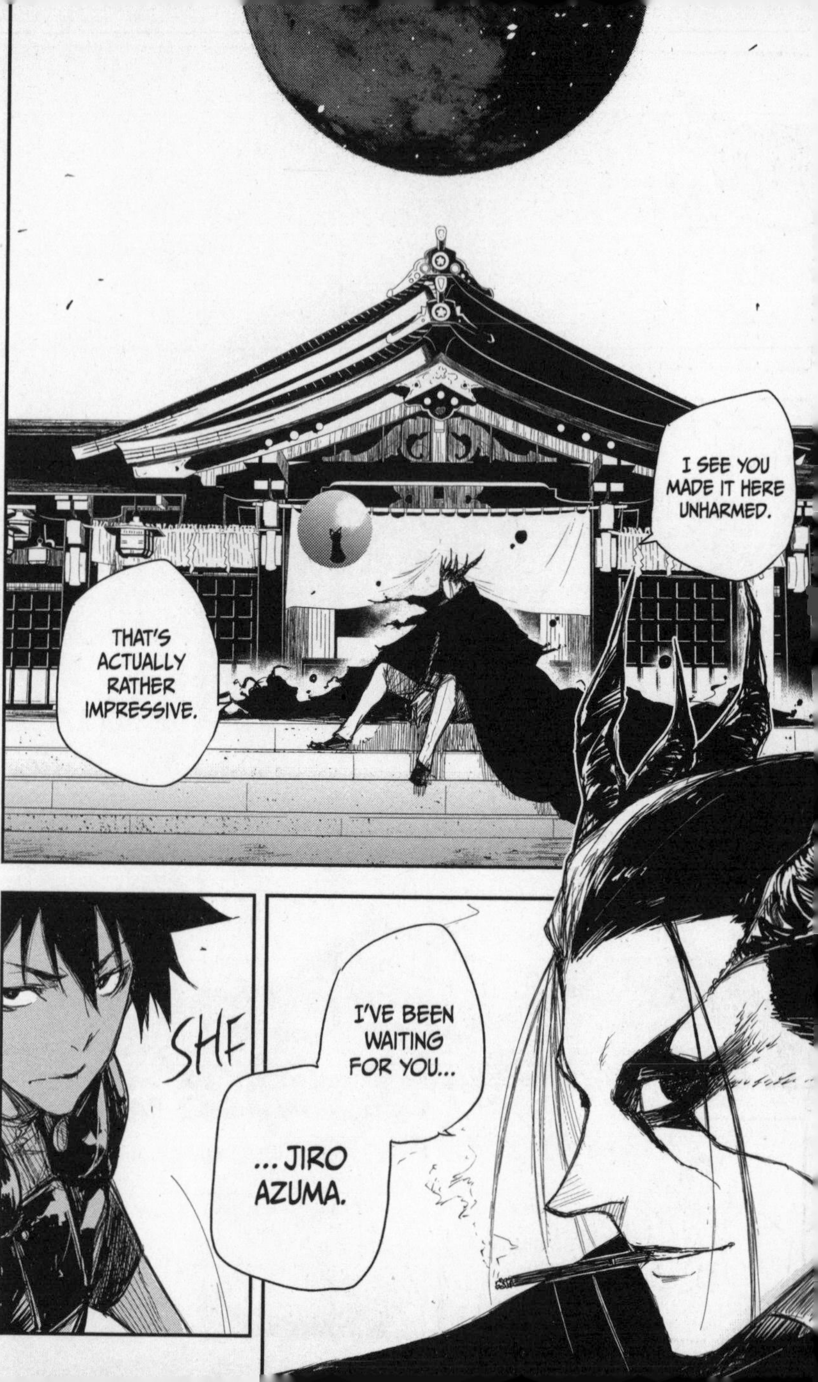
I SEE YOU MADE IT HERE UNHARMED.
THAT'S ACTUALLY RATHER IMPRESSIVE.
I'VE BEEN WAITING FOR YOU...
...JIRO AZUMA.
SHF

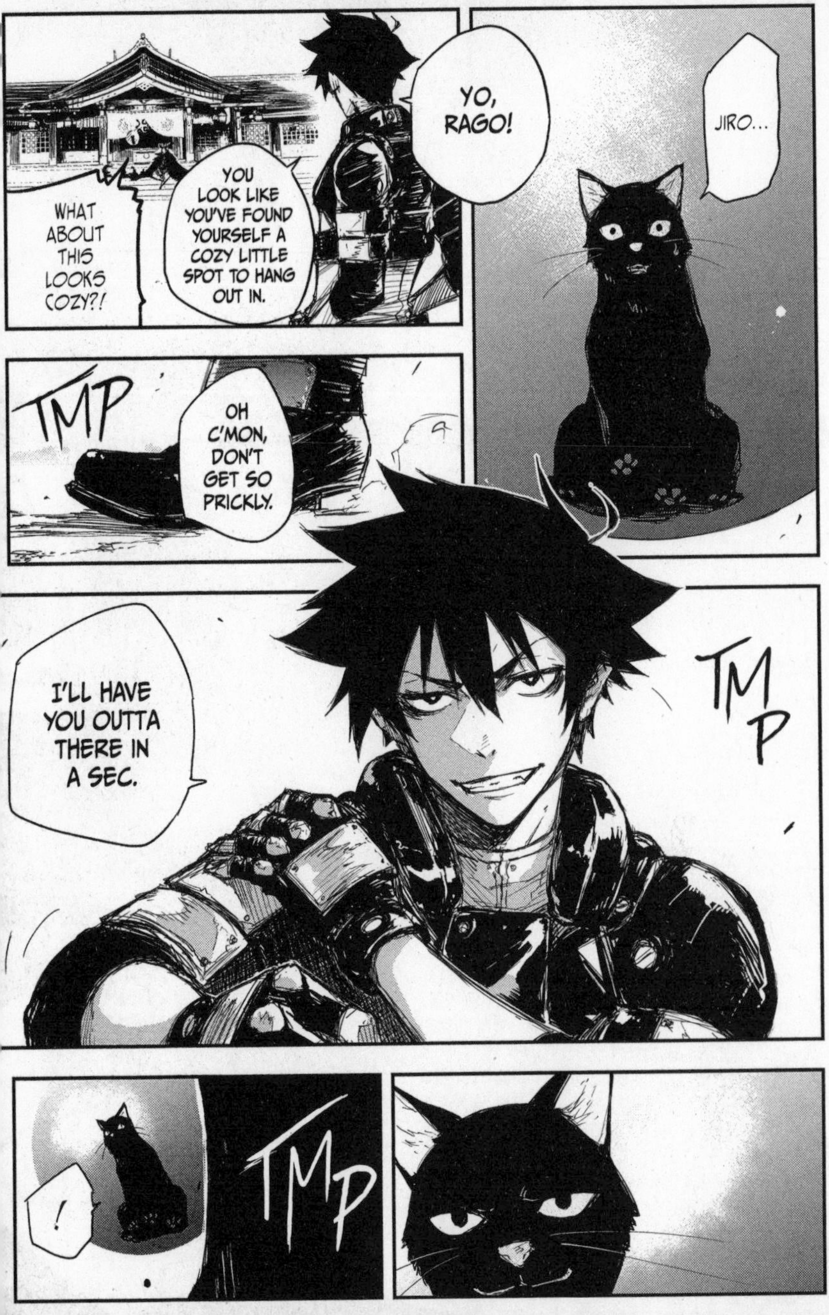
JIRO...
YO, RAGO!
YOU LOOK LIKE YOU'VE FOUND YOURSELF A COZY LITTLE SPOT TO HANG OUT IN.
WHAT ABOUT THIS LOOKS COZY?!
OH C'MON, DON'T GET SO PRICKLY.
TMP
TMP
I'LL HAVE YOU OUTTA THERE IN A SEC.
TMP
!

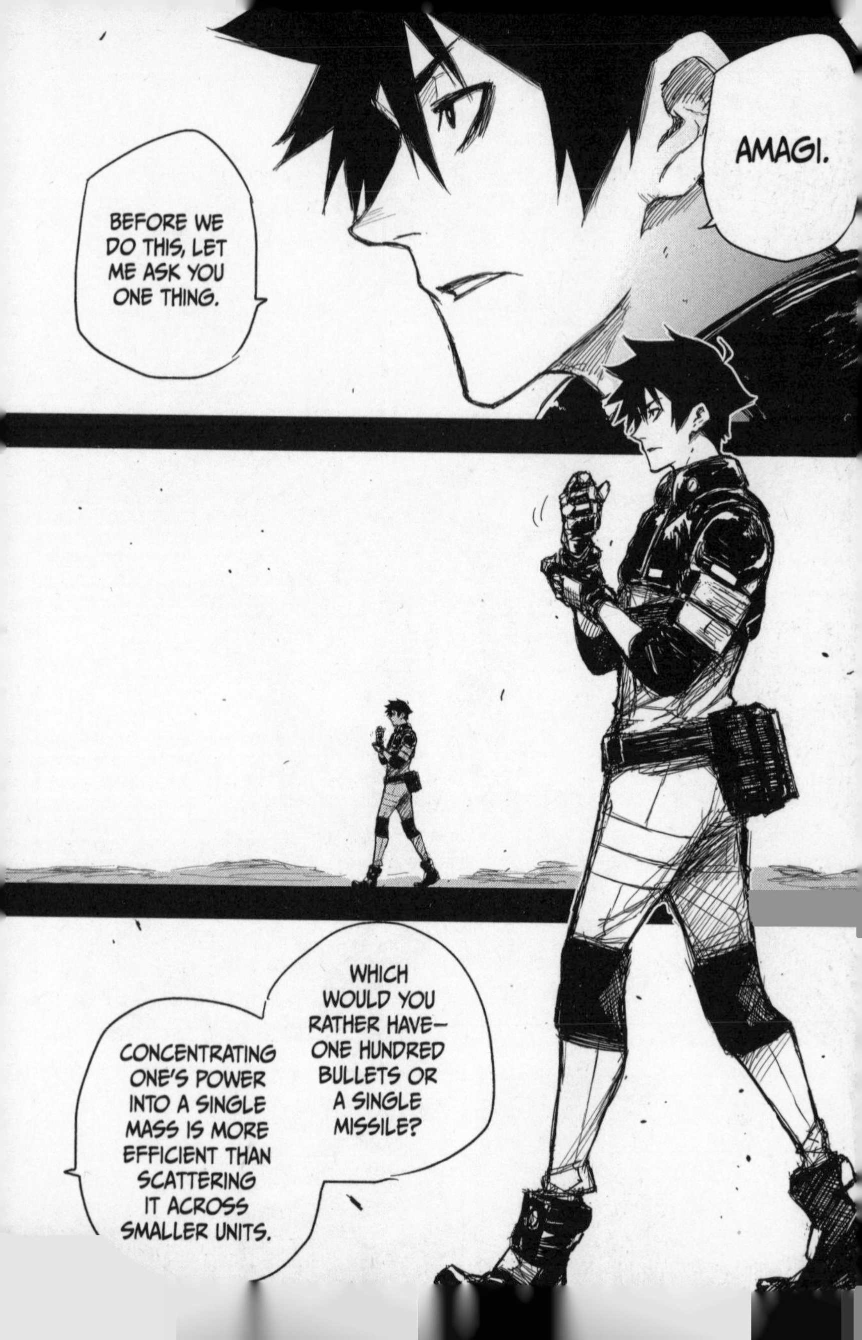
AMAGI.
BEFORE WE DO THIS, LET ME ASK YOU ONE THING.
WHICH WOULD YOU RATHER HAVE— ONE HUNDRED BULLETS OR A SINGLE MISSILE?
CONCENTRATING ONE'S POWER INTO A SINGLE MASS IS MORE EFFICIENT THAN SCATTERING IT ACROSS SMALLER UNITS.

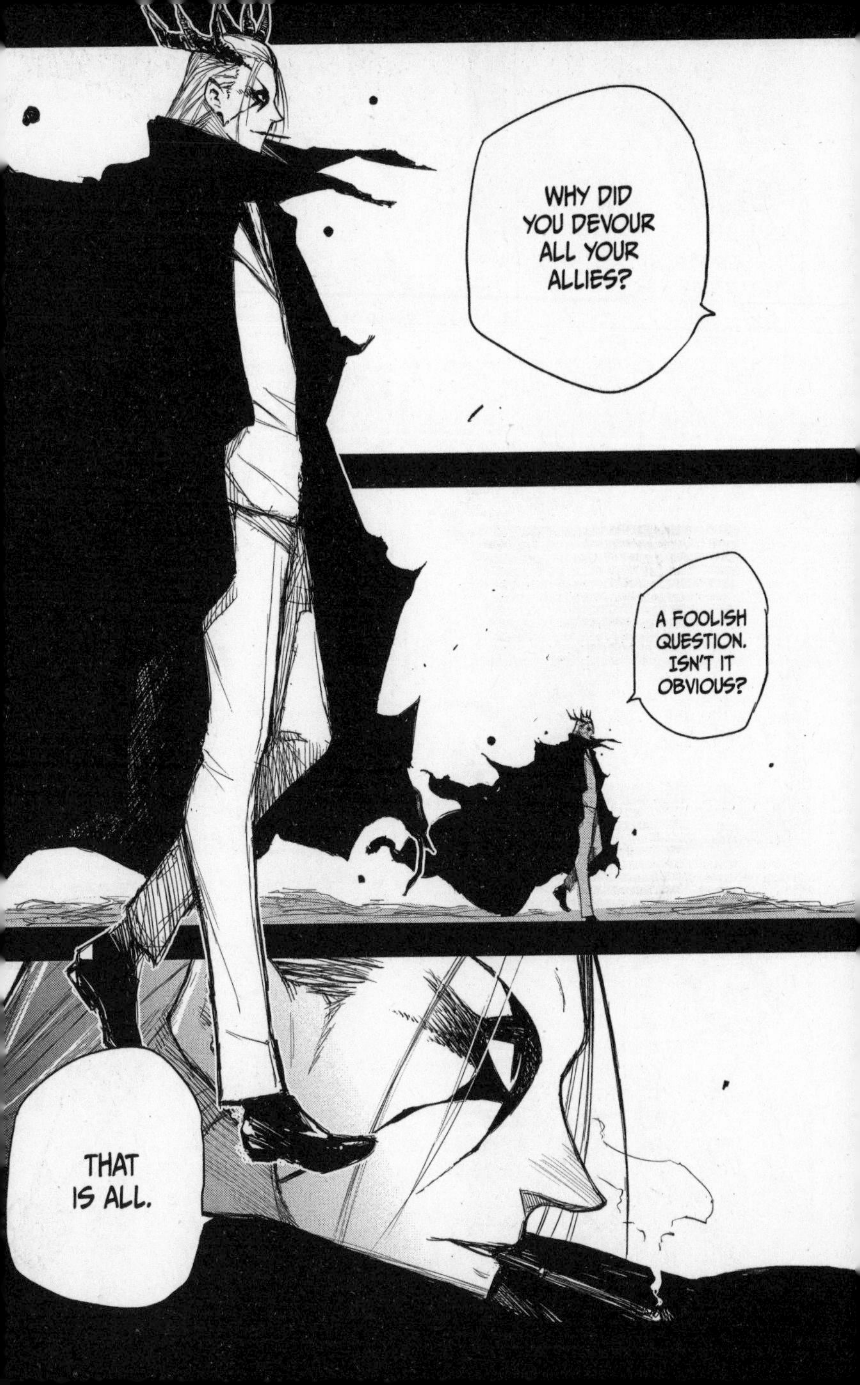
WHY DID YOU DEVOUR ALL YOUR ALLIES?
A FOOLISH QUESTION. ISN'T IT OBVIOUS?
THAT IS ALL.

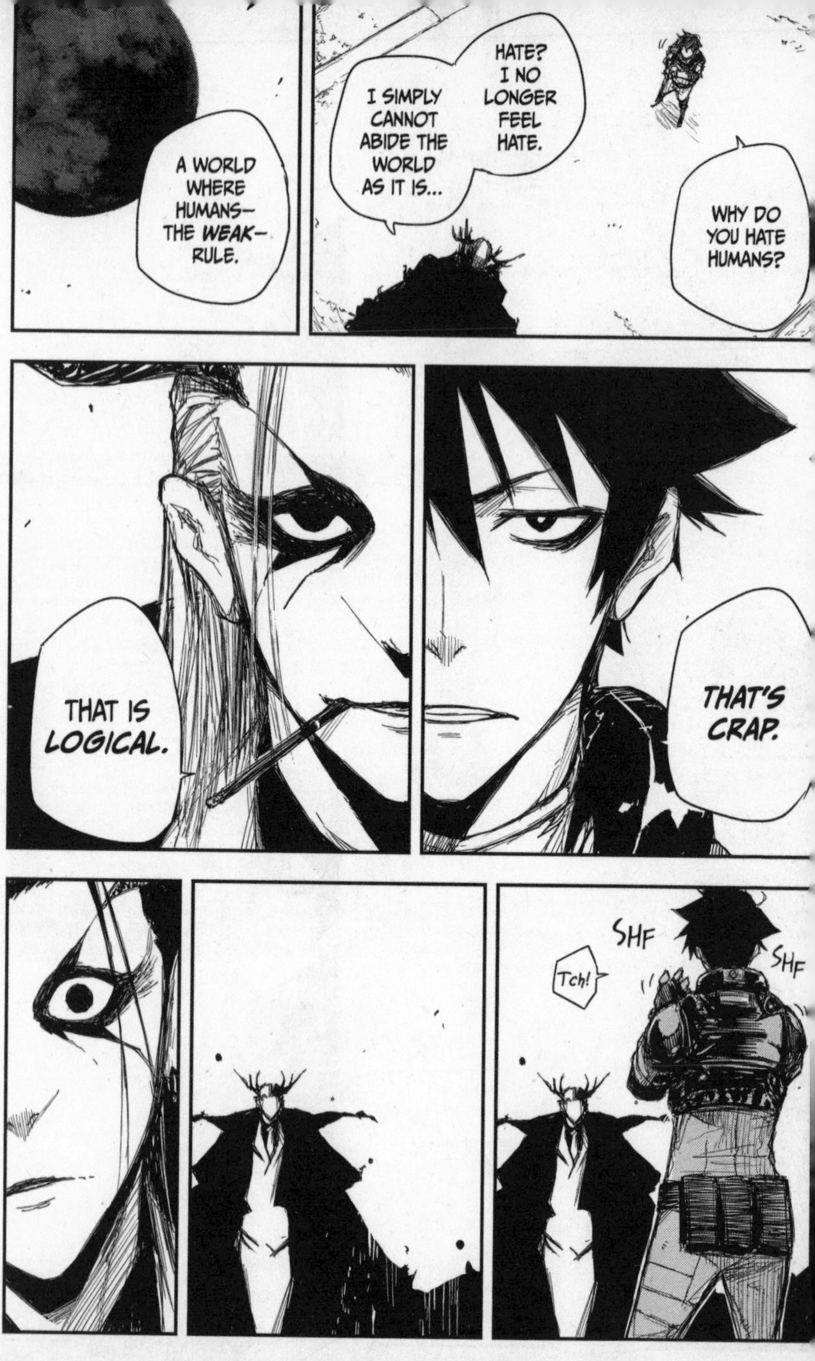
WHY DO YOU HATE HUMANS?
HATE? I NO LONGER FEEL HATE.
I SIMPLY CANNOT ABIDE THE WORLD AS IT IS...
A WORLD WHERE HUMANS— THE *WEAK*— RULE.
THAT'S CRAP.
THAT IS LOGICAL.
SHF
SHF
Tch!

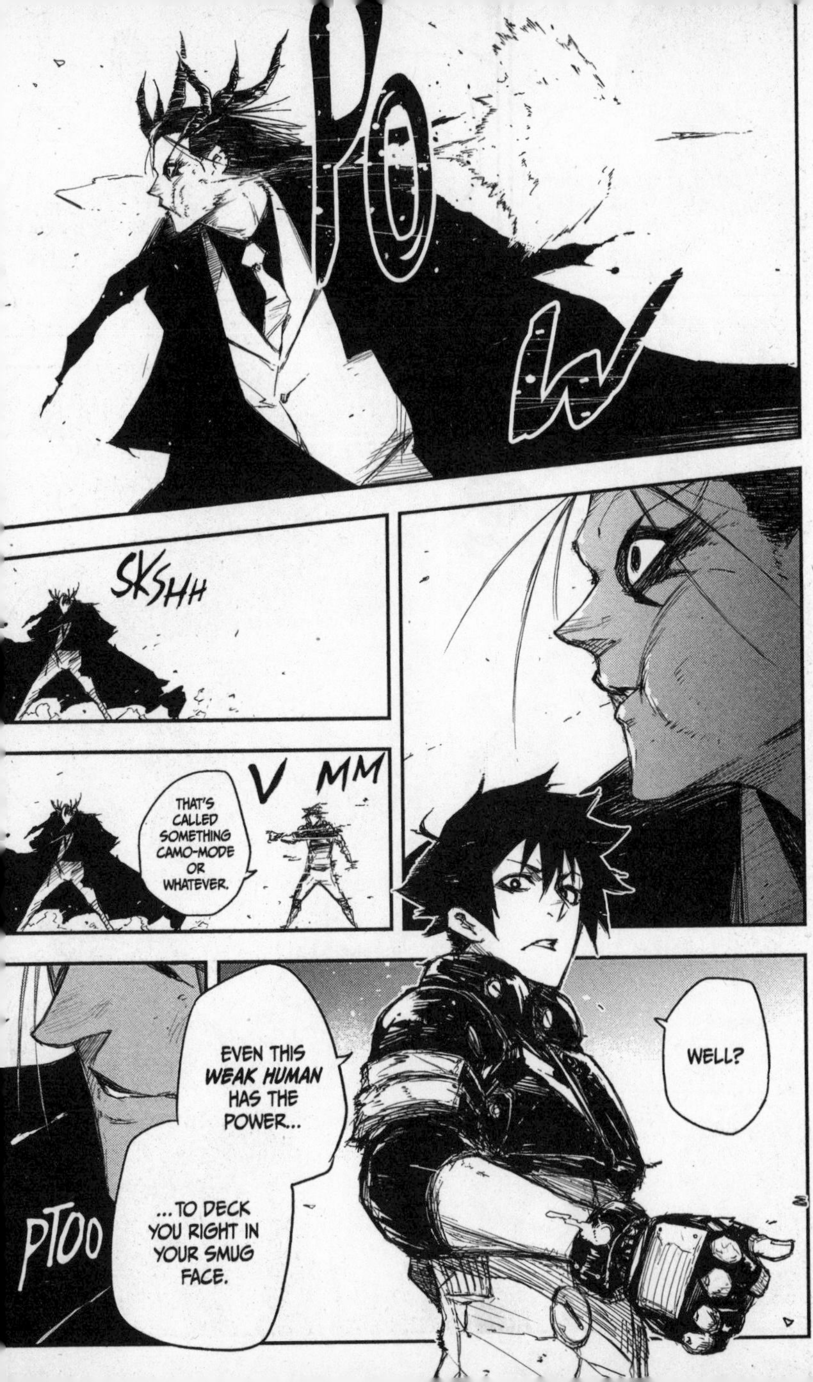
POW
SKSHH
V MM
THAT'S CALLED SOMETHING CAMO-MODE OR WHATEVER.
WELL?
EVEN THIS WEAK HUMAN HAS THE POWER...
...TO DECK YOU RIGHT IN YOUR SMUG FACE.
PTOO

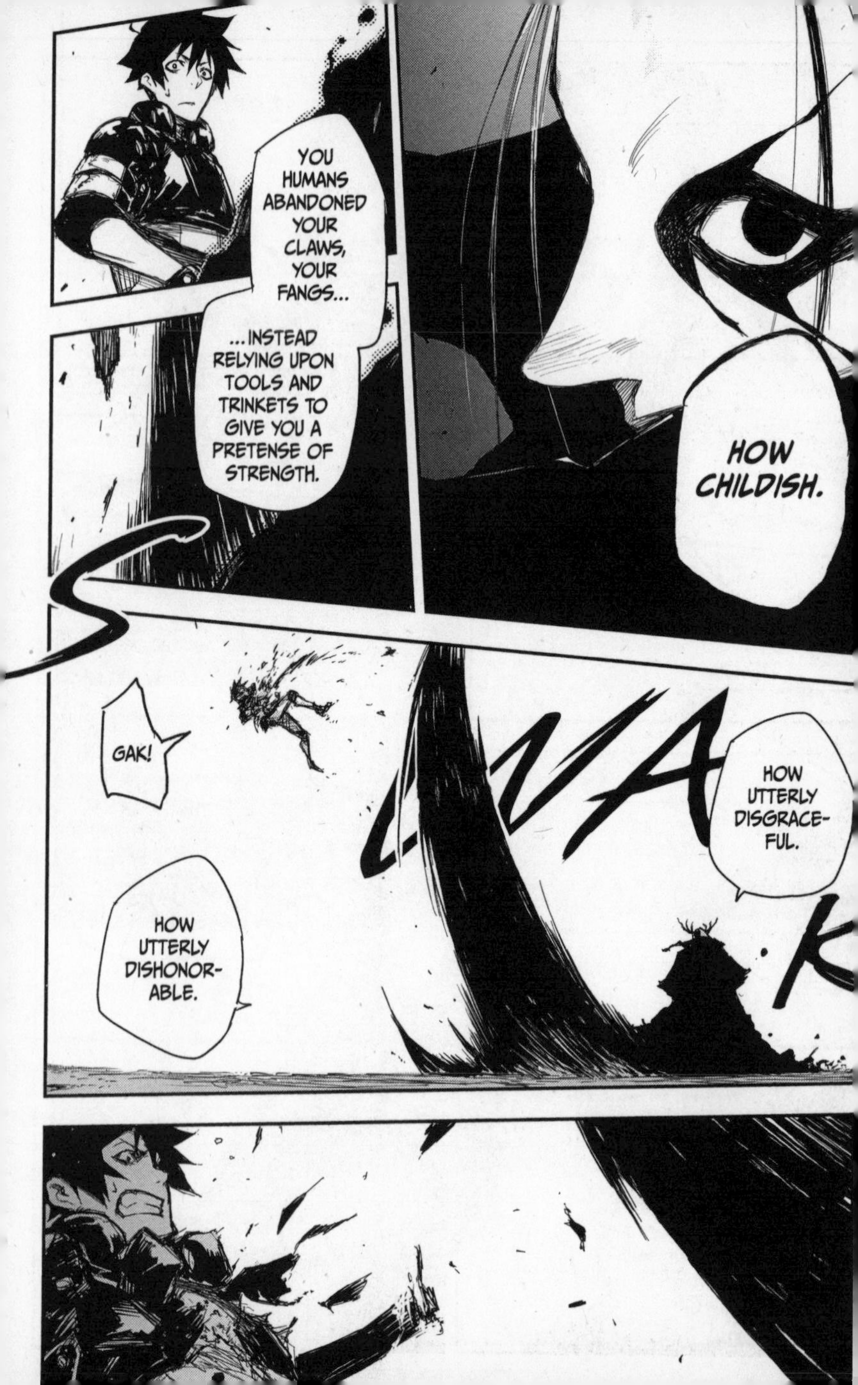
HOW CHILDISH.
YOU HUMANS ABANDONED YOUR CLAWS, YOUR FANGS...
...INSTEAD RELYING UPON TOOLS AND TRINKETS TO GIVE YOU A PRETENSE OF STRENGTH.
HOW UTTERLY DISGRACE-FUL.
SNAK
GAK!
HOW UTTERLY DISHONOR-ABLE.

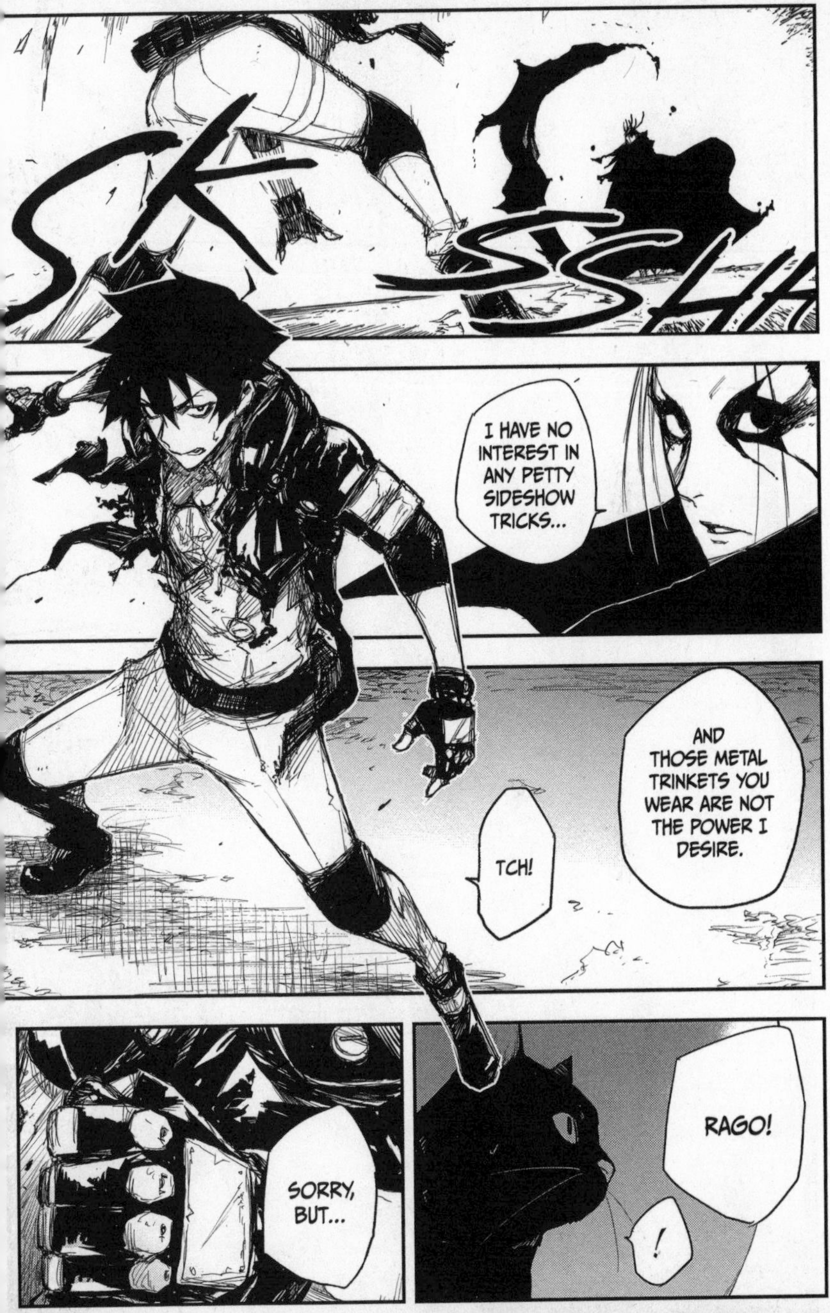
SK-SSHH
I HAVE NO INTEREST IN ANY PETTY SIDESHOW TRICKS...
AND THOSE METAL TRINKETS YOU WEAR ARE NOT THE POWER I DESIRE.
TCH!
RAGO!
!
SORRY, BUT...

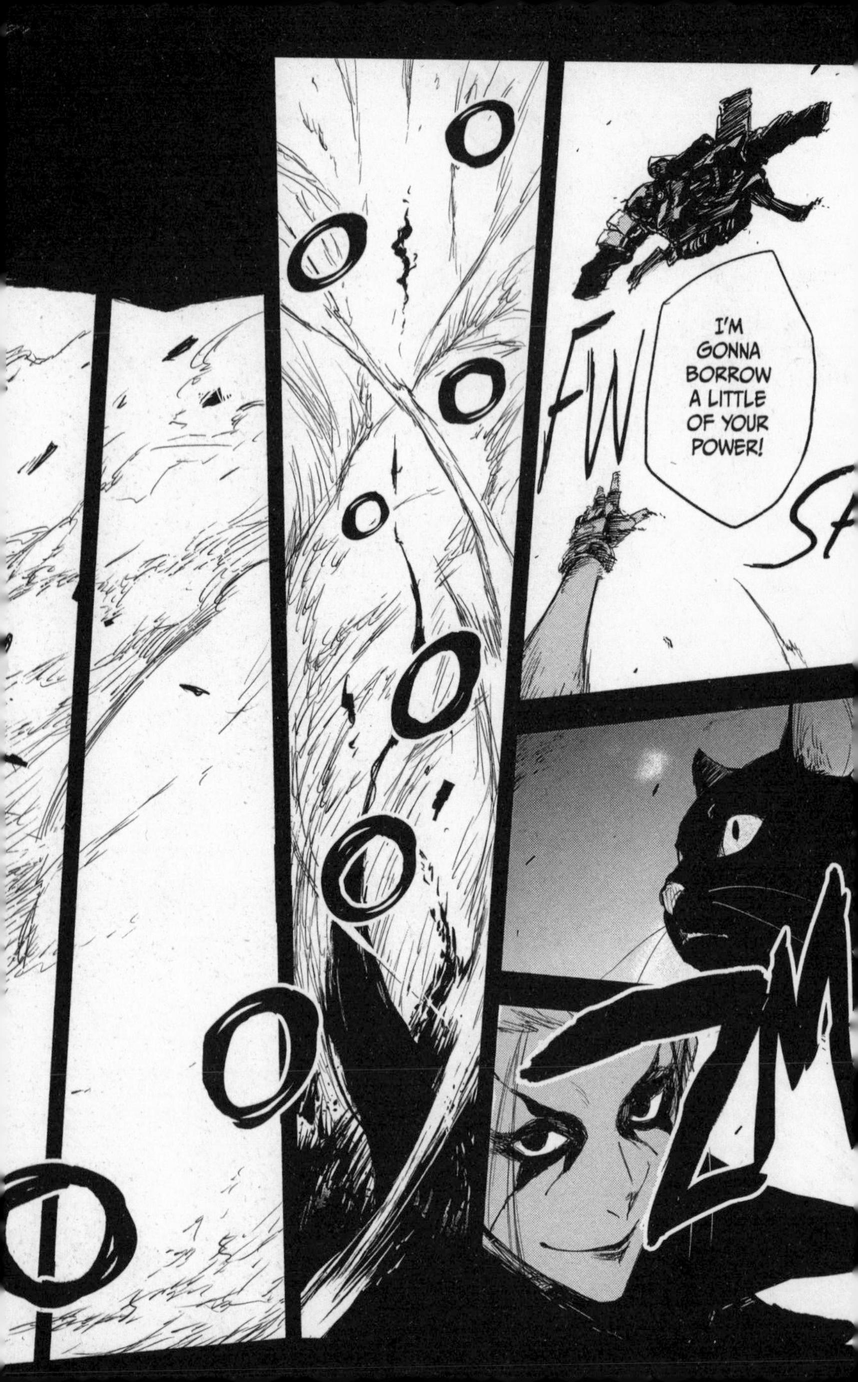
I'M GONNA BORROW A LITTLE OF YOUR POWER!
FW

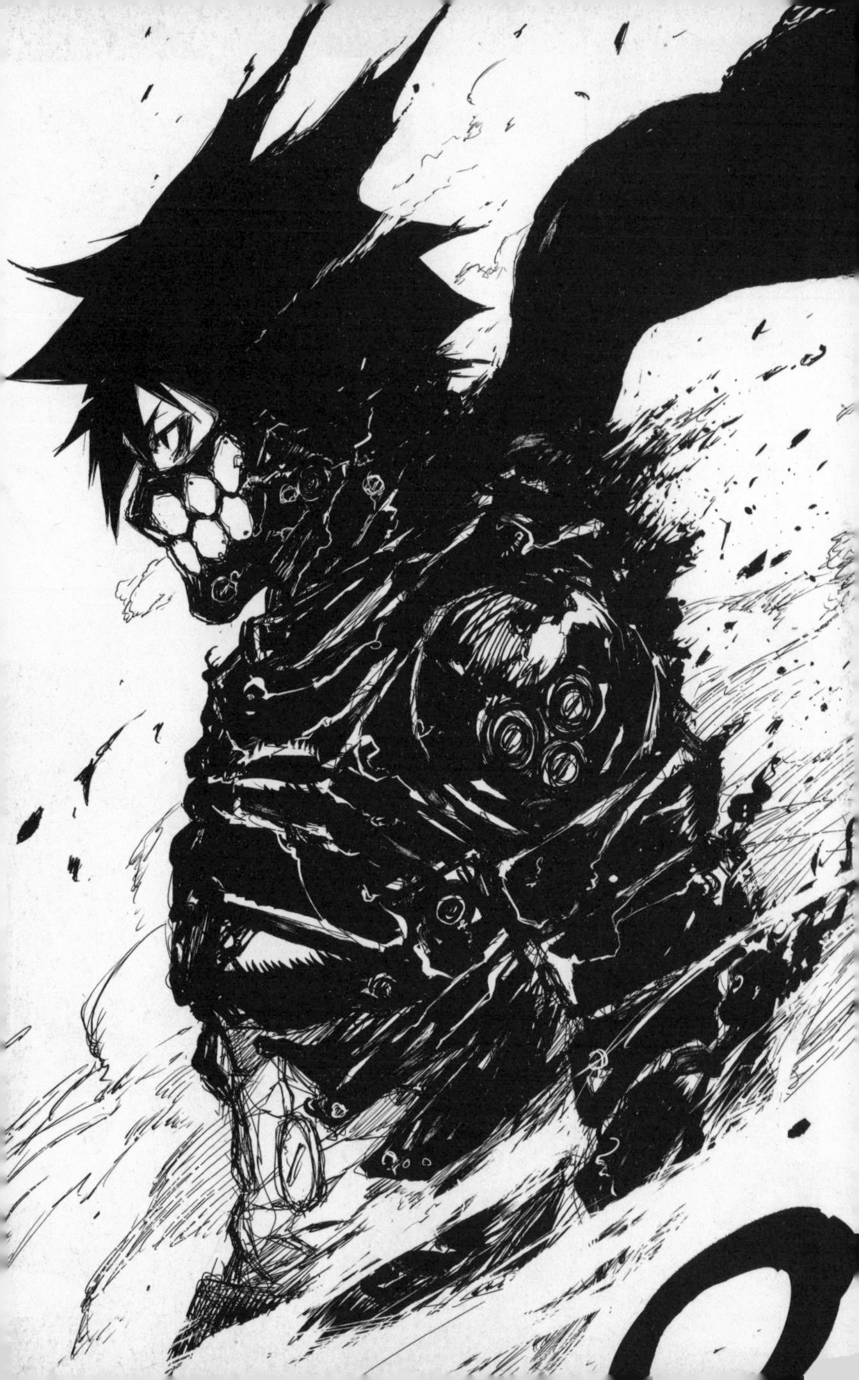

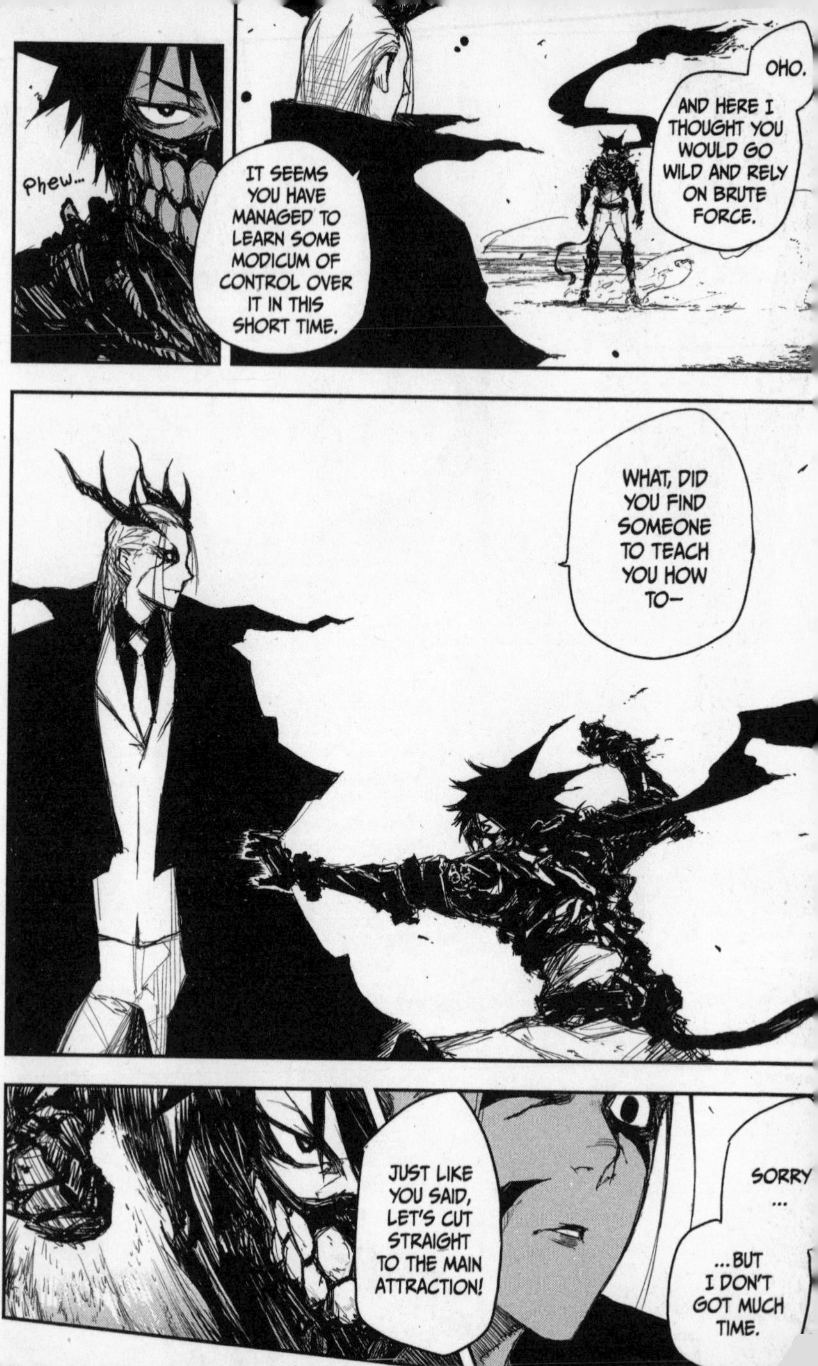
OHO.
AND HERE I THOUGHT YOU WOULD GO WILD AND RELY ON BRUTE FORCE.
IT SEEMS YOU HAVE MANAGED TO LEARN SOME MODICUM OF CONTROL OVER IT IN THIS SHORT TIME.
Phew...
WHAT, DID YOU FIND SOMEONE TO TEACH YOU HOW TO—
SORRY...
...BUT I DON'T GOT MUCH TIME.
JUST LIKE YOU SAID, LET'S CUT STRAIGHT TO THE MAIN ATTRACTION!

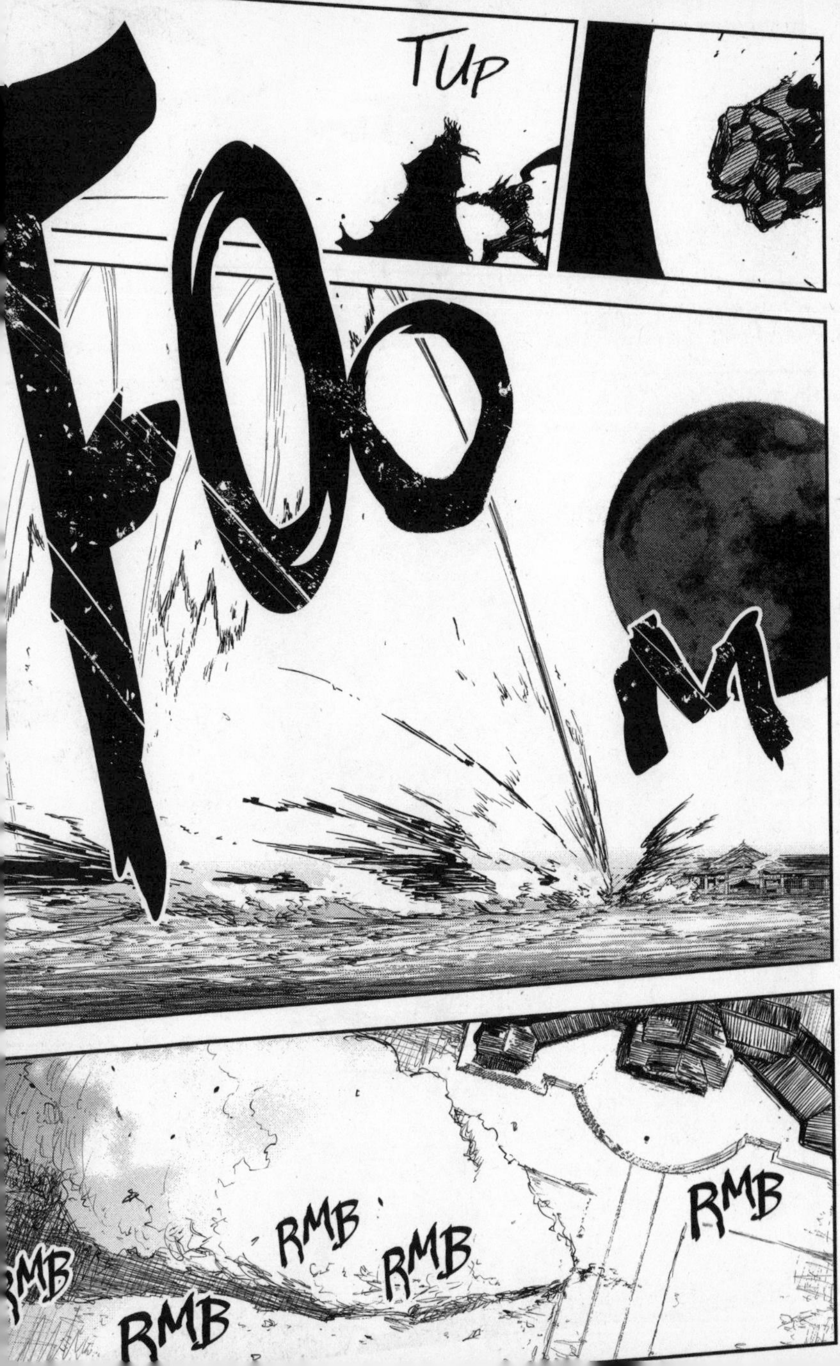
TUP
FOOOM
RMB
RMB
RMB
RMB

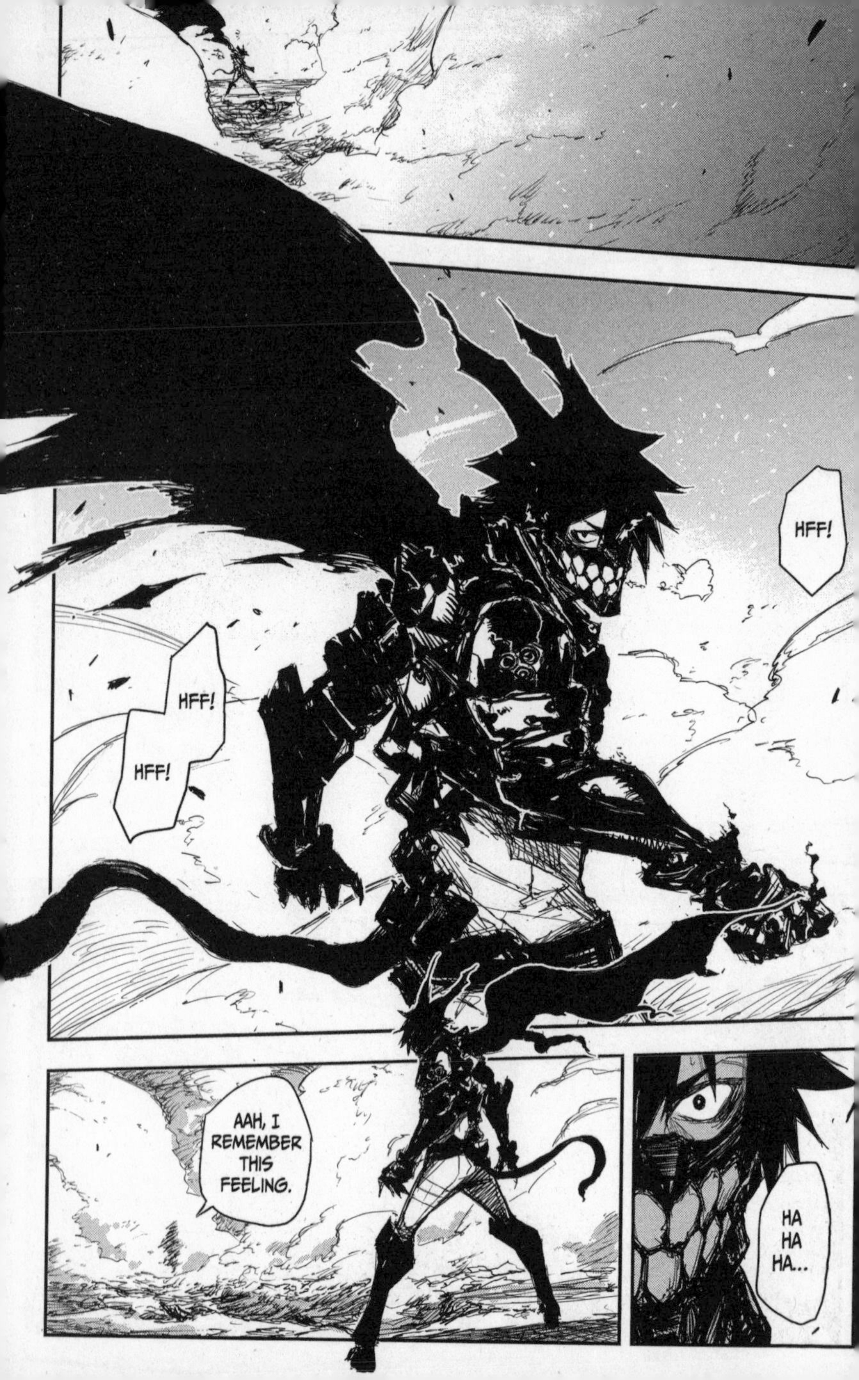
HFF!
HFF!
HFF!
HA HA HA...
AAH, I REMEMBER THIS FEELING.

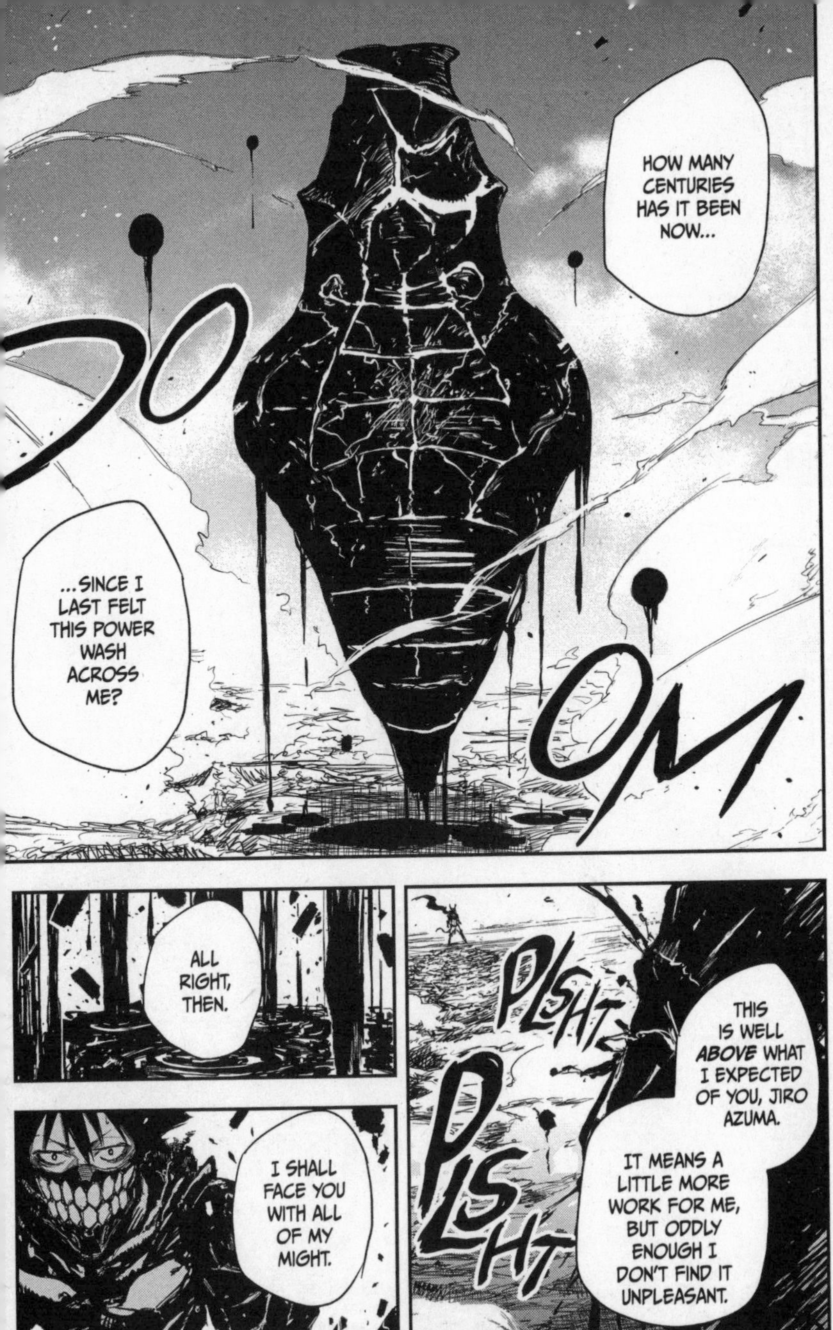
HOW MANY CENTURIES HAS IT BEEN NOW...
DOOM
...SINCE I LAST FELT THIS POWER WASH ACROSS ME?
PLSHT
PLSHT
THIS IS WELL *ABOVE* WHAT I EXPECTED OF YOU, JIRO AZUMA.
IT MEANS A LITTLE MORE WORK FOR ME, BUT ODDLY ENOUGH I DON'T FIND IT UNPLEASANT.
ALL RIGHT, THEN.
I SHALL FACE YOU WITH ALL OF MY MIGHT.

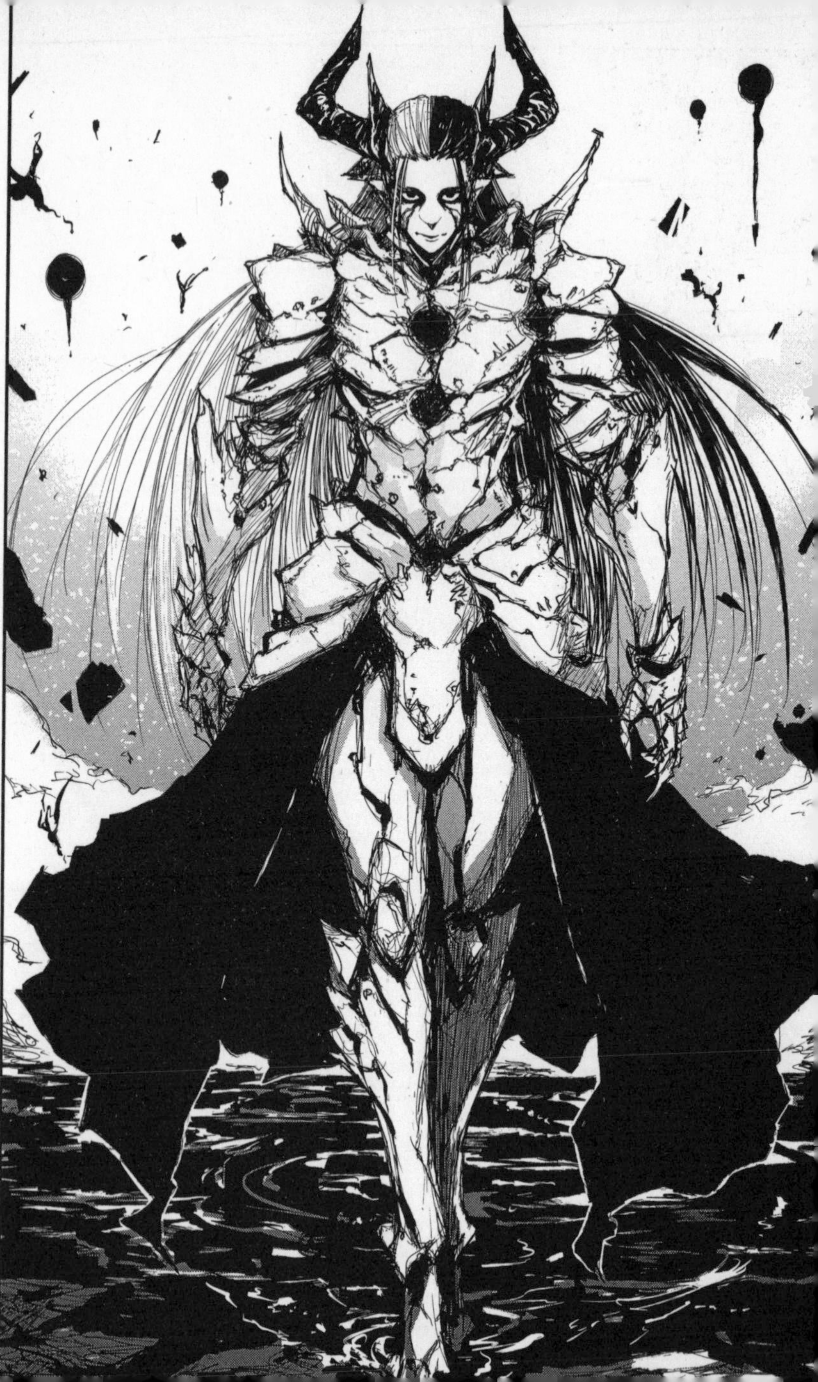

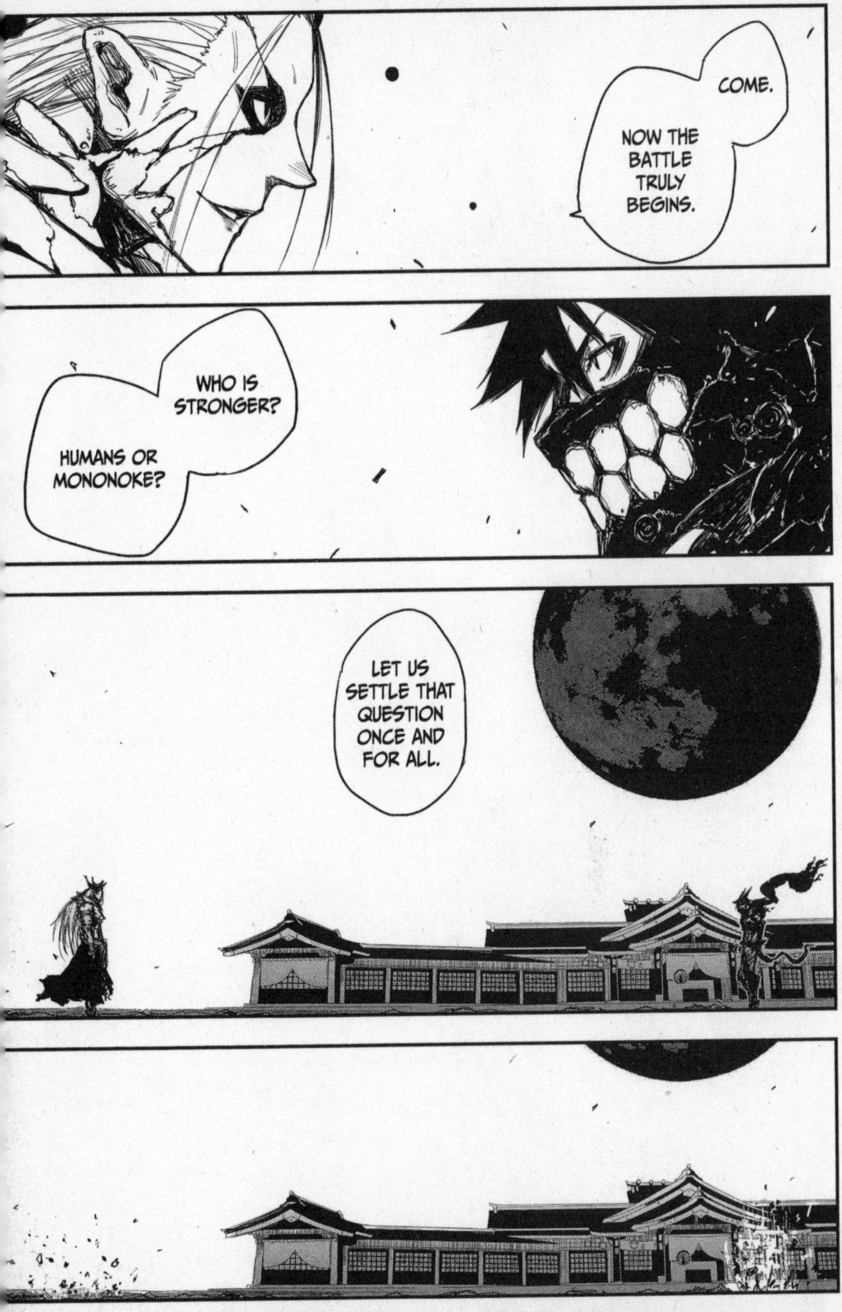
COME.
NOW THE BATTLE TRULY BEGINS.
WHO IS STRONGER?
HUMANS OR MONONOKE?
LET US SETTLE THAT QUESTION ONCE AND FOR ALL.

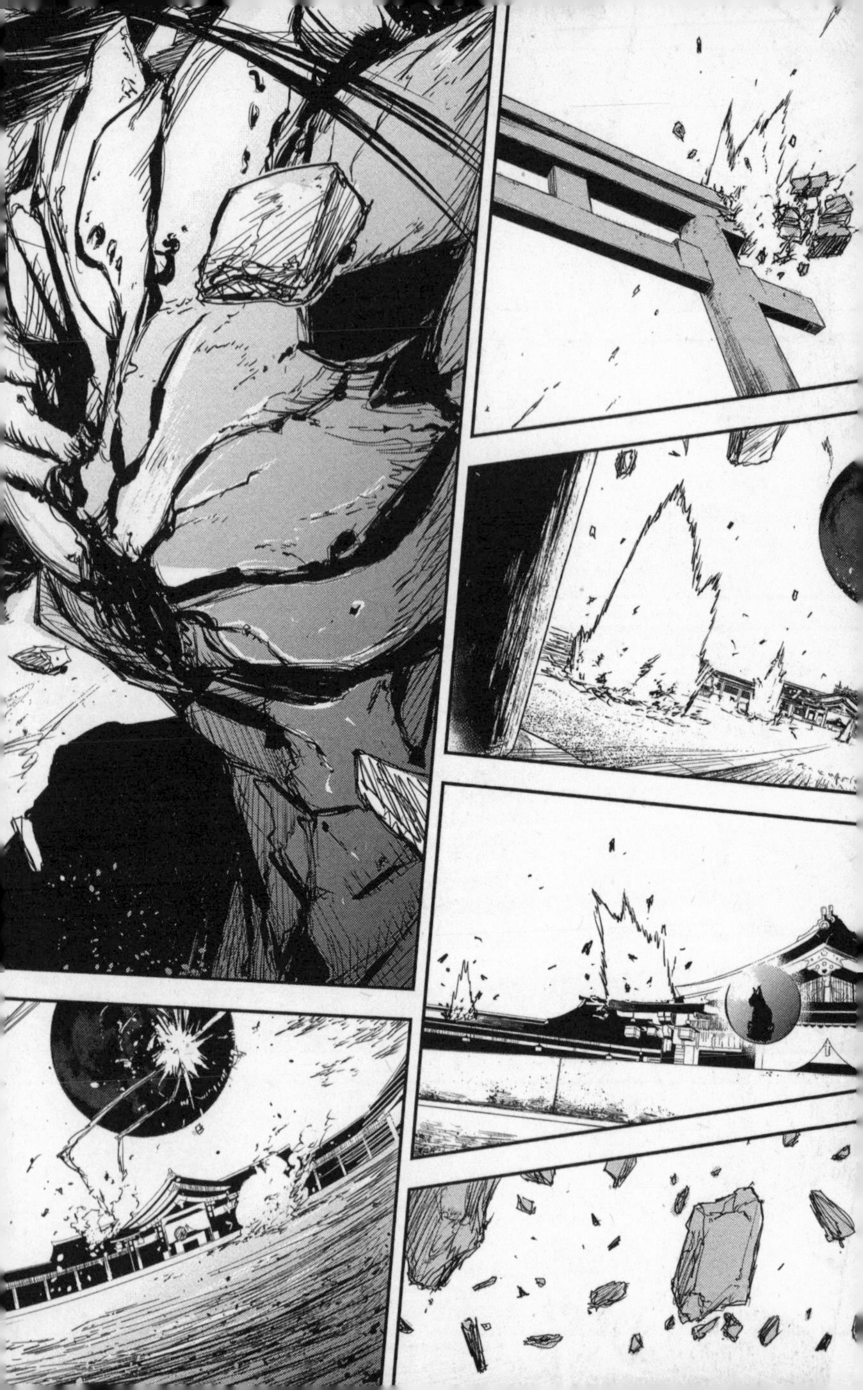

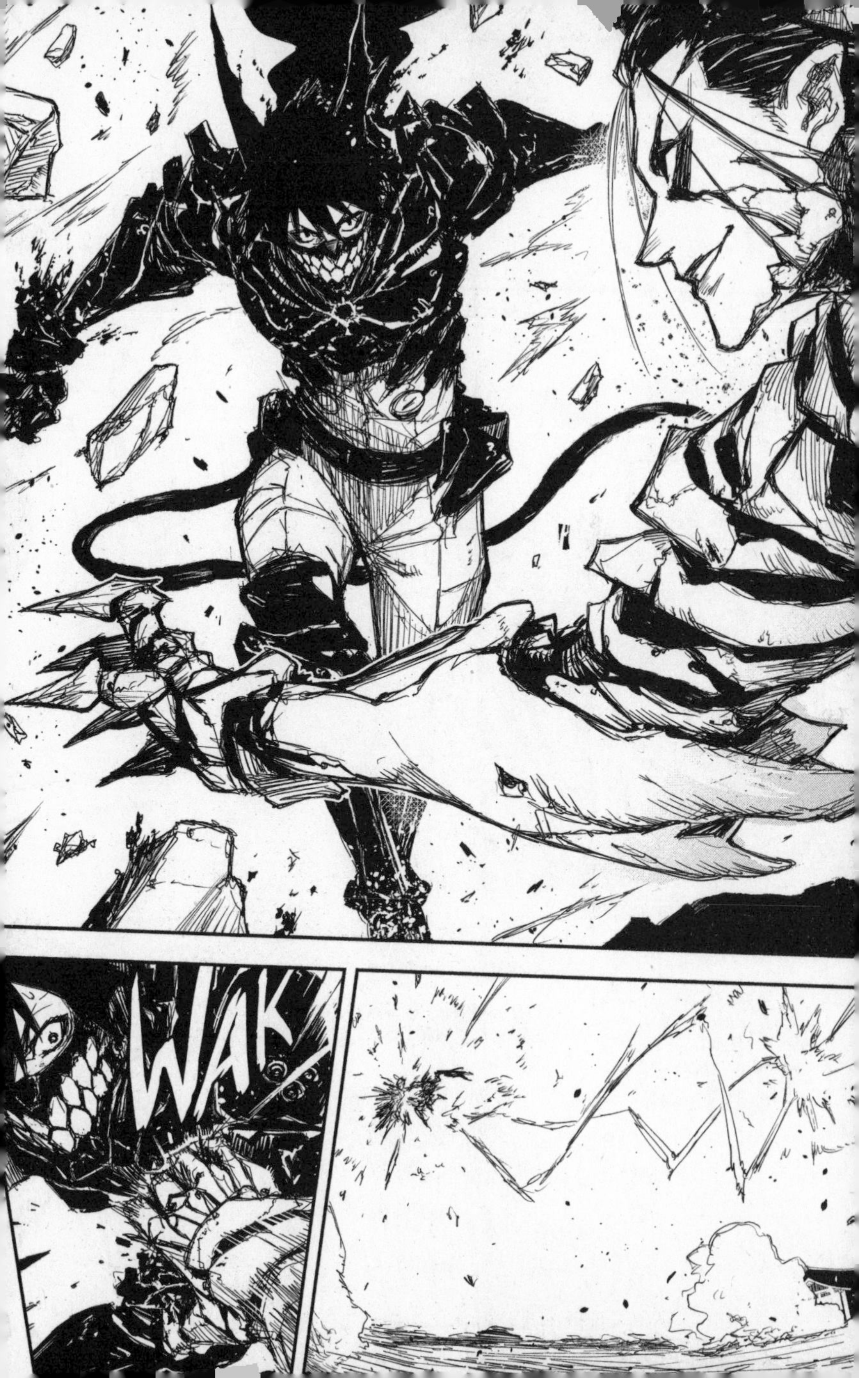
WAK

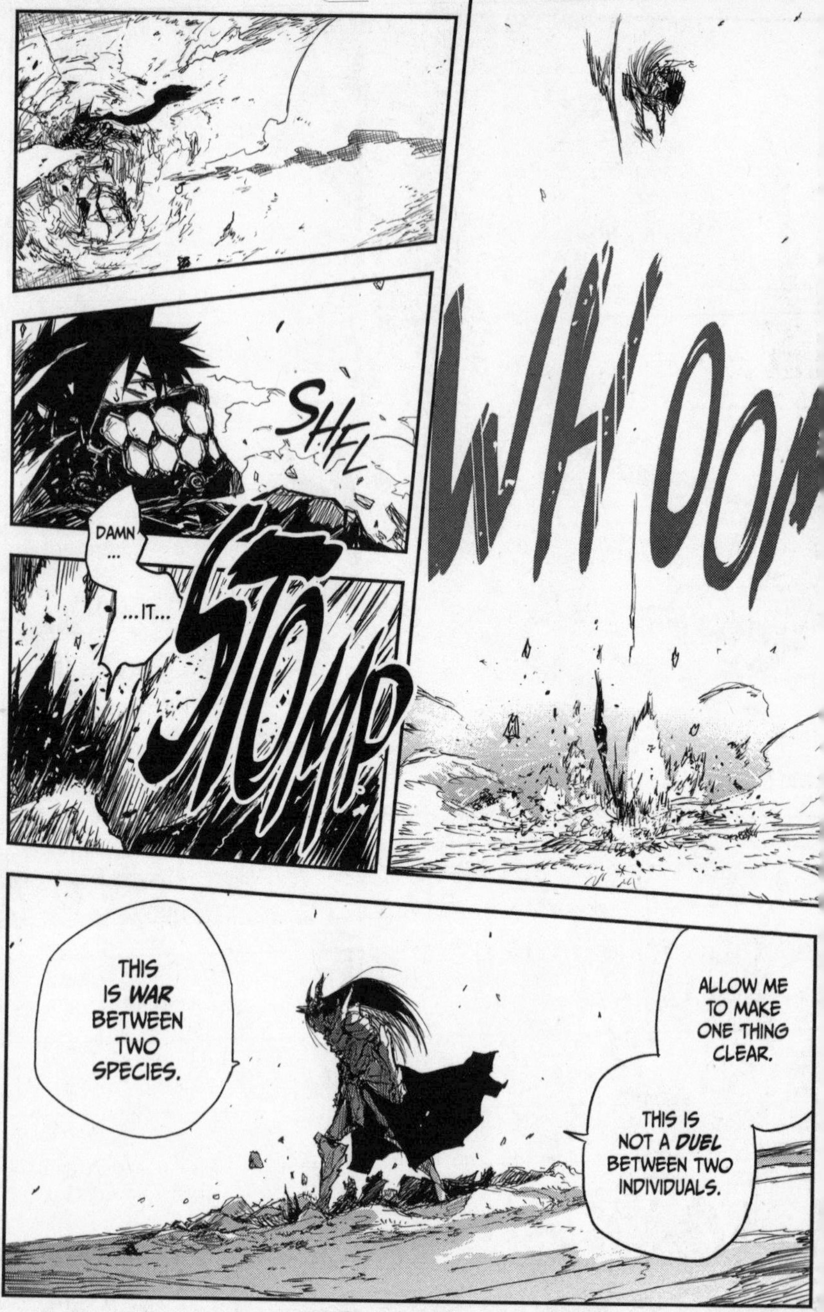
WHOOM
SHFL
DAMN ...
...IT...
STOMP
ALLOW ME TO MAKE ONE THING CLEAR.
THIS IS NOT A *DUEL* BETWEEN TWO INDIVIDUALS.
THIS IS *WAR* BETWEEN TWO SPECIES.

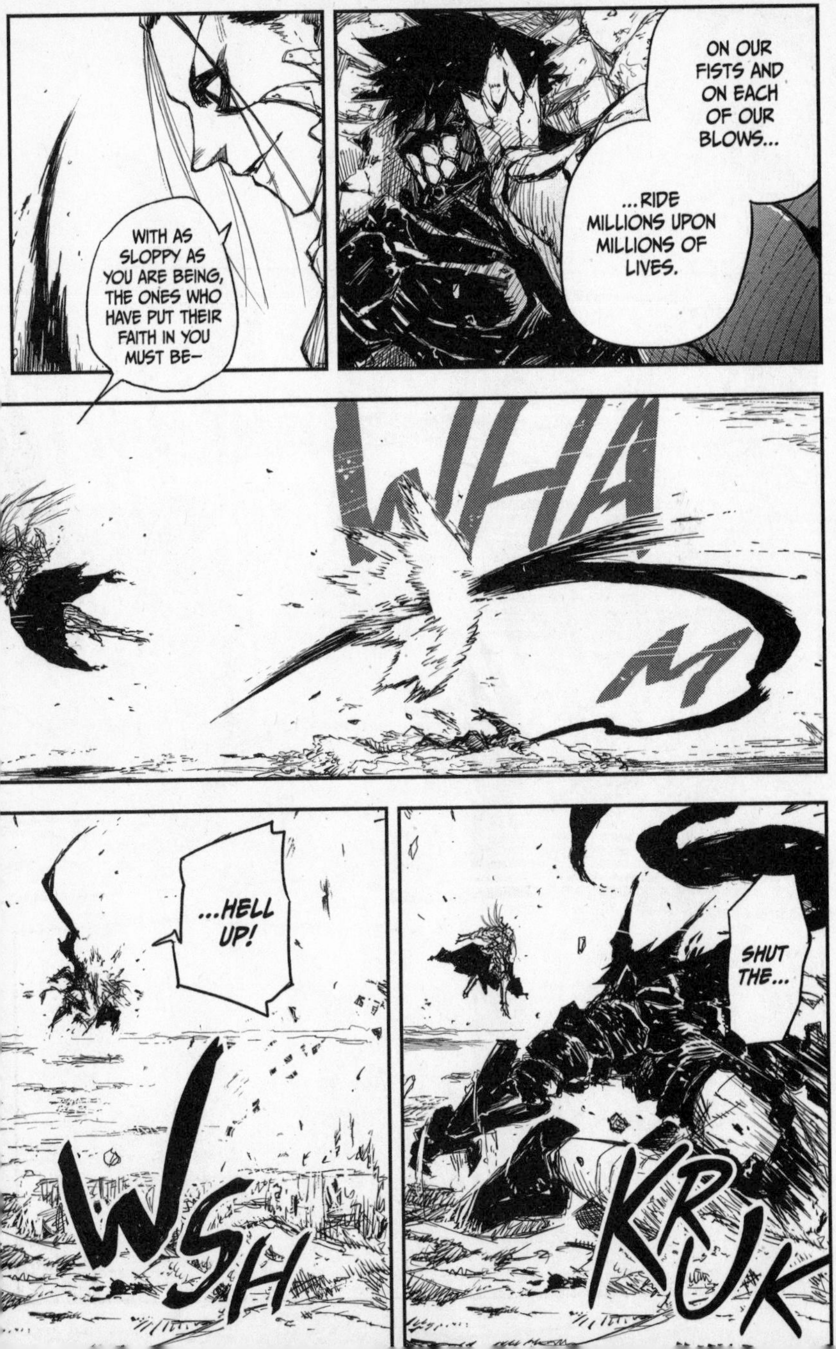
ON OUR FISTS AND ON EACH OF OUR BLOWS...
...RIDE MILLIONS UPON MILLIONS OF LIVES.
WITH AS SLOPPY AS YOU ARE BEING, THE ONES WHO HAVE PUT THEIR FAITH IN YOU MUST BE–
WHAM
SHUT THE...
KRUK
...HELL UP!
WSH

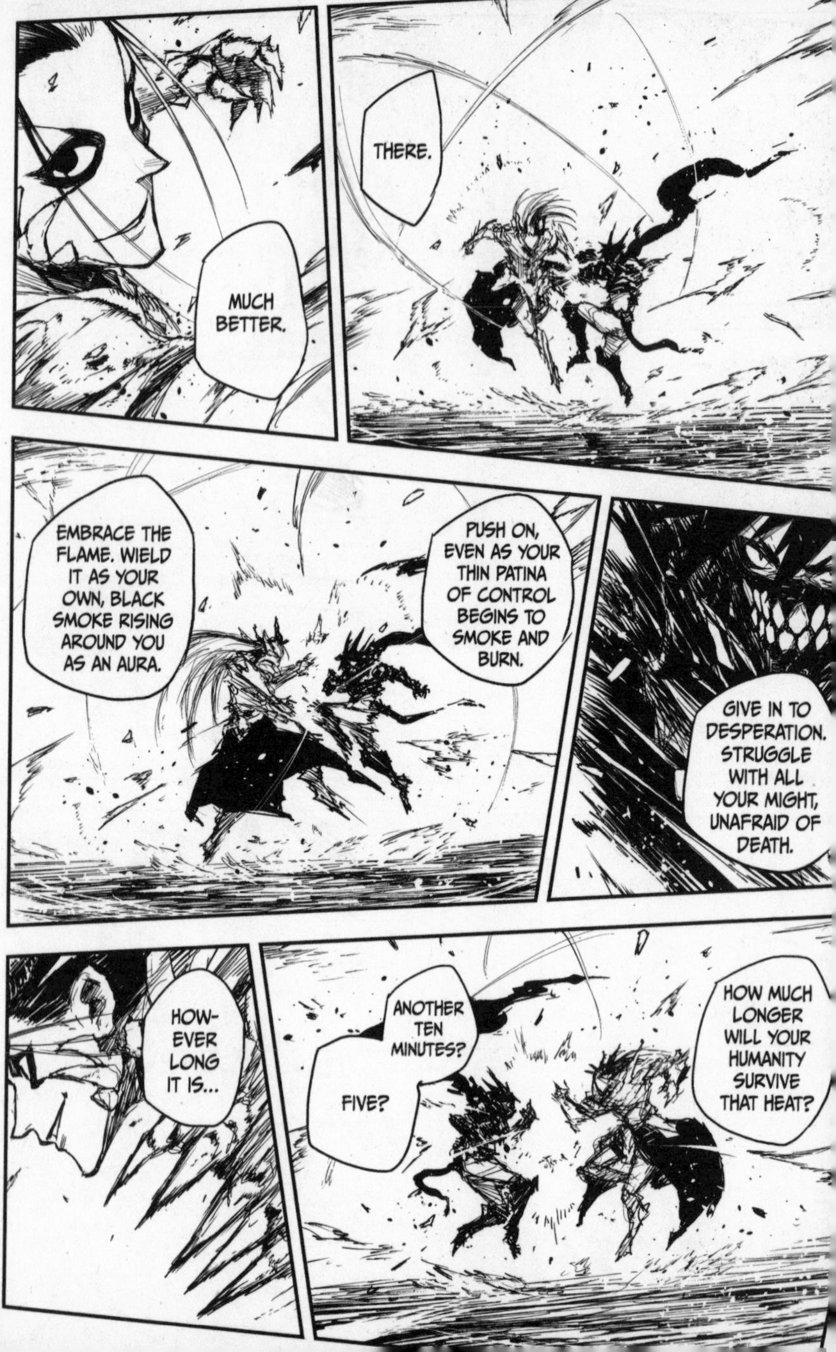
THERE.
MUCH BETTER.
GIVE IN TO DESPERATION. STRUGGLE WITH ALL YOUR MIGHT, UNAFRAID OF DEATH.
PUSH ON, EVEN AS YOUR THIN PATINA OF CONTROL BEGINS TO SMOKE AND BURN.
EMBRACE THE FLAME. WIELD IT AS YOUR OWN, BLACK SMOKE RISING AROUND YOU AS AN AURA.
HOW MUCH LONGER WILL YOUR HUMANITY SURVIVE THAT HEAT?
ANOTHER TEN MINUTES?
FIVE?
HOW-EVER LONG IT IS...

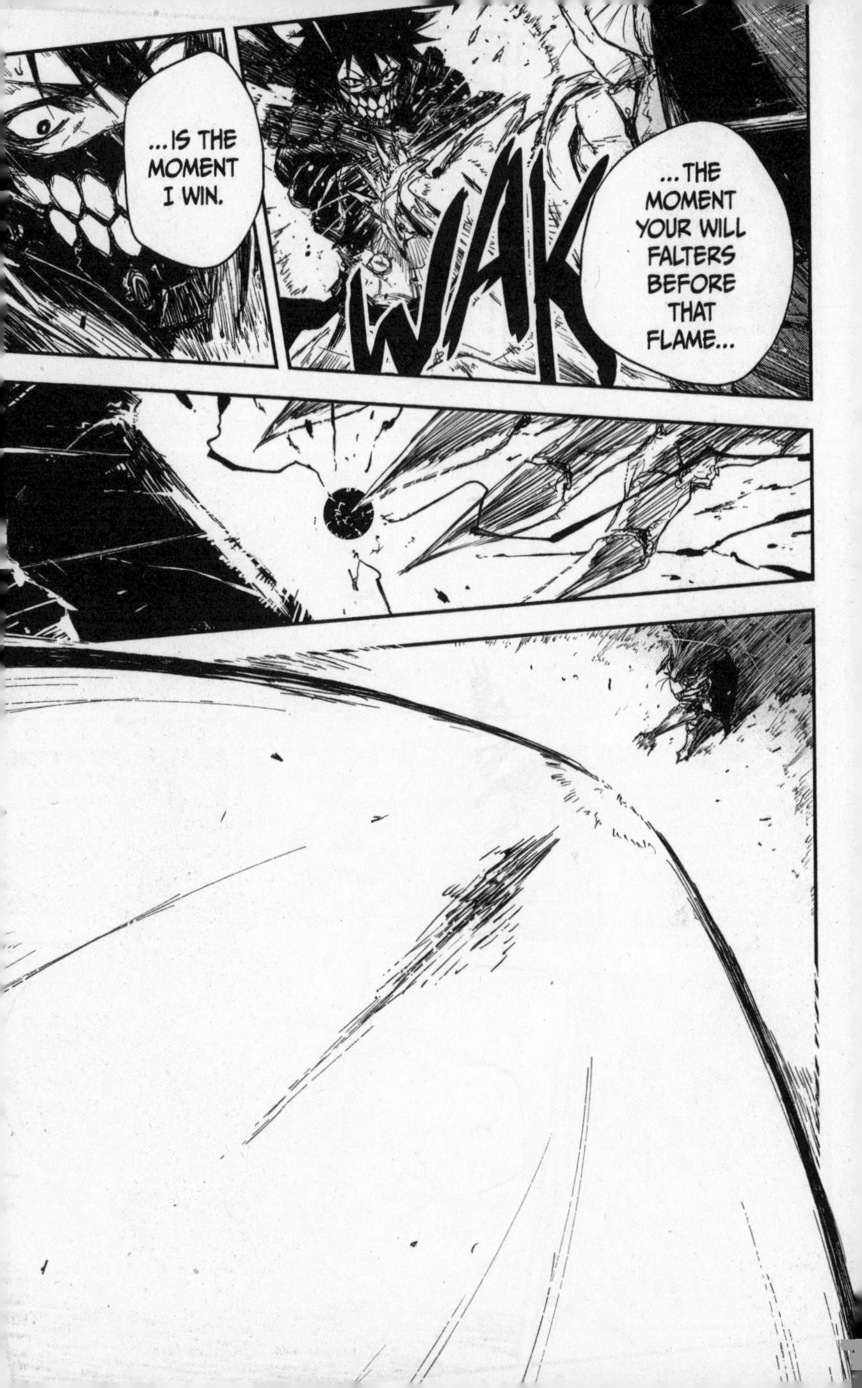
...THE MOMENT YOUR WILL FALTERS BEFORE THAT FLAME...
WAK
...IS THE MOMENT I WIN.

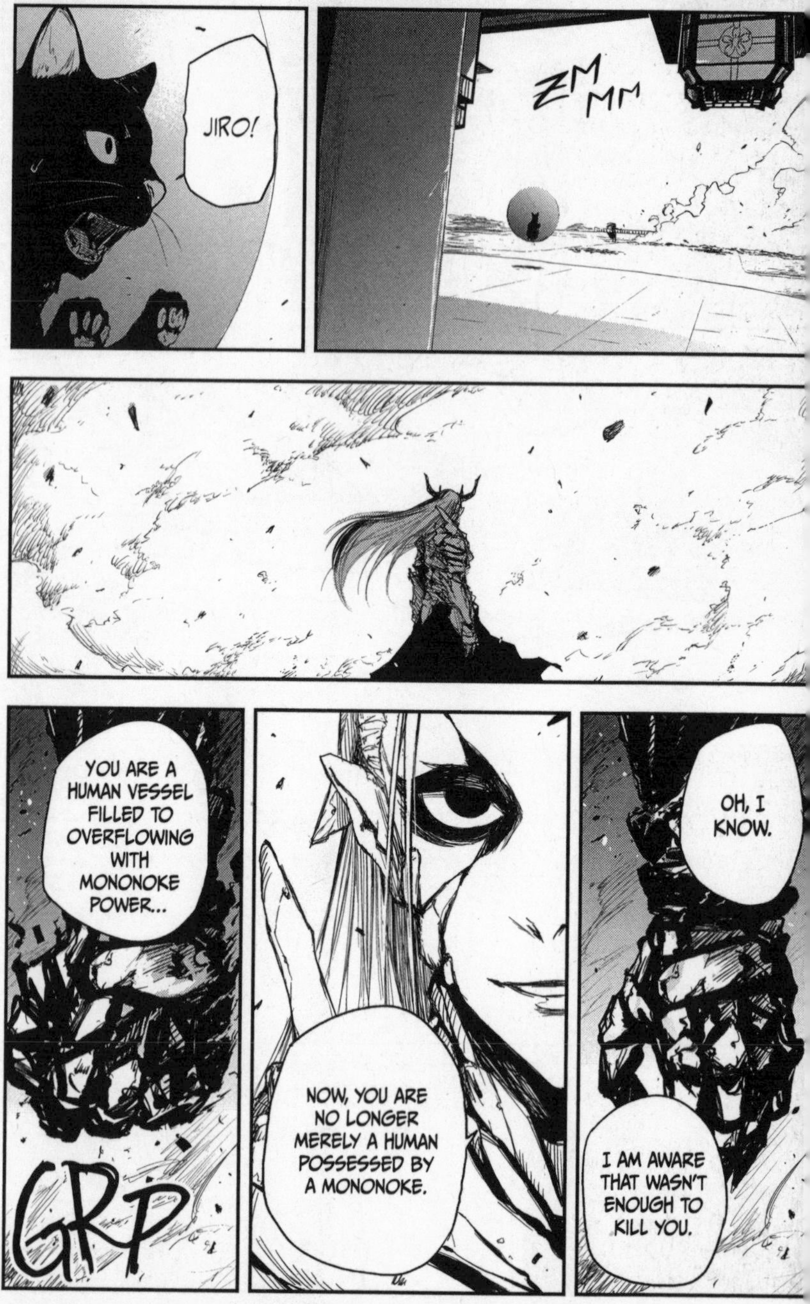
ZMMM
JIRO!
OH, I KNOW.
I AM AWARE THAT WASN'T ENOUGH TO KILL YOU.
NOW, YOU ARE NO LONGER MERELY A HUMAN POSSESSED BY A MONONOKE.
YOU ARE A HUMAN VESSEL FILLED TO OVERFLOWING WITH MONONOKE POWER...
GRP

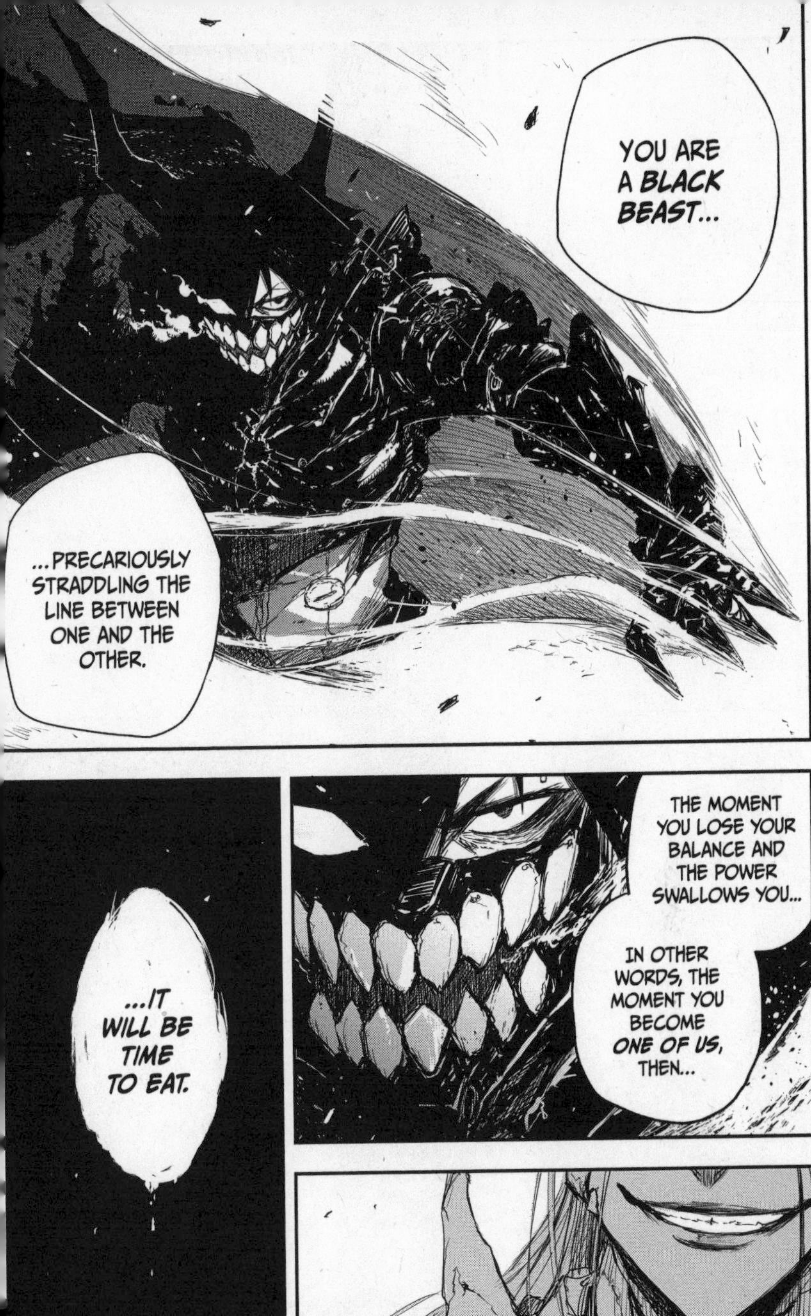
YOU ARE A *BLACK BEAST*...
...PRECARIOUSLY STRADDLING THE LINE BETWEEN ONE AND THE OTHER.
THE MOMENT YOU LOSE YOUR BALANCE AND THE POWER SWALLOWS YOU...
IN OTHER WORDS, THE MOMENT YOU BECOME *ONE OF US*, THEN...
...IT WILL BE TIME TO EAT.

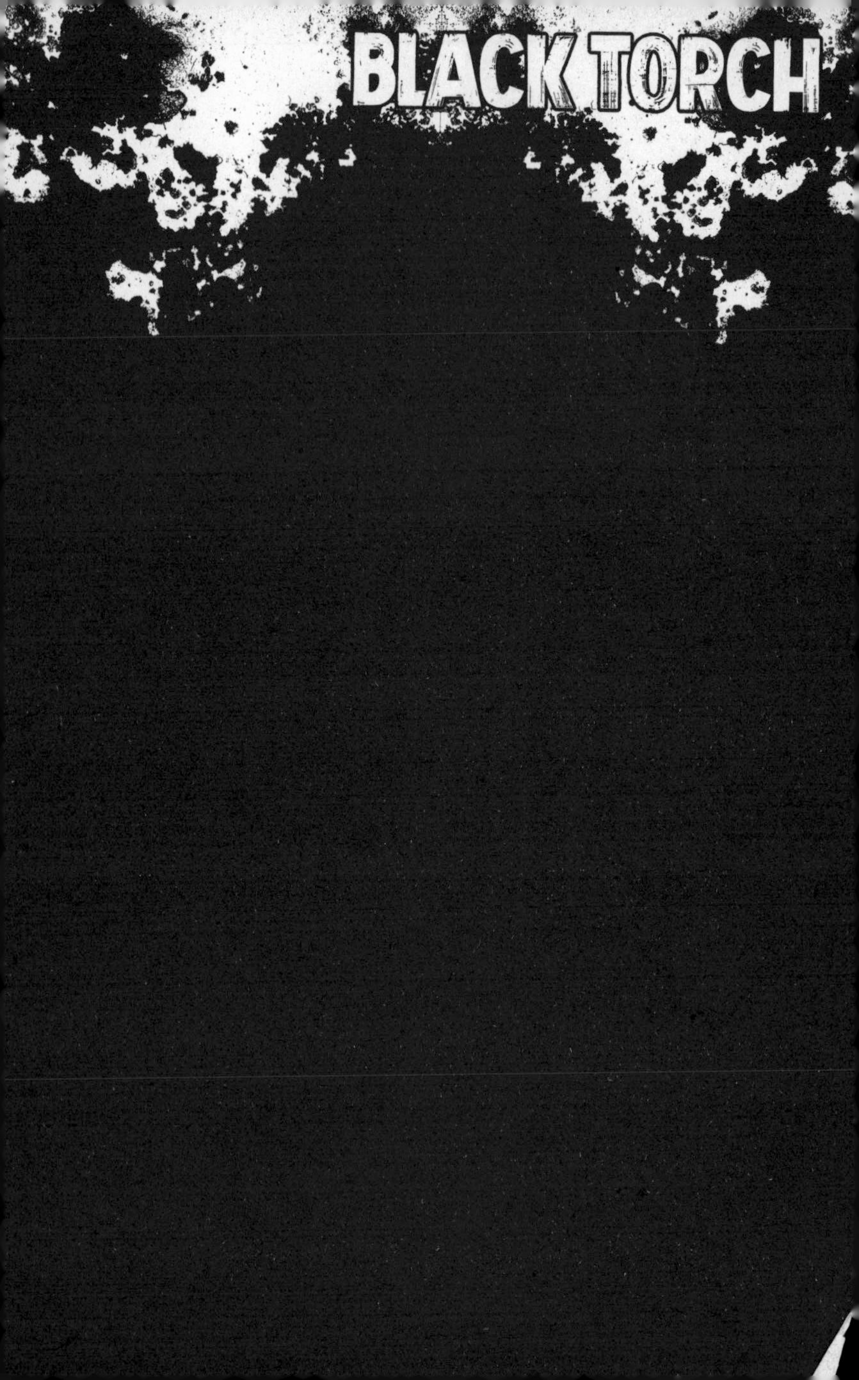
BLACK TORCH

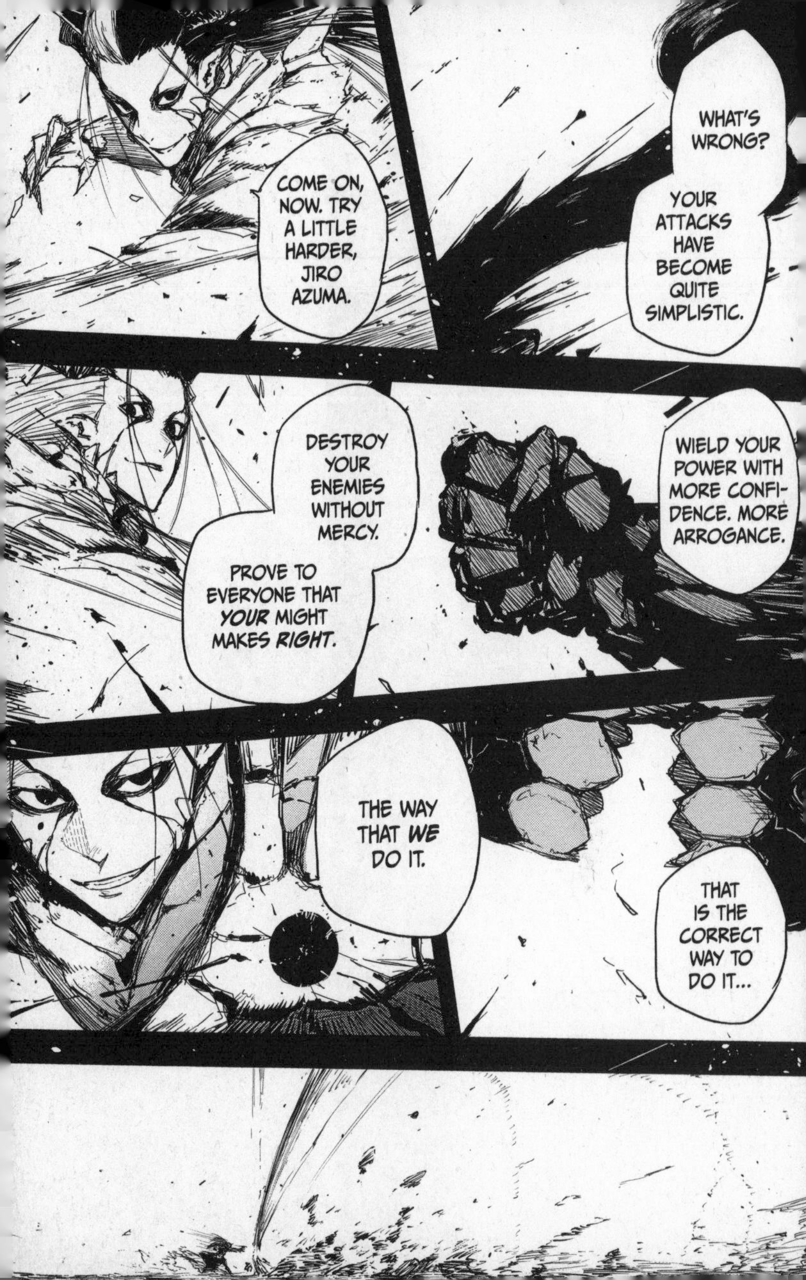
WHAT'S WRONG?
YOUR ATTACKS HAVE BECOME QUITE SIMPLISTIC.
COME ON, NOW. TRY A LITTLE HARDER, JIRO AZUMA.
WIELD YOUR POWER WITH MORE CONFIDENCE. MORE ARROGANCE.
DESTROY YOUR ENEMIES WITHOUT MERCY.
PROVE TO EVERYONE THAT *YOUR* MIGHT MAKES *RIGHT*.
THAT IS THE CORRECT WAY TO DO IT...
THE WAY THAT *WE* DO IT.

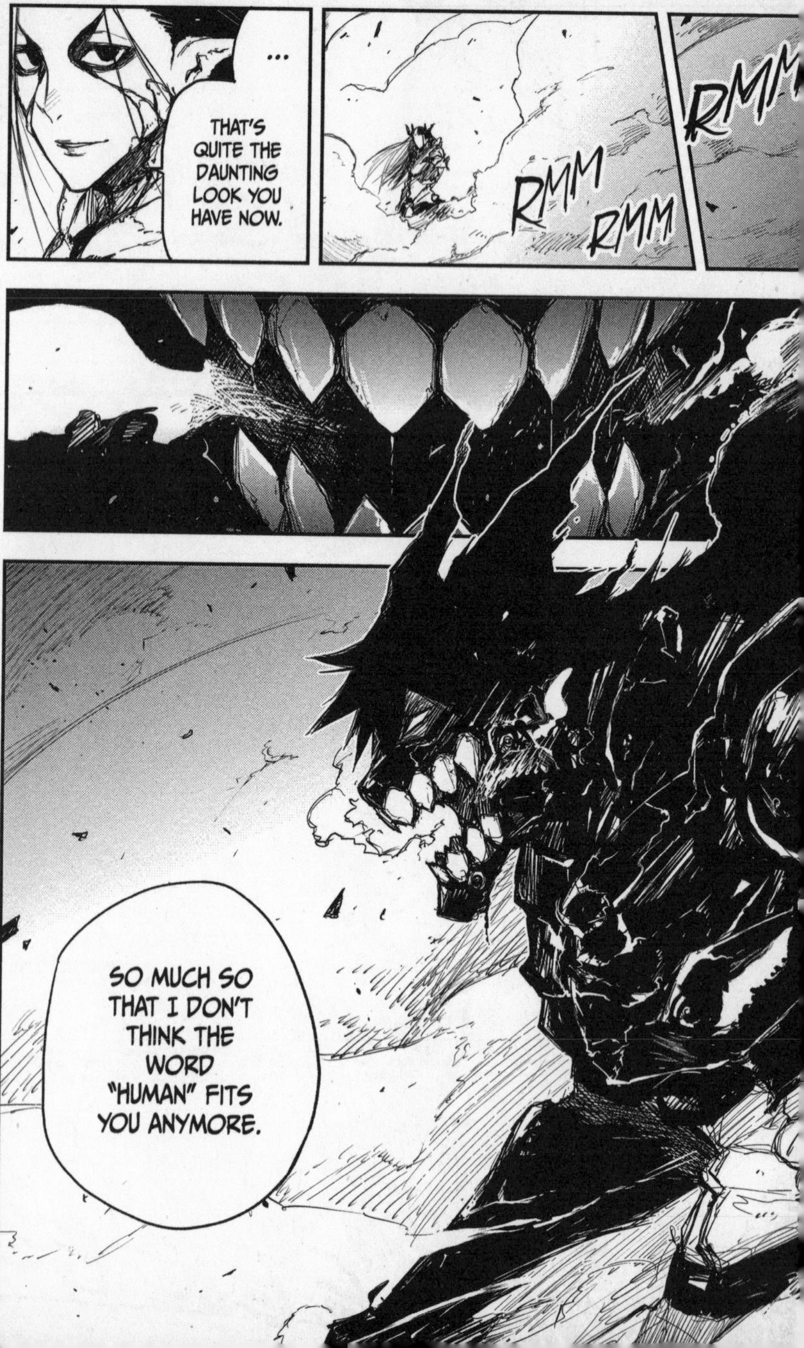
RMM
RMM
RMM
...
THAT'S QUITE THE DAUNTING LOOK YOU HAVE NOW.
SO MUCH SO THAT I DON'T THINK THE WORD "HUMAN" FITS YOU ANYMORE.

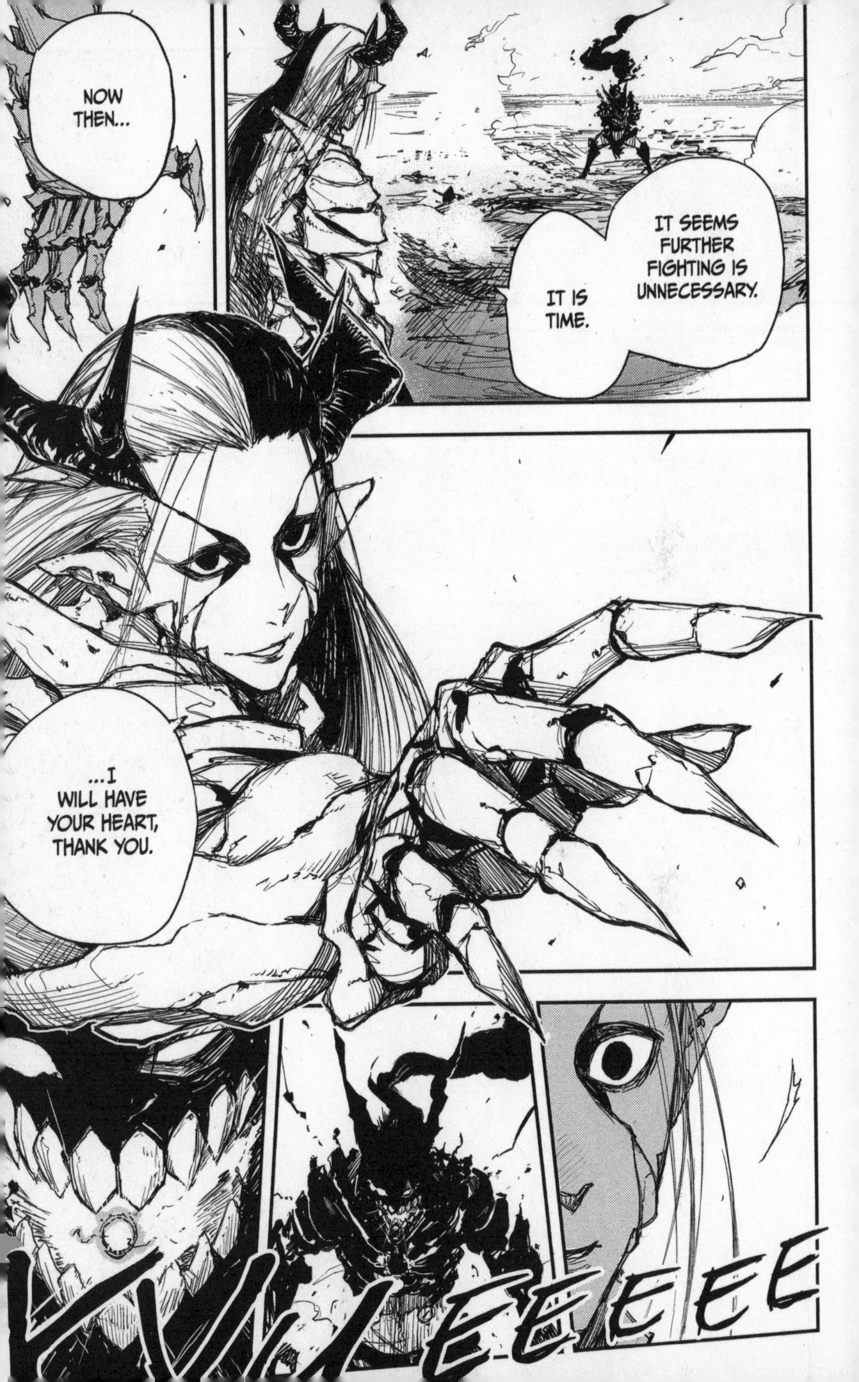
IT SEEMS FURTHER FIGHTING IS UNNECESSARY.
IT IS TIME.
NOW THEN...
...I WILL HAVE YOUR HEART, THANK YOU.

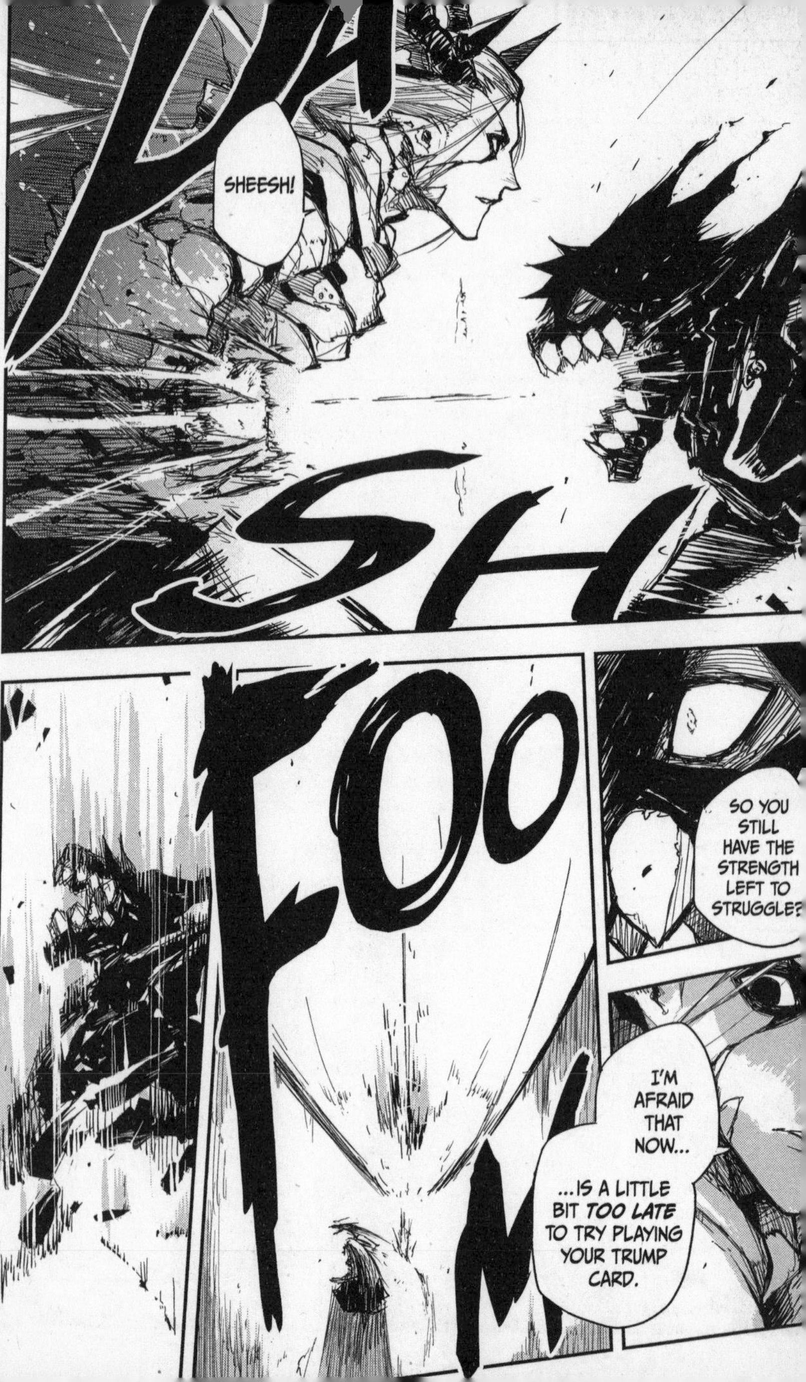
SHEESH!
SH
SO YOU STILL HAVE THE STRENGTH LEFT TO STRUGGLE?
I'M AFRAID THAT NOW...
...IS A LITTLE BIT *TOO LATE* TO TRY PLAYING YOUR TRUMP CARD.
FOOM

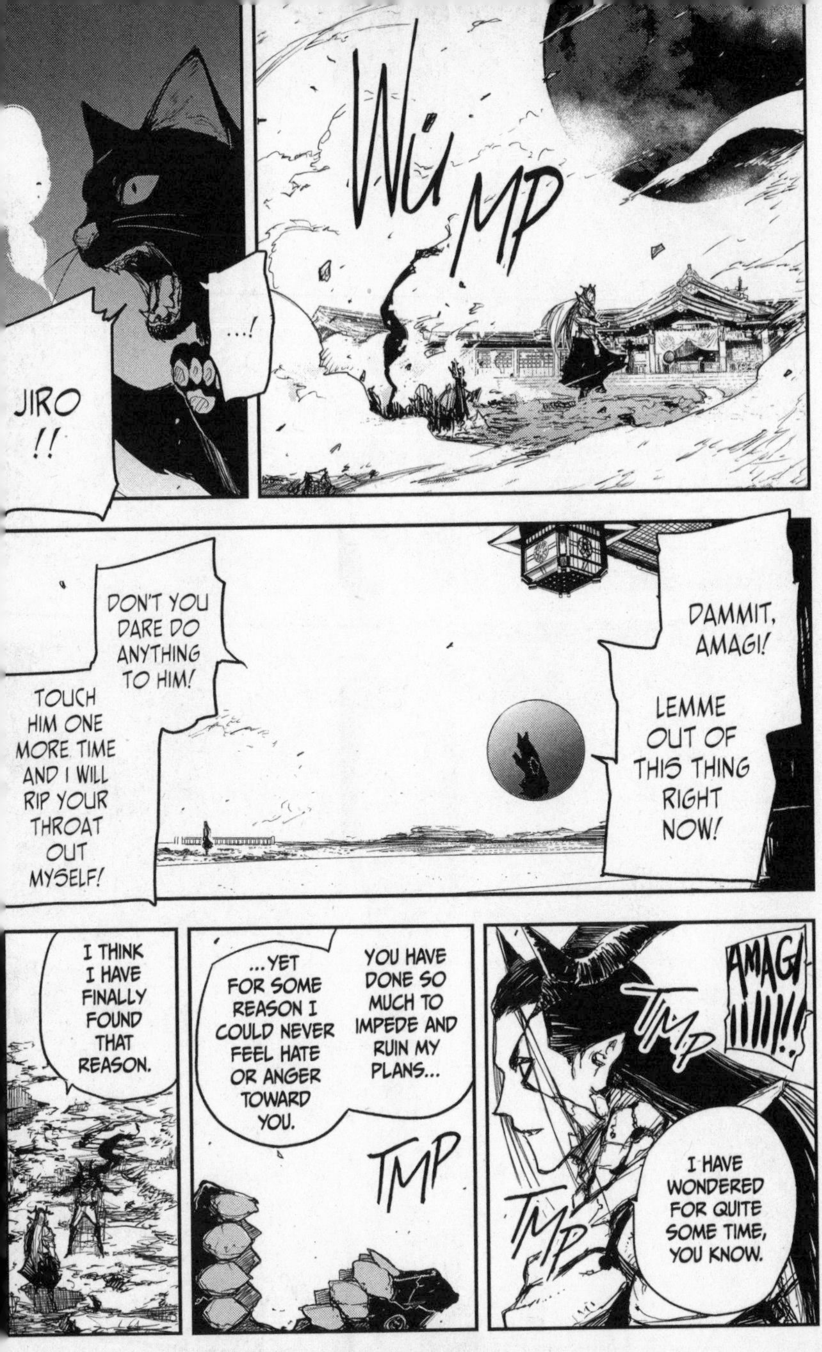
WUMP
...!
JIRO !!
DAMMIT, AMAGI!
LEMME OUT OF THIS THING RIGHT NOW!
DON'T YOU DARE DO ANYTHING TO HIM!
TOUCH HIM ONE MORE TIME AND I WILL RIP YOUR THROAT OUT MYSELF!
AMAGI !!!!!!!!..
TMP
TMP
I HAVE WONDERED FOR QUITE SOME TIME, YOU KNOW.
YOU HAVE DONE SO MUCH TO IMPEDE AND RUIN MY PLANS...
...YET FOR SOME REASON I COULD NEVER FEEL HATE OR ANGER TOWARD YOU.
TMP
I THINK I HAVE FINALLY FOUND THAT REASON.

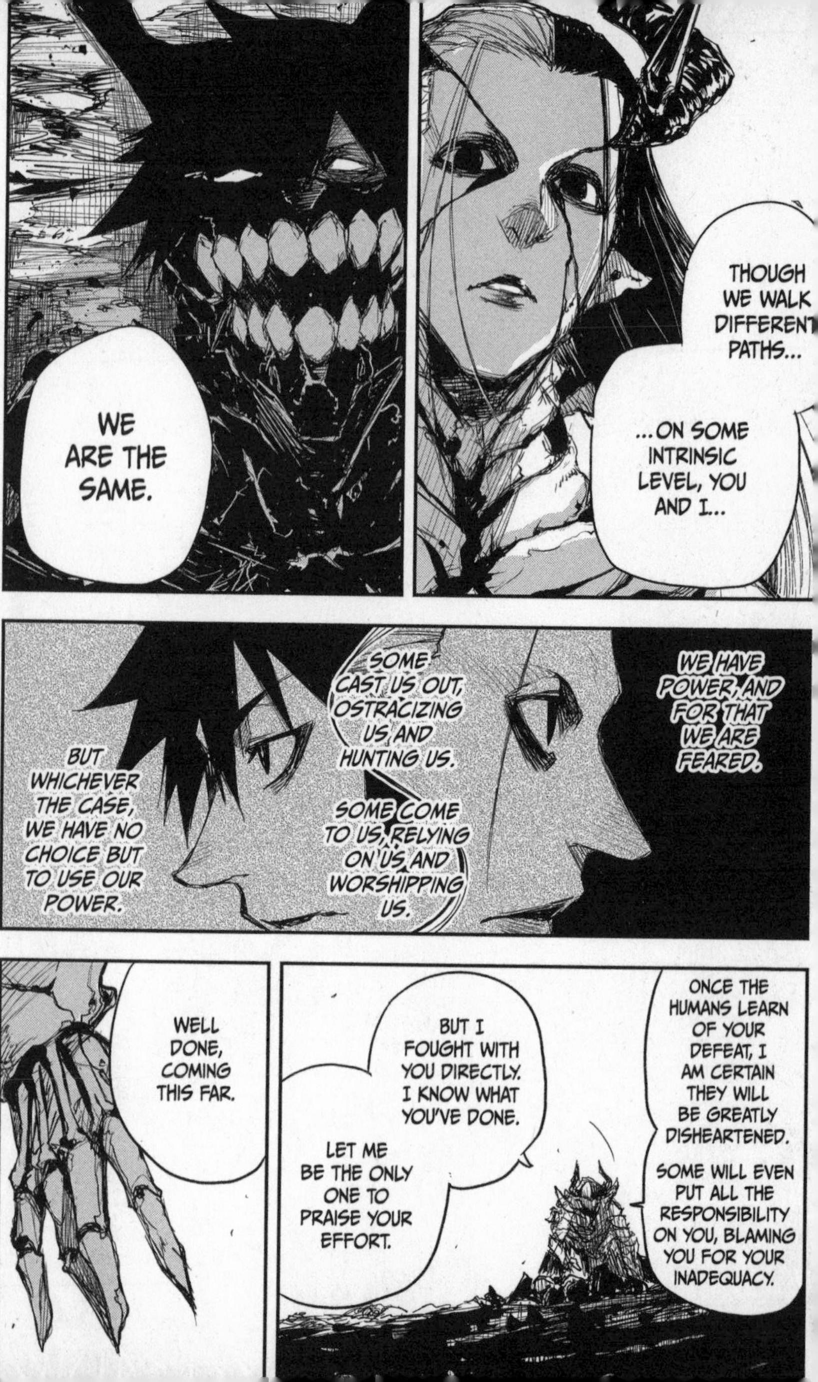
THOUGH WE WALK DIFFERENT PATHS...
...ON SOME INTRINSIC LEVEL, YOU AND I...
WE ARE THE SAME.
WE HAVE POWER, AND FOR THAT WE ARE FEARED.
SOME CAST US OUT, OSTRACIZING US AND HUNTING US.
SOME COME TO US, RELYING ON US AND WORSHIPPING US.
BUT WHICHEVER THE CASE, WE HAVE NO CHOICE BUT TO USE OUR POWER.
ONCE THE HUMANS LEARN OF YOUR DEFEAT, I AM CERTAIN THEY WILL BE GREATLY DISHEARTENED.
SOME WILL EVEN PUT ALL THE RESPONSIBILITY ON YOU, BLAMING YOU FOR YOUR INADEQUACY.
BUT I FOUGHT WITH YOU DIRECTLY. I KNOW WHAT YOU'VE DONE.
LET ME BE THE ONLY ONE TO PRAISE YOUR EFFORT.
WELL DONE, COMING THIS FAR.

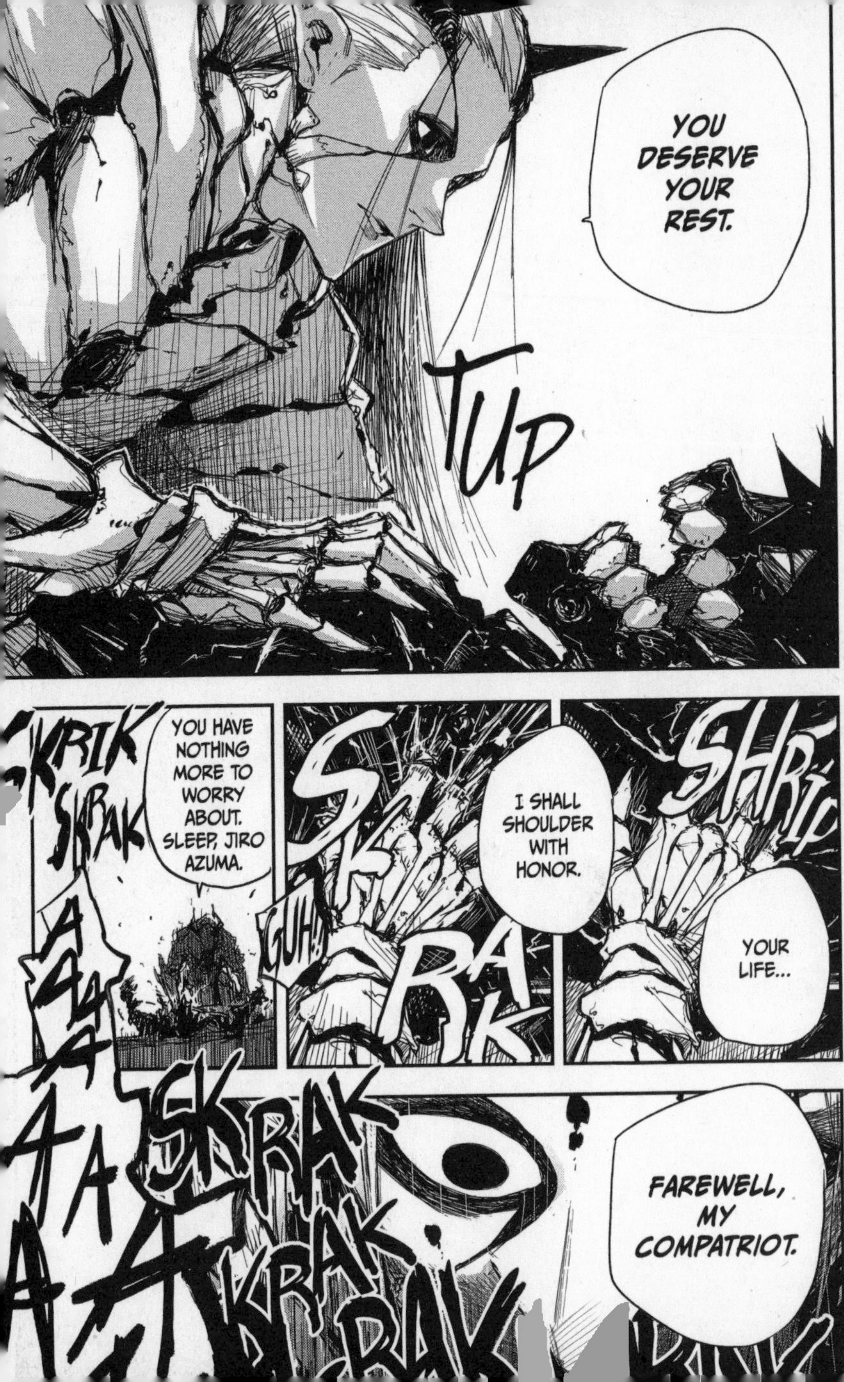
YOU DESERVE YOUR REST.
TUP
SHRIP
YOUR LIFE...
I SHALL SHOULDER WITH HONOR.
SK
BA
GUH!
SKRIK
SKRAK
YOU HAVE NOTHING MORE TO WORRY ABOUT. SLEEP, JIRO AZUMA.
FAREWELL, MY COMPATRIOT.
SKRAK
KRAK

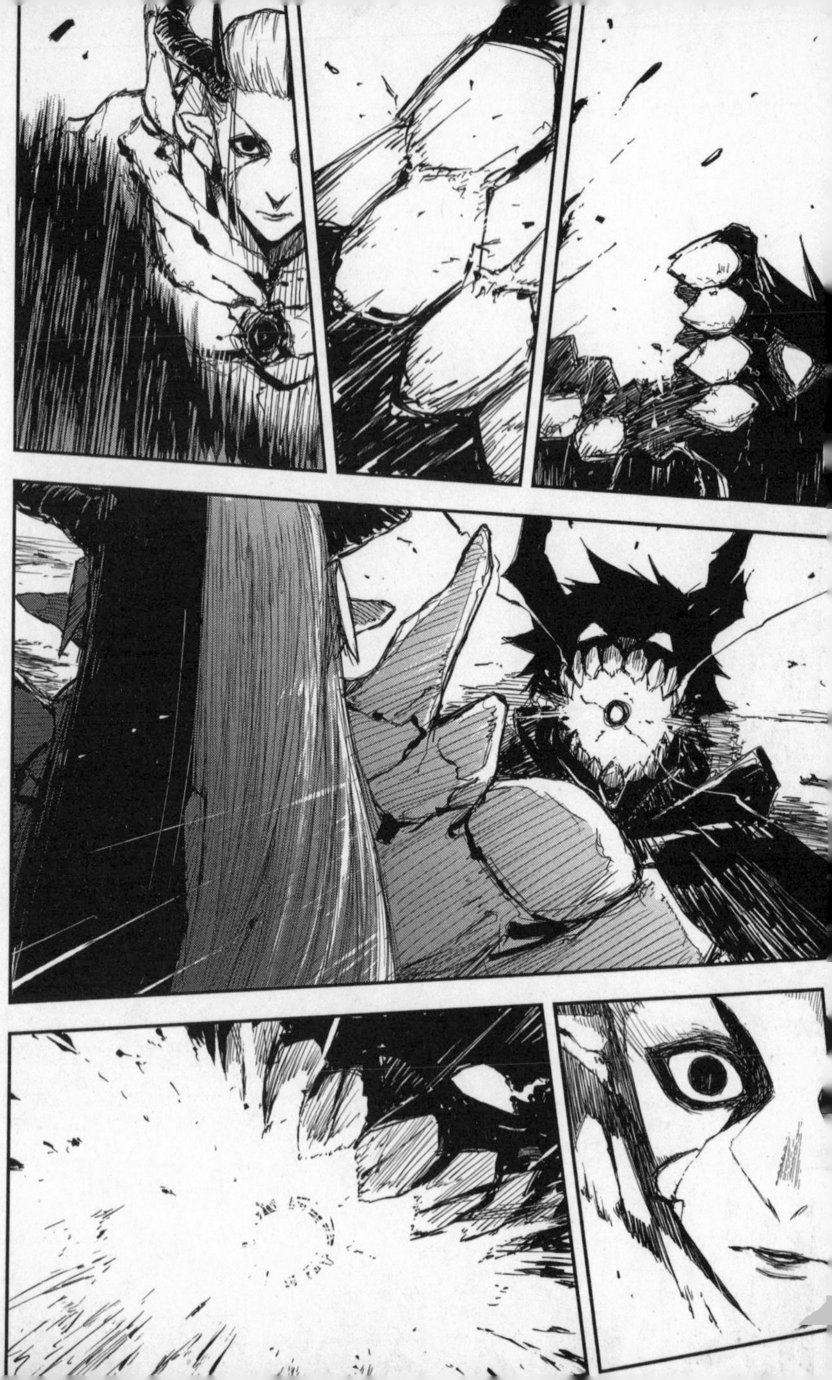

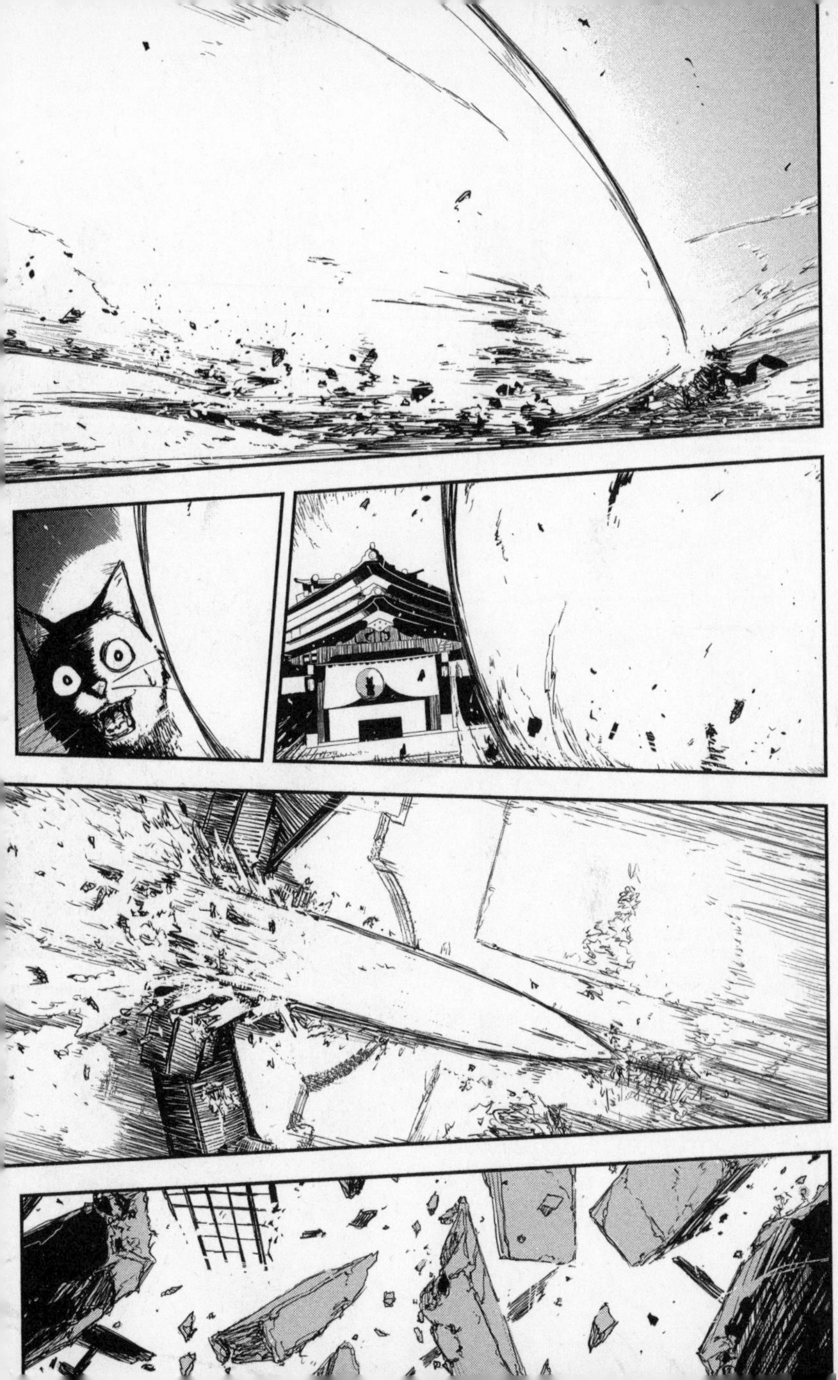

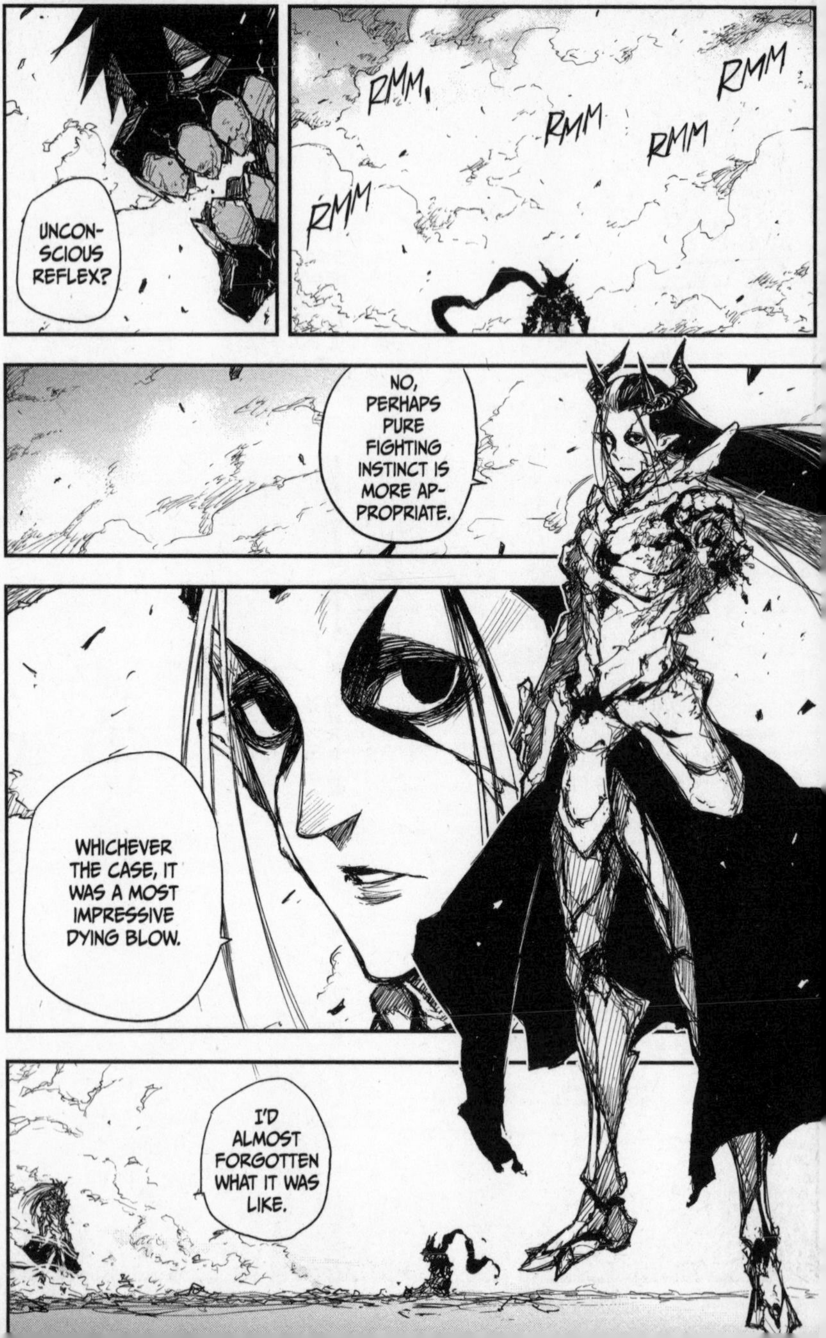
RMM
RMM
RMM
RMM
RMM
UNCON-SCIOUS REFLEX?
NO, PERHAPS PURE FIGHTING INSTINCT IS MORE AP-PROPRIATE.
WHICHEVER THE CASE, IT WAS A MOST IMPRESSIVE DYING BLOW.
I'D ALMOST FORGOTTEN WHAT IT WAS LIKE.

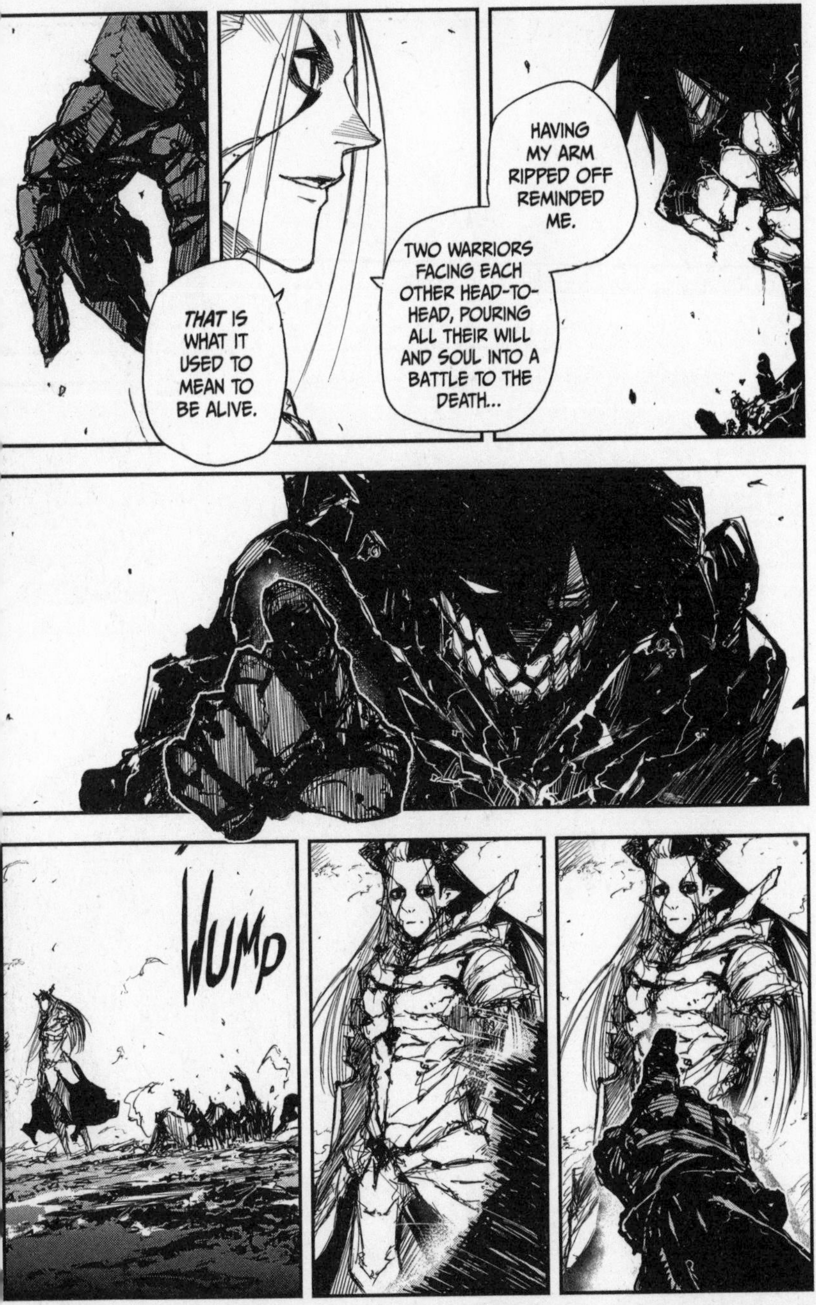
HAVING MY ARM RIPPED OFF REMINDED ME.
TWO WARRIORS FACING EACH OTHER HEAD-TO-HEAD, POURING ALL THEIR WILL AND SOUL INTO A BATTLE TO THE DEATH...
THAT IS WHAT IT USED TO MEAN TO BE ALIVE.
WUMP

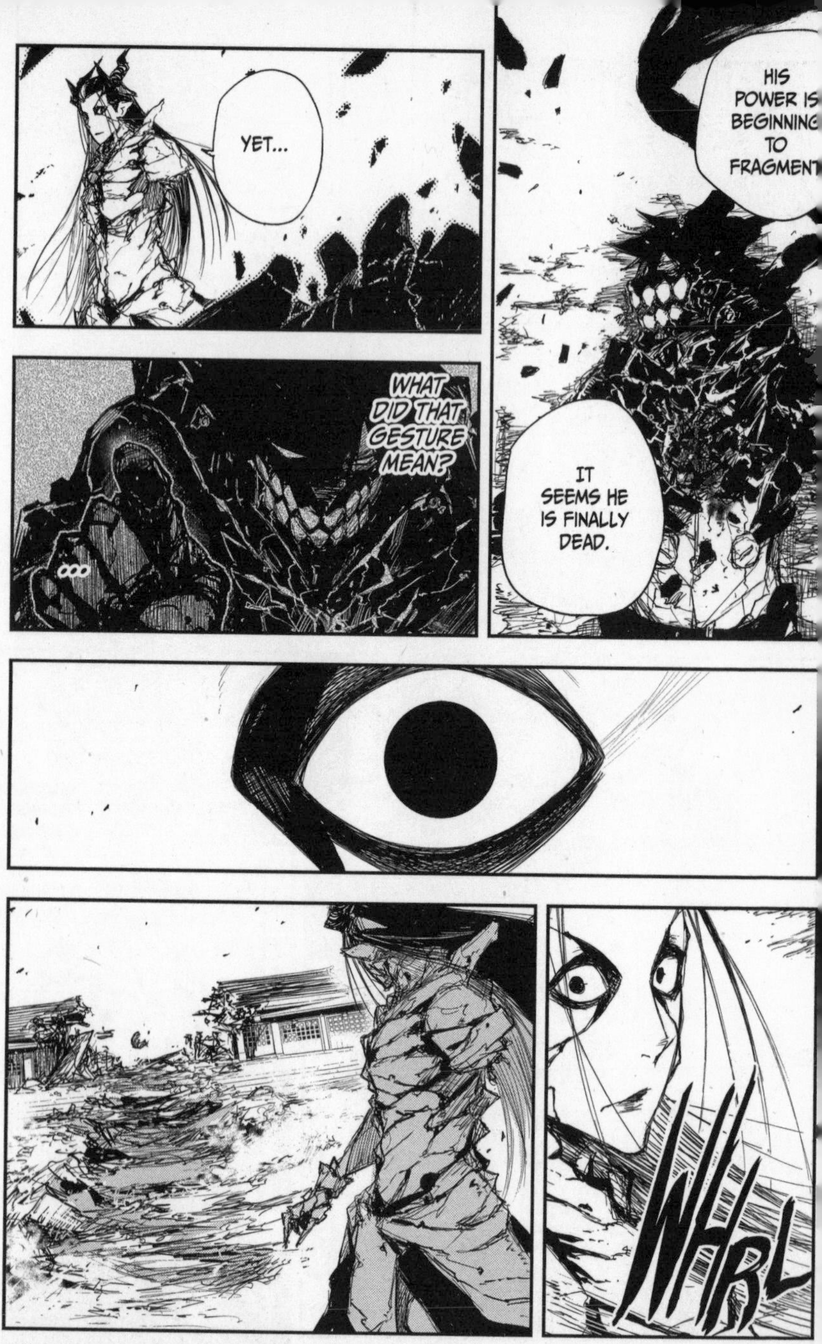
HIS POWER IS BEGINNING TO FRAGMENT
IT SEEMS HE IS FINALLY DEAD.
YET...
WHAT DID THAT GESTURE MEAN?
WHIRL

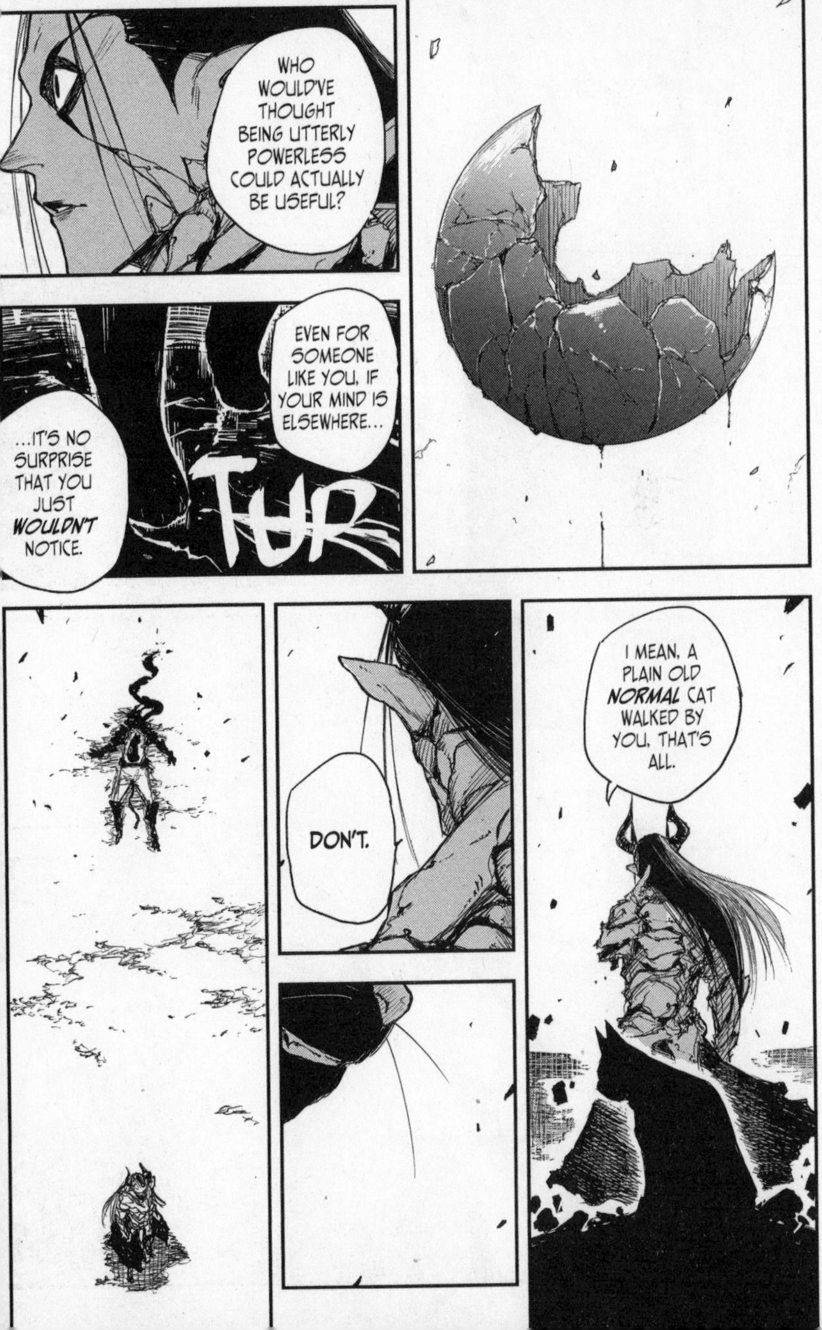
WHO WOULD'VE THOUGHT BEING UTTERLY POWERLESS COULD ACTUALLY BE USEFUL?
EVEN FOR SOMEONE LIKE YOU, IF YOUR MIND IS ELSEWHERE...
...IT'S NO SURPRISE THAT YOU JUST *WOULDN'T* NOTICE.
TUR
I MEAN, A PLAIN OLD *NORMAL* CAT WALKED BY YOU, THAT'S ALL.
DON'T.

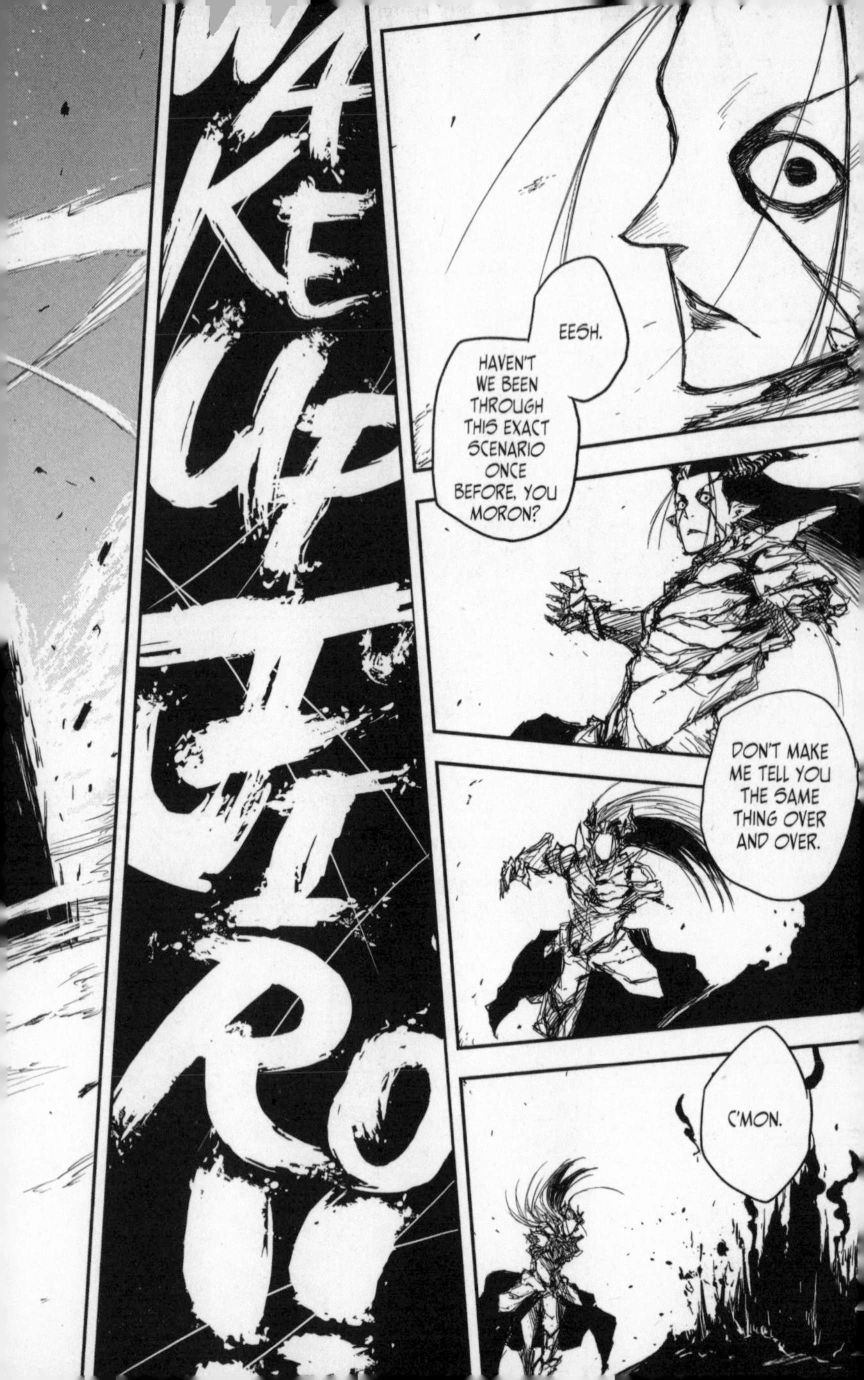
EESH.
HAVEN'T WE BEEN THROUGH THIS EXACT SCENARIO ONCE BEFORE, YOU MORON?
DON'T MAKE ME TELL YOU THE SAME THING OVER AND OVER.
C'MON.

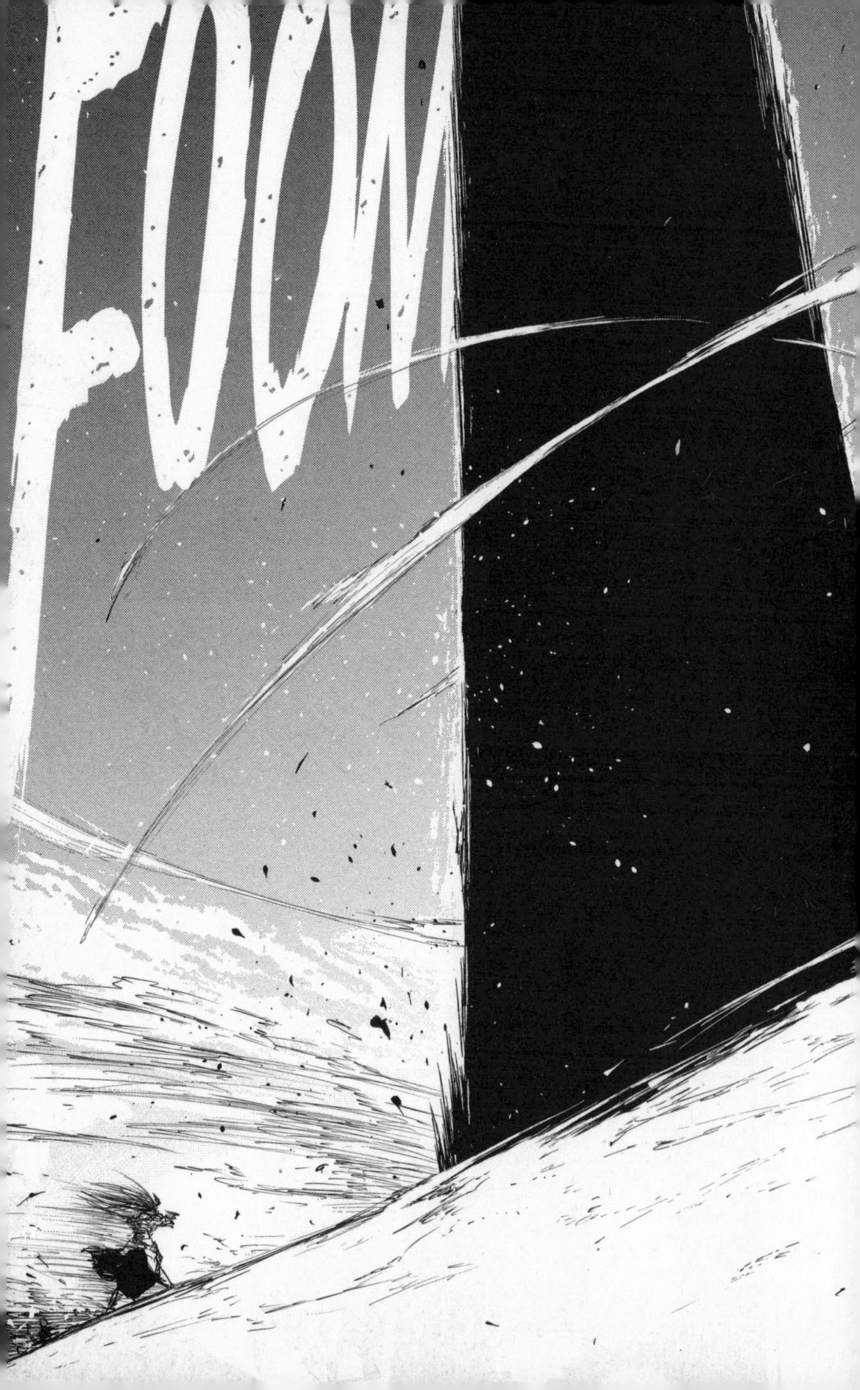
FOOM

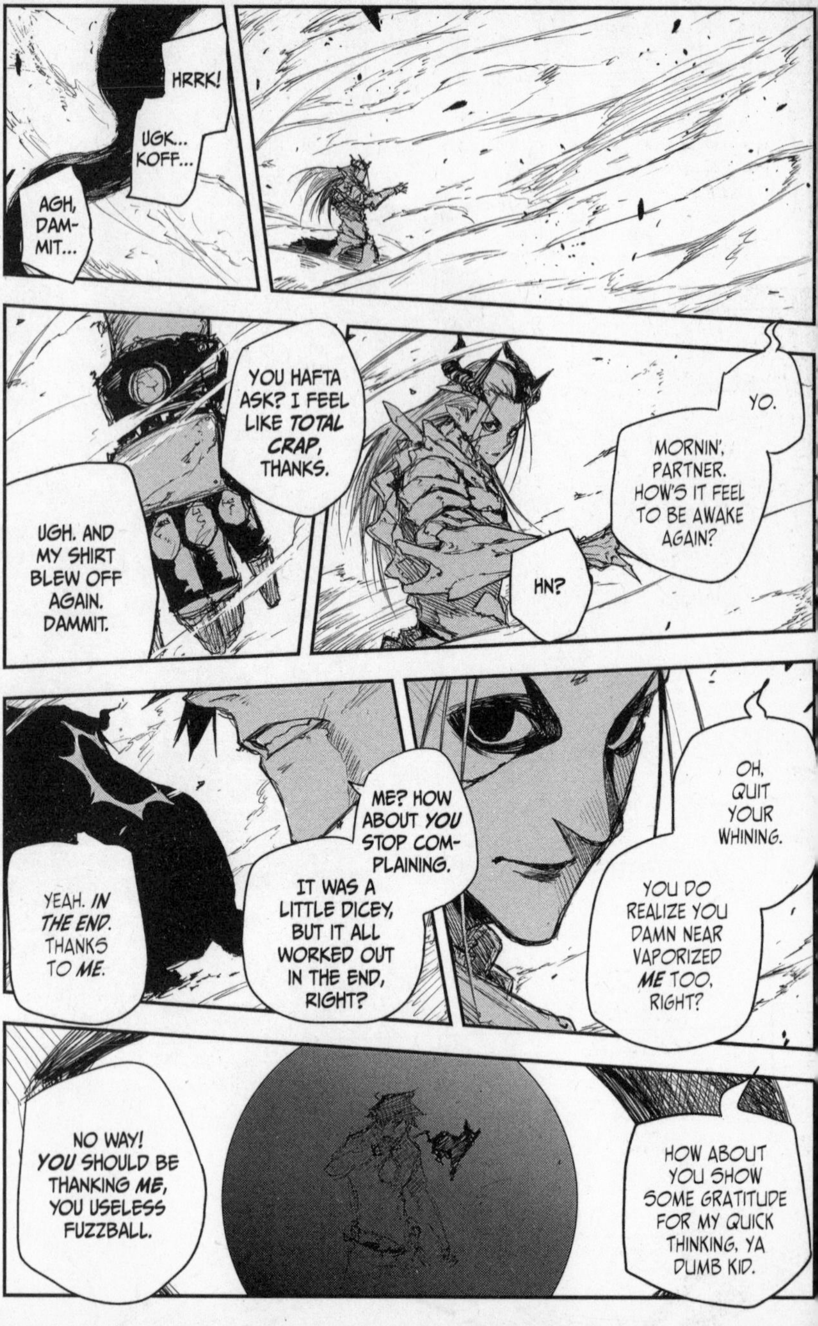
HRRK!
UGK... KOFF...
AGH, DAM-MIT...
YO.
MORNIN', PARTNER. HOW'S IT FEEL TO BE AWAKE AGAIN?
HN?
YOU HAFTA ASK? I FEEL LIKE *TOTAL CRAP*, THANKS.
UGH. AND MY SHIRT BLEW OFF AGAIN. DAMMIT.
OH, QUIT YOUR WHINING.
YOU DO REALIZE YOU DAMN NEAR VAPORIZED *ME* TOO, RIGHT?
ME? HOW ABOUT *YOU* STOP COM-PLAINING.
IT WAS A LITTLE DICEY, BUT IT ALL WORKED OUT IN THE END, RIGHT?
YEAH. *IN THE END*. THANKS TO *ME*.
HOW ABOUT YOU SHOW SOME GRATITUDE FOR MY QUICK THINKING, YA DUMB KID.
NO WAY! *YOU* SHOULD BE THANKING *ME*, YOU USELESS FUZZBALL.

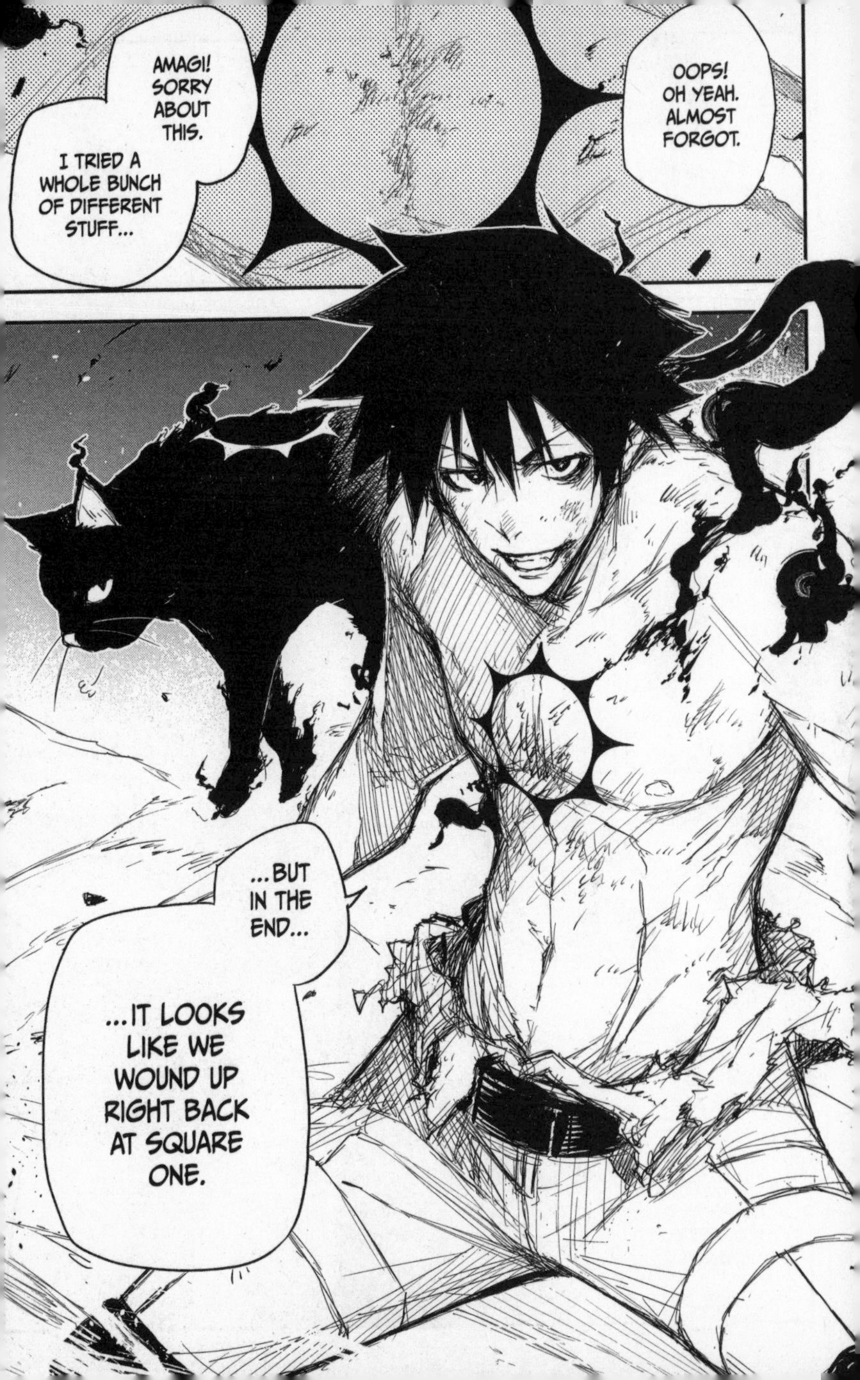
OOPS! OH YEAH. ALMOST FORGOT.
AMAGI! SORRY ABOUT THIS.
I TRIED A WHOLE BUNCH OF DIFFERENT STUFF...
...BUT IN THE END...
...IT LOOKS LIKE WE WOUND UP RIGHT BACK AT SQUARE ONE.

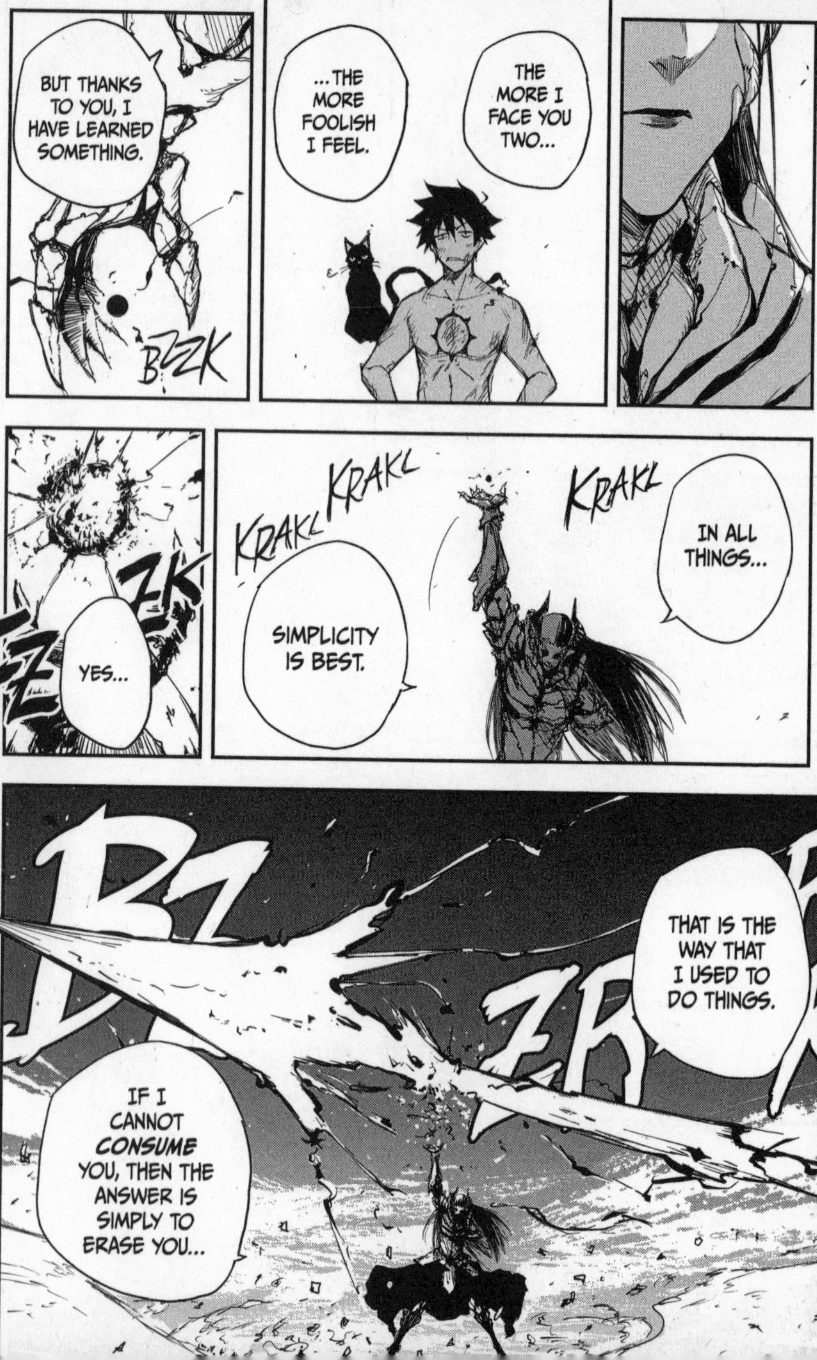
THE MORE I FACE YOU TWO...
...THE MORE FOOLISH I FEEL.
BUT THANKS TO YOU, I HAVE LEARNED SOMETHING.
BZZK
IN ALL THINGS...
KRAKL
KRAKL
KRAKL
SIMPLICITY IS BEST.
FZZK
YES...
THAT IS THE WAY THAT I USED TO DO THINGS.
IF I CANNOT ***CONSUME*** YOU, THEN THE ANSWER IS SIMPLY TO ERASE YOU...

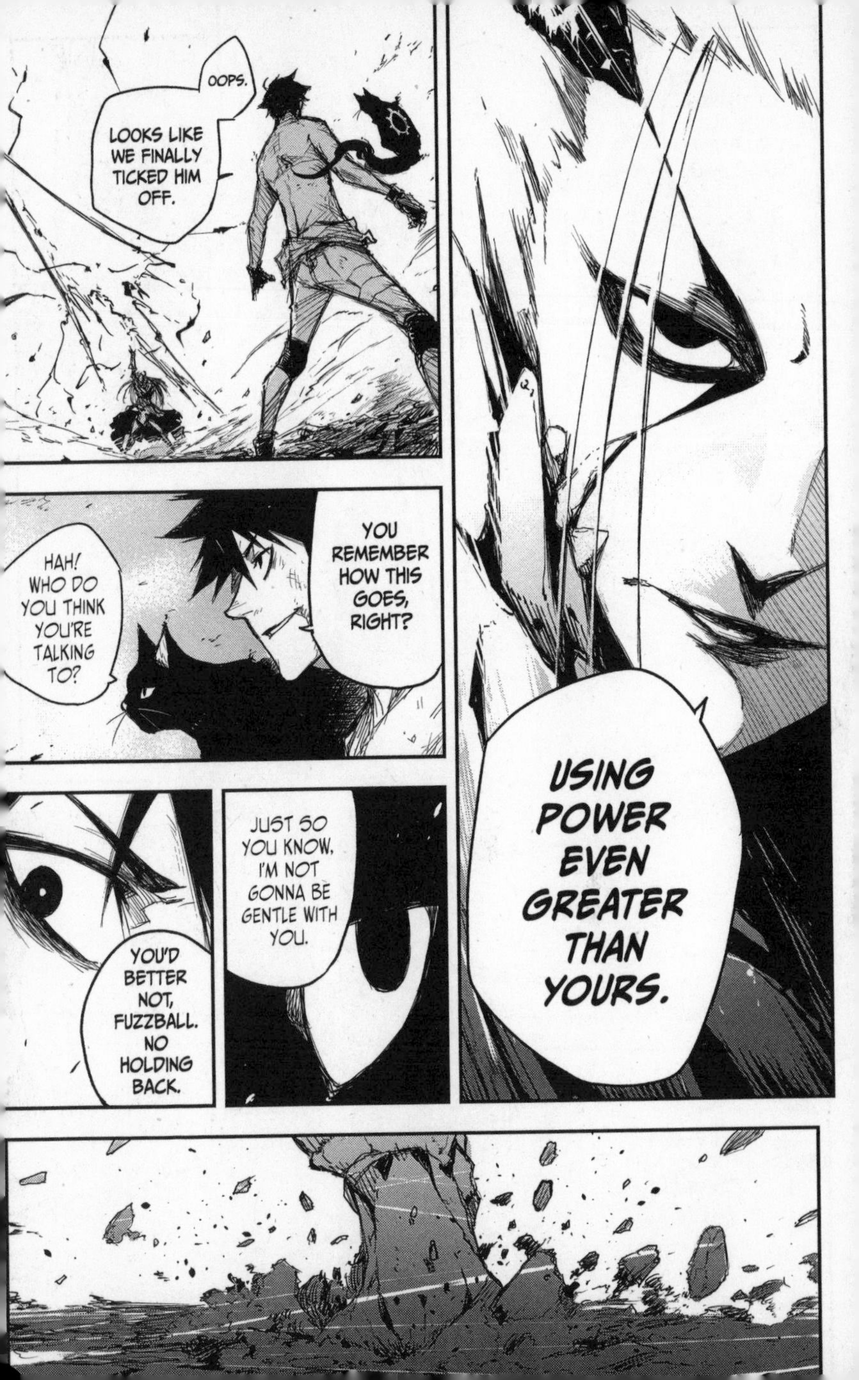
USING POWER EVEN GREATER THAN YOURS.
OOPS.
LOOKS LIKE WE FINALLY TICKED HIM OFF.
YOU REMEMBER HOW THIS GOES, RIGHT?
HAH! WHO DO YOU THINK YOU'RE TALKING TO?
JUST SO YOU KNOW, I'M NOT GONNA BE GENTLE WITH YOU.
YOU'D BETTER NOT, FUZZBALL. NO HOLDING BACK.

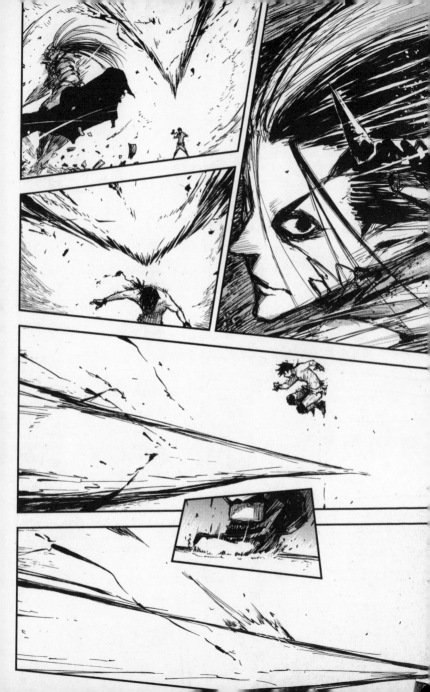

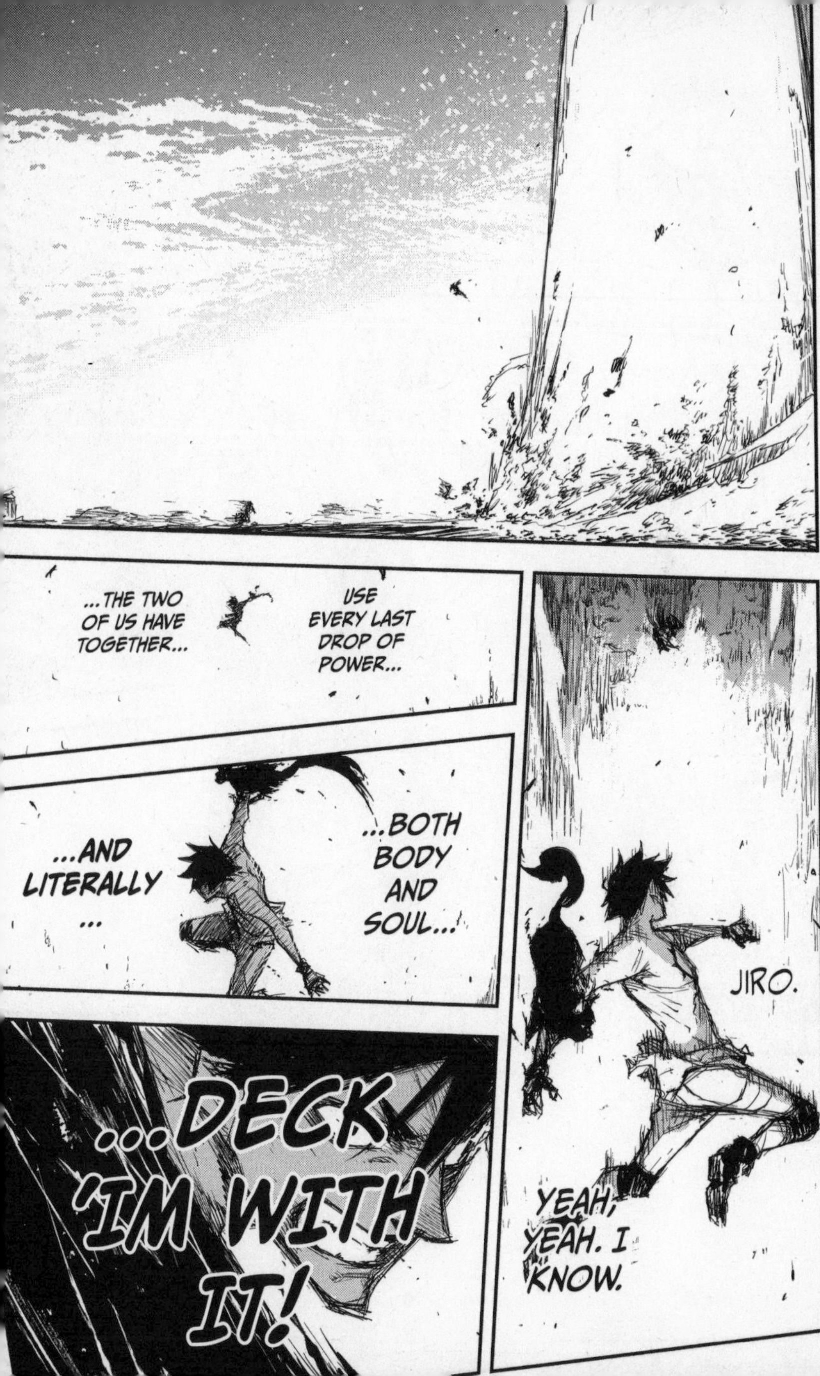
JIRO.
YEAH, YEAH. I KNOW.
USE EVERY LAST DROP OF POWER...
...THE TWO OF US HAVE TOGETHER...
...BOTH BODY AND SOUL...!
...AND LITERALLY...
...DECK 'IM WITH IT!

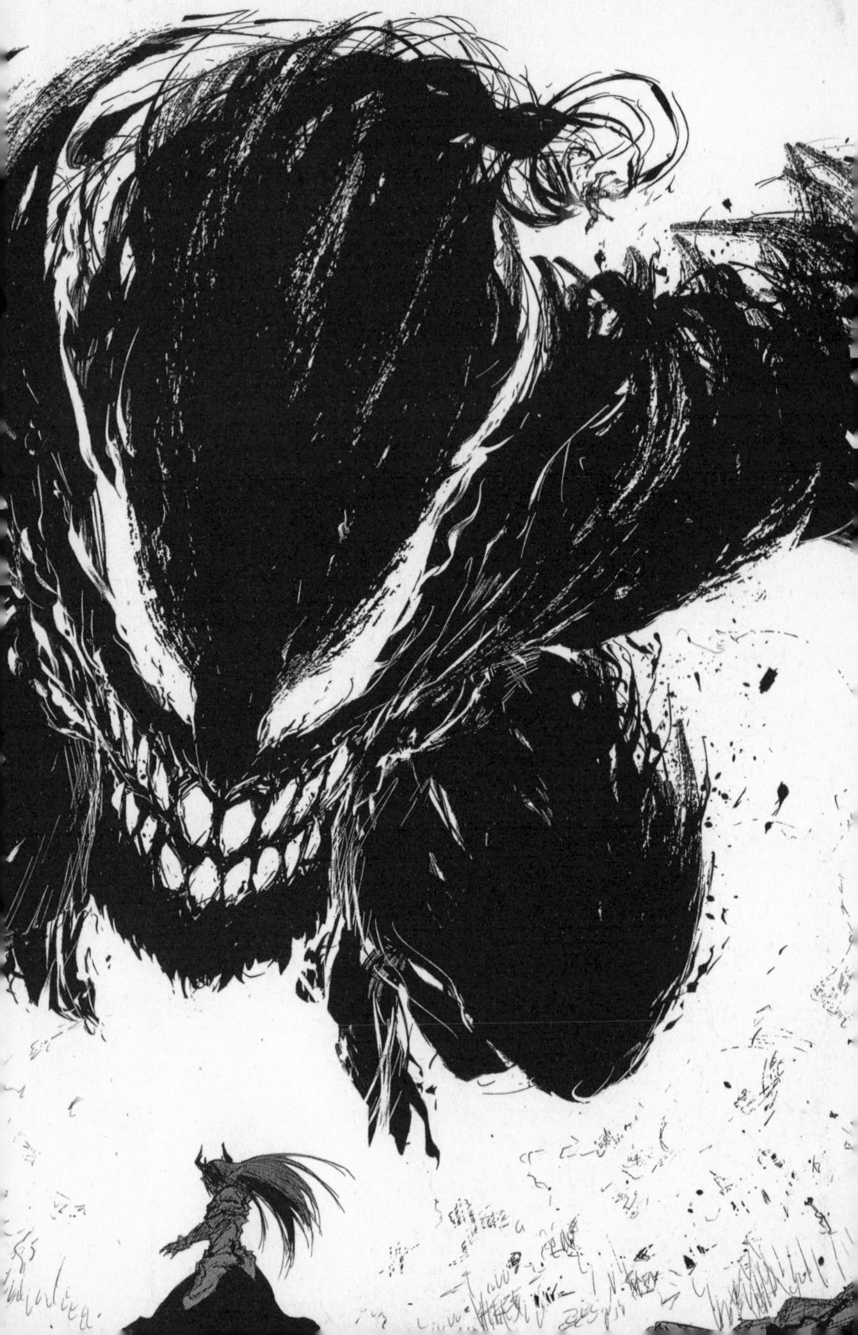

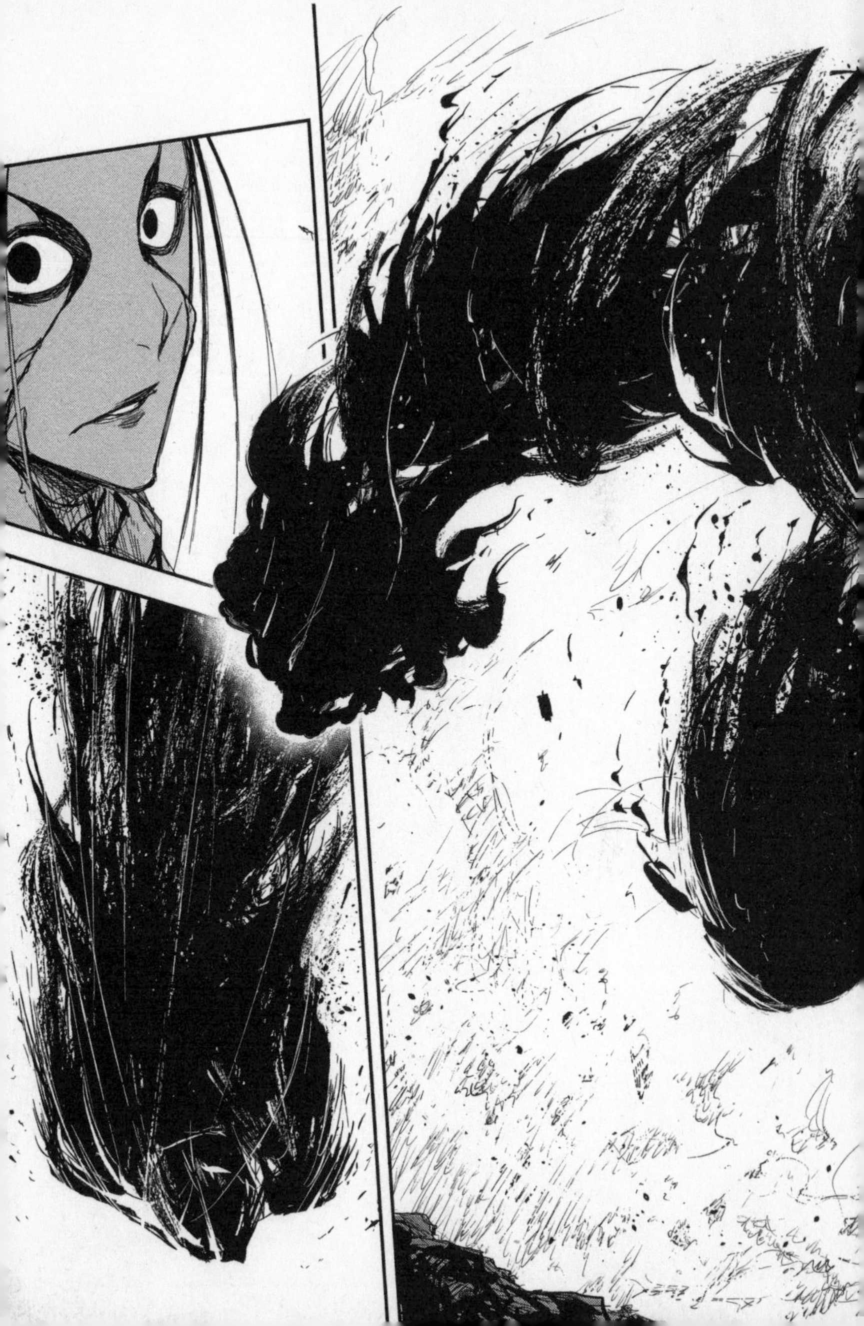

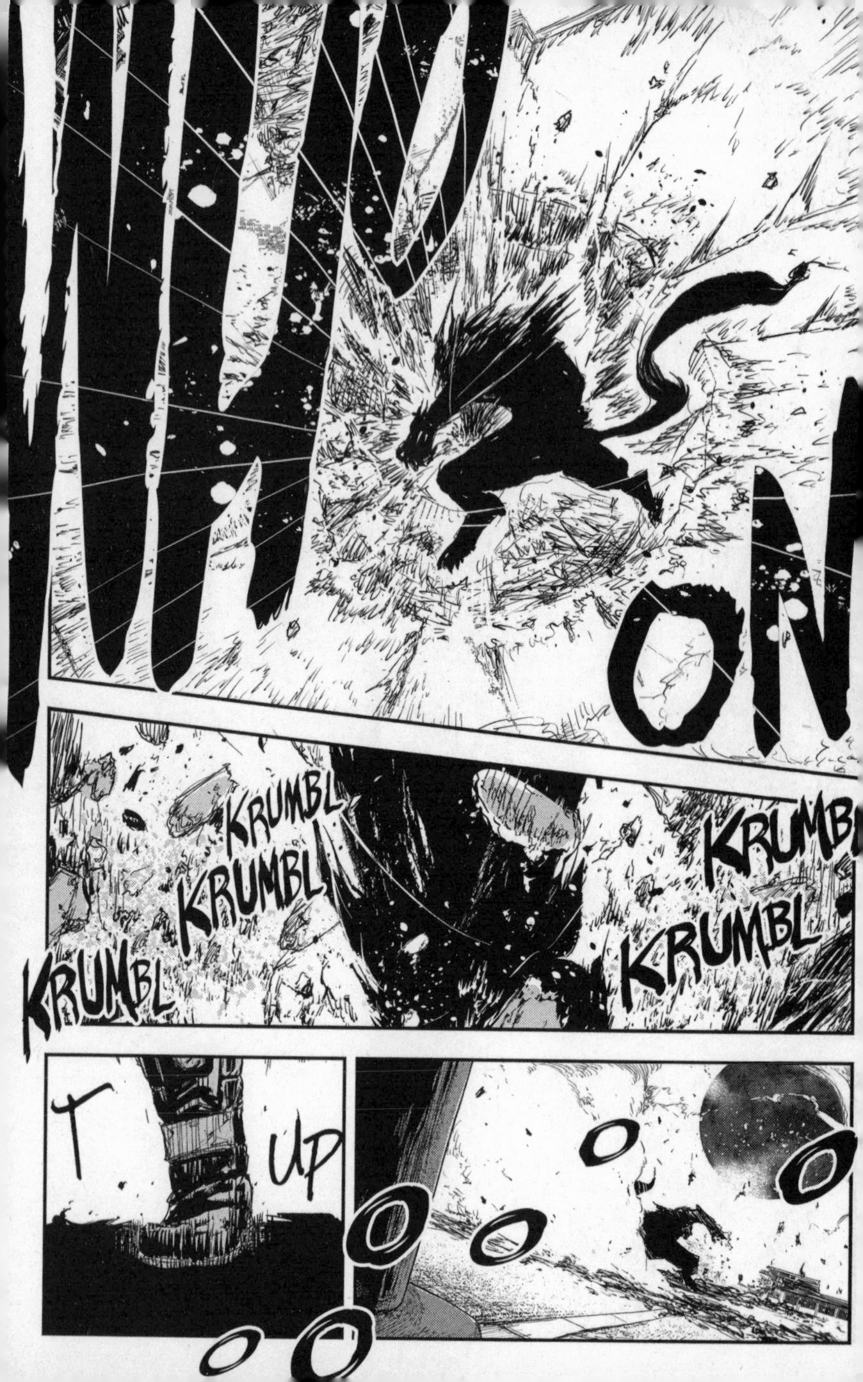
ON
KRUMB
KRUMBL
KRUMBL
KRUMBL
KRUMBL
O
O
O
O
O
O
O
T
UP

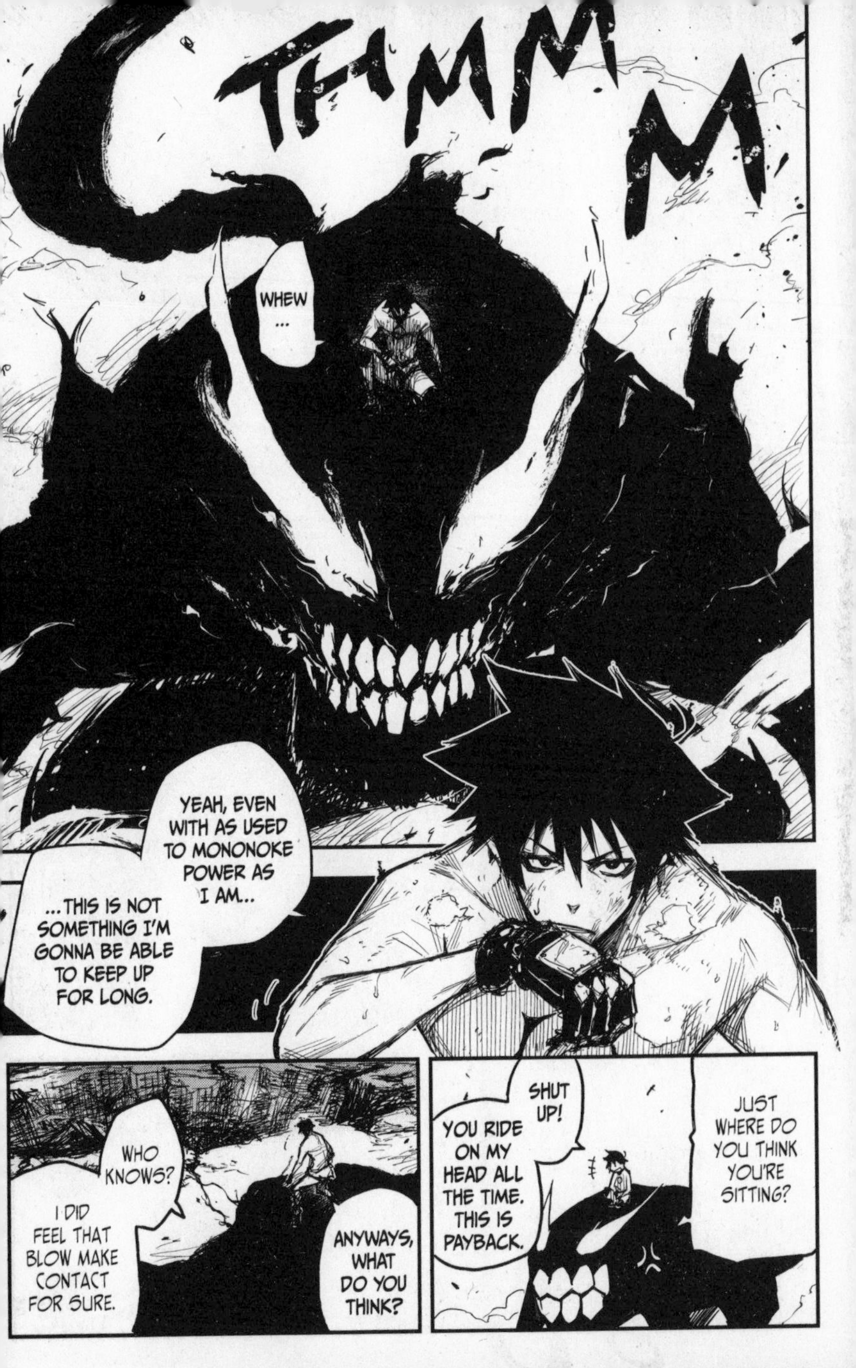
THMMM
WHEW...
YEAH, EVEN WITH AS USED TO MONONOKE POWER AS I AM...
...THIS IS NOT SOMETHING I'M GONNA BE ABLE TO KEEP UP FOR LONG.
JUST WHERE DO YOU THINK YOU'RE SITTING?
SHUT UP!
YOU RIDE ON MY HEAD ALL THE TIME. THIS IS PAYBACK.
ANYWAYS, WHAT DO YOU THINK?
WHO KNOWS?
I DID FEEL THAT BLOW MAKE CONTACT FOR SURE.

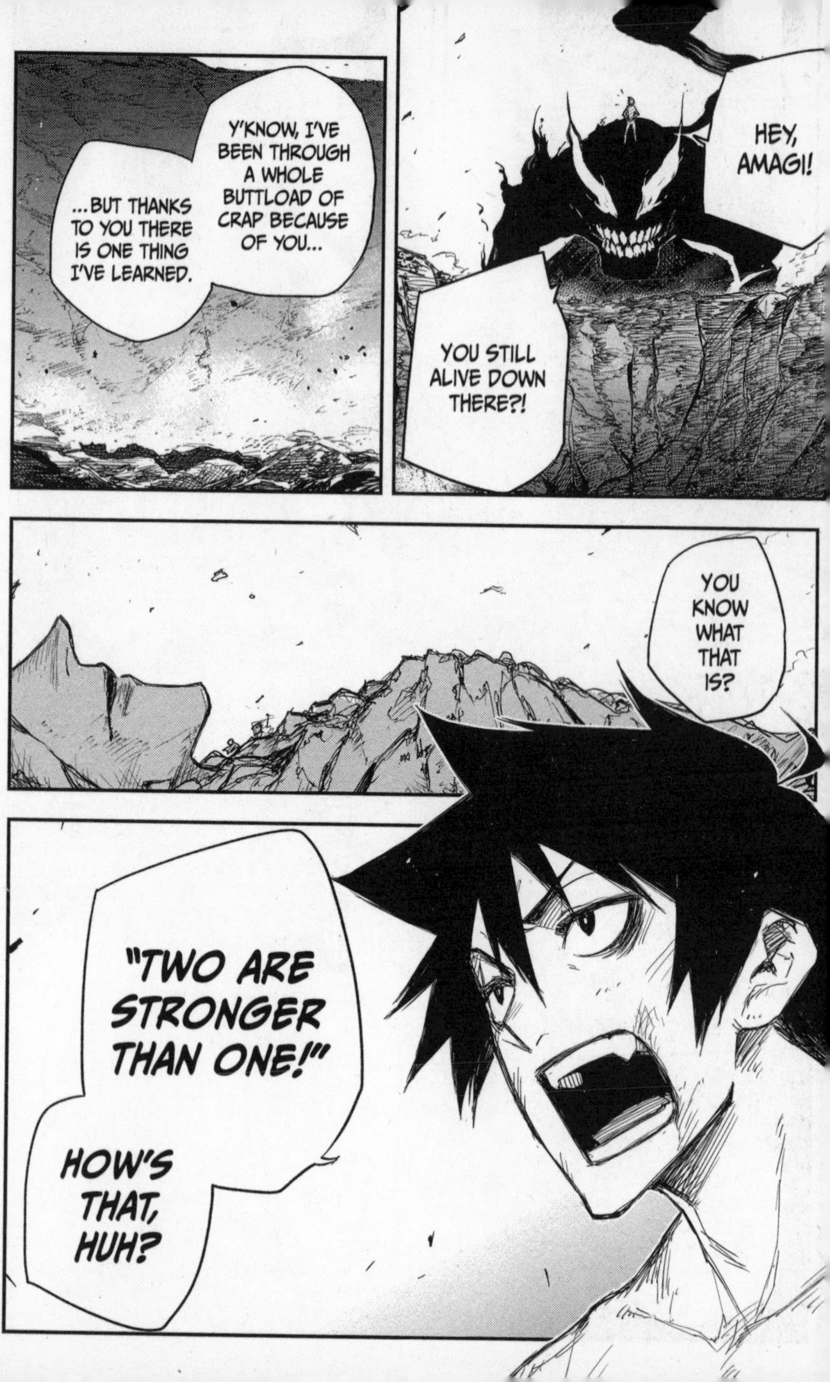
HEY, AMAGI!
YOU STILL ALIVE DOWN THERE?!
Y'KNOW, I'VE BEEN THROUGH A WHOLE BUTTLOAD OF CRAP BECAUSE OF YOU...
...BUT THANKS TO YOU THERE IS ONE THING I'VE LEARNED.
YOU KNOW WHAT THAT IS?
"TWO ARE STRONGER THAN ONE!"
HOW'S THAT, HUH?

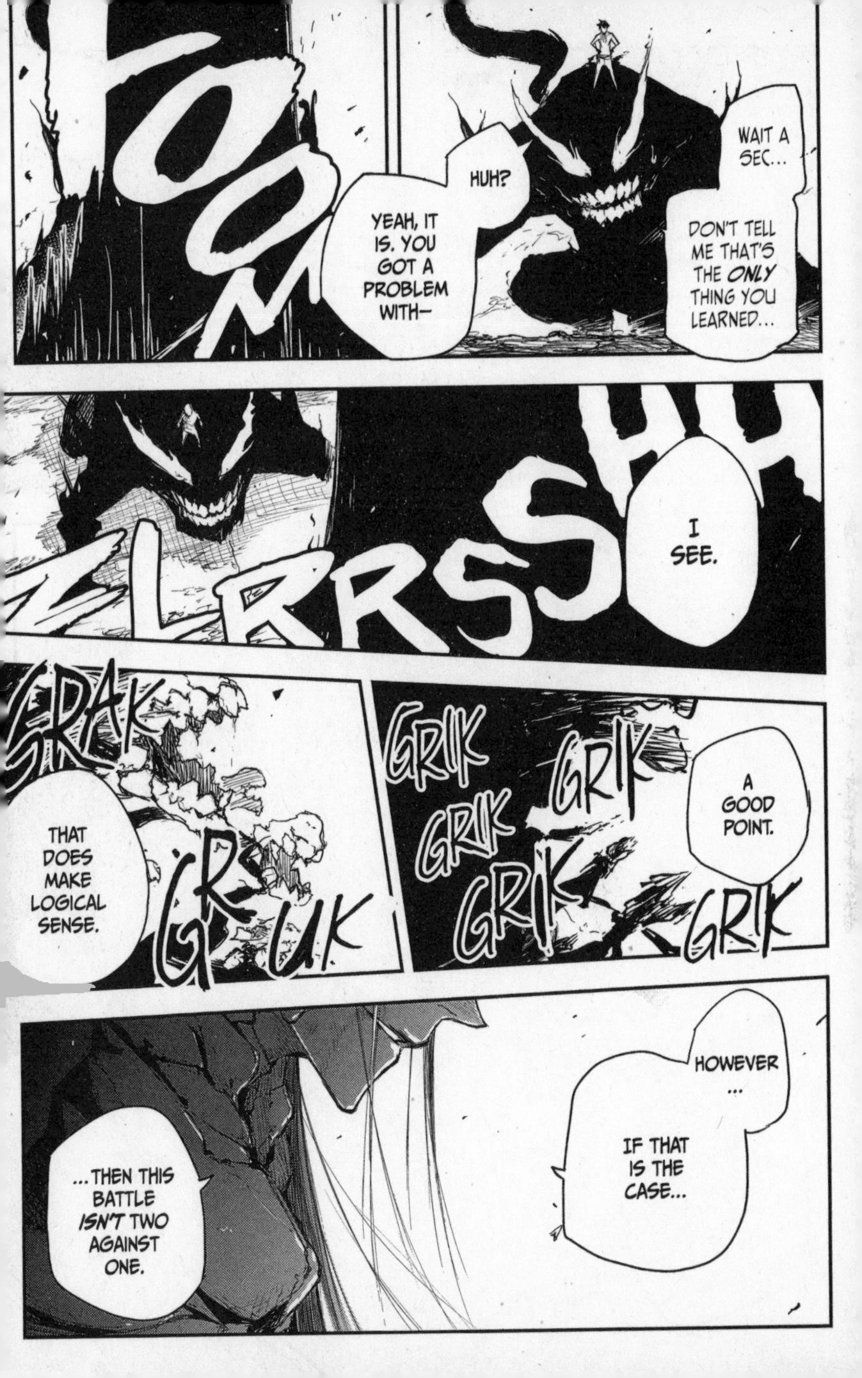
WAIT A SEC...
DON'T TELL ME THAT'S THE *ONLY* THING YOU LEARNED...
HUH?
YEAH, IT IS. YOU GOT A PROBLEM WITH—
I SEE.
GRIK GRIK GRIK GRIK GRIK
A GOOD POINT.
GRAK
THAT DOES MAKE LOGICAL SENSE.
HOWEVER...
IF THAT IS THE CASE...
...THEN THIS BATTLE *ISN'T* TWO AGAINST ONE.

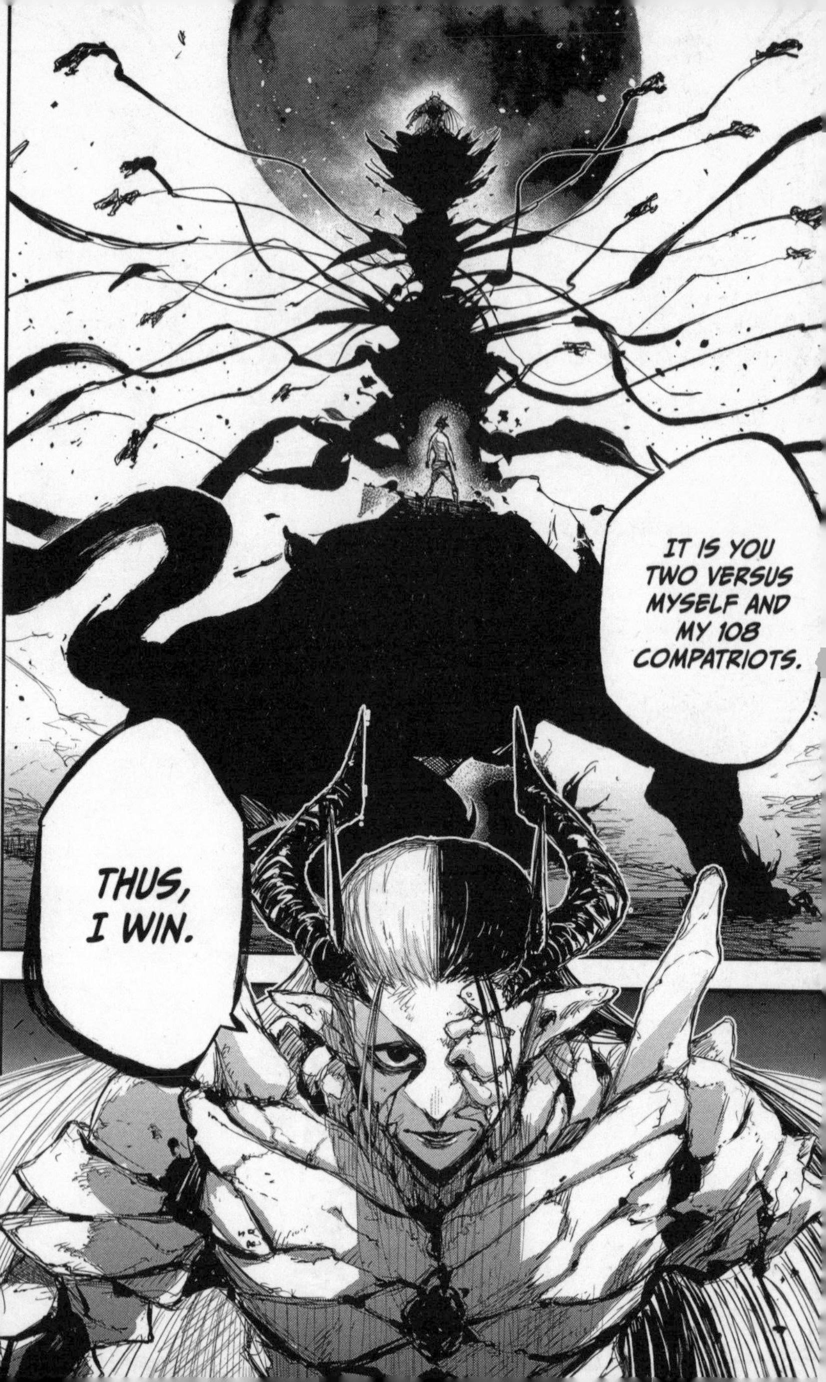
IT IS YOU TWO VERSUS MYSELF AND MY 108 COMPATRIOTS.
THUS, I WIN.

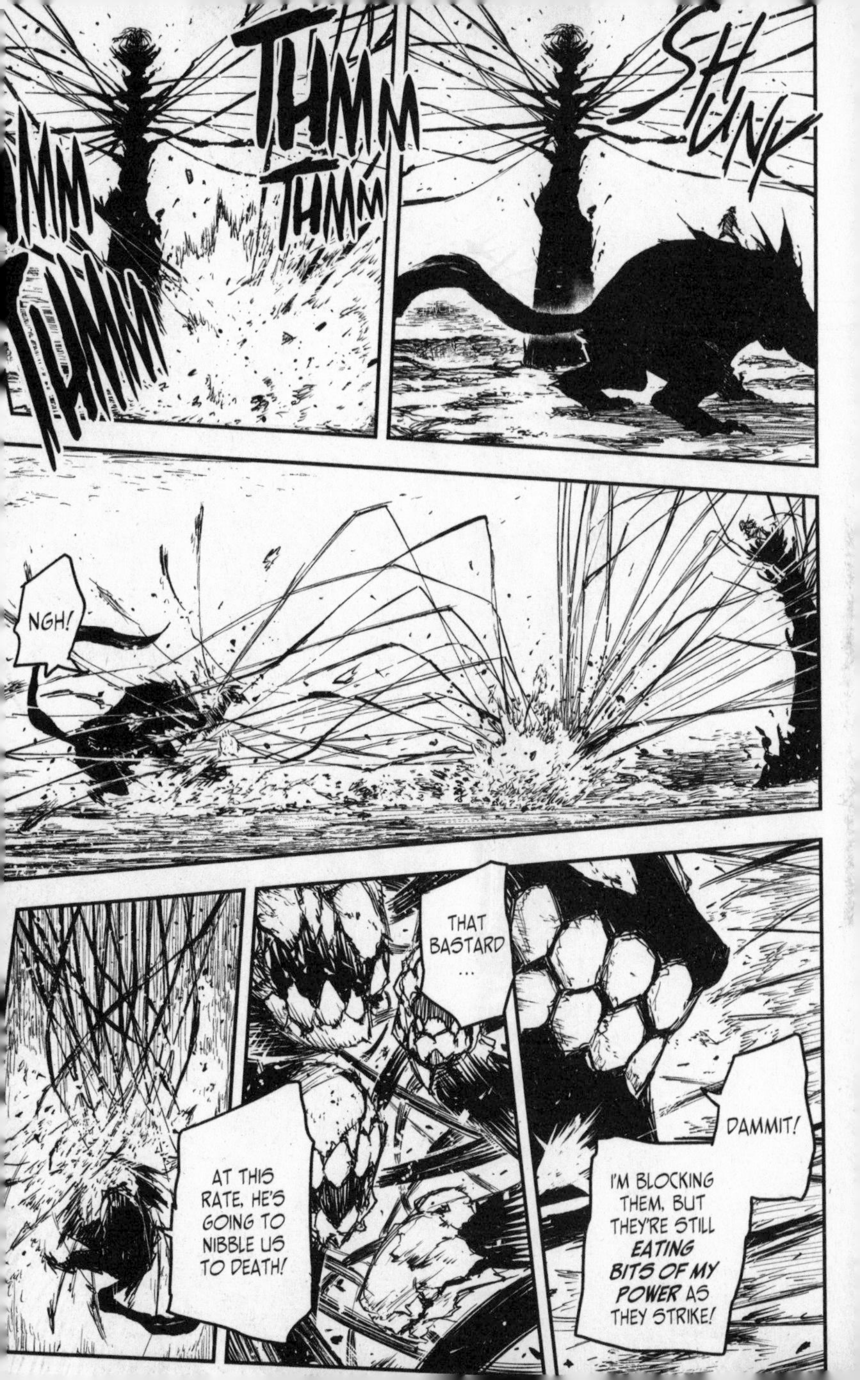
SHUNK
THMM
THMM
NGH!
DAMMIT!
I'M BLOCKING THEM, BUT THEY'RE STILL *EATING BITS OF MY POWER* AS THEY STRIKE!
THAT BASTARD ...
AT THIS RATE, HE'S GOING TO NIBBLE US TO DEATH!

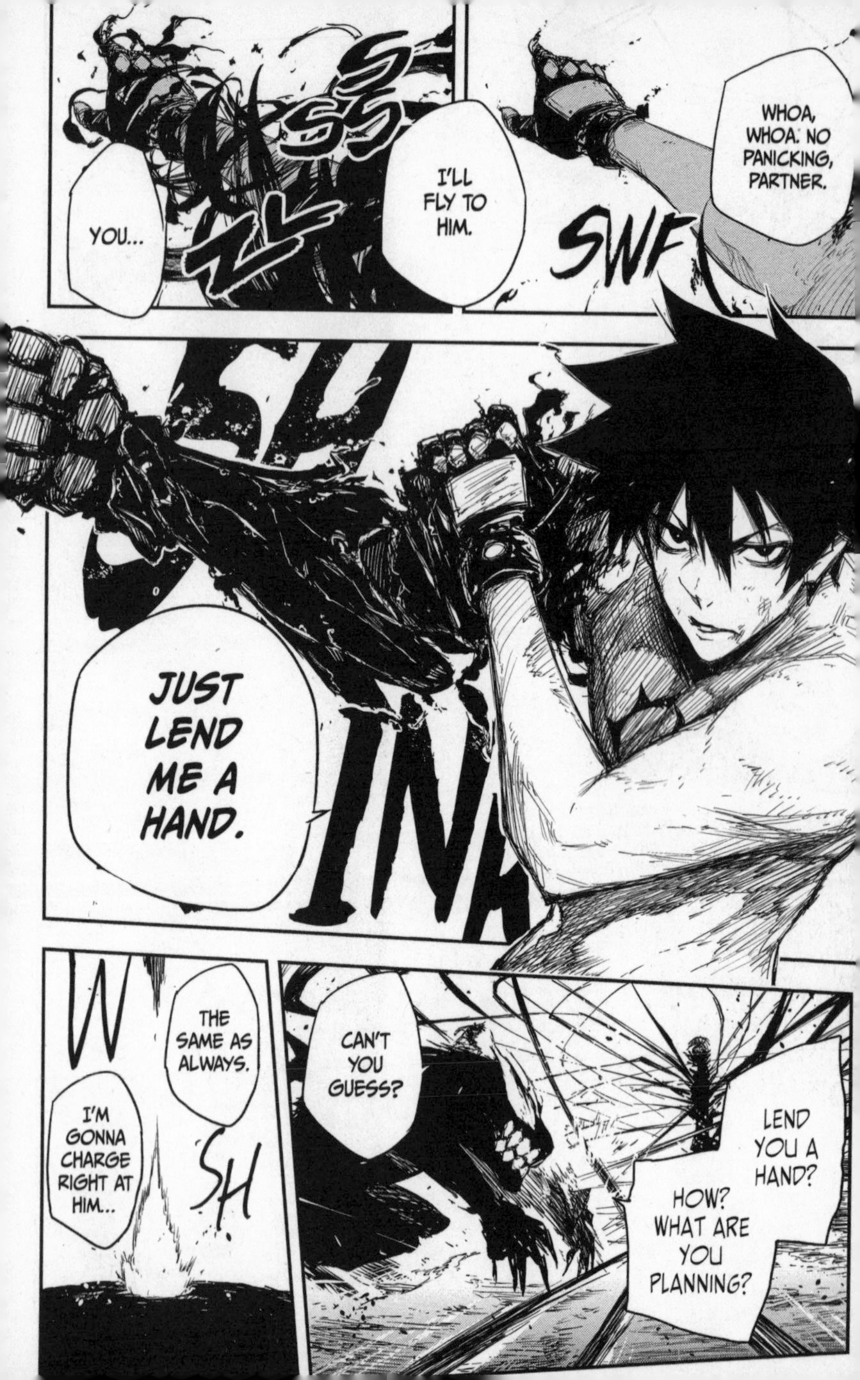
WHOA, WHOA. NO PANICKING, PARTNER.
SWF
I'LL FLY TO HIM.
YOU...
JUST LEND ME A HAND.
LEND YOU A HAND?
HOW? WHAT ARE YOU PLANNING?
CAN'T YOU GUESS?
THE SAME AS ALWAYS.
I'M GONNA CHARGE RIGHT AT HIM...

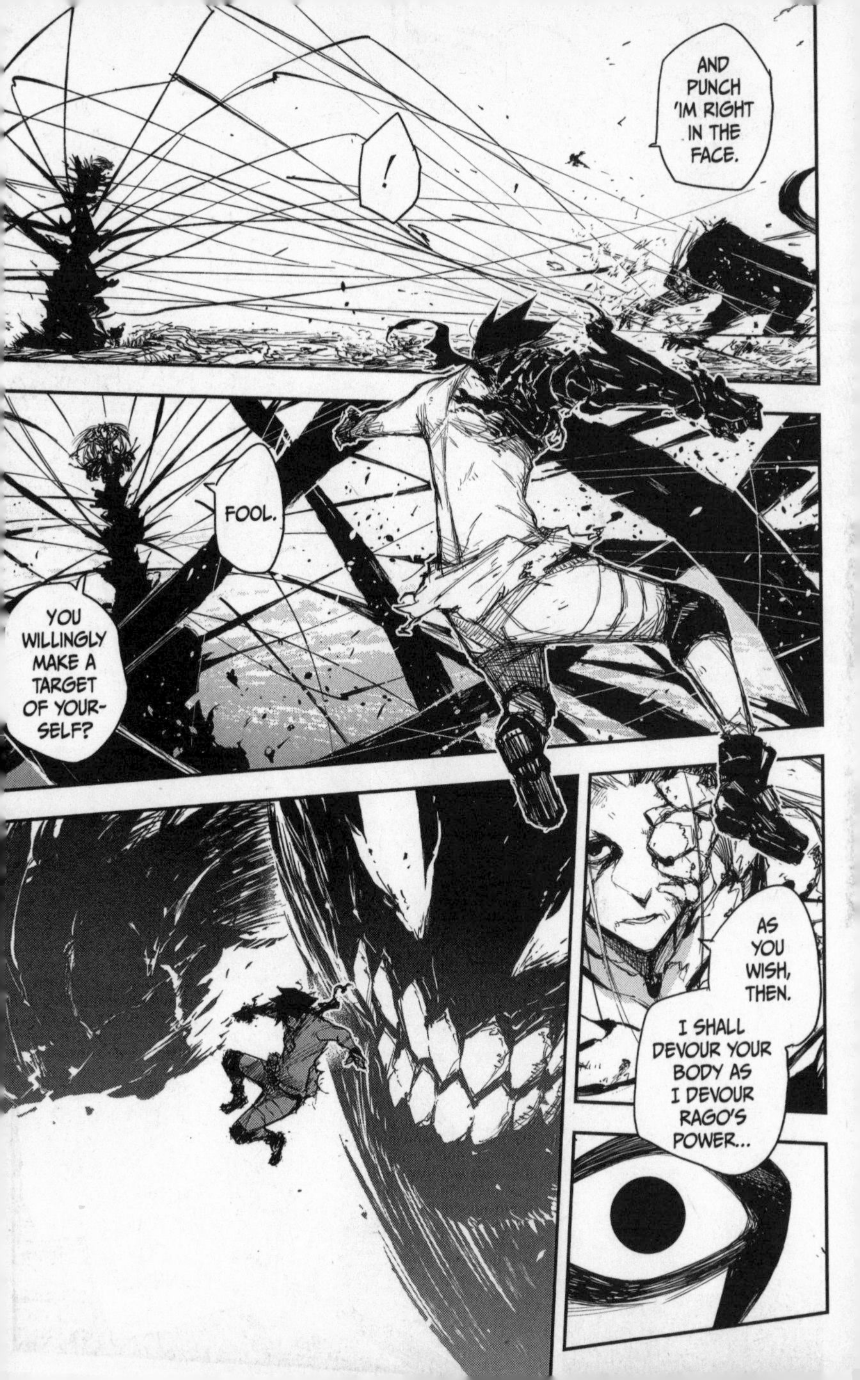
AND PUNCH 'IM RIGHT IN THE FACE.
!
FOOL.
YOU WILLINGLY MAKE A TARGET OF YOUR-SELF?
AS YOU WISH, THEN.
I SHALL DEVOUR YOUR BODY AS I DEVOUR RAGO'S POWER...

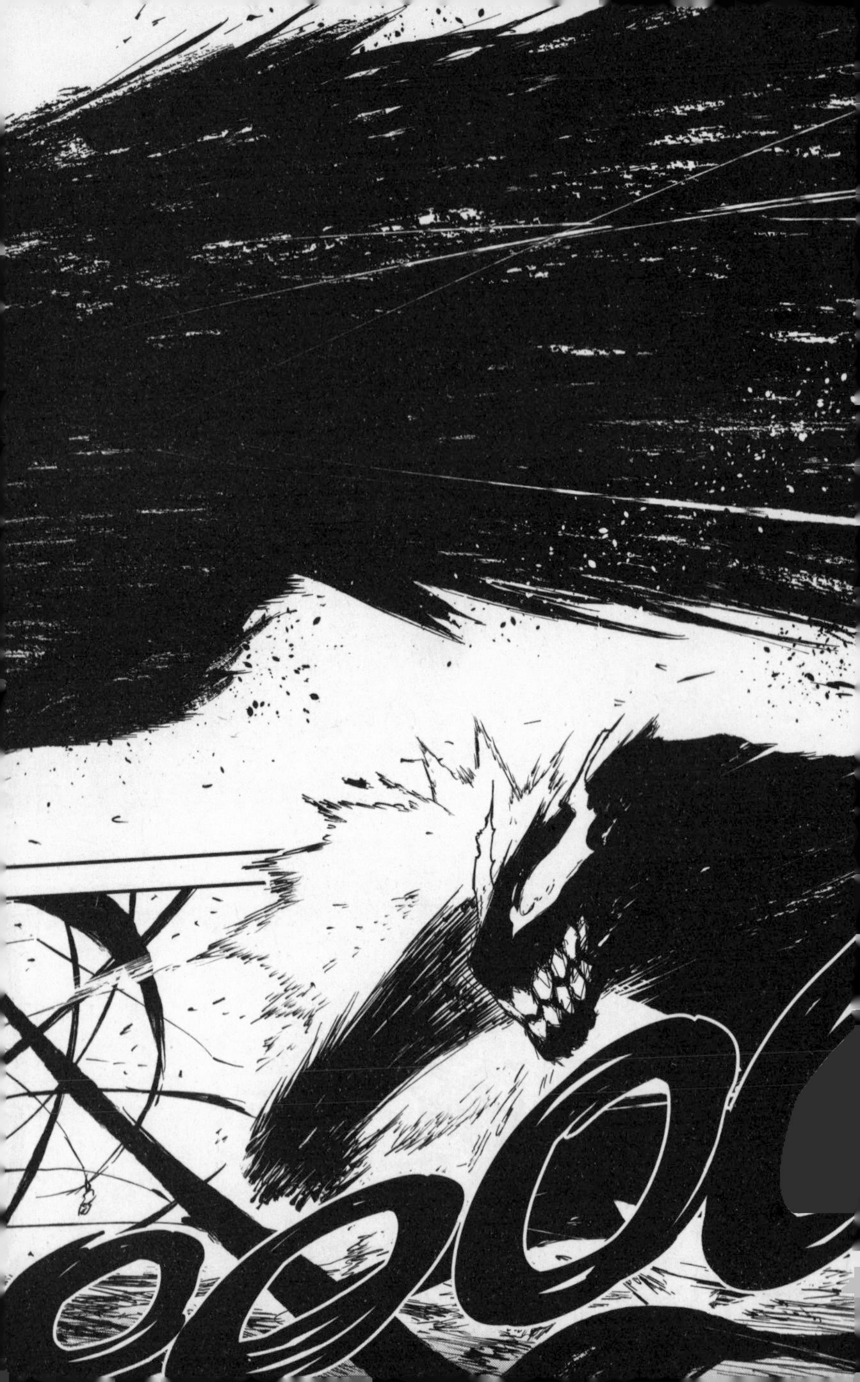

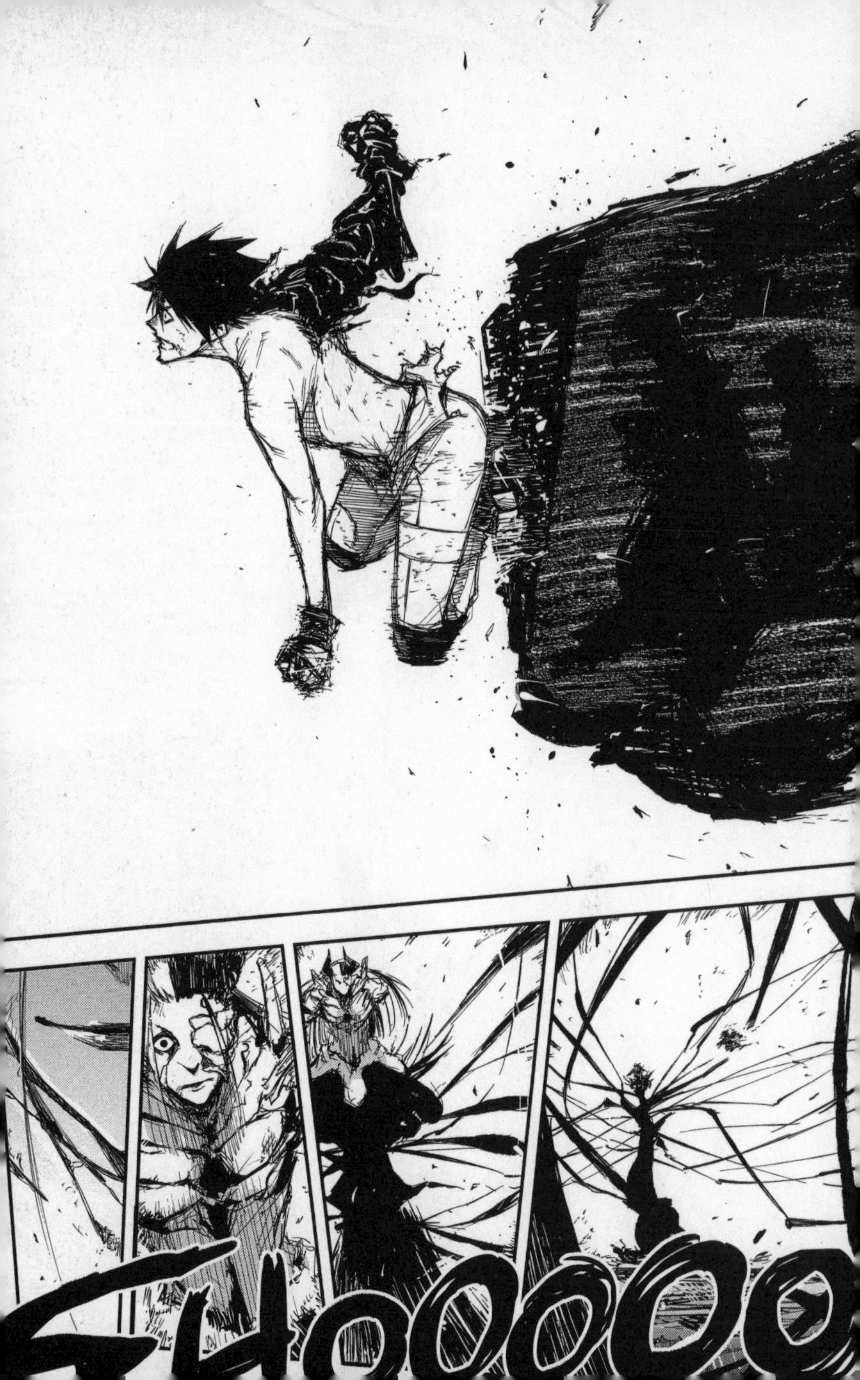
SHOOOOOO

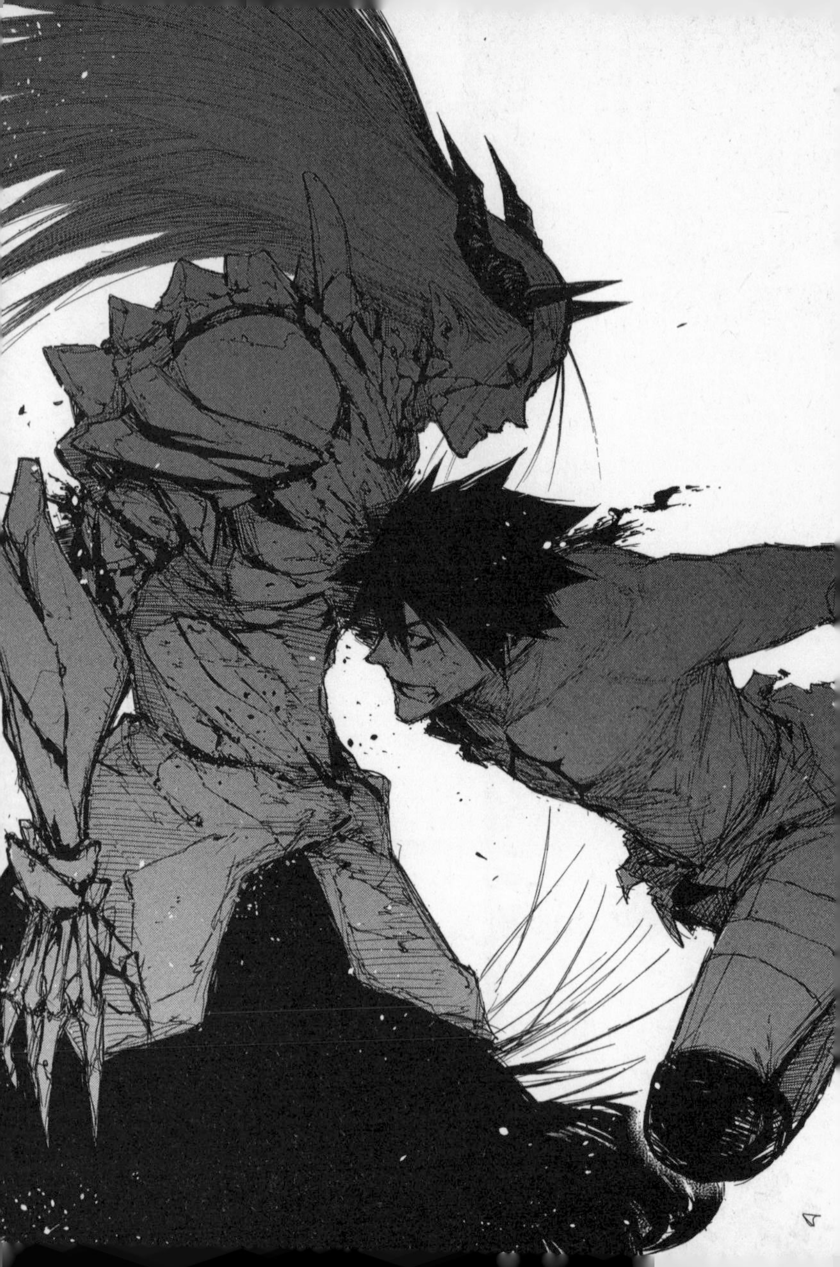

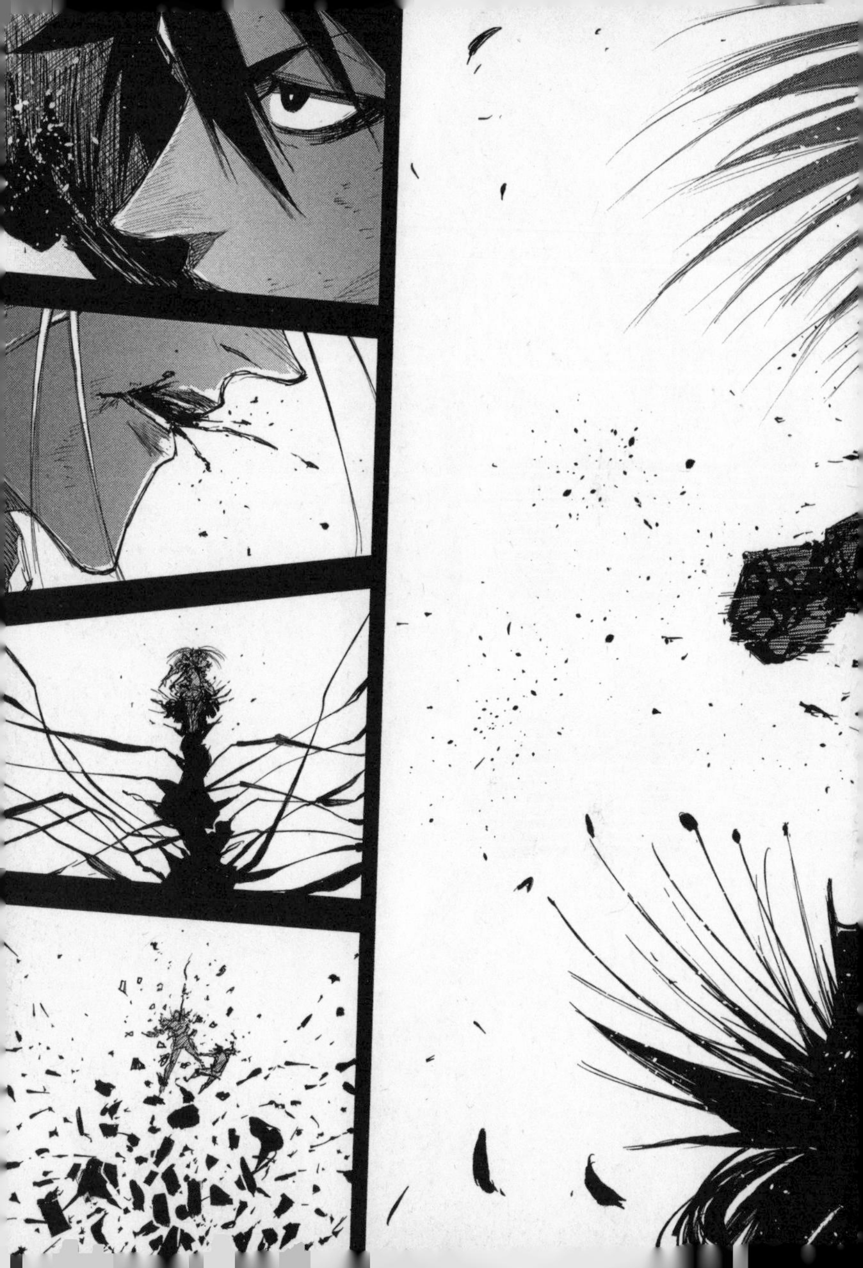

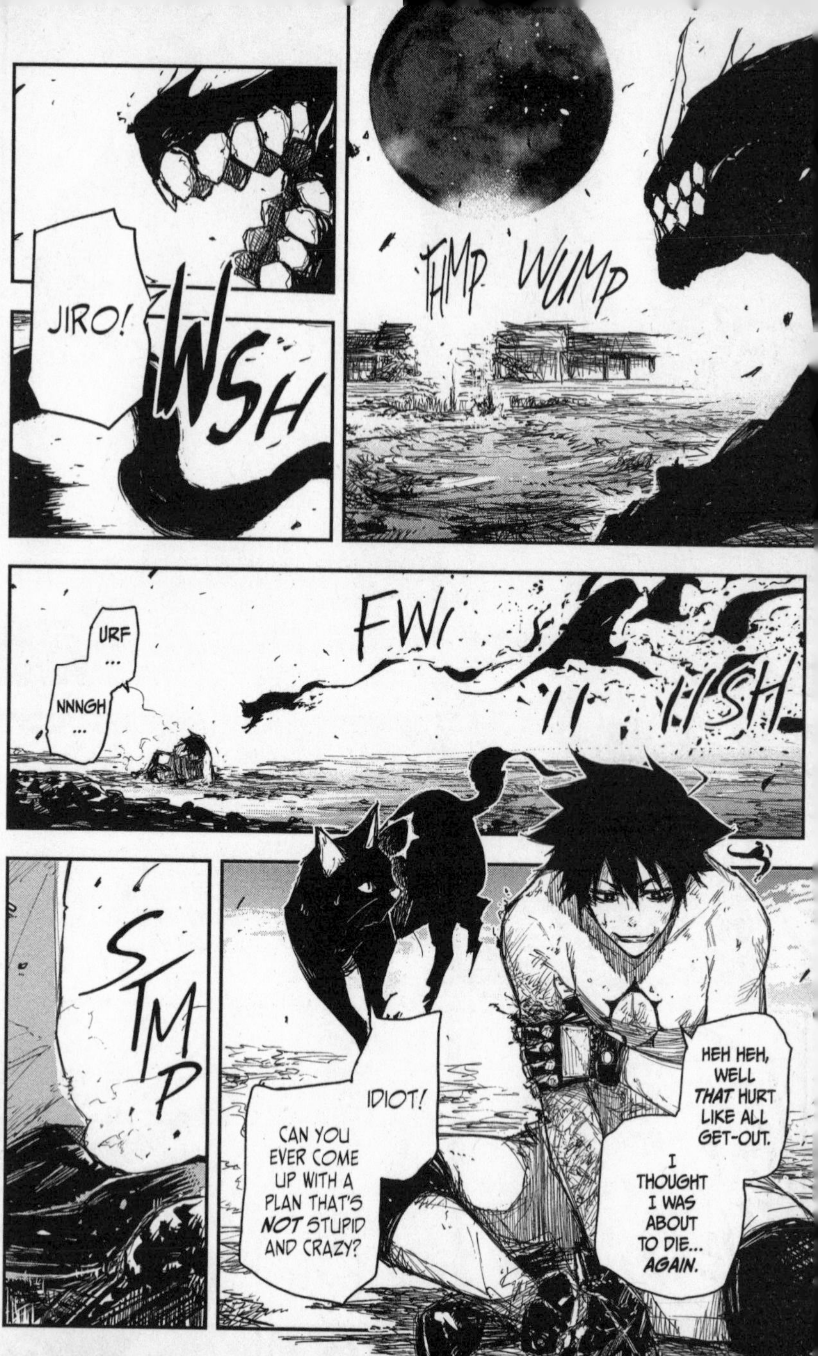
THMP WUMP
JIRO!
WSH
URF ...
NNNGH ...
FWI ISH
HEH HEH, WELL *THAT* HURT LIKE ALL GET-OUT.
I THOUGHT I WAS ABOUT TO DIE... *AGAIN*.
IDIOT!
CAN YOU EVER COME UP WITH A PLAN THAT'S *NOT* STUPID AND CRAZY?
STMP

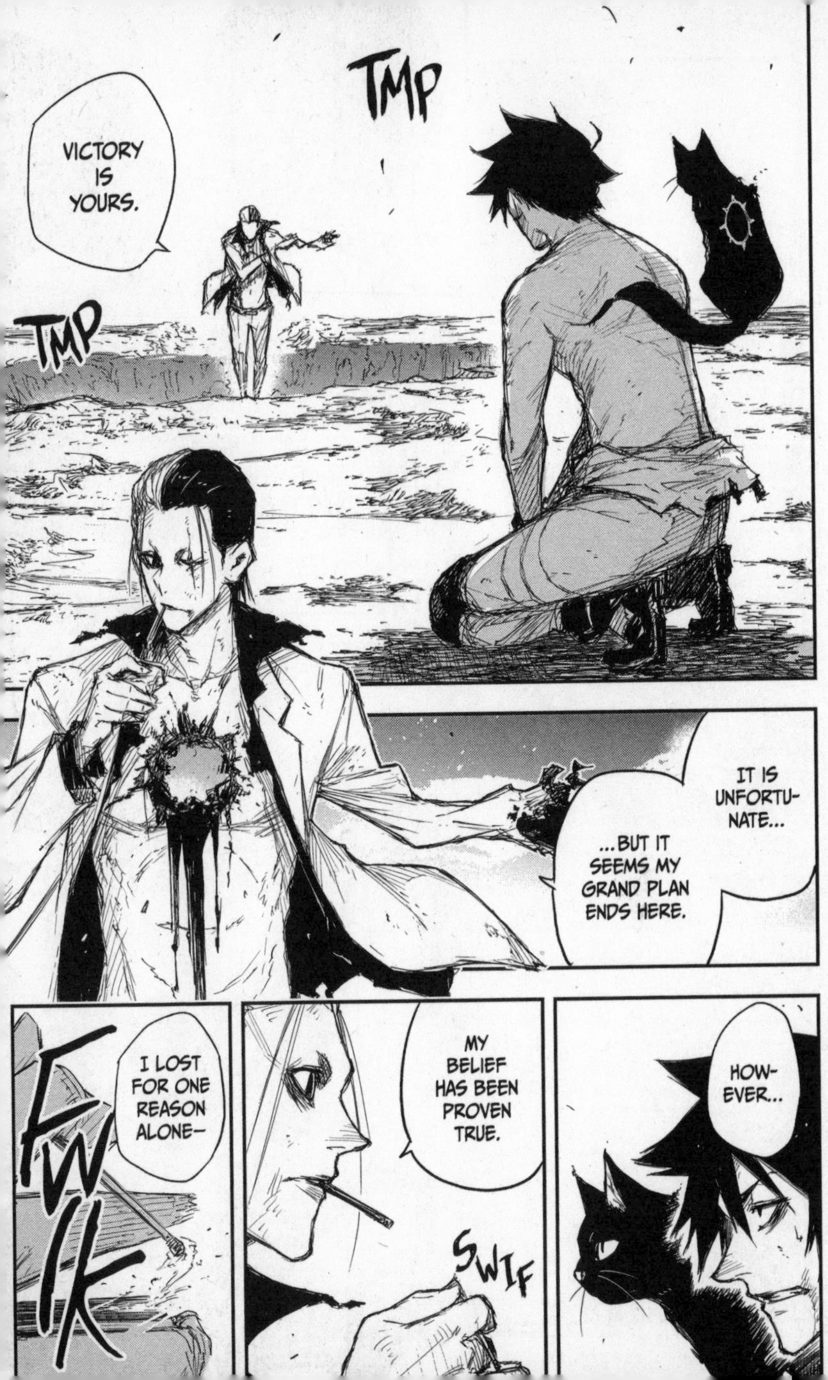
TMP
VICTORY IS YOURS.
TMP
IT IS UNFORTUNATE...
...BUT IT SEEMS MY GRAND PLAN ENDS HERE.
HOW-EVER...
MY BELIEF HAS BEEN PROVEN TRUE.
SWIF
I LOST FOR ONE REASON ALONE—
FWIK

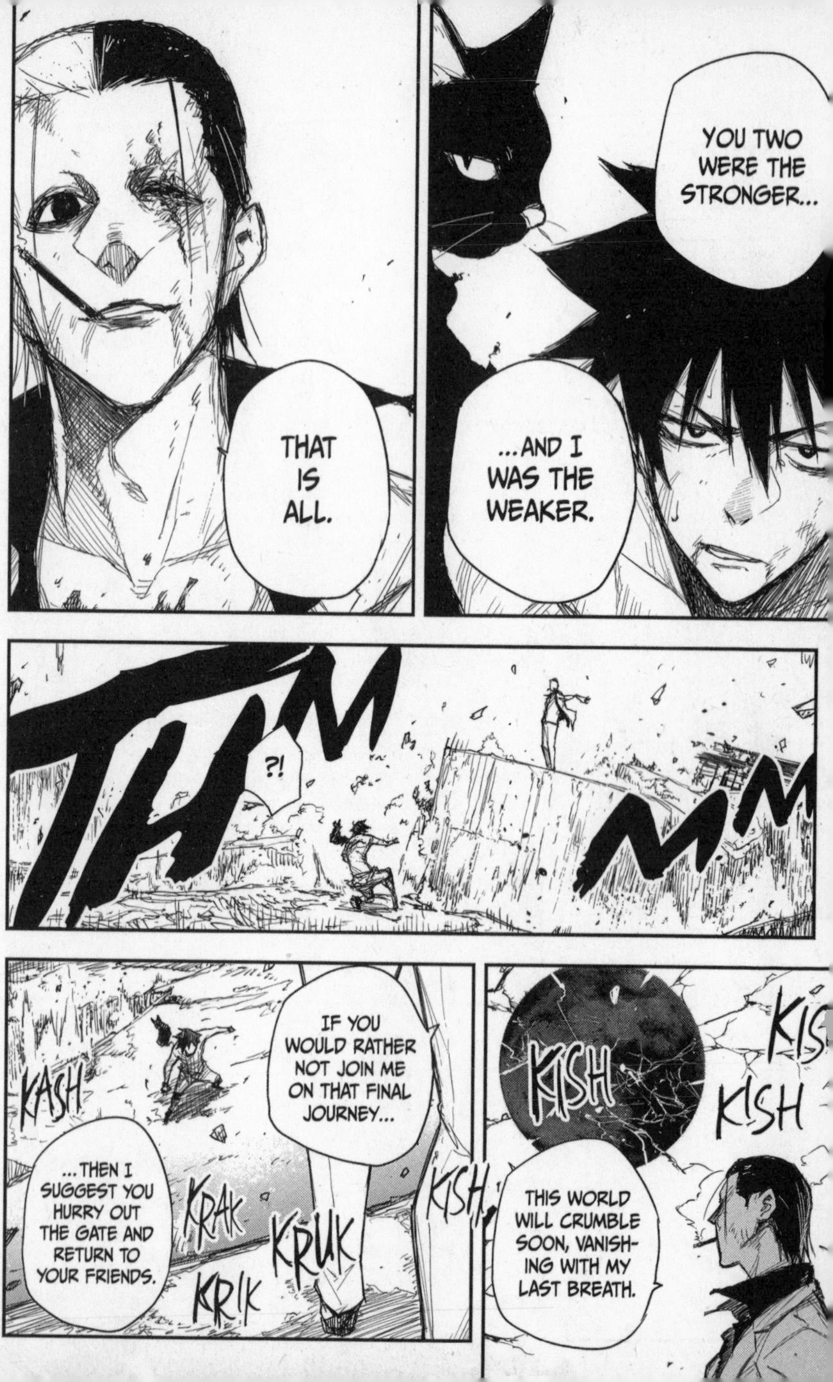
YOU TWO WERE THE STRONGER...
...AND I WAS THE WEAKER.
THAT IS ALL.
THMMM
?!
KISH
KISH
THIS WORLD WILL CRUMBLE SOON, VANISHING WITH MY LAST BREATH.
KISH
IF YOU WOULD RATHER NOT JOIN ME ON THAT FINAL JOURNEY...
...THEN I SUGGEST YOU HURRY OUT THE GATE AND RETURN TO YOUR FRIENDS.
KASH
KRAK
KRUK
KRIK

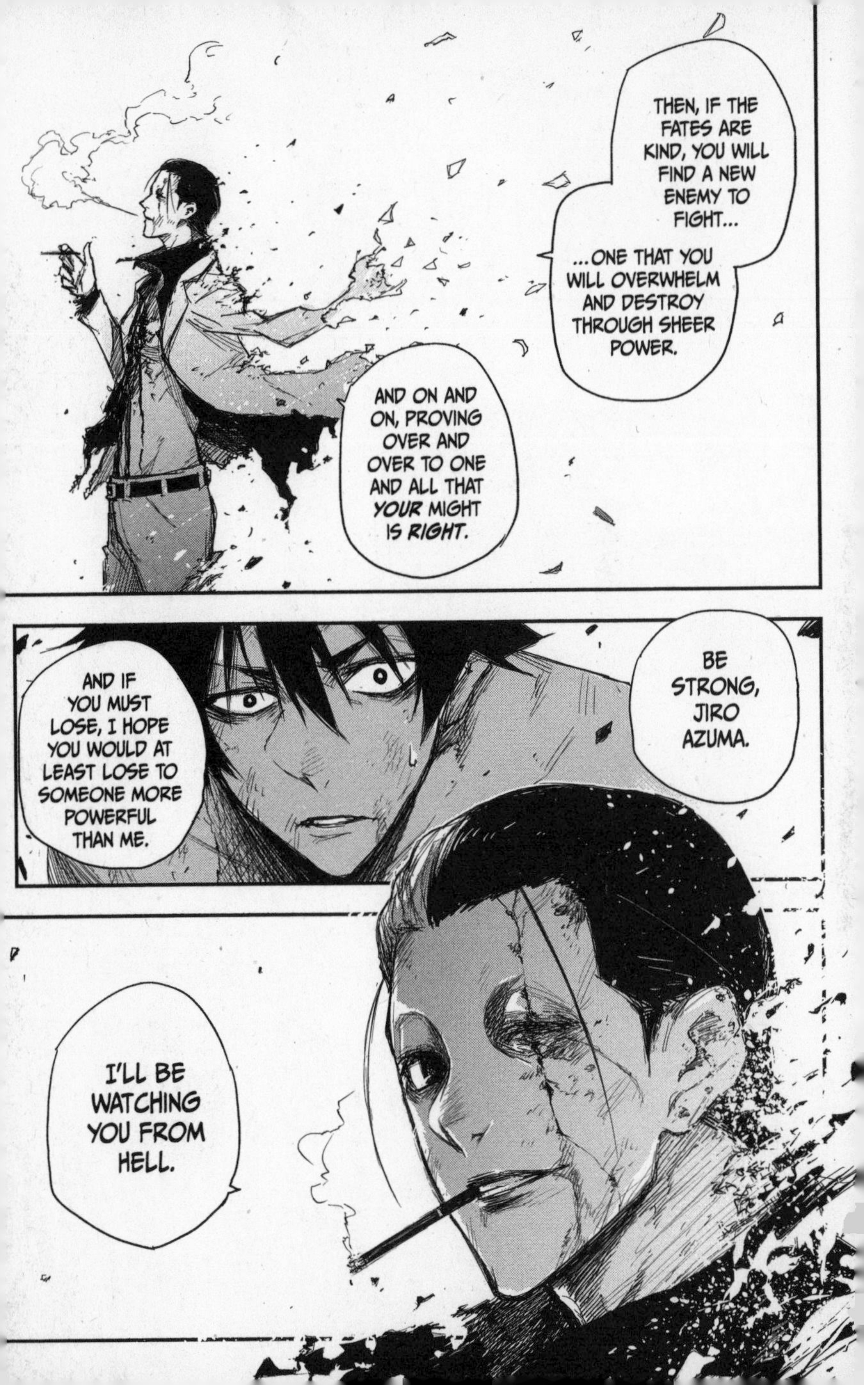
THEN, IF THE FATES ARE KIND, YOU WILL FIND A NEW ENEMY TO FIGHT...
...ONE THAT YOU WILL OVERWHELM AND DESTROY THROUGH SHEER POWER.
AND ON AND ON, PROVING OVER AND OVER TO ONE AND ALL THAT *YOUR* MIGHT IS *RIGHT*.
BE STRONG, JIRO AZUMA.
AND IF YOU MUST LOSE, I HOPE YOU WOULD AT LEAST LOSE TO SOMEONE MORE POWERFUL THAN ME.
I'LL BE WATCHING YOU FROM HELL.

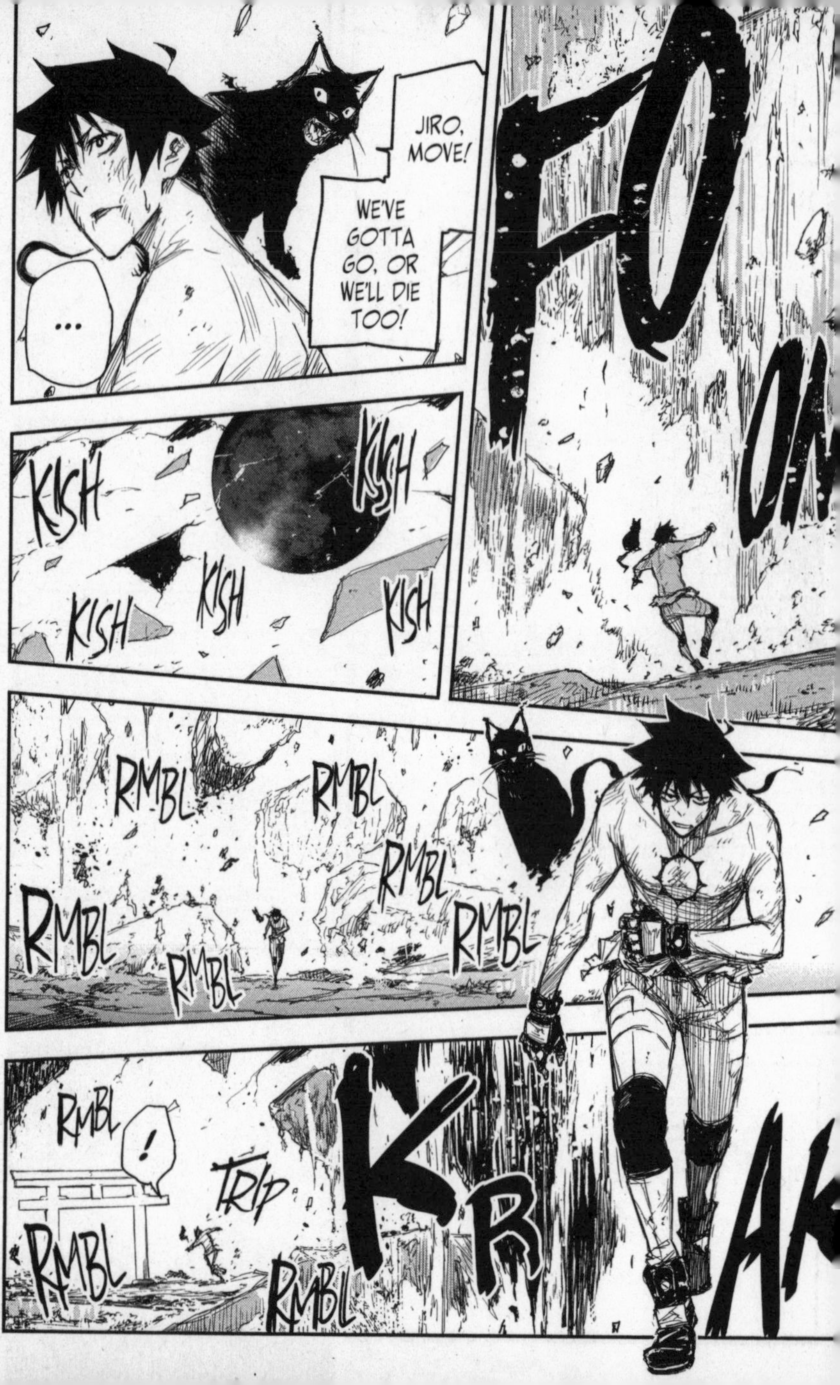
FOOM
JIRO, MOVE!
WE'VE GOTTA GO, OR WE'LL DIE TOO!
...
KISH
KISH
KISH
KISH
KISH
RMBL
RMBL
RMBL
RMBL
RMBL
RMBL
KRAK
TRIP
RMBL
!
RMBL
RMBL

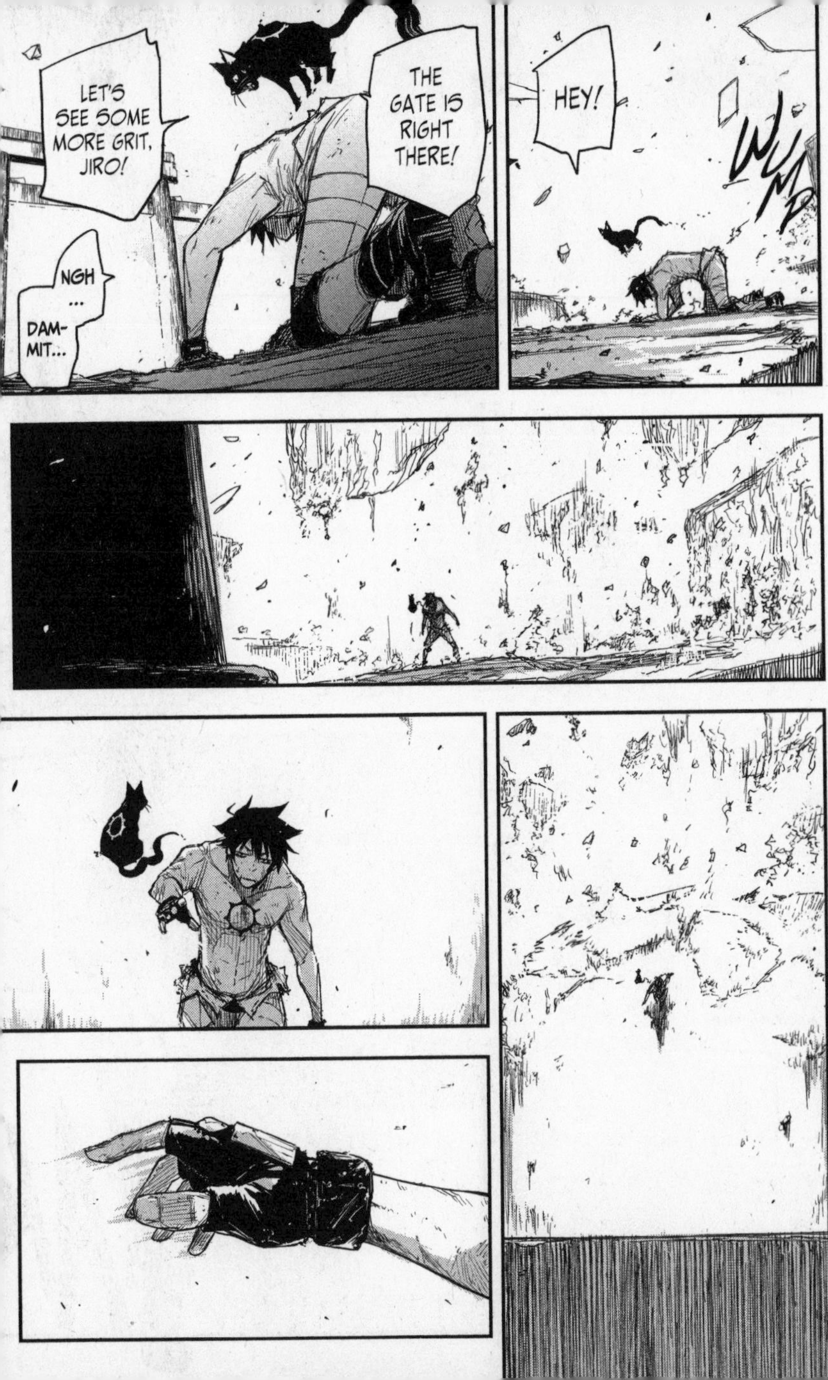
HEY!
WUMP
THE GATE IS RIGHT THERE!
LET'S SEE SOME MORE GRIT, JIRO!
NGH... DAM-MIT...

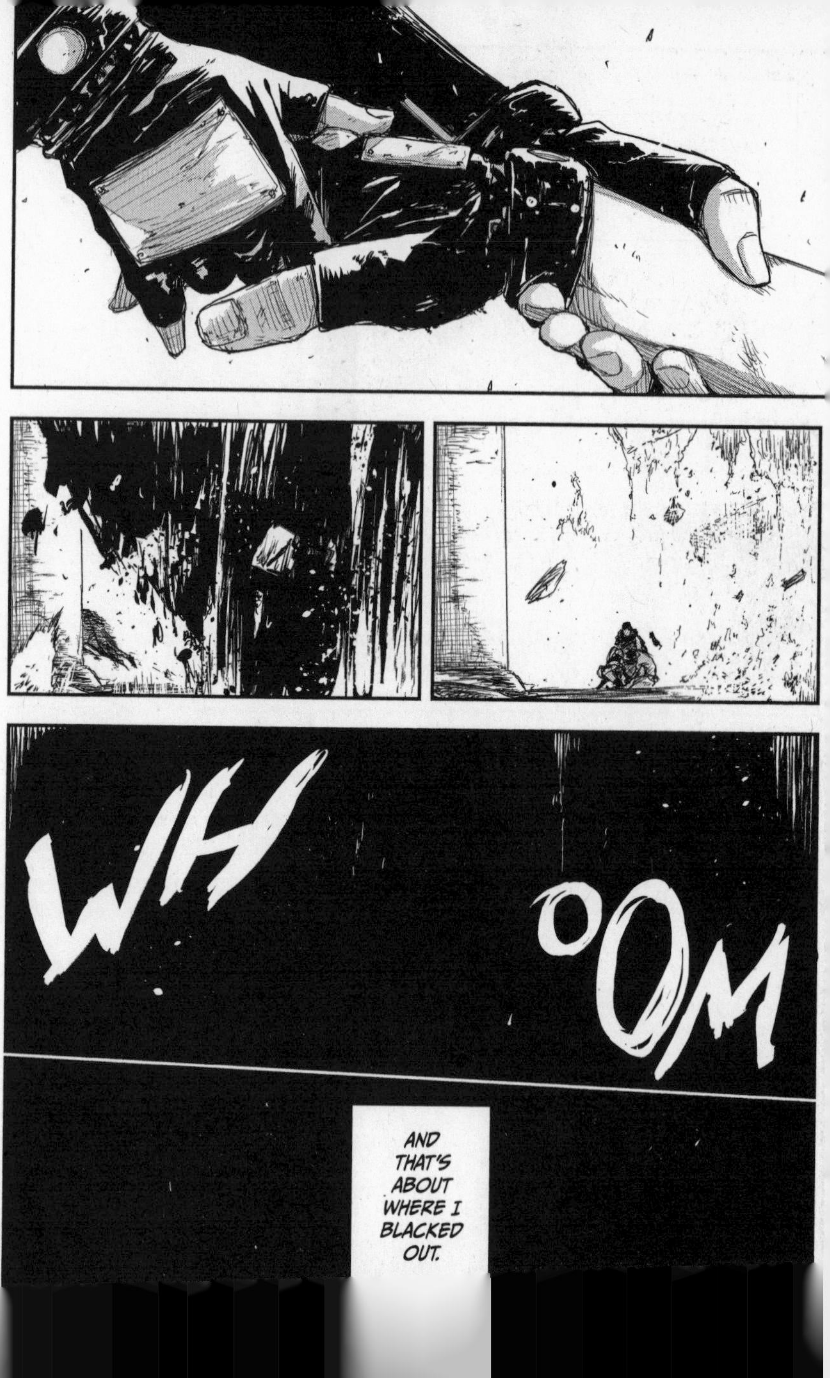
WH OOM
AND THAT'S ABOUT WHERE I BLACKED OUT.

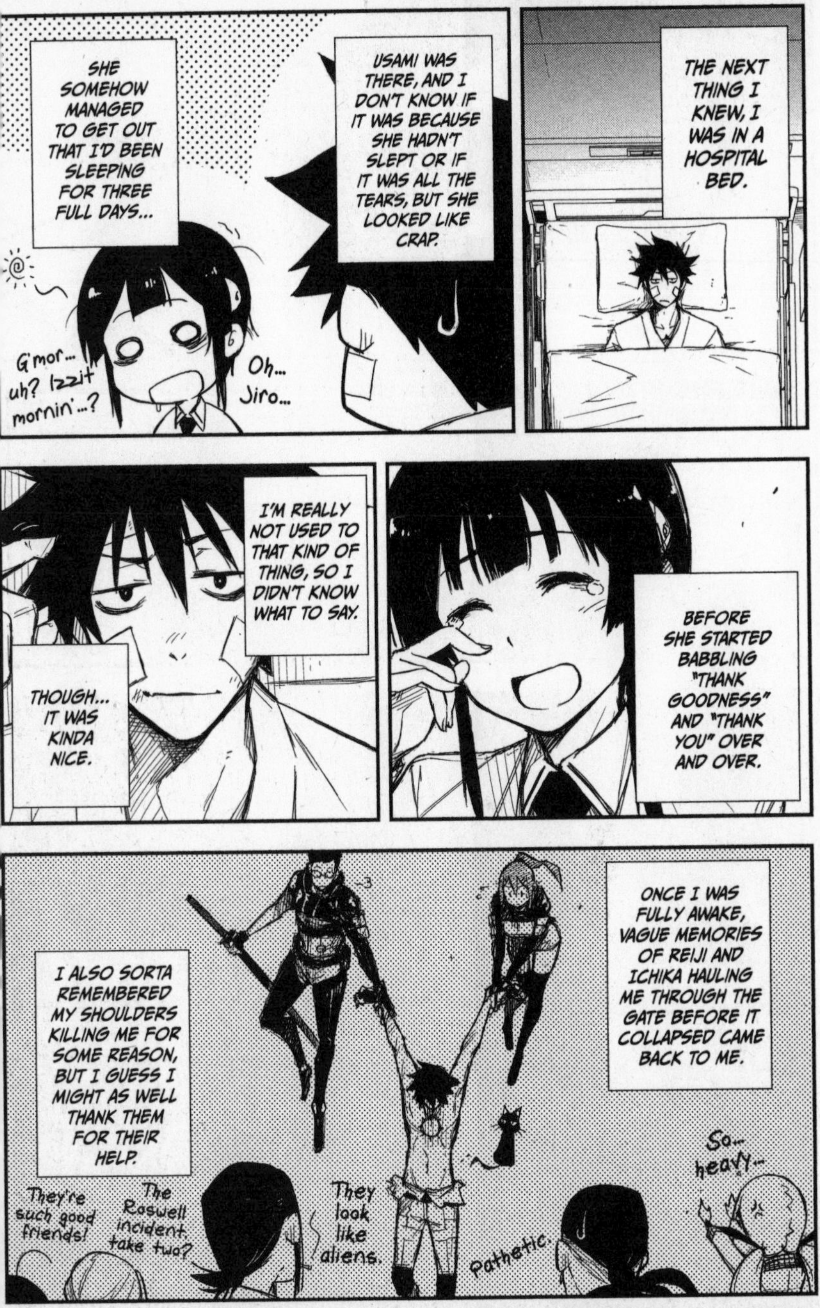
THE NEXT THING I KNEW, I WAS IN A HOSPITAL BED.
USAMI WAS THERE, AND I DON'T KNOW IF IT WAS BECAUSE SHE HADN'T SLEPT OR IF IT WAS ALL THE TEARS, BUT SHE LOOKED LIKE CRAP.
SHE SOMEHOW MANAGED TO GET OUT THAT I'D BEEN SLEEPING FOR THREE FULL DAYS...
Oh... Jiro...
G'mor... uh? Izzit mornin'...?
BEFORE SHE STARTED BABBLING "THANK GOODNESS" AND "THANK YOU" OVER AND OVER.
I'M REALLY NOT USED TO THAT KIND OF THING, SO I DIDN'T KNOW WHAT TO SAY.
THOUGH... IT WAS KINDA NICE.
ONCE I WAS FULLY AWAKE, VAGUE MEMORIES OF REIJI AND ICHIKA HAULING ME THROUGH THE GATE BEFORE IT COLLAPSED CAME BACK TO ME.
So... heavy...
I ALSO SORTA REMEMBERED MY SHOULDERS KILLING ME FOR SOME REASON, BUT I GUESS I MIGHT AS WELL THANK THEM FOR THEIR HELP.
Pathetic.
They look like aliens.
The Roswell incident take two?
They're such good friends!

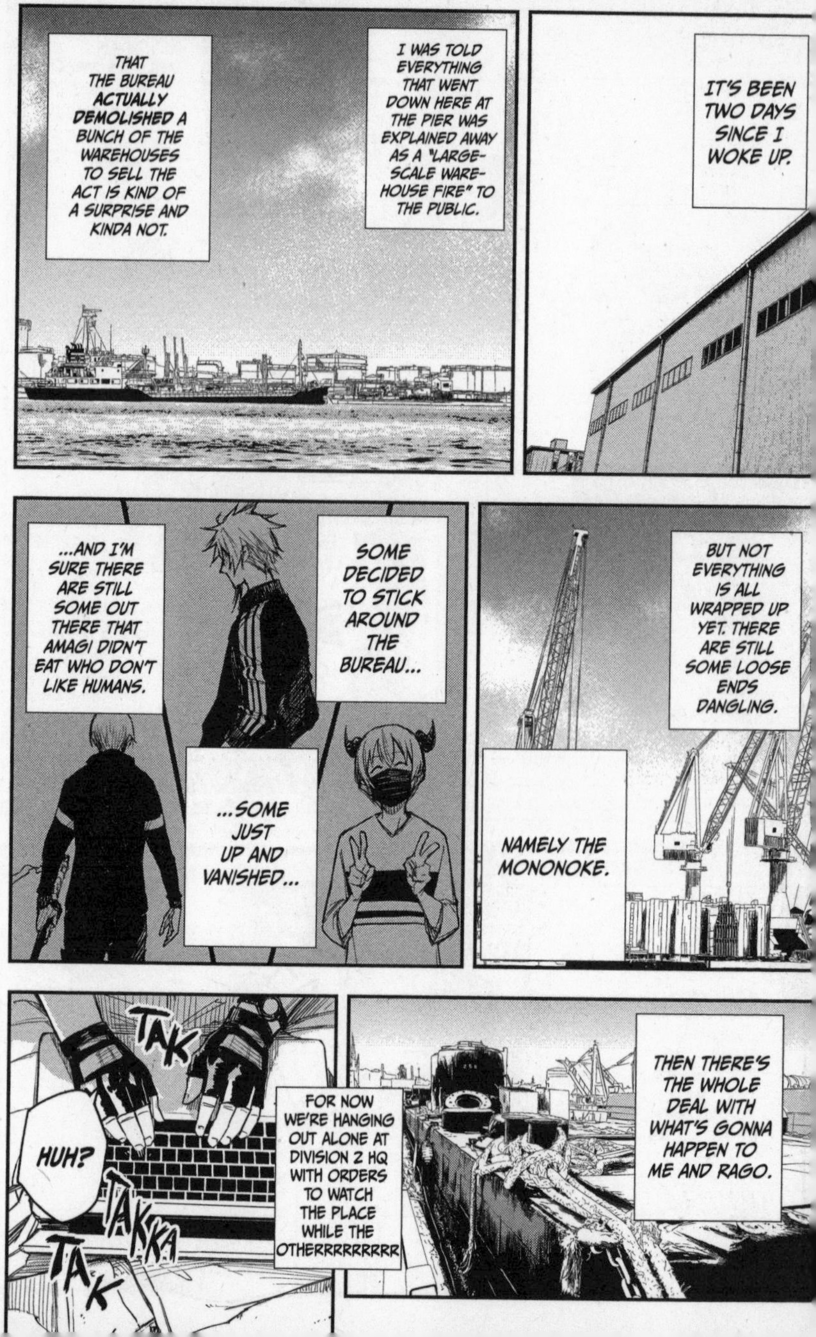
IT'S BEEN TWO DAYS SINCE I WOKE UP.
I WAS TOLD EVERYTHING THAT WENT DOWN HERE AT THE PIER WAS EXPLAINED AWAY AS A "LARGE-SCALE WAREHOUSE FIRE" TO THE PUBLIC.
THAT THE BUREAU ACTUALLY DEMOLISHED A BUNCH OF THE WAREHOUSES TO SELL THE ACT IS KIND OF A SURPRISE AND KINDA NOT.
BUT NOT EVERYTHING IS ALL WRAPPED UP YET. THERE ARE STILL SOME LOOSE ENDS DANGLING.
NAMELY THE MONONOKE.
SOME DECIDED TO STICK AROUND THE BUREAU...
...SOME JUST UP AND VANISHED...
...AND I'M SURE THERE ARE STILL SOME OUT THERE THAT AMAGI DIDN'T EAT WHO DON'T LIKE HUMANS.
THEN THERE'S THE WHOLE DEAL WITH WHAT'S GONNA HAPPEN TO ME AND RAGO.
TAK
FOR NOW WE'RE HANGING OUT ALONE AT DIVISION 2 HQ WITH ORDERS TO WATCH THE PLACE WHILE THE OTHERRRRRRRRR
HUH?
TAKKA
TAK

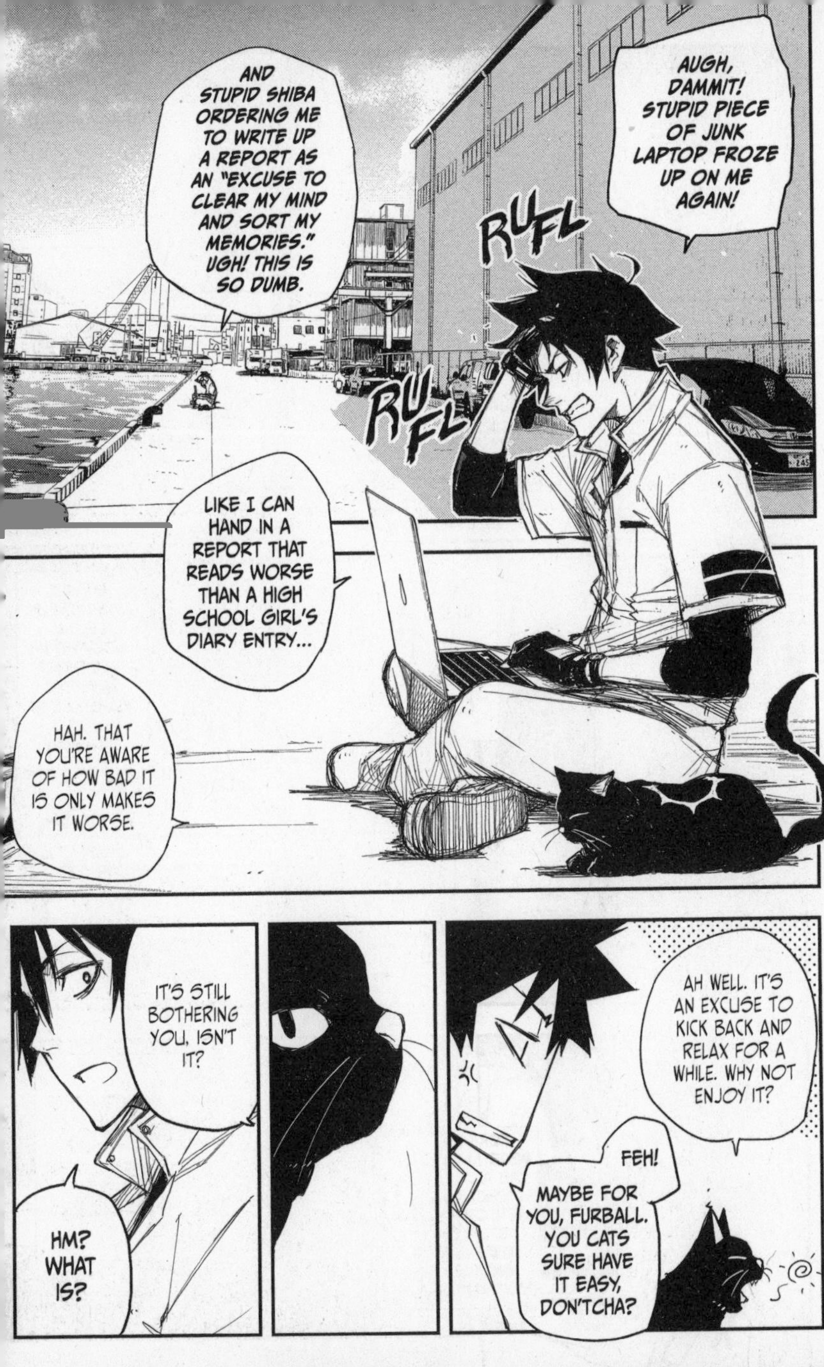
AUGH, DAMMIT! STUPID PIECE OF JUNK LAPTOP FROZE UP ON ME AGAIN!
RUFL
RUFL
AND STUPID SHIBA ORDERING ME TO WRITE UP A REPORT AS AN "EXCUSE TO CLEAR MY MIND AND SORT MY MEMORIES." UGH! THIS IS SO DUMB.
LIKE I CAN HAND IN A REPORT THAT READS WORSE THAN A HIGH SCHOOL GIRL'S DIARY ENTRY...
HAH. THAT YOU'RE AWARE OF HOW BAD IT IS ONLY MAKES IT WORSE.
AH WELL. IT'S AN EXCUSE TO KICK BACK AND RELAX FOR A WHILE. WHY NOT ENJOY IT?
FEH!
MAYBE FOR YOU, FURBALL. YOU CATS SURE HAVE IT EASY, DON'TCHA?
IT'S STILL BOTHERING YOU, ISN'T IT?
HM? WHAT IS?

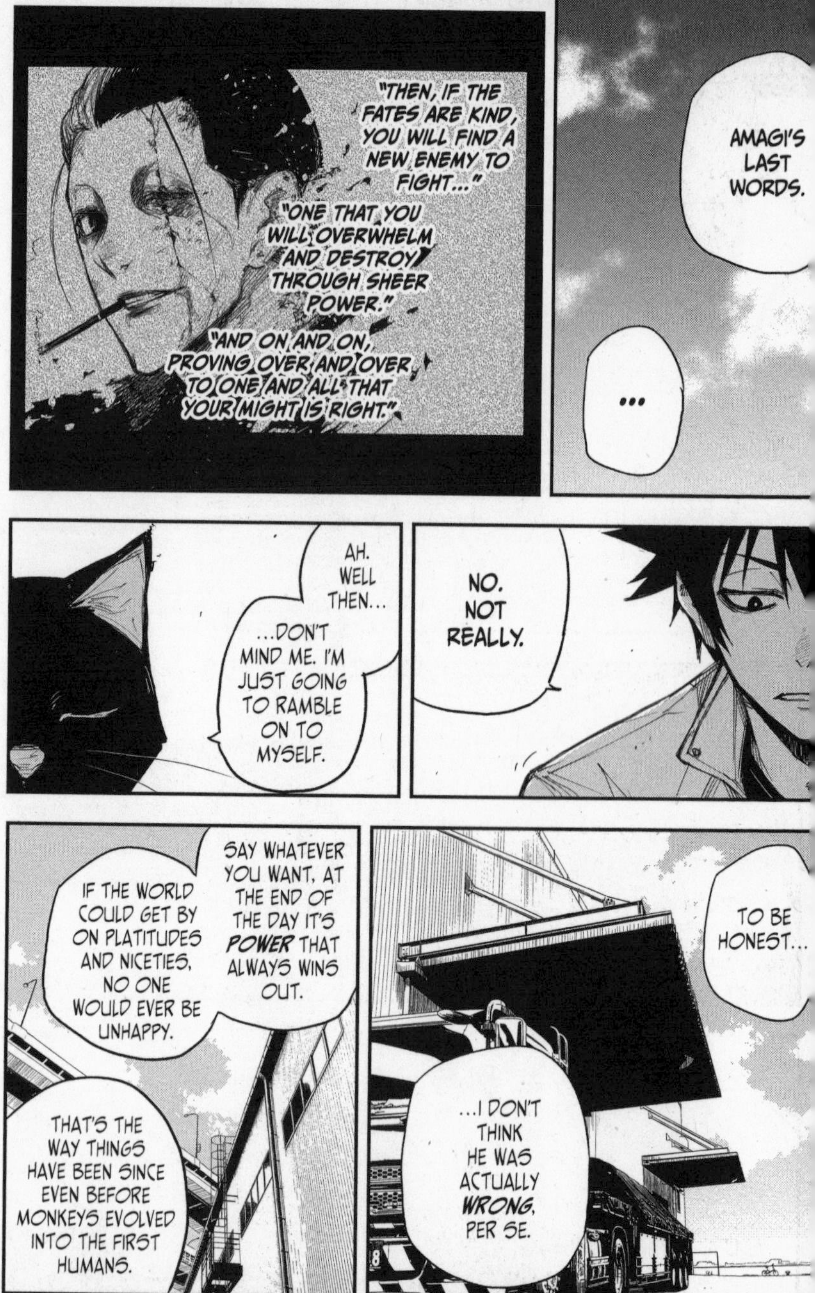
AMAGI'S LAST WORDS.
...
"THEN, IF THE FATES ARE KIND, YOU WILL FIND A NEW ENEMY TO FIGHT..."
"ONE THAT YOU WILL OVERWHELM AND DESTROY THROUGH SHEER POWER."
"AND ON AND ON, PROVING OVER AND OVER TO ONE AND ALL THAT YOUR MIGHT IS RIGHT."
NO. NOT REALLY.
AH. WELL THEN...
...DON'T MIND ME. I'M JUST GOING TO RAMBLE ON TO MYSELF.
TO BE HONEST...
...I DON'T THINK HE WAS ACTUALLY *WRONG*, PER SE.
SAY WHATEVER YOU WANT, AT THE END OF THE DAY IT'S *POWER* THAT ALWAYS WINS OUT.
IF THE WORLD COULD GET BY ON PLATITUDES AND NICETIES, NO ONE WOULD EVER BE UNHAPPY.
THAT'S THE WAY THINGS HAVE BEEN SINCE EVEN BEFORE MONKEYS EVOLVED INTO THE FIRST HUMANS.

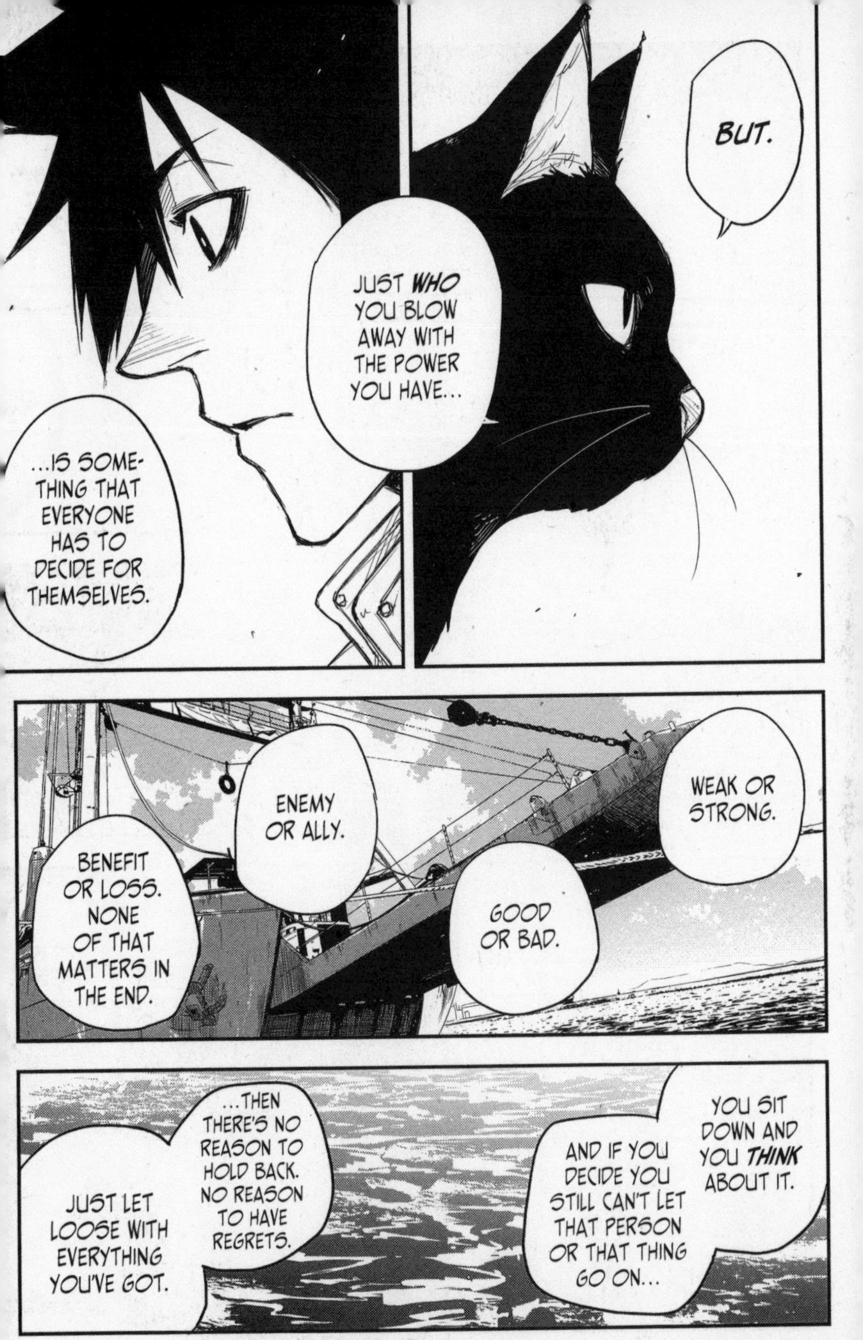
BUT.
JUST WHO YOU BLOW AWAY WITH THE POWER YOU HAVE...
...IS SOMETHING THAT EVERYONE HAS TO DECIDE FOR THEMSELVES.
WEAK OR STRONG.
GOOD OR BAD.
ENEMY OR ALLY.
BENEFIT OR LOSS. NONE OF THAT MATTERS IN THE END.
YOU SIT DOWN AND YOU THINK ABOUT IT.
AND IF YOU DECIDE YOU STILL CAN'T LET THAT PERSON OR THAT THING GO ON...
...THEN THERE'S NO REASON TO HOLD BACK. NO REASON TO HAVE REGRETS.
JUST LET LOOSE WITH EVERYTHING YOU'VE GOT.

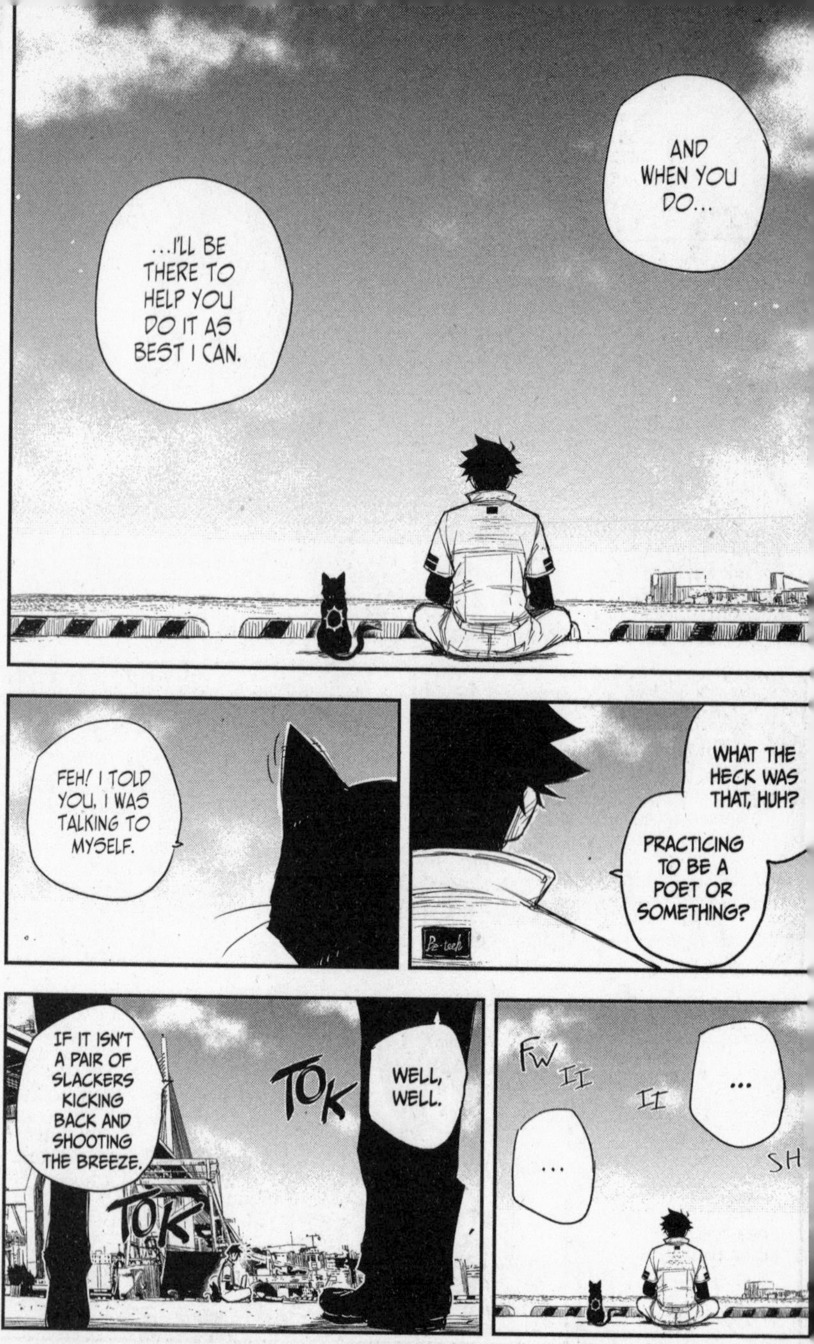
AND WHEN YOU DO...
...I'LL BE THERE TO HELP YOU DO IT AS BEST I CAN.
WHAT THE HECK WAS THAT, HUH?
PRACTICING TO BE A POET OR SOMETHING?
FEH! I TOLD YOU, I WAS TALKING TO MYSELF.
FWIIIISH
...
...
TOK
WELL, WELL.
IF IT ISN'T A PAIR OF SLACKERS KICKING BACK AND SHOOTING THE BREEZE.
TOK

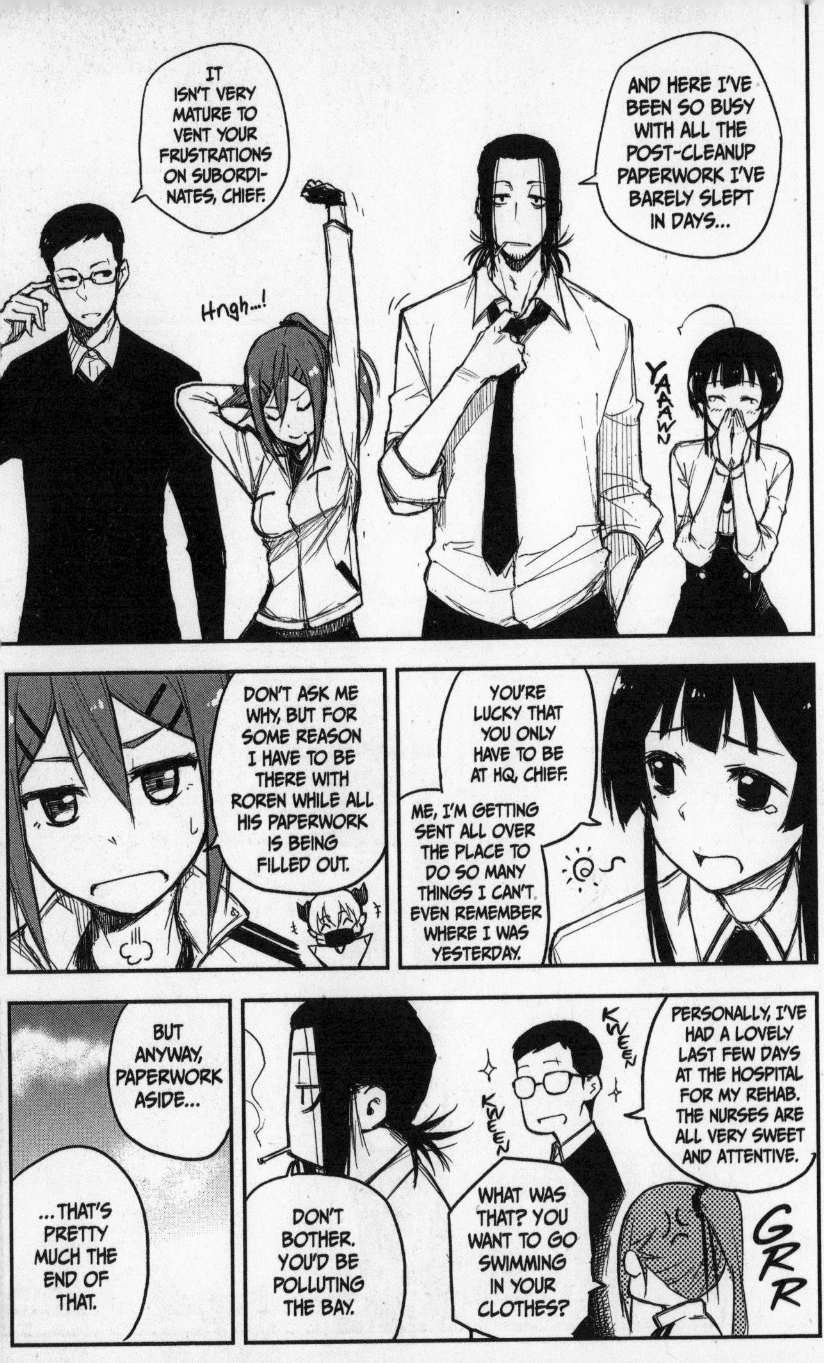
AND HERE I'VE BEEN SO BUSY WITH ALL THE POST-CLEANUP PAPERWORK I'VE BARELY SLEPT IN DAYS...
YAAAWN
Hngh...!
IT ISN'T VERY MATURE TO VENT YOUR FRUSTRATIONS ON SUBORDI-NATES, CHIEF.
YOU'RE LUCKY THAT YOU ONLY HAVE TO BE AT HQ, CHIEF.
ME, I'M GETTING SENT ALL OVER THE PLACE TO DO SO MANY THINGS I CAN'T EVEN REMEMBER WHERE I WAS YESTERDAY.
DON'T ASK ME WHY, BUT FOR SOME REASON I HAVE TO BE THERE WITH ROREN WHILE ALL HIS PAPERWORK IS BEING FILLED OUT.
PERSONALLY, I'VE HAD A LOVELY LAST FEW DAYS AT THE HOSPITAL FOR MY REHAB. THE NURSES ARE ALL VERY SWEET AND ATTENTIVE.
KWEEN
KWEEN
GRR
WHAT WAS THAT? YOU WANT TO GO SWIMMING IN YOUR CLOTHES?
DON'T BOTHER. YOU'D BE POLLUTING THE BAY.
BUT ANYWAY, PAPERWORK ASIDE...
...THAT'S PRETTY MUCH THE END OF THAT.

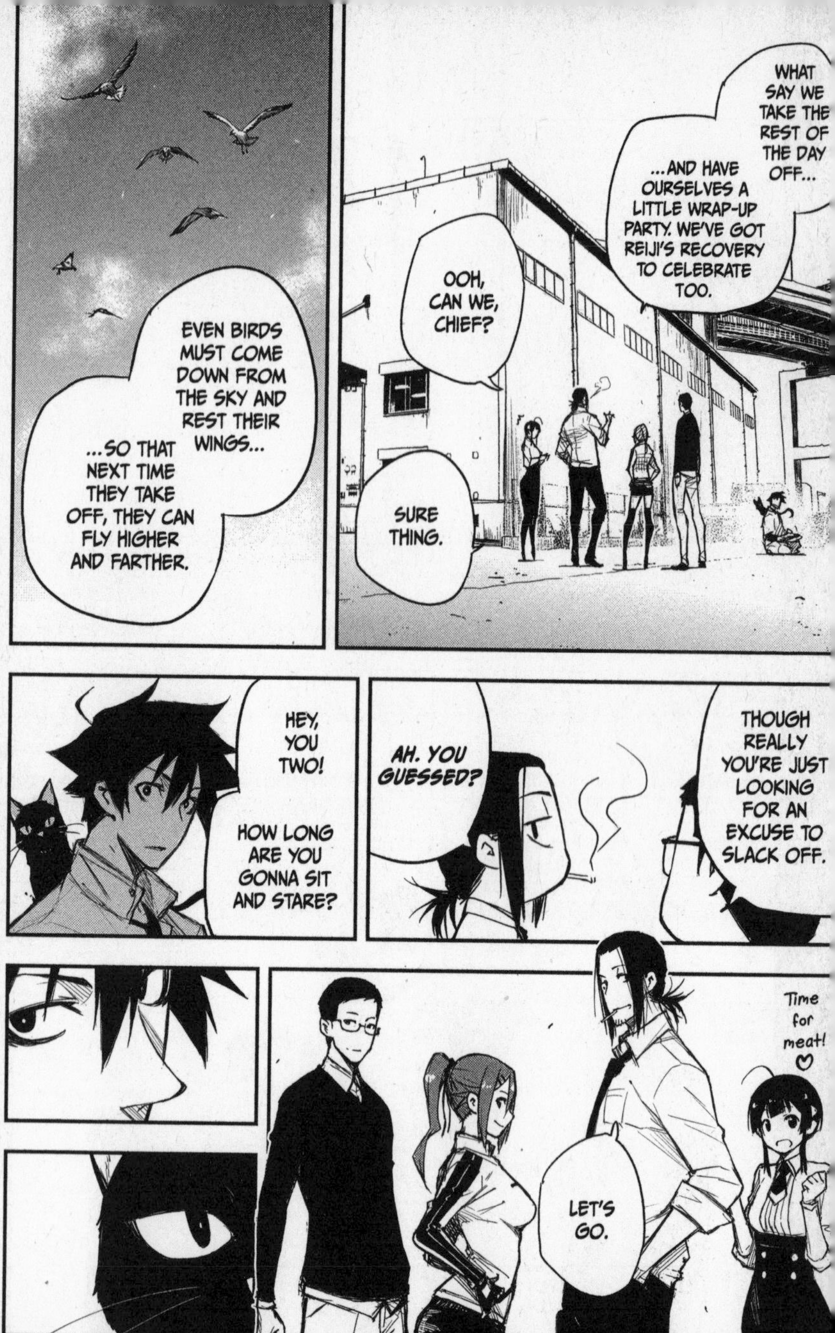
WHAT SAY WE TAKE THE REST OF THE DAY OFF...
...AND HAVE OURSELVES A LITTLE WRAP-UP PARTY. WE'VE GOT REIJI'S RECOVERY TO CELEBRATE TOO.
OOH, CAN WE, CHIEF?
SURE THING.
EVEN BIRDS MUST COME DOWN FROM THE SKY AND REST THEIR WINGS...
...SO THAT NEXT TIME THEY TAKE OFF, THEY CAN FLY HIGHER AND FARTHER.
THOUGH REALLY YOU'RE JUST LOOKING FOR AN EXCUSE TO SLACK OFF.
AH. YOU GUESSED?
HEY, YOU TWO!
HOW LONG ARE YOU GONNA SIT AND STARE?
Time for meat! ♡
LET'S GO.

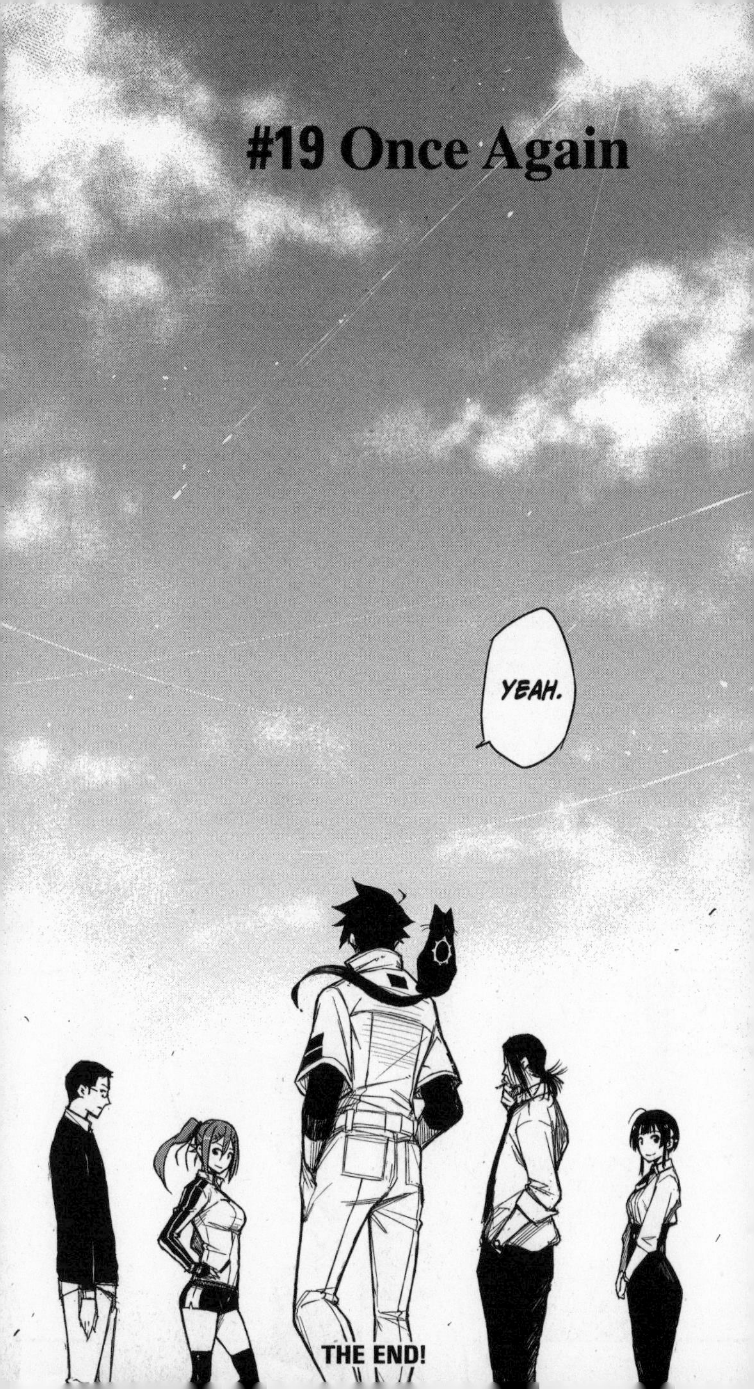
#19 Once Again
YEAH.
THE END!

*TO EACH, THEIR
OWN HISTORY...
TO EACH, THEIR
OWN FUTURE...*

BLACK TORCH #XXX

OUTRO

*TO EACH, THEIR
OWN STORY...*

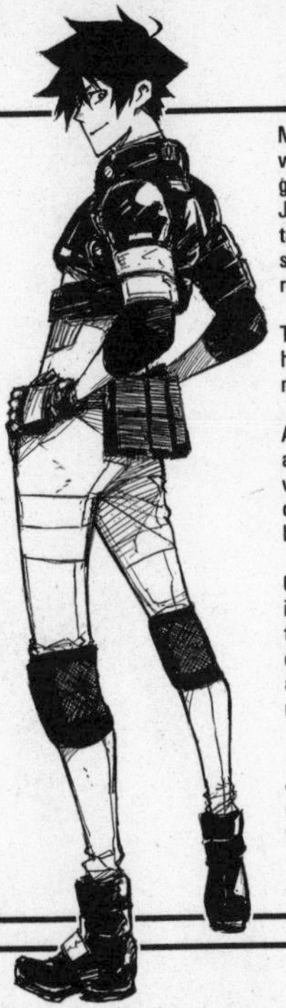

JIRO AZUMA

Many centuries ago, a mononoke gifted the ancestor of the Azuma Clan with heightened athleticism and the power to speak to animals. All later generations inherited these abilities to a greater or lesser degree, though in Jiro's case they came through particularly strongly. His eye-opening physical talent and ability to speak to any animal right away (when it usually requires spending a lot of time together to learn to speak with even a single animal) result from this.

Toshimasa is Jiro's maternal grandfather. Since his mother died shortly after he was born, Jiro was effectively raised by Toshimasa. He has never even met his father.

After the battle with Amagi, the Bureau recognizes Jiro as an official onmitsu agent. They also enroll him in a special high school they directly sponsor, which Reiji and Ichika also attend. Being a high school student and an onmitsu specializing in mononoke cases means Jiro's life grows exponentially busier, but he doesn't seem to mind.

One day, the Bureau acquires information that a certain massive corporation is secretly in league with mononoke, contracting with them for assassinations and dangerous experiments. What first seemed to be a cut-and-dried case of corporate espionage soon turns into a sprawling conspiracy involving assassination of Bureau VIPs, exporting mononoke to foreign countries, replacing powerful politicians with imposters, and more.

The secret war against mononoke grows fiercer. Plots and plans on a level Jiro doesn't truly grasp grow more devious. All Jiro knows is that he's getting perilously close to having too many absences from school. But through all the whirlwind of activity, he starts catching glimpses of his father.

And so the story of Jiro and his friends continues...

Rago once mentioned to Jiro about "living for eternity." That was no exaggeration. Rago is over a thousand years old. In his youth, when Rago still preferred human form, he became friends with the lord of a powerful family. However, in time, having Rago's power at his disposal made that lord grow arrogant. Giving in to ambition, he started more and more wars for land until his many enemies finally wiped out his entire clan in revenge. After that, Rago began avoiding relationships, giving up human form for the cat body he wears to this day.

At least, that's what Rago believes. Most of those memories are still vague thanks to his time fused to the killing stone. All that he really remembers is a vague "fear of commitment."

Centuries later, in the present day, Rago meets Jiro. Though it wasn't his first choice, Rago winds up growing close to humans again and begins to rethink his old beliefs.

After the battle with Amagi, Jiro gains at least a basic ability to control Rago's power somewhat by himself, freeing Rago to concentrate on devouring as little of Jiro's vital essence as possible. However, Rago is still very aware that he is a burden on Jiro and believes that, someday, the two of them need to be separated once again.

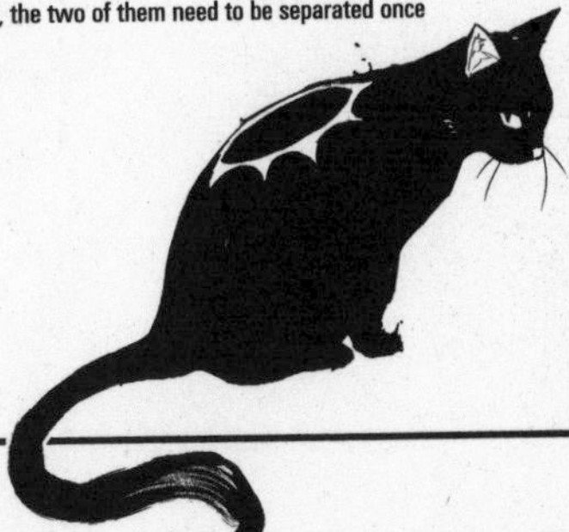

RAGO

REIJI KIRIHARA

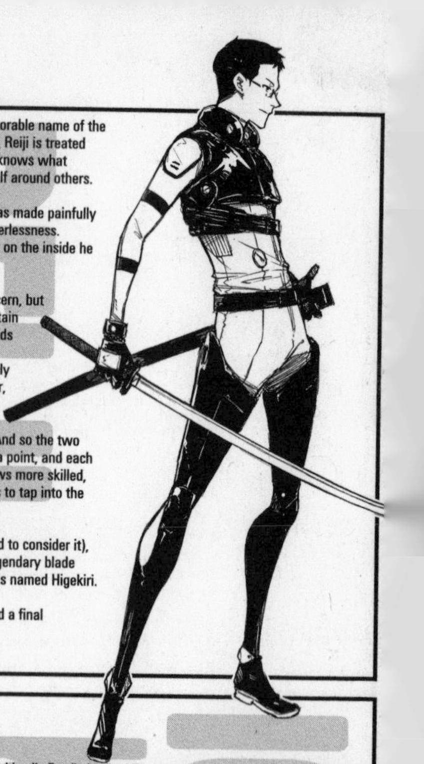

"Family heir murders own father." The once proud and honorable name of the Kirihara family has fallen into disgrace. Even in the Bureau, Reiji is treated as a pariah. Thus Division 2, where no one (except Shiba) knows what happened, has become a rare place where he can be himself around others.

During his encounter with Shinji in Hirasaka Town, Reiji was made painfully aware of both what his older brother felt and his own powerlessness. Though on the surface he remains as easygoing as always, on the inside he just can't forget what happened.

It's unclear whether Shiba was aware of Reiji's secret concern, but one day he gives the young man a mission to request a certain mononoke assist the Bureau. On this solo mission, Reiji heads deep into the mountains, where he meets the one-armed tengu crow demon, Tarobo. Tarobo, a human hater, obviously turns down Reiji's request. Reiji refuses to give up, however, and when Tarobo discovers he is a swordsman he jokingly offers to consider the request if Reiji can score a point on him in a sparring match. Reiji accepts the offer. And so the two spar, time and again. Each time Reiji loses without scoring a point, and each time Tarobo gives him some harsh but fair advice. Reiji grows more skilled, and eventually scores a point. It happens when he manages to tap into the latent talent he had unconsciously smothered as a child.

In the end, Tarobo still refuses the request (he only promised to consider it), but he does gift Reiji with a special sword. This sword, a legendary blade that a certain ancient warrior used to cut off Tarobo's arm, is named Higekiri.

His new sword at his belt, Reiji continues his journey toward a final showdown with his brother...

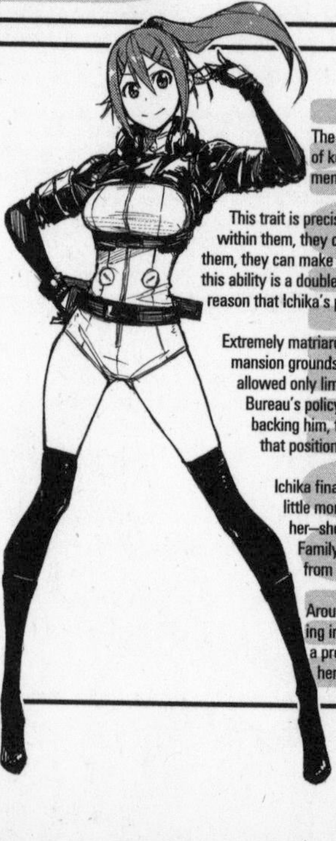

The Kishimojin Family is an oddity even among the Bureau, being a lineage of kunoichi female shinobi. Together with their fired hair, only the female members of this family inherit the special trait called flameblood.

This trait is precisely what it says on the tin—flaming blood. By igniting it as it flows within them, they can gain bursts of inhuman speed and power. When it bleeds out of them, they can make it burn with a fire that only goes out if they will it. While powerful, this ability is a double-edged sword that exacts a heavy price from the wielder. It is for that reason that Ichika's parents didn't want her to become an onmitsu.

Extremely matriarchal, the Kishimojin family forbids the presence of any man within their mansion grounds. Even Ichika's father, who officially married into the family, is allowed only limited access. Still alive, he presently holds a top position in the Bureau's policy-making division. While he did have the power of the Kishimojin name backing him, to avoid being called a "gold digger" he worked toward and earned that position primarily on his own merit.

Ichika finally hears about all of this directly from her father and, to become a little more like the mother she admired—and to find the mononoke who killed her—she begins training to control her ability. With the help of the Kishimojin Family's special maids (who are actually a Kishimojin branch family, sprung from a second son), Ichika eventually masters her flameblood talent.

Around that time, Ichika hears rumors of people turning into stone happening in connection with a corporate espionage case. Finally finding a precious clue, Ichika takes her newfound ability and pushes onward in her quest to save her mother...

ICHIKA KISHIMOJIN

RYOSUKE SHIBA

The only son of an affluent middle-class family, Ryusuke had a perfectly normal life until he was in elementary school. That was when his mother discovered his father cheating on her. She flew into a rage, stabbing his father to death and then killing herself. The one to first discover the grisly scene when he came home from school that day, Ryusuke has had something of a self-destructive streak ever since.

He lived in an orphanage through high school, using college as an excuse to move out on his own. However, he dropped out after only one semester. Looking for cheap thrills, he got involved in illegal gambling, earning cash at underground casinos and mahjong parlors. Eventually, he caught the eye of a yakuza gang and wound up employed by them as a pro gambler. Unfortunately for them, Ryusuke had no sense of loyalty whatever.

Working in the underworld, he heard rumors of mononoke and the Bureau. Though most believed they were just urban legends, Ryusuke was curious enough to dig into them. He eventually discovered that the Bureau was, in fact, real. In most cases, anyone finding the Bureau would have their memories modified or be erased entirely, but given that Ryusuke found them by his own talents, he was scouted instead. After a probation period, he was hired. Joining at the same time as Toko Kusumi, both began training under Toshimasa.

Ryusuke primarily made a name for himself in information manipulation and investigating dangerous organizations. But his tendency to disobey orders and take independent action led to him being ostracized by his peers and frowned on by his superiors. As a result, he was "promoted" to Director of the skeletal remains of Division 2 just so they could be rid of him.

However, after the Amagi incident, the higher-ups could not deny that not just Division 2, but the whole of Bureau needed a vast overhaul. One again, they were faced with the problem of what to do with Ryusuke. Who can say whether Ryusuke himself was aware of the headaches he was causing, but for now he continues to lazily pass the time, smoking his cigarettes and waiting for the next thrill to come along...

Hana grew up idolizing her parents, both of whom were police officers, and dreaming of the day she, too, could be a "hero of justice." Serious and studious, she earned excellent grades in school. She also trained in judo from elementary school through college, consistently placing in the top ranks at tournaments. However, perhaps because of some issue handling pressure, she never managed to take the top spot.

Graduating college, she finally achieved her dream of joining the police, where she was assigned to the Security Bureau of the Metropolitan Police Department. As an SP in the department, she functioned as a bodyguard for both foreign and domestic VIPs. Her skill, along with her pleasant and honest personality, made her a highly valued employee to the MPD.

Not long into her career, she was scouted by the Bureau. She quickly passed her training period to become an official onmitsu. However, disaster struck during one of her missions to apprehend a dangerous criminal. The target resisted capture, pulling a hidden gun. Though her orders changed from capture to kill, Hana was not able to pull the trigger. Instead, one of the other agents destroyed the target. Though she was capable of doing her best to protect someone, she could not put the same effort into killing.

After that incident, the Bureau labeled her "incompatible with field missions" and banished her to a desk job in Division 2.

Even with the Amagi Incident over, Hana still does as she always has, working her hardest to support Division 2 and Black Torch. But seeing Jiro and the others put their lives in danger awoke something in her. When she had the time, she began seeking out Toshimasa for some one-on-one combat training, so that this time, when the time came, she could once again give her all to protect the ones dear to her...

HANA USAMI

FUYO

Despite her looks, Fuyo is over 500 years old. Though she doesn't have much in the way of physical abilities, she is a master of the magical arts, being adept with illusions and all other ways to use a mononoke's inherent power. This has earned her the nickname of "Division 2's Handywoman."

For several decades now, Fuyo has been in charge of the Bureau's anti-mononoke defense training. Toshimasa underwent that training during his time as a rookie and wound up fainting once. Fuyo still uses it as joke fodder to this day.

Many centuries ago, Fuyo and Ibuki were best friends. That they still wear the same style of hair ribbon is a sign of that. However, when the Oniwaban began gaining power, Fuyo decided to join the humans while Ibuki chose isolation, and the two friends parted. They remained apart until Jiro's training gave Fuyo the excuse to see Ibuki for the first time in centuries.

At first the two were frosty toward each other, but that Ibuki came to respect Jiro helped Fuyo warm back up to her old friend.

After the Amagi Incident, Fuyo began visiting Ibuki regularly under the pretext of being the Bureau's watchdog over a "rogue" mononoke, and the two would share drinks and stories.

Fuyo has always been friendly toward humans. Before the Oniwaban was founded, she was the local deity of a small village. She enjoys watching human culture and society change over time, as well as occasionally partaking in human hobbies and pastimes. Her favorite foods are cheesecake and inari sushi. When asked what she thinks of mononoke who eat humans, she said she could not comprehend why they would go out of their way to eat something that tasted so disgusting.

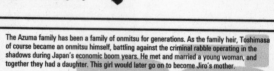

The Azuma family has been a family of onmitsu for generations. As the family heir, Toshimasa of course became an onmitsu himself, battling against the criminal rabble operating in the shadows during Japan's economic boom years. He met and married a young woman, and together they had a daughter. This girl would later go on to become Jiro's mother.

Toshimasa's wife passed away of illness while their daughter was in high school. He had no intent to remarry and, for his late wife's sake, he didn't want to force his daughter into becoming an onmitsu, either. Thus he decided that he would be the last Azuma onmitsu. It is for this reason that he stubbornly opposed Jiro becoming an onmitsu.

But one day his daughter came home pregnant by a man he didn't even know, and to top it off she passed away in childbirth. This drove Toshimasa over the edge. He pulled in favors at the Bureau, using their information network for his personal hunt. He even resorted to illegal methods, but in the end he was unable to track down Jiro's father.

While he was searching, Jiro grew into a healthy, energetic young boy. The passage of time and watching Jiro get bigger and bigger helped cool Toshimasa's temper. Eventually he decided to spend the rest of his days raising his grandson, and he retired from the Bureau.

After the Amagi Incident, he returned to active duty as a special advisor at the Bureau, training new recruits and the regular foot soldiers.

Later, certain events would set Jiro on the path to finding his father, but as Toshimasa wasn't present he would not learn of this until much, much later...

TOSHIMASA AZUMA

TOKO KUSUMI

Born and raised in a strict family, Toko attended an all-girls boarding school from middle through high school, after which she attended a prestigious foreign college. There she studied law and criminal psychology, graduating with honors. She returned to Japan and promptly joined the Public Security Intelligence Agency.

It was during an investigation of a certain religious cult as a Public Security agent that Toko learned of the Bureau and mononoke. Apparently, the cult worshipped a mononoke as their deity, so Public Security and the Bureau opened a joint investigation. When the cult was exposed, both the mononoke and the cultists resisted fiercely. Though Public Security and the Bureau prevailed in the end, it was not without casualties. Toko herself wound up with scars she would bear for the rest of her life.

After that incident, Toko petitioned for a transfer into the Bureau. At the time, Toshimasa was still the director of Division 2, and it was under him that she trained and performed her first missions as an onmitsu agent. It was then that she met Shiba, as he joined up about the same time.

Toko posted excellent results with astonishing speed. Thus, when the previous director of Division 1 passed away from illness, she was immediately appointed as his replacement despite her relatively young age.

Cold, cruel and eminently logical, the members of Division 1 fear and respect Toko as an "Ice Queen." Not a one of them knows that her secret hobby is reading sappy shojo romance manga (probably a reaction to her overly strict upbringing).

Though she definitely has some attraction to Shiba, who is her polar opposite, the two have not started a relationship.

Originally a mercenary hit man, Banjuro fled to the mainland to avoid pursuit by police and enemy yakuza gangs. Travelling from the Korean Peninsula through China, he went back into business as a hit man in Russia. There, he picked up the Russian language as well as the Russian martial art of Systema, folding it into his own personal assassination style. With the collapse of the Soviet Union, Banjuro returned to Japan and once again began working in the Japanese underworld.

During one job he found himself battling his target's bodyguard, who happened to be a mononoke. Though he came out of the fight gravely wounded, he still managed to get the job done. Onmitsu hunting the mononoke arrived in time to get Banjuro medical care and, after a period of detention, he was officially recruited into the Bureau.

As an onmitsu, he carried out assassinations of terrorists and dangerous criminals. Quickly amassing an impressive record, he was soon assigned to the elite squad, Black Cloak. Given his talents both for work and in practical matters, the higher-ups even thought about promoting him to an upper-level managerial role, but when they considered his history prior to joining the Bureau that promotion was dropped. Not only that, Banjuro himself said that he did not have the personality or the qualifications to be a leader of others. Instead, he said, he was more fit to be used as a tool by others, like a knife or a gun, and had no intention of accepting any further promotion.

Banjuro always speaks and acts in a pleasant, polite manner, however this is mostly a tactic for getting by that he learned working in the underworld. Perhaps because of that natural poker face, he is extremely good at cards, mahjong and any other gambling game played against other people. Inui in particular routinely gets flfleeced.

Toshimasa has said this about Banjuro: "To him, human life—even his own—is just an object. If told to kill, he'll kill. If told to protect, he'll protect. It's that cut-and-dried to him. Personally, there are lots of mononoke out there I'd rather as an enemy than him."

BANJURO TOKIEDA

TAKERU INUI

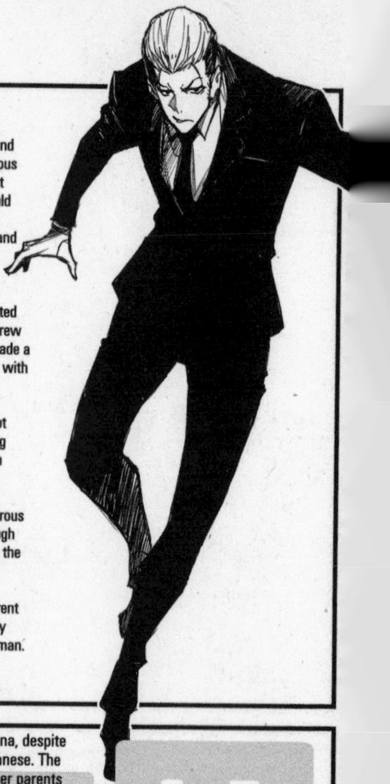

A large man at close to six and a half feet tall, Inui grew up in a single-parent household with his mother and three little sisters. Extra tall ever since he was young, he was the star player on his school's basketball team in both middle and high school. He may look like a typical delinquent, but he's actually a very serious and responsible guy. He could have gone to college on a sports scholarship, but instead he chose to enlist in the Japanese Self-Defense Force (JSDF) so he could support his family and send his little sisters to college by sending most of his paycheck home to them. It was during this time when he learned martial arts and how to use guns, putting his already impressive athletic talent to good use.

While he was in the JSDF, he heard about foreign private military contractors (PMC). Interested in the higher pay PMCs receive, he promptly went to the United States after his term in the JSDF was up. Taking on odd jobs of all kinds, he threw himself into learning English and, working out at the gym one day, he finally made a contact in a PMC. Passing their rigorous hiring exam, Inui landed an official job with them. As a side note, his coworkers at this time nicknamed him "ninja man."

Inui's new job took him to war zones across the world, where he picked up a lot of practical experience. Through sheer happenstance, an onmitsu agent working abroad caught sight of him and scouted him. Hearing that the Bureau paid even better, he promptly transferred in.

As a Bureau agent, Inui's missions were mostly infiltrating and exposing dangerous organizations and other rough-and-tumble jobs. Recently, he finally gained enough recognition for his accomplishments that he was assigned to Black Cloak. With the extra hazard pay he gets now, he is quite satisfied with his salary.

Inui's hobbies are working out, cooking and tending his kitchen garden. His current worry is his younger sisters. They have all reached their teen years and are very attractive. He's constantly concerned they might fall in with the wrong kind of man.

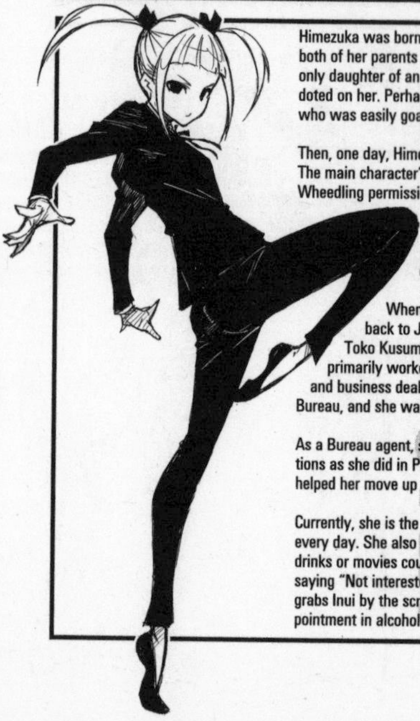

Himezuka was born and raised in China, despite both of her parents being native Japanese. The only daughter of an affluent family, her parents doted on her. Perhaps because of that, when she was little she was a shy, bashful girl who was easily goaded to tears by her friends' teasing.

Then, one day, Himezuka watched a certain Hong Kong action movie with her father. The main character's kungfu skills impressed her so much she was immediately smitten. Wheedling permission out of her reluctant parents, she began attending a martial arts dojo that taught kenpo, where her latent talents quickly began to shine. Growing stronger and more confident by the day, she was soon winning junior martial arts tournaments and even holding her own against adults.

When Himezuka was ready to attend college, she and her parents moved back to Japan. Upon graduation, she went straight into the same agency as Toko Kusumi did—Public Security. She took advantage of her background and primarily worked on investigations and intelligence gathering on shady corporations and business deals in Chinese-speaking areas. Her record quickly caught the eye of the Bureau, and she was scouted.

As a Bureau agent, she worked on cases that dealt with the same kind of shady corporations as she did in Public Security, her missions were just more dangerous. Her abilities helped her move up the ranks rapidly, and before long she was placed in Black Cloak.

Currently, she is the partner/trainer of new recruit Inui, to whom she shows tough love every day. She also hero-worships Toko Kusumi, and has invited her out to after-work drinks or movies countless times. However, every time Kusumi turns her down cold, saying "Not interested," or "I fail to see the necessity." And every time that happens, she grabs Inui by the scruff and drags him to a bar with her, where she drowns her disappointment in alcohol and alternately lectures him or cries on his shoulder.

BANRI HIMETSUKA

ROREN

Roren never actually believed in Amagi's cause. Instead, he was instructed by another mononoke to infiltrate Amagi's group and keep an eye on him. Using Amagi's planned uprising to his advantage, he scouted out the Bureau's power and, in a stroke of good luck, even found a way into that organization himself.

After the Amagi Incident, he was formally inducted as a member of the Bureau, but he of course never intended to give his loyalty to humanity. His plan was to act as a mole and gather what information he could. Unfortunately for him, since he was previously an enemy agent, the Bureau has been keeping close tabs on his every move, severely curtailing his ability to do any snooping. But Roren has always been of the "If you can't beat them, join them" mind-set. If the Bureau proves to be more powerful than the mononoke that originally employed him, he will promptly turn his coat without a second thought.

A self-centered hedonist, he doesn't have any great ambitions of his own. He is, in that way, a stark contrast to Amagi. His feelings for Ichika are no lie, either, but it is difficult to tell if he is or isn't hamming it up a little.

As a new incident begins brewing, Roren makes a show of cooperating with the Bureau, but on the inside he is constantly watching to see which side looks like the better prospect to give his (temporary) loyalty to.

In general, Roren holds humanity in contempt. However, he has no problems accepting and even enjoying those parts of human culture (music, fashion) that he likes.

Ibuki is called an Ogre Lord by many, and she has the power to back it up. Though fully capable of using mystical spells, she doesn't like to rely on them in battle. She prefers a brawler style, using her powers to increase her physical strength and abilities, making her the opposite of her old friend Fuyo.

After the Amagi Incident, Jiro began to visit her regularly for training in Rago's powers. Though she prefers solitude she doesn't go out of her way to avoid people. She just doesn't care for shallow, superficial relationships. If it is someone she can speak to bluntly and honestly she will call them friend, whether they are mononoke or human. It's for this reason that Monjumaru eventually got through to her and earned her love after half a century of effort, earning her love and respect. Ibuki is generally the one who wears the pants in that relationship, though when she gets drunk she will suddenly turn snuggly and affectionate.

Monjumaru did not spend all 50 years chasing Ibuki, of course. After his first defeat he went back to working as an onmitsu with the Oniwaban, using what spare time he could find between missions to go back and challenge her again. He was actually an exceptional agent, talented at information gathering, spying and battle. However, even with all his skill he could not put a scratch on Ibuki.

After 50 years, an old Monjumaru approached Ibuki for a last time. The two fought viciously, and Monjumaru was severely wounded. Without thinking, Ibuki ran to his side and gently lifted him up. Monjumaru said that, if he had to die, it would be an honor to do so by her hand. That was the point at which Ibuki finally gave in. She gave him a portion of her powers, healing his injuries and, across many following decades, taught him how to use them. Because of that, Monjumaru lost his humanity to become a mononoke, and Ibuki's overall power was reduced to about half of what she had at her strongest. However, neither regrets their decision.

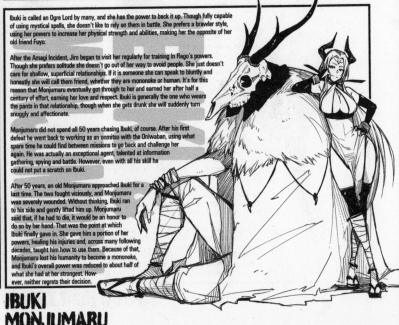

IBUKI
MONJUMARU

SHINJI KIRIHARA

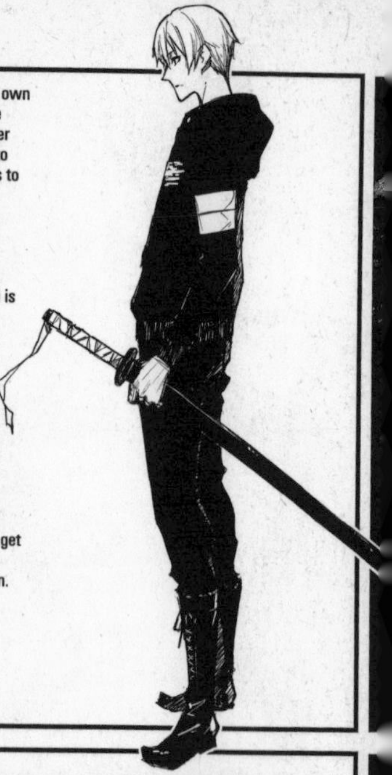

Shinji has been on the Bureau's most-wanted list ever since he killed his own father, but even after the Amagi Incident he is still at large. However, the Bureau effectively hamstrung itself in its search, because in order to cover up the truth behind the murder, they had to declare Shinji dead. Thanks to that, they can't make use of the police and other governmental resources to conduct a full criminal search.

As Shinji and his father once said, the cursed blade Hell Wind has no consciousness of its own. It cannot manipulate Shinji. Instead, the foul aura of its power resonated with Shinji's own repressed pain and desire, amplifying them and bringing them to the fore. In a sense, the way Shinji is now is the true him.

After he left Amagi, Shinji went into hiding, carefully watching for his chance to challenge Reiji to a rematch. But before long, he received an unexpected visitor—Roren. Roren had followed the lingering traces of Hell Wind's aura to search for him, and he assures Shinji he wasn't there to turn him in, he just introduces him to the mononoke Roren actually works for. And so Shinji winds up working for another mononoke organization that opposes the Bureau.

Shinji does it all for the chance to fight Reiji at his full strength and beat him. How much meaning would there be to such a fight? What would he get should he manage to kill Reiji at his best? None of that matters anymore. Shinji is no longer capable of turning back. He cannot repent and try again. All he can do is keep moving forward, keep swinging Hell Wind...

Even if all that awaits him is destruction.

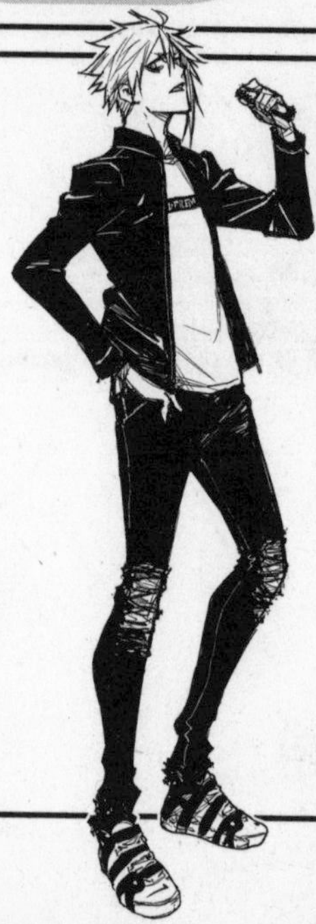

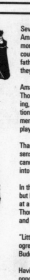

Seventeen years ago, two men created a new mononoke. One of those men was Amagi. The other was Jiro's father. The mononoke created was Kouga. In nature, mononoke spontaneously coalesce into being. The experiment was to see if one could be artificially created. Amagi offered a portion of his power while Jiro's father offered the resources and the technology. After several years of failures, they finally created Kouga.

Amagi, of course, never bothered to educate Kouga in the truth of his birth. Though Jiro's father visited several times to observe how Kouga was progressing, Amagi only ever introduced him as a "compatriot" assisting with the acquisition of Rago's power. Now, with Amagi gone, it is unclear what exactly the two men intended to do with Kouga, but it is very likely that they both had interest in playing god and creating life.

Thanks to that, Kouga was not yet fully stable emotionally, and had only a vague sense of self. Though he did show strong attachment to some things (Rago, candy bars), most of his thoughts and opinions were ones that Amagi imprinted into him.

In the confusion around the Amagi Incident, Kouga escaped from the Bureau, but had little idea where to go next. Wandering aimlessly, he eventually arrived at a little temple deep in the mountains maintained by a single old, blind monk. Though the monk realizes Kouga is a mononoke, he still provides him with food and shelter.

"Little baby ogre," the monk tells Kouga, "Whether you go on to become an ogre lord or a hell demon, or perhaps revert into a minor, mewling imp, even the Buddha himself cannot say. It is all up to you."

Having met this strange old man in his lonely temple, Kouga gets the opportunity to step back and take a hard look at himself...

KOUGA

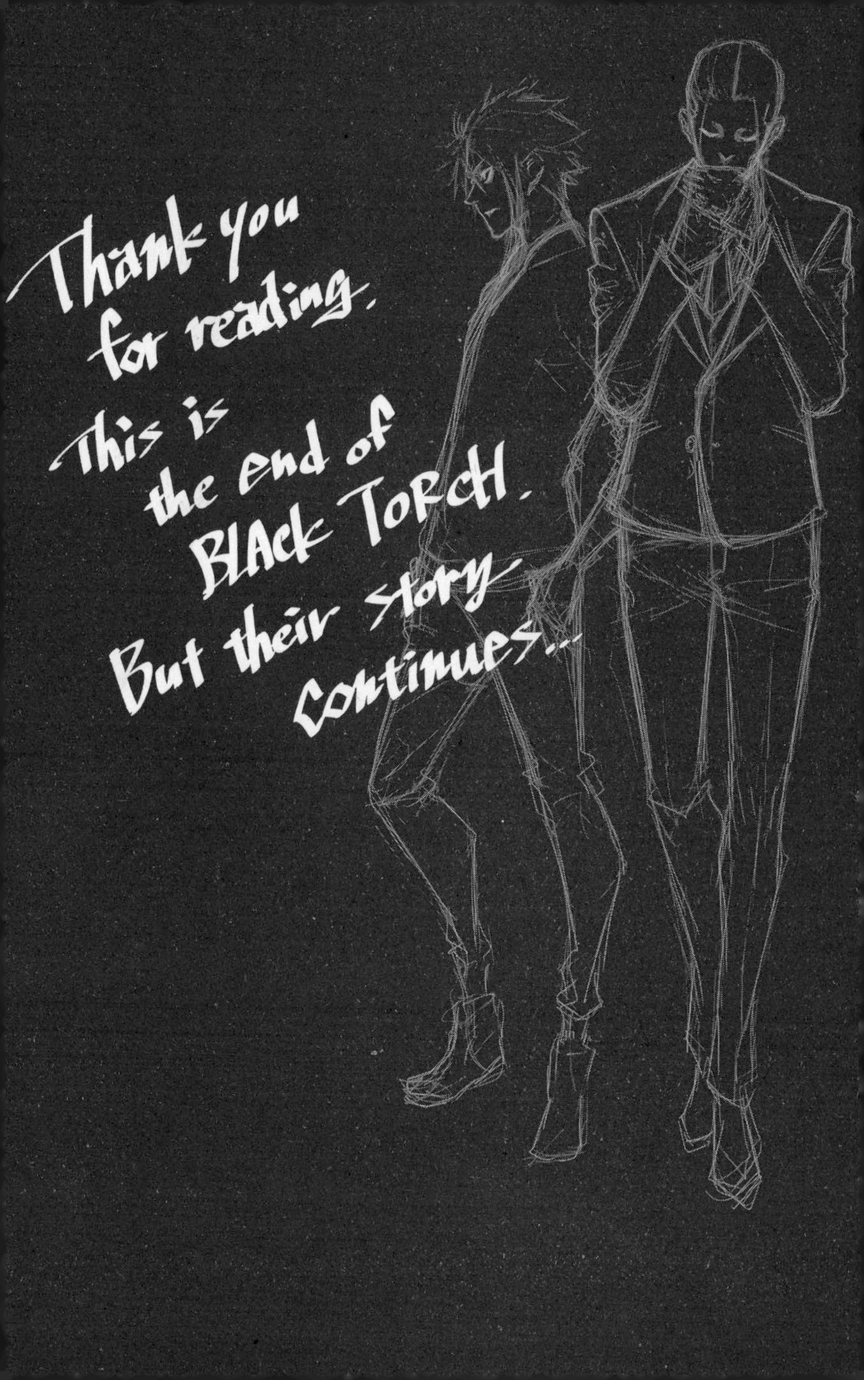
Thank you for reading.
This is the end of BLACK TORCH.
But their story continues...

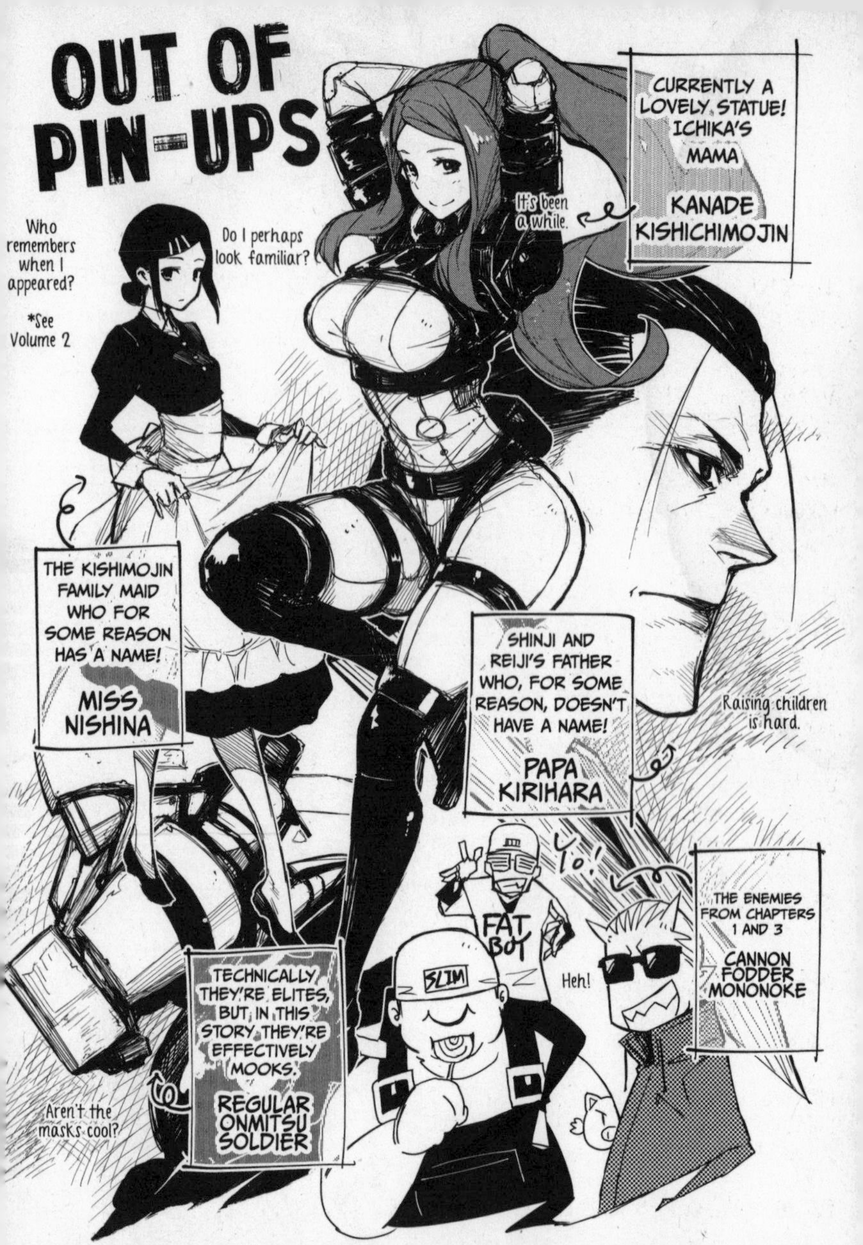
OUT OF PIN-UPS
CURRENTLY A LOVELY STATUE! ICHIKA'S MAMA
KANADE KISHICHIMOJIN
It's been a while.
Do I perhaps look familiar?
Who remembers when I appeared?
*See Volume 2
SHINJI AND REIJI'S FATHER WHO, FOR SOME REASON, DOESN'T HAVE A NAME!
PAPA KIRIHARA
Raising children is hard.
THE KISHIMOJIN FAMILY MAID WHO FOR SOME REASON HAS A NAME!
MISS NISHINA
THE ENEMIES FROM CHAPTERS 1 AND 3
CANNON FODDER MONONOKE
Yo!
FAT BOY
Heh!
SLIM
TECHNICALLY THEY'RE ELITES, BUT IN THIS STORY THEY'RE EFFECTIVELY MOOKS.
REGULAR ONMITSU SOLDIER
Aren't the masks cool?

BLACK TORCH 5

STORY & ART
TSUYOSHI TAKAKI

Poorly Written Afterword!

THANK YOU FOR MAKING YOUR WAY TO THE END OF THE BOOK! I'M TAKAKI. UNFORTUNATELY ENOUGH, THIS IS THE END OF *BLACK TORCH*.

IF THERE IS ONE THING I WANT TO MAKE SURE TO GET ACROSS OVER ANYTHING ELSE, IT IS— AT THE RISK OF REPEATING MYSELF—HOW GRATEFUL I AM TO EVERYONE WHO READ AND ENJOYED THIS SERIES.

MY FIRST ORIGINAL TITLE. MY FIRST TIME DOING EVERYTHING DIGITALLY. MY FIRST TIME BEING INTRODUCED AROUND AT BOOKSELLERS AND SIGNING BOOKS. MY FIRST REPRINTED VOLUME. MY FIRST TIME BEING A GUEST AT AN EVENT. MY FIRST TIME DOING AN AUTOGRAPH SESSION.

I EXPERIENCED THOSE FIRSTS AND MANY MORE WORKING ON THIS TITLE. ALL HYPERBOLE AND FLATTERY ASIDE, I DO BELIEVE THAT IT WAS ALL THANKS TO READERS LIKE YOU.

THIS IS ONLY MY PERSONAL OPINION, BUT TO ME A MANGA IS NOT "COMPLETE" WHEN THE ARTIST FINISHES DRAWING IT. ONLY AFTER THE PUBLISHER HAS PUBLISHED IT AND A READER HAS READ AND FELT SOMETHING FROM IT, IS THE WORK FINALLY COMPLETE.

WHO READ THIS WORK TO THIS POINT? WHAT DID THEY FEEL AS THEY "COMPLETED" THE STORY? I CAN ONLY IMAGINE. WAS IT FUN? WAS IT BORING? DID THEY WISH THERE WAS MORE? DID THEY WISH IT HAD FINISHED SOONER?

WHATEVER YOU AND ALL THE OTHER READERS FELT, YOU ARE STILL HERE WITH ME AT THE VERY END, HAVING HELPED ME COMPLETE MY STORY. I AM GRATEFUL FOR THAT.

THIS MAY NOT HAVE BEEN THE GREATEST MASTERWORK EVER, BUT FOR ALL ITS GOOD AND BAD PARTS, IT IS STILL MY BABY. IT HAS TAUGHT ME MANY INVALUABLE THINGS, AND I WILL TREASURE IT FOREVER.

I PROMISE I WILL PUT TO GOOD USE EVERY LAST THING I HAVE LEARNED, GROWING AND IMPROVING WITH EVERY DAY SO THAT, HOPEFULLY, SOMETIME SOON, I CAN INTRODUCE YOU ALL TO MY NEW BABY.

BUT FOR NOW, REGRETFULLY, IT IS TIME THAT WE MUST PART.

UNTIL NEXT TIME. MAY WE MEET AGAIN WITH A SMILE.

Tsuyoshi Takaki

2018.7.9

NIECE, WHO SUDDENLY ARRIVED DURING SERIALIZATION.

TSUYOSHI TAKAKI

THE TITLE OF THIS SERIES, BLACK TORCH, IS NOT ONLY A REFERENCE TO JIRO'S POWERS, BUT ALSO TO A LIGHT—A TORCH—THAT LIGHTS THE SURROUNDING DARKNESS.

THIS SERIES HAS BEEN A LITTLE OF THAT FOR ME, GROPING ABOUT IN THE DARKNESS OF THE UNKNOWN WORLD OF MANGA PUBLISHING. BUT THANKS TO MY FAMILY, MY FRIENDS, MY STAFF, MY EDITOR, MY DESIGNER AND ALL THE READERS WHO HAVE BEEN WITH ME ALONG THE WAY...THE LIGHT OF ALL OF YOUR "TORCHES" HAS HELPED ME MAKE THE SLOW, SLIGHTLY FRIGHTENING, BUT ALWAYS FUN JOURNEY FORWARD.

THAT'S ALL FOR *BLACK TORCH*. THANK YOU FOR READING UNTIL THE END.

Tsuyoshi Takaki published his first one-shot, *Freaks*, in *Jump SQ Crown* in Japan in 2016. He began serialization of *Black Torch* in *Jump SQ* later that year.

BLACK TORCH

VOLUME 5

SHONEN JUMP Manga Edition

STORY AND ART BY **TSUYOSHI TAKAKI**

Translation/Adrienne Beck
Touch-Up Art & Lettering/Annaliese Christman
Design/Julian [JR] Robinson
Editor/Marlene First

BLACK TORCH © 2016 by Tsuyoshi Takaki
All rights reserved. First published in Japan in 2016 by
SHUEISHA Inc., Tokyo. English translation rights arranged by
SHUEISHA Inc.

The stories, characters and incidents mentioned in this
publication are entirely fictional.

Published by VIZ Media, LLC
P.O. Box 77010
San Francisco, CA 94107

Printed in the U.S.A.

10 9 8 7 6 5 4 3 2 1
First printing, August 2019

viz.com

shonenjump.com

PARENTAL ADVISORY
BLACK TORCH is rated T+ for Older Teen
and is recommended for ages 16 and up.
This volume contains violence and gore.

Black ❖ Clover

STORY & ART BY YŪKI TABATA

Asta is a young boy who dreams of becoming the greatest mage in the kingdom. Only one problem—he can't use any magic! Luckily for Asta, he receives the incredibly rare five-leaf clover grimoire that gives him the power of anti-magic. Can someone who can't use magic really become the Wizard King? One thing's for sure—Asta will never give up!

SHONEN JUMP

VIZ media

www.viz.com

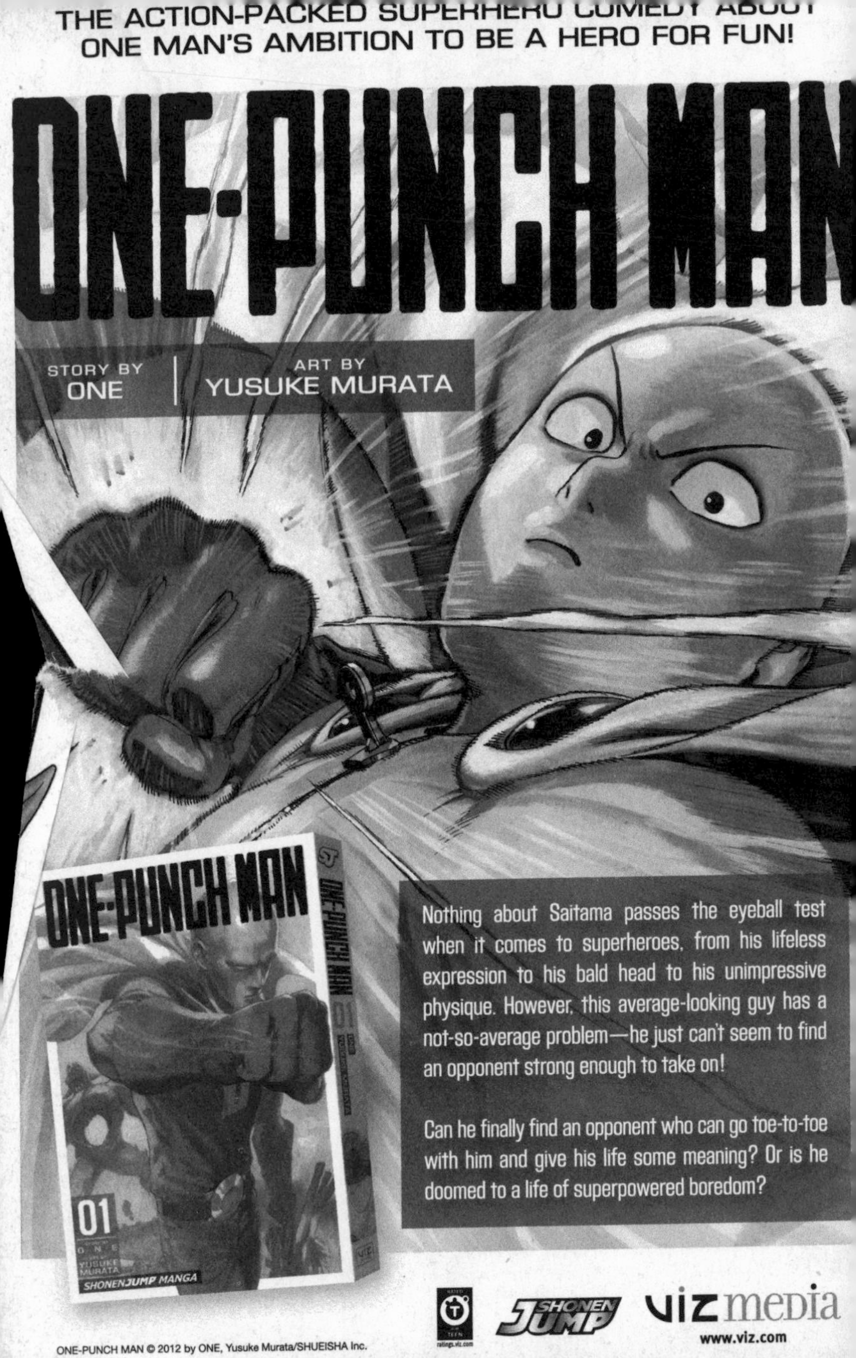
THE ACTION-PACKED SUPERHERO COMEDY ABOUT
ONE MAN'S AMBITION TO BE A HERO FOR FUN!
ONE-PUNCH MAN
STORY BY
ONE
ART BY
YUSUKE MURATA
ONE-PUNCH MAN
01
ONE
YUSUKE MURATA
SHONEN JUMP MANGA
Nothing about Saitama passes the eyeball test when it comes to superheroes, from his lifeless expression to his bald head to his unimpressive physique. However, this average-looking guy has a not-so-average problem—he just can't seem to find an opponent strong enough to take on!
Can he finally find an opponent who can go toe-to-toe with him and give his life some meaning? Or is he doomed to a life of superpowered boredom?
SHONEN JUMP
VIZ media
www.viz.com

DRAGON BALL SUPER

STORY BY **Akira Toriyama**   ART BY **Toyotarou**

Goku's adventure from the best-selling classic manga *Dragon Ball* continues in this new series written by Akira Toriyama himself!

Ever since Goku became Earth's greatest hero and gathered the seven Dragon Balls to defeat the evil Boo, his life on Earth has grown a little dull. But new threats loom overhead, and Goku and his friends will have to defend the planet once again!

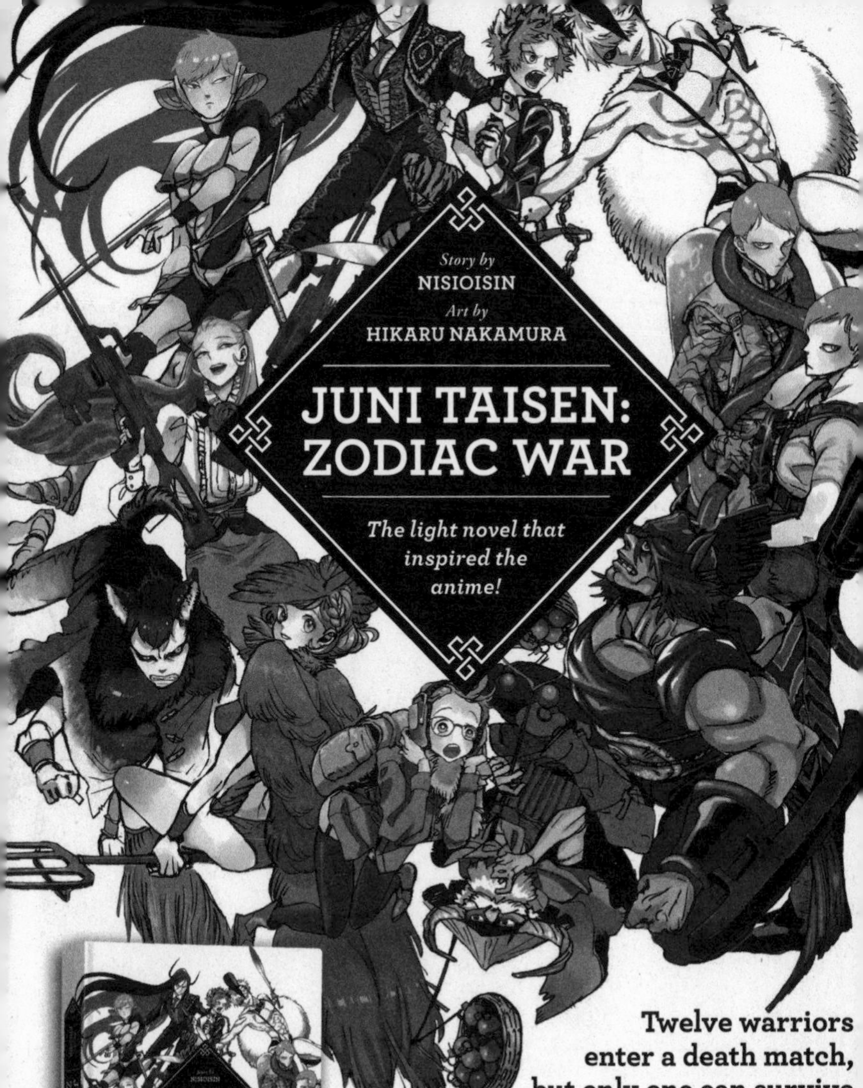
Story by
NISIOISIN
Art by
HIKARU NAKAMURA
JUNI TAISEN: ZODIAC WAR
The light novel that inspired the anime!

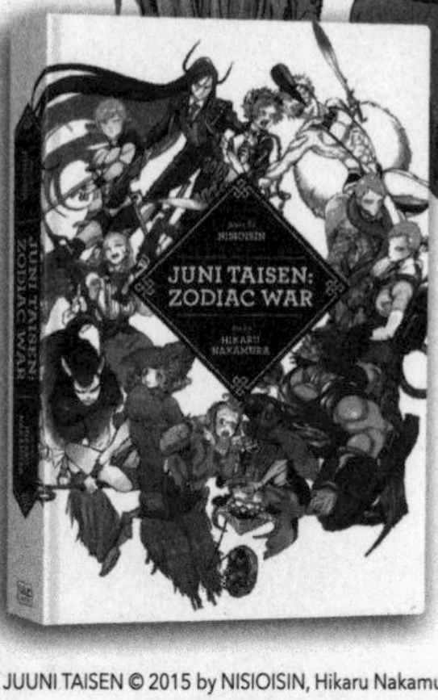
NISIOISIN
JUNI TAISEN: ZODIAC WAR
HIKARU NAKAMURA

YOU ARE READING THE WRONG WAY

Black Torch reads from right to left, starting in the upper-right corner. Japanese is read from right to left, meaning that action, sound effects, and word-balloon order are completely reversed from English order.

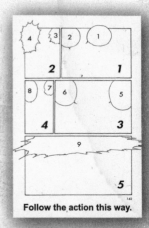

Follow the action this way.